Financial Risk Management

Francisco Javier Población García

Financial Risk Management

Identification, Measurement and Management

palgrave
macmillan

Francisco Javier Población García
European Central Bank
Frankfurt am Main, Germany

ISBN 978-3-319-41365-5 ISBN 978-3-319-41366-2 (eBook)
DOI 10.1007/978-3-319-41366-2

Library of Congress Control Number: 2016958311

Cover design by Tom Howey

Printed on acid-free paper

This Palgrave Macmillan imprint is published by Springer Nature
The registered company is Springer International Publishing AG
The registered company address is: Gewerbestrasse 11, 6330 Cham, Switzerland

Freedom, Sancho, is one of the most precious gifts that heaven has bestowed upon men; no treasures that the earth holds buried or the sea conceals can compare with it; for freedom, as for honour, life may and should be ventured . . .

(*Don Quixote of La Mancha*, Chapter LVIII, second part: *The Ingenious Gentleman Don Quixote of La Mancha*, Miguel de Cervantes Saavedra)

To my father

Preface

In recent times, risk analysis and management has become of great importance in the world of business, but unfortunately, as highlighted by the deep economic crisis we have become immersed in, this management has not always been based on purely financial criteria, mainly due to ignorance of such in certain areas. Perhaps that is what has driven me to write this book.

However, I think my underlying motivation to continue and complete this task has been the desire to show that risk is not something negative but quite the opposite, something very positive, as it is the inevitable consequence of freedom. In other words, if there were no risk, there would be no freedom, and as was taught by the famous one-armed man of Lepanto (the name given to Cervantes after fighting in the Battle of Lepanto) through his most famous fictional character, the ingenious gentleman Don Quixote of La Mancha: "Freedom is one of the most precious gifts that heaven has bestowed upon men." Certainly the existence of freedom, and therefore risk, allows humankind to acquire human dignity, as one can read in another bestseller completed in the Middle East almost 2,000 years ago.

For this reason, the fact that risk exists must be thought of not as a problem but as an opportunity—an opportunity for people to reach their full potential. In any event, this is neither the time nor the place to further discuss this interesting theological dilemma, because this book is not about risk in general but specifically about financial risk and, more specifically, financial risk in an industrial company.

On another subject and to conclude this short prologue, I would like to mention that I wrote the first version of this book in Spanish and in doing so received a tremendous amount of help. First of all, I would like to thank my former graduate students from CUNEF, Ana Belen Calvo Gago and Manuel Esteban García González, who collaborated closely with me on the preparation of this manuscript.

Secondly, I especially appreciate the help I received from Rachel Well in translating the book from Spanish to English. I have to say that Rachel is one of the best professionals with whom I have worked.

I would also like to thank Andrés García Mirantes, Juan Manuel Martín Prieto and Gregorio Serna Calvo for sharing so many years of work with me, during which I have learnt everything I know about risk analysis and management. Without them I would not have been able to write this book.

I would also like to thank, and dedicate this book to, all the members of the risk department at Repsol YPF—whether I have worked with them or not—the creation of which was inspired by Luis Manas Anton and which was so efficiently directed by Juan Manuel Martín Prieto.

Finally, I cannot fail to mention the fact that it is God who makes everything possible, including of course the elaboration of this book.

Contents

List of Figures

List of Tables

Part I

Introduction and Perspectives

1

Introduction

1.1 General Principles

In general, it can be said that risk has always been present in companies and therefore, measurement and management of risk has always been important. In recent times, due to the increasing internationalisation of corporations and the fact that economic activity is increasingly dependent on technology, risk measurement and management has become critical in all companies, regardless of their sector of activity.

The results of a company are subject to risks arising from the management of its assets and the development of its business strategy. All economic activity, even buying government debt, is subject to risk since, as has recently been demonstrated, there is always a risk that the state cannot pay its debts or cannot do so in the time and manner agreed at the time of issue. Even if the debts are paid in this time and manner, a great deal of value can be lost (currency depreciation, hyperinflation, etc.).

Therefore, although there is often no awareness of this, risks are run and it is unclear which carries more risk: to take a specific action, to take a number of actions or not to take any action at all. For this reason, the first

F.J. Población García, *Financial Risk Management*,
DOI 10.1007/978-3-319-41366-2_1

thing that has to be done to analyse a company's risk is to define some general principles and concepts.

1.1.1 Risk

The word risk has multiple meanings. Thus, it is necessary to specify what is understood when discussing the concept of risk. For the purposes of this book, we define risk as the degree of uncertainty that exists about the return of future net cash flows generated by making a particular investment.

This definition is very general and involves many different aspects which will be dealt with in detail throughout this book. For the moment, based on this general definition, this first chapter will try to shed some light on the purpose of risk management in an industrial company.

1.1.2 The Purpose of Corporate Risk Management: The Natural Risk Profile

The purpose of a business is to develop economic activity and this involves managing risk, which is why the first step must be to define the company's "natural" risk profile.

The "natural" risk profile of a company is defined as the recurrent risk derived from the efficient management of assets, with purchases and sales carried out in accordance with standard market practices. Bearing this definition in mind, the purpose of corporate risk management is to determine the risk profile that the company intends to offer its investors based on a cost–benefit analysis of natural risk profile alternatives. That is to say, the primary objective of the directors of a company is to maximise its value, or in other words to maximise the value of its shares. As far as risk management is concerned, the company responsible must offer investors, who are potential buyers of its shares, a risk profile that best fits their demand.

In an ideal world, the investor's risk aversion should not be relevant for this analysis, since the investor can diversify their portfolio. This implies that if the investor is averse to risk, they can invest in different assets and thus achieve a level of risk with which they feel comfortable. However, principal–agent problems are always present, that is, the directors have more information about the company than the investors. The investors may become wary of companies which they perceive to be high risk, even if they are expected to be highly profitable.

In addition, hedging risks helps avoid costs related to "financial distress", that is, costs (direct and indirect) associated with defaults and bankruptcy. This includes premiums payable to counterparties (customers, employees, partners, manufacturers, etc.) during a period of financial distress. At a time when a company is close to bankruptcy, the best employees go to other companies, industry partners become wary and are unwilling to collaborate in economic activities, suppliers tend not to provide goods due to the threat of defaults, customers do not buy from the company as in the future they will not be able to find parts for their products, and so on.

In addition, it must be taken into account that the opportunity to participate in potentially profitable investment projects is lost if there is a lack of liquidity, since in times of financial distress banks, along with international investors, are very reluctant to provide funding. This is particularly relevant in leading technology sectors, in which a novel discovery or development could present an immediate need to make large investments which could not be carried out without sufficient financial leverage.

On the other hand, it has to be said that selective risk hedging could create value in the company, increasing its borrowing capacity (with the tax benefits that entails) without compromising financial flexibility.

Given the above, it is possible to establish the general principle that, in an ideal world, a company's hedging strategies should focus on aspects over which it has no control or competitive advantage. In other words, hedging strategies should enable the company to focus on its "competitive advantages". Ideally, if hedging instruments incurred no costs, companies would strictly moderate the intrinsic risk of the business. However, typically hedging comes at considerable cost (as indicated above, principal–agent problems, including financial distress, must be taken into account).

In addition, other factors have to be considered when determining the risk profile of a company, two of which must be highlighted above all others: the impact on accounting and the preference that potential clients have for certain risk profiles. Financial statements collect information which is released into the market and is validated by an independent third party. The financial statements themselves do not generate either profits or losses. However, as a rule, accounting standards and the relative recognition of hedging, especially International Accounting Standard (IAS) 39, are general, of a conservative nature and unable to adapt to each individual case, and therefore they do not always allow accounting statements to reflect the results of hedging strategies in the most appropriate way. These "imperfections" together with disproportionate information problems could cause concern for investors and, as a result, a fall in the value of shares. It is for this reason that the possible modification of the natural risk profile is always considered. It is essential to consider the accounting aspect. The case could arise, and in fact has arisen, in which hedging is perfect economically (or, from an economic-financial point of view, the risk being covered has almost completely disappeared) but is not perceived as such from an accounting perspective. This is particularly likely to happen when the accounting standard requires the asset (which may be a permanent investment for the company) to be recorded at its purchase price, while its hedging (usually a financial derivative) is recorded at the market price at the time. This causes accounting distortions which are difficult for the company to explain and difficult to understand in the market.

On the other hand, we must also consider that different investors from different sectors ("retail"/institutional, local/international, etc.) may have a preference for different risk profiles. Taking the hedging practices of the sector into account, the company may choose to offer its investors a definite risk profile or offer specific investment products. In other words, the goal of the company is to create value for its shareholders and, in particular, to try to increase the value of their shares as much as possible. Thus, when choosing the risk profile of the company, it is important to take into account what the market is demanding in terms of risks.

Although ideally companies should monitor their intrinsic business risk, in practice, as will be demonstrated, in many cases this is not desirable or appropriate once the costs have been analysed.

1.1.3 Cost–Benefit Analysis

Obviously, in order to modify the natural risk profile of a company, there must be another person or entity (counterparty) willing to take the part of the risk that the company does not want to accept. To perform this risk transfer, some type of financial instrument must be used, for example derivative assets.[1] In addition, both finding and convincing a counterparty to assume the risks that the company will not, and the instruments which are used to transfer this risk, come at a price. To clarify, these costs can be divided into three categories.

The first category corresponds to what are known as intermediation costs. These costs are related to the fact that both the counterparty and the agencies that create the financial instruments necessary for risk transfer charge all kinds of commission. Similarly, the market clearly shows that the price a counterparty is willing to pay will be lower than the price it is willing to sell for (the "bid–ask spread"), which is, in one way or another, an expense.

The second category relates to what is known as counterparty risk. Although counterparty risk will be dealt with in subsequent chapters, this can be defined simply as the risk resulting from the possibility that, at the time of settlement, the counterparty fails to meet its commitments. This counterparty risk can be minimised using periodic settlement mechanisms (which is expensive), or using clearing houses that charge fees specifically for hedging against counterparty risk. Furthermore, these mechanisms lead to a risk of liquidity.[2]

The third category consists of administration and control costs. As its name suggests, this is the cost of managing the company and of monitoring counterparties and instruments used to modify the natural risk profile. Although these costs are usually not too high, they can become especially significant when considering complex hedging strategies which require constant modifications (such as regular adjustments to the portfolio).

[1] Subsequent chapters will discuss the concept of a derivative asset in more detail.

[2] All of these concepts (periodic settlement, clearing, counterparty risk, risk of liquidity, etc.) will be developed in detail in subsequent chapters.

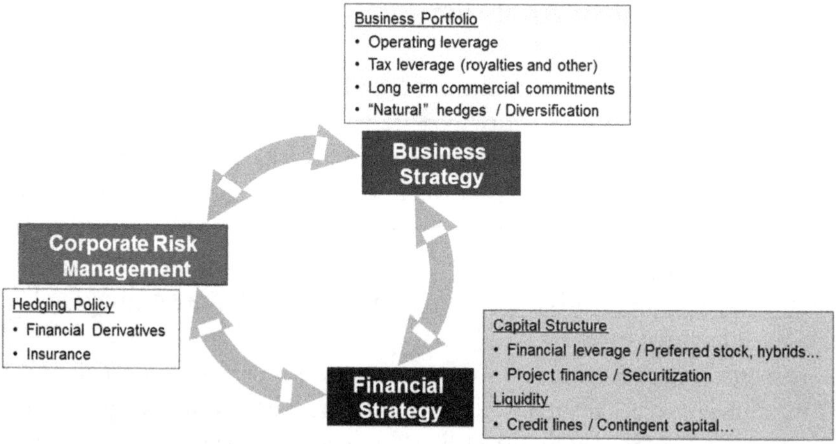

Fig. 1.1 Corporate risk management, business strategy and financial strategy

Considering all the factors described above, the cost–benefit analysis of alternatives which modify the risk profile of a company should result in a set of principles and rules to be followed. In addition, these principles and rules should be closely linked to the financial and business strategy of the company, designed to be stable over time and to provide transparency and stability in risk management activities (Fig. 1.1).

1.1.4 Hedging Versus Trading

One aspect to consider when defining the risk profile of a company is that corporate risk management is conceptually different from and independent from the function of "trading/risk taking". Corporate risk management does not focus on sporadic and opportunistic hedging based on an idea that the manager has at a particular moment.

The use of opportunistic and unrestricted hedging is a legitimate activity that can create, and actually does create, value for the company; however, this activity cannot be treated as a corporate function. Instead, this activity must have a separate income statement, have objectives, be monitored and so on—in other words, be a classic trading/risk taking activity.

Therefore, efforts to alter the natural risk profile in order to adapt it to a certain level ("benchmark") can be defined as "hedging".[3] In this case, the gains or losses of the hedging instrument cannot be considered as such, as they are offset by the losses or gains of hedging the assets. Conversely, deviations from this particular level (benchmark), based on opportunistic decisions in an attempt to obtain exceptional returns, should be defined as "speculative positions" ("trading positions"). Thus, the key question in determining the nature of a position is as follows: Is the position the result of an unrestricted action or is it the result of the application of predetermined rules, previously communicated to the investors?

The classic trading activity is different from hedging in one essential element: the benchmark, that is, a given level of risk that is considered appropriate for the management of the company. This benchmark is defined by senior management and determines risks for which the trading unit manager is not responsible.

Deviations from this benchmark are decided by the trading unit managers and are subject to trading business standards: risk limits and income statements. In other words, this must be considered not only as an operation but as a business activity, which is allocated resources, given objectives, allowed to run risks to a certain point, monitored and judged based on the results obtained, in the same way as the company's other business activities. Thus, the managers of this line of business take positions according to their own estimations and experience and are judged on this.

1.1.5 Accounting Recognition

As stated above, accounting regulation, which allows a hedging strategy to be recognised as "hedge accounting", does not follow the logic that is being discussed here. The two main accounting bodies are the FAS (Federal Accounting Standards), which is valid in the USA, and the IAS (International Accounting Standards), which is valid in the other OECD

[3] Subsequent chapters will define the concept of hedging in more detail.

(Organisation for Economic Co-operation and Development) countries. Except for slight differences (which in some cases could be of great importance), the legislations are virtually identical.

According to these regulations, a hedging strategy may be designated as "hedge accounting" if it is "highly effective" in offsetting the risk generated by an asset or a transaction, without having an impact on the overall risk of the company. This definition provides some flexibility, since at the beginning of the process a measurement can be chosen to evaluate hedging performance ("fair value hedge", "cash flow hedge", "net investment hedge", etc.). In addition, the asset to be hedged and the instrument used to do so can be chosen without considering the impact on the overall risk of the company.[4]

However, this definition is not without its constraints. The fact that it has to be highly effective means there are limits in recognising complex and/or dynamic hedging strategies. Furthermore, a mismatch in timing and/or underlying assets can lead to severe limitations. As noted above, while being perfect or near perfect hedging from an economic-financial standpoint, it may not be viewed as such from an accounting perspective, which can lead to serious distortions in the income statement and/or the company balance sheet. The distortions themselves neither create nor destroy value, that is, the company's fundamentals and prospects remain the same. However, in such a highly globalised world, the company's relationship with investors is crucial and investors, unlike managers, are only provided with accounting information which indicates the status of the company in question. Therefore, distortions in the company's accounting statements may be perceived by investors as the result of mismanagement, leading to funding restrictions and/or reductions in the value of shares. Considering that large multinational companies have a huge and constant demand for institutional investors, this could have disastrous consequences for the company.

---

[4] All the concepts mentioned here (definition of hedge accounting, types of hedge accounting, highly effective hedge, etc.) will be discussed in depth in subsequent chapters.

1.1.6 Corporate Strategies: Systemic Risk Versus Idiosyncratic Risk

The classic risk theory divides the risk of a corporation into two categories. The first of these is systemic (or non-diversifiable) risk, which is simply the risk derived from factors that affect the whole economy and not just one particular company. In other words, when the economy is in an expansion phase, the value of all companies tends to rise regardless of the managers' performance and the industry's prospects, whereas in a recession phase the opposite occurs. Thus, the factors causing these variations are systemic risk factors. By contrast, idiosyncratic (or diversifiable) risk is derived from factors that only affect one particular company or industry. These factors are linked to the company's own idiosyncrasy (such as market share, manager performance, operating costs, their profit margin or leverage) and to their sector of activity (for example, whether their industry is developed, in a period of expansion or in a period of recession).

As previously stated, the investor's risk aversion should not be relevant for this analysis, since the investor can diversify their portfolio. Although this is true, the problem is that the investor can only diversify idiosyncratic risk, not systemic risk. In other words, by investing in various assets an investor can ensure that if one asset goes badly as a result of its own idiosyncrasy, this is offset by the other assets because some other asset or assets will perform better than expected. On average, the investor will get a return that does not depend solely on the performance of one particular asset in their portfolio, that is, their average return will not be affected by the idiosyncratic risk of every individual asset. Conversely, in times of recession the value of their portfolio will undoubtedly fall, while in times of expansion the value will increase regardless of how varied their portfolio is; in other words, there is no way to diversify systemic risk.

Furthermore, the manager's ultimate goal should be to maximise the company's value, that is, to maximise the value of its shares. Thus, the manager is responsible for making the company's shares as attractive as possible for the investor and the only way of doing this is by improving the risk–return equation of the company, in other words, increasing profitability and reducing risk. For this reason, company shares can be considered as a product which has an expected return and a risk. This risk, as stated, can be divided into idiosyncratic risk and systemic risk.

Moreover, the managers modify the company's natural risk profile using a cost–benefit analysis in order to offer investors a different risk profile. In this cost–benefit analysis managers must be aware that for the investor systemic risk is not the same as idiosyncratic risk, because the latter can be diversified while the former cannot. This means that in general company activity, and in particular the management of corporate risk, should aim to maximise the value of its shares or, what amounts to the same, the managers' ultimate goal must be to ensure that demand for shares of their company is as high as possible. From this perspective, based on a cost–benefit analysis, the risk profile of the company must aim to achieve the following goal: to achieve a demand for shares which is as high as possible, considering the type of risk that investors are demanding at a particular moment.

1.2 Individual and Savings Bank Risk Management

The issues that have already been analysed could give the impression that risk management is a discipline which is independent of the object to which it is applied, that is, that the principles of risk management can be applied to industrial companies, savings banks and individual investors in the same way. However, as the following explanation indicates, this is not the case.

1.2.1 Individual Risk Management

In the same way as a business, an individual's economic activity (work, investments, etc.) is also subject to risk and susceptible to management. Many of the issues that have been discussed in relation to companies can also be applied to individuals. However, there are two important (interrelated) differences between individual investors and firms: limited liability and risk aversion.

Most countries have laws which state that when a company goes bankrupt it has limited liability, which means that the owners, the managers and the employees don't pay the debts, and only the assets of the company respond. This is essential for an economy's business development, as demonstrated by John Ford's companies, which went bankrupt several times before Ford came to "invent" mass production.

Conversely, an individual responds to any contracted debts using their assets, and it is false that if an individual fails to pay the fees on a bank loan, for example a mortgage, the bank seizes the collateral and the payment obligation is cancelled. It is increasingly evident nowadays that in the case of default, the collateral goes to public auction and if what is made at auction does not manage to fully recover the debt, the individual retains the remaining debt with the bank. In this case, the bank may take, and indeed does take, legal action against the individual to demand that the remaining debt is paid and if this occurs, the individual's assets are used to respond to this demand (accounts, wages, property, etc. can be seized.) These legal actions usually take a lot longer than it takes to execute a mortgage, and because lawyers, trials and so on are expensive for both parties, in many cases agreements are reached. On this basis, the individual cannot be considered to have limited liability in any way, but this is not entirely true.

Besides the fact that individuals do not have limited liability and companies do, another difference is that an individual's risk aversion is usually greater than that of a company. There are many reasons for this, one of which is that without limited liability, greater risk aversion is needed. "Bankruptcy costs" and "financial distress" are other reasons for individuals' greater risk aversion compared to companies, as these costs are much higher for the former. "Losing your home and sleeping on the street" is not the same as "losing your office and ceasing economic activity", and "not having money to buy food" is not the same as "not having money to pay employees, suppliers and so on." Similarly, on reaching a certain level of income, an additional monetary unit creates much greater "utility" in the company's case than in the individual's, because the individual reaches a stage at which this factor improves living standards very little, whereas the company distributes dividends to many shareholders.

For all the reasons previously outlined, it is perfectly legitimate for a business manager to manage company risk differently than their own individual risk. In other words, the "utility function" of an individual is less linear—it is more concave than that of a company. Limited liability and risk aversion means that an individual's risk management is performed in a much more conservative way than a company's, and therefore a manager cannot be criticised in any way for taking many more risks when managing the company than when managing their own assets.

However, there are other factors that cause risk management in a company to be different from that of an individual. It is clear that the individual does not have the "accounting problems" or agency problems that exist in a company. Similarly, in many cases the individual does not have the same resources as a company. These considerations, together with the aforementioned cases of risk aversion and limited liability, further support the argument that a manager not only can but must manage the company assets in a different way to their own personal assets.

1.2.2 Risk Management in Savings Banks

Savings banks are firms in which the main activity is to take the depositors' money and lend it to individuals and businesses. The risk related to this mainly arises from the default risk and credit risk of the borrowers. For this reason, the majority of what has been demonstrated previously in the case of industrial companies can also be applied in this case. However, there is one significant difference that has important consequences: the liability of a savings bank is mainly made up of demand deposits and/or term deposits, usually around 90 %, while the remaining liability is made up of capital and other savings bank or central bank loans.

In order to protect the depositors' money and the stability of the financial system, savings banks are subject to specific regulations and close supervision by the central bank, which in theory should prevent savings banks from facing bankruptcy or even financial distress. The concept of protecting depositors stems from the fact that the liability, which does not come from business capital, lies mainly in the hands of banks and institutional investors, both of whom are assumed to have the ability to analyse and understand the risks they are taking. Conversely, it is not usually possible for the depositor to ascertain the bankruptcy risk of a savings bank, and thus logically it should be the government that protects their interests. In addition, depositors generally do not receive any remuneration for their investment and if they do, it is usually at much lower rates than those in the market. For the economy to function properly, as a rule, it is necessary for the public to deposit their savings in a savings bank or use them to make investments, but due to risk aversion the public always demands safe investments. Thus, for normal economic development it is desirable to protect the depositors' money.

On the other hand, as previously noted, the stability of the financial system must be protected as the liability of savings banks is usually made up of "demand deposits", money that the depositor may withdraw at any time, while its assets are usually made up of much larger instalment loans. In fact, mortgage loans represent a high percentage within the loan portfolio, usually about 50 %, and have a payback period of around 30 years. For this reason, if the depositor is not absolutely certain that their money is completely safe, there could be a huge number of requests for deposit withdrawals that could not be realised, which would cause "panic". If panic is widespread, the government and the central bank can do very little to avoid the bankruptcy of the financial system.

Given the above, savings banks have specific regulations and are subject to close supervision, meaning they do not have the freedom to take the same risks as industrial companies and may have to accept many restrictions depending on the risks being taken. In other words, their utility function is "less linear", and therefore their behaviour is more conservative than that of an industrial company.

2

Risk Quantification

2.1 Basic Concepts

As indicated in Chap. 1, risk is defined as a degree of uncertainty; therefore, when quantifying it, it should be noted that when an investment is made, the profitability of it is uncertain or equivalently a random variable and must be treated as such. In this regard, when an investment is made only the value of the moments (mean, standard deviation, etc.) associated with it can be quantified.

For this reason, the first thing that must be taken into account when quantifying risk is the type of exposure it has. For example, if the investment concerns buying a share, the future value of this investment can be quantified from the expected value or average of these share prices in the future while, as will be discussed in subsequent chapters, its risk can be quantified using standard deviation. On the other hand, if future purchase rights on a share are being acquired, both the future value and the risk of these rights must be quantified using the expected value and standard deviation of the possible outcomes caused by these rights. This quantification is much more complicated, as different scenarios must be taken into consideration. Namely, when share price values are high, the

F.J. Población García, *Financial Risk Management*,
DOI 10.1007/978-3-319-41366-2_2

purchase rights will be valuable, while in the opposite scenario, when share price values are low, the purchase rights will not be valuable.

Although all types of exposure can be considered unique, it is easy to demonstrate that any exposure, however complex, can be broken down into one of two types: linear and "option type". For this reason, the first part of this chapter will focus on characterising each of them, introducing some concepts beforehand.

2.1.1 Long Positions and Short Positions

The classic characteristic of an investment strategy is to establish the assets to be acquired to form a portfolio. Once the portfolio has been formed, existing assets from it can be sold or other new ones can be purchased, varying the investment profile. Similarly, in most financial markets, assets can be sold provided they are not under commitment and are guaranteed to be returned in the future (short-selling). This is like the stock market temporarily lending an asset to an investor, so that they can sell it, with a commitment from the investor that in the near future this asset will be returned to the stock market from which it was borrowed. Thus, if the price of the asset in question rises, the investor makes a loss, whereas if it decreases they make a profit.

Thus, within an investment strategy, it is said that the investor takes a long position or buyer position on a specific asset when they perform an action whereby if the price of that asset rises in the future, they make a profit or stop suffering a loss, while if the price of the asset decreases, the investor suffers a loss or stops making a profit. In contrast, it is said that the investor takes a short position or seller position on an asset when they perform an action whereby if the price of that asset rises in the future, they suffer a loss or stop making a profit, while if the price of the asset decreases, the investor makes a profit or stops suffering a loss. The classic example of a long position is acquiring an asset, while an example of a short position is selling one, whether it is a short selling or not.

2.1.2 Derivative Assets

A financial asset is an instrument used to channel savings into investment. In their search for funding, companies can enter into the market through financial assets issuing equity claims (shares) or debt claims (bonds). Shares grant the right to participate in ownership, and thus the shareholder is a partner, is involved in results and is a co-owner. A share is defined as the proportional part of a corporation's registered capital which enables the shareholder to use authorised shares to subscribe preferably to new shares issued as capital increases, to receive dividends, to vote at general meetings and to participate in the distribution of the company's assets in case of the company's liquidation. When the company is listed in the stock market, shares can be bought or sold there, and their price is always referred to as a spot price, as opposed to a future price which will be discussed later. Market capitalisation (the value of the company) is calculated by multiplying the price of a share by the number of existing shares. For this reason, the stock market is considered an "indication" of the state of the economy.

On the other hand, companies can seek funding through fixed-income securities by releasing shares, which causes their owners to also become their creditors. With these assets, unlike shares, investors know beforehand the monetary flows they are going to receive. Debt security holders have three fundamental rights: receiving predetermined interest rates, repayment of main assets once the product life has come to an end and being the first to collect payment in the event of the corporation's liquidation. In addition, fixed-income securities are divided into two large groups according to their maturity: the first group consists of money market assets, which are short-term assets and generally enjoy high liquidity (certificates of deposit, treasury bills, etc.), while the second group is made up of debentures and bonds, which are instruments that take longer than a year to mature. The investor becomes a lender of the issuing company.

By definition, a derivative, also known as a derivative asset or financial derivative, is a contract that both parties sign at a given point in time whereby future payments arising from it depend on the price of another asset, the underlying asset. Therefore, a derivative cannot truly be considered a financial asset as a derivative does not make a saver's capital available to the investor; it does, however, allow two agents in the economy to mutually transfer risk. However, although they are not pure financial assets, the derivative products can be broadly considered as financial assets as they are negotiated in the same way and in the same places (stock exchanges) as financial assets.

The two simplest derivative assets are future and European option derivatives. A future, or forward, is an agreement between two parties whereby a future buyer agrees to buy a particular asset and a future seller agrees to sell the asset (the underlying asset) at some point in the future (when the asset reaches maturity) at a price which is determined when the agreement is made. The fact that the underlying asset will be exchanged in the future for a price which is determined today causes the future value to fluctuate over time, depending on how the value of the underlying asset varies. Figures 2.1 and 2.2 demonstrate the variations in the future value for both the buyer and the seller according to the variations in the value of the underlying asset.

In the case of European options, there are two types: purchase options and sale options. The purchase European option ("European call") is an

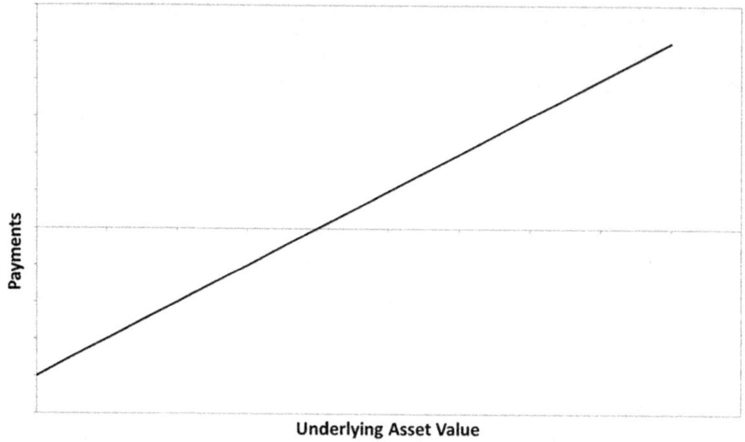

Fig. 2.1 Future buyer payment (Author's own composition)

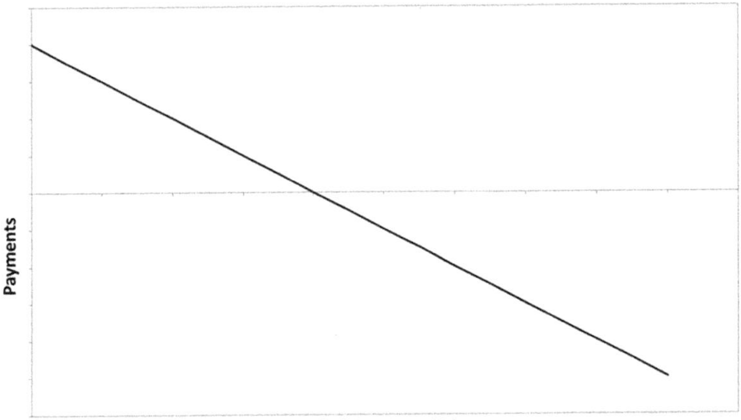

Fig. 2.2 Future seller payment (Author's own composition)

agreement that is signed between two parties whereby one party (the buyer of the option) has the right (but not the obligation) to purchase a particular asset (the underlying asset) from the other party (the seller of the option) at some point in the future (when the option reaches maturity) at a price (the exercise price or "strike") that is determined when the agreement is made. For the seller of the option (who only has obligations and not rights) to accept this contract, the buyer (who only has rights and not obligations) must compensate them with a premium today. In the same way as before, the fact that the strike is determined now is what causes the value of the options to fluctuate over time depending on the underlying asset. Figures 2.3 and 2.4 demonstrate how the value of the European call varies for both the buyer and the seller, depending on the changes in the value of the underlying asset.

The sale European option ("European put") is an agreement that is signed between two parties whereby one party (the buyer of the option) has the right (but not the obligation) to sell a particular asset (the underlying asset) to the other party (the seller of the option) at some point in the future (when the option matures) at a price (the exercise price or "strike") that is determined at that time. In the same way as before, for the seller of the option (who only has obligations and not rights) to accept

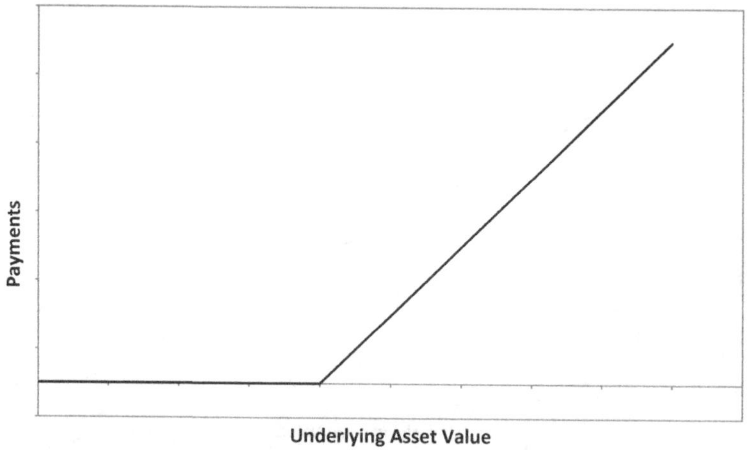

Fig. 2.3 European call buyer payment (Author's own composition)

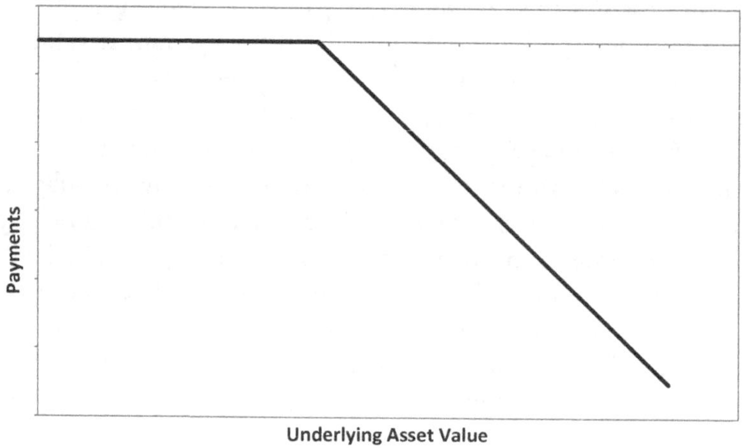

Fig. 2.4 European call seller payment (Author's own composition)

this contract, the buyer (who only has rights and not obligations) must compensate them with a premium when the agreement is made (Figs 2.5 and 2.6).

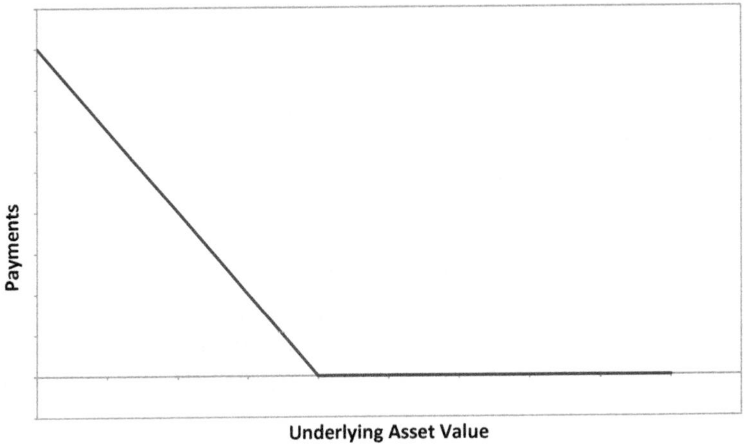

Fig. 2.5 European put buyer payment (Author's own composition)

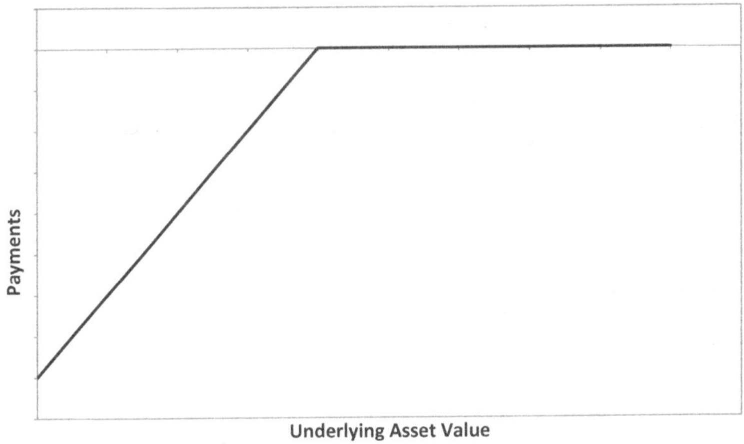

Fig. 2.6 European put seller payment (Author's own composition)

Even the most simple derivative assets are futures/forwards and European options, there is a great variety of derivative assets. There are also abundant ranking criteria, so any list must inevitably be incomplete; however, the most common ones can be defined as:

- European options have already been defined above; options in general can be divided according to payment structure into:
  - **Call option:** Grants the right (not the obligation) to buy an asset at a predetermined strike price.
  - **Put option:** Grants the right (not the obligation) to sell an asset at a predetermined strike price.

  In accordance with the exercise they can be divided into:
  - **European**: They can only be exercised at the end of the period.
  - **American**: They can be exercised at any time until expiration.
  - **Bermudan**: They can be exercised during specific periods up to and including the expiration date.

Since the European and American (and sometimes Bermudan) put and call options are the simplest ones, they are known as "vanilla options". However, there is an endless list of more complicated options which are known as "exotic options" (barrier, binary, lookback, Asian, etc.).

- A Swap is a contract through which the nature of the flows generated in a financial transaction are exchanged or altered; the fact that a swap is a set of long and short positions on futures is easily demonstrated. Although, as in the case of options, there is an endless list, the most important are:
  - **Interest rate swap (IRS)**: one party agrees to pay the other a fixed interest rate applied to a reference amount agreed in advance for a certain period of time on certain dates, in exchange for receiving a variable interest rate on that amount from the other party.
  - **Cross currency rate swap (CCRS)**: one party pays the other an amount in currency for a certain period of time on certain dates, in exchange for another amount in a different currency.
  - **Credit default swap (CDS)**: this is a credit derivative which is implemented through a swap contract on a particular credit instrument, usually a bond or a loan, where the buyer of the swap makes a series of periodic payments, called spread, to the seller and in

exchange is paid an amount of money if the title that serves as the underlying asset to the contract is unpaid at maturity or the issuer defaults.

- **Swaption:** this is an option in which the underlying asset is a swap. Although there are a wide variety of swaps, the most common swaptions are options on interest rate swaps.

2.1.2.1 Greek Letters

Greek letters are defined as the sensitivity of the price of an option (or a derivative in general) to a change in the underlying parameters on which the value of the underlying asset and/or the value of the derivative is dependent. Although there are many Greek letters in finance, only the most important ones will be presented here.

- The "delta" (Δ) is the most famous Greek letter and measures the rate of change in the derivative value with respect to changes in the price of the underlying asset. Mathematically the "delta" is the first derivative of the value of the option relating to the price of the underlying instrument. As can be inferred from previous charts, in "plain vanilla" options the "delta" is the $[-1, 1]$ range.
- The "gamma" (Γ) measures the rate of change in the "delta" with respect to changes in the price of the underlying asset. Mathematically the "gamma" is the second derivative of the value of the option relating to the underlying price. Options buyers have positive "gamma" whereas options buyers have negative "gamma".
- The "vega" (ν) measures the sensitivity of the value of the derivative to volatility. Mathematically the "vega" is the derivative of the option value with respect to the volatility of the underlying asset.
- The "theta" (Θ) measures the sensitivity of the value of the derivative to time (or to be more precise to the "time decay").
- The "rho" (ρ) measures the sensitivity of the derivative to the interest rate. Mathematically it is the derivative of the option value with respect to the risk free interest rate.

The Greek letters are very important risk management tools because each Greek letter measures the sensitivity of the value of the derivative to a small change in a given underlying parameter, allowing each component of the risk to be treated in isolation. Moreover, the Greek letters in "plain vanilla" options are relatively easy to calculate, which is very convenient for derivatives traders, especially those who seek to hedge their positions against undesirable changes in the market.

2.1.3 Linear Exposure

As indicated previously, when buying a share the future value of this investment can be quantified by the expected value, or average, of the share price in the future. The payment function of this investment will be identical to that for the future buyer, as the price for which the share has been acquired will represent the future price. In the same way, if the investment strategy involves selling a share when overdrawn, the payment function will be identical to that for the future seller. As demonstrated in the future payment graphs for the buyer and the seller, in both cases the value of the investment and the value of the underlying asset in question develop in a linear manner. When the current and future payment function and the value of the asset in question develop linearly the investments are known as linear exposures.

The value of this type of exposure today is calculated in a very simple way:

The value of the buyer position (long position) today is:

$$E\left[e^{-rT}\{S_T - K\}\right] = e^{-rT}\{E[S_T] - K\}.$$

The value of the seller position (short position) today is:

$$E\left[e^{-rT}\{K - S_T\}\right] = e^{-rT}\{K - E[S_T]\}.$$

In the above equations $E[\ ]$ represents the mathematical expectation (expected value), K represents the updated value of the investment, with a risk free interest rate ("r") at a future moment in time "T", and S_T represents the price of the underlying asset at a future moment in time

"T". As it is a linear payment function, this type of investment is relatively easy to assess. The only thing that can be complicated to determine is $E[S_T]$, which depends on underlying asset price dynamics. However, in the case of fluctuating interest rates, the expected mathematical value of S_T is simply the initial value of the underlying asset (S_0) updated with the risk free interest rate at a future time "T", in other words $E[S_T] = S_0e^{rT}$.[1]

The reason for this is the fact that an investor can enter into the market at $t = 0$ and apply for funding to acquire a share with a price equivalent to S_0, and therefore, if $E[S_T]$ were different from S_0e^{rT}, the investors would act in the market in the following way until $E[S_T] = S_0e^{rT}$: if $E[S_T] > S_0e^{rT}$ investors would ask to borrow at $t = 0$ an amount of money equal to S_0, they would acquire a share to keep until the moment "T" at which point it would be sold and on average would make a profit, as the money that has to be repaid is S_0e^{rT} (which was applied for with interest) while the amount of money obtained from the sale is normally $E[S_T]$ which has a higher value than S_0e^{rT}. Continuing in this way, buying shares at $t = 0$, the initial price of those shares, namely S_0, would rise until $E[S_T] = S_0e^{rT}$. On the other hand, if $E[S_T] < S_0e^{rT}$ the procedure followed by investors to make money would be the opposite: at $t = 0$ they would sell shares obtaining S_0 for every share and the money they received would be invested in the risk free rate so that at the time "T" the value of this money would be S_0e^{rT} which, on average, would exceed the value of the sold share. Continuing in this way, selling shares at $t = 0$ the price, S_0, would decrease until $E[S_T] = S_0e^{rT}$.

For these reasons, in the future market, the future exercise price (K) is $K = E[S_T] = S_0e^{rT}$ whereby the initial value of the long position is equal to the value of the short position and equal to zero. A future price which causes the initial buyer and seller positions to have the same value can be called a future price, future value or future (Ft, T, where t is the initial time and T is the future maturity) and, as indicated previously, in the case of variable equity the future price is $F_{0,T} = S_0e^{rT}$.

[1] In fact this only occurs in an environment of risk neutrality. However, considerations of this type are beyond the scope of this book.

Although this activity is still relevant, measuring the risk of such exposures is not characterised by great mathematical complexity, which is not always the case with "option type" exposures.

2.1.4 Option Type Exposure

The other type of exposure, "option type" exposure, is closely related to the definition of an option discussed previously. Unlike linear exposure, this kind of exposure is characterised by the fact that its payment function does not vary linearly with the value of the underlying asset, but instead when the value of the underlying asset changes at some point, the investment payment function changes "abruptly" without a definite derivative. In other words, at some point in the development of the underlying asset price the payment function experiences a change of trend. In all cases in which the payment function has a change of trend, the exposure can be broken down into linear exposure and option type exposure whereby the payment function is identical to that of the options.

Thus, the value of this type of exposure, which can be broken down into linear exposure and option type exposure, will be the sum of the value of linear exposure, whose calculation method was detailed previously, plus the value of the option premium that characterises this exposure. As previously indicated when discussing options in Sect. 2.1.2, there are four different option positions, as both the "European call" and the "European put" have a buyer and seller position.

The option premium is more complex to assess because the payment formula is not linear. In the case of the "European call":

The value of the buyer position (long position) today is: $E[e^{-rT}\max\{S_T - K; 0\}]$

The value of the seller position (short position) today is: $E[e^{-rT}\min\{S_T - K; 0\}]$

In the case of the "European put":

The value of the buyer position (long position) today is: $E[e^{-rT}\max\{K - S_T; 0\}]$

The value of the seller position (short position) today is: $E[e^{-rT}\min\{K - S_T; 0\}]$

As demonstrated, these expected values are much more complex to calculate, as in addition to the inherent complexity of S_T dynamics, there is the complexity arising from having maxima and minima in a mathematical expectation function. For a general S_T dynamic, the previous mathematical expectations cannot be calculated in an analytical manner and can only be calculated numerically. However, in the case of equity, as we shall see in later chapters, the dynamics of S_T are relatively simple. In 1972 Black and Scholes were able to analytically deduce the value of those expectations and in doing so they revolutionised the world of finance. The analytical expressions for this case are listed below:

- $E[e^{-rT}\max\{S_T - K;0\}] = e^{-rT}*(E[S_T]*N(d_1) - K*N(d_2))$
- $E[e^{-rT}\min\{S_T - K;0\}] = e^{-rT}*(K*N(d_2) - E[S_T]*N(d_1))$
- $E[e^{-rT}\max\{K - S_T;0\}] = e^{-rT}*(K*N(-d_2) - E[S_T]*N(-d_1))$
- $E[e^{-rT}\min\{K - S_T;0\}] = e^{-rT}*(E[S_T]*N(-d_1) - K*N(-d_2))$

where K represents the "strike", σ the volatility, T the time of maturity, $N()$ the cumulative probability of standard normal distribution (normal distribution of mean 0 and standard deviation 1) and:

- $d_1 = (\ln(E[S_T]/K) + T*\sigma_2/2)/(\sigma*T^{1/2})$
- $d_2 = d_1 - \sigma*T^{1/2}$

If it is already difficult to calculate the expected value in this type of exposure, as previously demonstrated, then measuring the risk of such exposures would require great mathematical complexity and can usually only be estimated using simulation methods as opposed to analytical formulas. A more detailed explanation of this concept will be given in subsequent chapters.

Therefore, it can be concluded that when a corporation analyses the risk of a specific balance sheet position, close attention must be paid to the type of position concerned because, as previously demonstrated, "similar" positions can generate very different risks, that is, the valuation and hedging of these risks can come to be very different from one position to another.

2.2 Types of Risk

Once the possible types of exposure have been established, the next step in quantifying the risk is to ascertain the type of risk they are exposed to. The next section provides an overview of the different types of risk affecting a company. Subsequent chapters will develop all the concepts mentioned here in much greater detail.

2.2.1 Market Risk

When managing the risk of a non-financial company the most important risk by far is market risk, as this refers to the uncertainty of future earnings resulting from changes in market conditions (share prices, interest rates, exchange rates, commodity prices, etc.). In other words, market risk is the uncertainty of all economic and financial variables which affect the results of a company. Thus, there are many kinds of market risk:

2.2.1.1 Equity

According to financial theory, the share price at a given time reflects all the information made available to the market up to that point. As all market information is included in the price, it is urgent to verify that, as indicated previously, in an environment of risk neutrality, the mathematical expectation of the price at a future time is simply the price today updated with a risk free interest rate $E[S_T] = e^{rT} * S_0$, where S_T is the share price at a future time "T", while S_0 represents the share price today.

Additionally, two shares from different companies will have the same systemic risk; however, each one will have its own idiosyncratic risk. The idiosyncratic risk causes the risk to be different for two different shares. In other words, with the exception of systemic risk, each share will have its own risk which will be different to that of the other shares. Therefore, it can be concluded that the quantification of risk in equities is not very complex, as there is not a close relationship between the risk of one share and the risk of another. For the same reason, it is also easy to hedge equity risk with futures or options because $E[S_T] = e^{rT} * S_0$.

2.2.1.2 Interest Rate

The risk management of fixed income (interest rate risk) is much more complex, as bonds are very different and depend on several variables such as issuer, maturity, coupons and so on. In other words, in the market there is a wide variety of bonds with many similar, but not identical, characteristics, and proposing a model that coherently represents them all is complicated.

Interest rate risk is essentially a particular type of market risk as it is "the uncertainty of future earnings resulting from changes in market conditions" (in this case changes in the market interest rate), but due to its complexity it is usually studied separately and in relation to the exchange rate risk.

In relation to the issuer, bonds can be divided into default risk bonds, corporate bonds and bonds without default risk (government debt). It is assumed, although it is not always the case, that government debt cannot default; for this reason, the difference between the interest paid by a corporate bond and a government bond is called a risk premium, "spread." For a particular corporate bond, the value of the risk premium varies over time and thus there is a very close relationship between corporate bonds and government bonds, which makes the issue more complex.

Also, the bonds listed in the market have very different maturities, from very short term, which could be less than a month, to very long term, which could be 30 years. Thus, there are interest rates with very different terms; the daily interest rate is fixed by the central bank of the currency zone in question, while interest rates with longer maturities are set by the market. As will be discussed in subsequent chapters, in fixing these interest rates to different terms, various other factors come into play such as demand for bonds with different maturities (more short-term bonds are demanded than long-term), risk (which also grows with the term) and so on. There is also a close relationship between interest rates at different terms, because there cannot be a big difference between interest rates from one year to the next. If this were the case it would mean that in a year's time the annual interest rate (the implicit annual rate) would be expected to be very different from what it is now, which is not very reasonable. In addition, as there is greater demand for short-term bonds, short-term interest rates are usually lower than long-term rates and the variation in the rates from one date to another is "gradual" because of the close relationship that exists between them. All this increases the complexity of managing this risk.

The coupon bond is closely related to maturity because the older the coupon, the sooner the borrowed money will be repaid (the average payment date is closer to the original date).

In short, fixed-income dynamics are very complex as a result of two main factors: the great diversity of products and the close relationship that exists between them. It can be concluded, as will be discussed in subsequent chapters, that the quantification and hedging of interest rate risks are very complex issues.

2.2.1.3 Exchange Rate

As in the case of interest rates, exchange rate dynamics are also rather complex. There are "spot" exchange rate markets, in which one currency can be exchanged for another instantly, but there are also future exchange rate markets, in which today's market participants commit to exchange currency in the future at an exchange rate that is fixed today.

Additionally, as is to be expected, there is a very close relationship between spot exchange rates and future exchange rates, and this close relationship also exists between different interest rates. The relationship is clear: investing a euro in buying a European bond annually must be the equivalent of exchanging a euro for a dollar today, investing the dollar in North American bonds today and signing a contract agreeing on a future exchange rate to convert the money back from dollars to euros after a year. Otherwise, you could make money without taking any risks, which is not possible in a perfect market. This relationship is called covered exchange rate parity.

Therefore, it can be concluded that there are complexities involved in quantifying and hedging exchange rate risks.

2.2.1.4 Commodities

All the financial products that have been dealt with so far (shares, bonds, exchange rate agreements, etc.) have an electronic format, and therefore, unlike "commodities", these products do not incur any storage costs. In order to manage the market risk associated with commodities, storage costs must be taken into account in addition to the factors considered for other product types.

Similarly, another peculiarity of commodities compared to other types of financial assets is what is known as a "convenience yield". As will be discussed in subsequent chapters, in a formal definition a convenience yield could be described as the value accumulated for the holder of a spot asset compared to the value accumulated for those with a futures contract on the asset. In a more simple and direct way, in the case of commodities, it can be said that the convenience yield refers to the yield generated for a particular owning entity from their necessary commodities. For example, if a refinery has crude oil in storage, the problems associated with disruptions in supply are avoided. This does not occur if the refinery has no crude oil in storage and has only future assets of the crude material. This gain is known as the convenience yield.

The fact that commodities present storage costs and convenience yields, among other things, causes their price dynamic to be very complex and thus makes it very difficult to quantify and hedge the risk. The first consequence of storage costs and convenience yields is that, while share prices follow a simple random process (standard Brownian), commodity prices have some degree of mean reversion. In the case of shares, as all the information is included in the price, the price will be the same tomorrow as it is today updated with the interest rate, plus a simple random noise representing the new information available tomorrow ("shocks"), while in the case of commodities, even in the presence of these factors their prices have some degree of mean reversion.

Nor can we forget that at specific times of year supplies of many commodities are lower and demand for them cannot be met, causing their prices to reflect seasonality, that is, substantially different prices at different times of year.

2.2.2 Credit Risk

Broadly speaking, credit risk is the risk that a customer does not pay for the products or services they have demanded. This risk is usually not the most important risk in industrial companies, particularly in companies where the business focuses on the end client, because in these cases the "delivery and payment" criterion makes it virtually impossible to default. However, in many industrial sectors institutional clients are charged at 60, 90,120 or 180 days so in this case credit risk is also present. In contrast, this risk is of vital importance to banks, as their business involves lending money which should be returned over time and in some cases, as in the case of mortgages, the repayment period may exceed 30 years.

The quantification and management of this risk is radically different to market risk, mainly because market risk focuses on changes in asset prices, which offers an infinite set of possibilities, whereas the phenomenon of default is dichotomous by its very nature, in other words, the debt is either paid or unpaid. Therefore, credit risk management focuses on three features of the default phenomenon: the probability of default, the loss in case of default and the exposure when default occurs.

In order to characterise the likelihood of clients defaulting in the future, companies develop "credit scoring" models. These models assign a rating depending on the characteristics of each individual client: accounting statements (income, debt, margin, etc.), industry, size and so on, and the probability of default is associated with this credit rating. There are also companies that specialise in assigning credit ratings, such as Standard & Poor's, Moody's and Fitch. As will be discussed in subsequent chapters, the loss in case of default is closely linked to the value of its warranty, if it has a warranty, in the same way as it is to economic cycles, whereas the default exposure is not always known accurately, as there are some types of loans, such as credit accounts or cards, in which the borrower has the right to have more cash available to them at any time.

It should also be noted that accurately measuring the credit risk of a given client is usually complicated due to asymmetric information problems: the client knows their exact ability to pay, while external analysts for the company only have the information contained in financial statements that do not accurately reflect the risk of the company. Conversely, when there are a large number of clients, it is easier to characterise the average credit risk of the portfolio, as it is possible to know quite accurately that the average default probability of firms of a certain size and a given sector is XX %, even though it is not known which customers will default. In addition, it is also simple to establish the average loss in case of default and the default exposure.[2]

From the previous explanation it can be concluded that hedging this risk is very complex. Therefore, explicit hedging is not usually performed on it, but rather the portfolio tends to be diversified. However, in recent times banks have turned to derivatives to hedge overall credit risk. As will be discussed in more detail in subsequent chapters, these derivatives are implemented in such a way that a set of creditors with the same credit rating provide default hedging above the average probability. However, the recent crisis has shown that the market is not yet mature enough for the widespread use of these products, as instruments of this type that were extremely liquid a year earlier have become completely illiquid (their liquidity has "evaporated").

2.2.2.1 Counterparty Risk

A derivative credit risk, also known as counterparty risk, is related to credit risk. When a contract is signed for a derivative to hedge a risk, another risk is created: the risk that if this case arises, the counterparty with whom the contract has been signed does not meet their obligations. In this type of operation a service is not provided, or a product that has been provided is not paid for by the client, but rather a position is simply taken on a

[2] In other words, the law of large numbers is followed in this type of risk.

derivative. Over time, depending on how the underlying asset varies, it can generate a positive or negative value for the contractors, as can be seen in the Figures in Sect. 2.1.2. (Figs. from 2.1 to 2.6). Counterparty risk describes a risk whereby the derivative in question produces a positive value for the contractor over time and the counterparty fails to meet its obligations.

This is an increasingly important risk, as it is becoming more common to sign derivative asset contracts; however, there are mechanisms to reduce it. The first is to sign a contract for derivatives in organised markets (stock exchanges). In these markets all participants sign a contract with the market and the possible losses are hedged by the fees charged, that is, these markets have a clearing house. Furthermore, at the end of each day a settlement of gains and losses is generally required which involves settling the gains or losses made during the day instead of waiting for maturity. Another possibility to reduce this risk is the collateral requirement that can be quickly implemented if the counterparty fails to meet their obligations, whether the derivative contract is signed in an organised market or not.

2.2.3 Other Risks

Apart from the risks already outlined, there are many more (liquidity risks, operational risks, country risks, regulatory risks, reputational risks, etc.) which will be discussed in more depth in subsequent chapters. However, by way of introduction, in this section operational and liquidity risks will be presented briefly.

2.2.3.1 Operational Risk

Operational risk is a risk which has always existed but which has become critically important in recent times due to the increasing internationalisation of businesses and the increasing dependence on new technology. It is not easy to establish a precise definition of this risk (examples will be provided in later chapters) but it can be defined simply as the risk of loss resulting from a failure in business processes. These can be productive processes or any other of the company's activities, which may range from payroll to system maintenance, while faults can be caused by external or internal agents.

The measurement and management of this risk is based on the same principles as in the case of credit risk but with a unique characteristic which results in a significant increase in the complexity of its measurement: in many cases, operational risk events are very low probability events but when they occur they cause very high losses.

2.2.3.2 Liquidity Risk

When a contract is signed for a derivative, or any other product, to hedge a given risk or to speculate, we must rely on its liquidity, as it could be that the risk disappears and there is a need to sell it. It is also necessary to rely on liquidity when there is a need to buy rather than sell it at some point in the future. In either case, it is possible that when the time of sale or purchase comes, this cannot be accomplished without incurring a significant loss due to lack of counterparties in the market. This uncertainty is what is known as a liquidity risk.

It must be taken into account that liquidity varies over business cycles, as in times of crisis it decreases while in times of prosperity it grows, which in many cases leads traders to believe that liquidity will be much greater than it really is, even in moments of crisis.

2.3 The Accounting Impact of Hedging

Although this will be covered in detail in subsequent chapters, this chapter would be incomplete without briefly mentioning the significance of the accounting impact of hedging in quantitative terms.

As indicated in Chap. 1, a hedging strategy may be designated as "hedge accounting" if it is "highly effective" in offsetting the risk generated by an asset or a transaction without having an impact on the overall risk of the company. Thus, if an instrument is designated as hedge accounting of a balanced asset, the rule states that profits or losses of one can be compensated for by the gains or losses of another and they do not need to be shown in the results, regardless of how each of them is recorded. Conversely, if at the start or during the period of time agreed between two consecutive presentations of results hedging is no longer effective, both the asset to be hedged and the hedging instrument must be recorded with standard criteria. In most cases this means that the asset to be hedged is recorded at its historical value, since it is usually a permanent investment, while the hedging instrument is recorded at its market value, which varies at different periods.

The formal definition of "highly effective" states that for hedging to be referred to in this way two conditions must be met: the first is that at the beginning and during every period from then on, the hedging instrument is expected to be highly effective in offsetting changes in the value of the hedging instrument in the future, while the second states that in each period the actual results of dividing the change in value into the hedging instrument and the asset to be hedged are in the range of 80–125 %.

The condition of being "highly effective" established here is very reasonable and seems simple to comply with. However, in the actual operating of a company its compliance may not be free of great complexity, as it is not always possible to find a hedging instrument with exactly the same characteristics as the asset to be hedged and which is, therefore, able to ensure full compliance with the conditions previously established. Consequently, the high risk of signing a hedge contract for an asset that, on balance, is considered a permanent investment is that if at the beginning or during the hedging period the definition of hedge accounting is not complied with, it will lead to the asset to be hedged being recorded at its acquisition value in the company's financial statements, while the hedging instrument is recorded at its market value, which can cause large variations in value that undoubtedly must be shown in the results, even though they are compensated for economically, at least in part, by the change in the value of the asset to be hedged.

Part II

Market Risk

3

One-Dimensional Market Risk; Equity Risk

3.1 Basic Concepts

As defined in Chap. 1, risk is the degree of uncertainty regarding future net returns that will be obtained by making an investment. Similarly, in Chap. 2 it was established that market risk is the uncertainty that exists about future earnings arising from changes in market conditions (share prices, interest rates, exchange rates, commodity prices, etc.). In other words, market risk is the uncertainty that exists regarding all economic and financial variables which affect the results of a company.

In this chapter, as in Chap. 4, the characterisation, quantification and management of this risk will be described in greater depth, firstly from a one-dimensional perspective in which only two periods are considered: the current time (when the investment to be made is defined) and a future moment in time (at which the value of that investment is measured). Chapter 4 will discuss the multidimensional case, in which various moments in time will be considered.

Equity risk is the most frequently discussed type of market risk. It is the uncertainty that exists about future profits resulting from changes in share

F.J. Población García, *Financial Risk Management*,
DOI 10.1007/978-3-319-41366-2_3

price. It is for this reason that this specific risk rather than general market risk will be referred to in many parts of this chapter. However, not only equity risk, but all the other concepts addressed here, correspond with the general definition of market risk and at most these variations may occasionally alter the probability model.

3.1.1 Terminology

Before analysing this concept in detail, the terminology that will be used should be clearly established. First of all, at each moment in time t, the price of any share will be given by P_t. Additionally, only two periods will be considered: the time of investment ($t = 0$) and the time when the value of this investment is measured ($t = 1$). Thus, the absolute deviation is defined as $D = P_1 - P_0$, the relative deviation as $R = \frac{P_1 - P_0}{P_0}$ (which is the exact profit per unit invested), whereas gross yield is defined as $\frac{P_1}{P_0} = 1 + R$ (which is the result per unit invested).

However, price logarithms are often used instead of prices as they have better operating properties due to the fact that, by definition, prices cannot be negative whereas their logarithms can take any real value. This enables normal distribution to be used, while in the other case asymmetric and truncated distributions set at zero must be used. In turn, the logarithms transform products into sums and quotients into subtractions, greatly simplifying operations, especially when working with various periods. In the same way, logarithm variations are independent of price level, which greatly facilitates comparisons. Thus, lowercase letters will be used for quantities equivalent in logarithms, that is, the price in logarithms is $p_t = \text{Ln}(P_t)$, while the continuous yield will be defined as $r = p_1 - p_0 = \text{Ln}\left(\frac{P_1}{P_0}\right) = \text{Ln}(1 + R)$.

The following example demonstrates the simplification arising from the use of logarithms: initially an investment is made in a share $t = 0$ and two future moments in time are considered $t = 1$ and $t = 2$. This allows two yields to be obtained: $R_1 = \frac{P_1 - P_0}{P_0}$ and $R_2 = \frac{P_2 - P_1}{P_1}$. The question is: what are the final and the average yields per period? In this case the following is achieved: $(1 + R_{Tot}) = (1 + R_1)(1 + R_2)$, thus the total yield is: $R_{Tot} = (1 + R_1)(1 + R_2) - 1$ while the average yield is defined by the following relationship: $(1 + R_{Med})^2 = (1 + R_1)(1 + R_2)$, from which $R_{Med} = \sqrt{(1+R_1)(1+R_2)} - 1$.

Note the difference working in logarithms: $r_{Tot} = \text{Ln}(1 + R_{Tot}) = \text{Ln}[(1 + R_1)(1 + R_2)] = \text{Ln}(1 + R_1) + \text{Ln}(1 + R_2) = r_1 + r_2$, in other words, $r_{Tot} = r_1 + r_2$, while the average yield is defined by $2r_{Med} = \text{Ln}[(1 + R_{Med})^2] = \text{Ln}[(1 + R_1)(1 + R_2)] = r_1 + r_2$ from which it can be concluded that $2r_{Med} = r_1 + r_2$ therefore, the average yield is $r_{Med} = \frac{r_1+r_2}{2}$.

Consider the extent to which the calculation would be simplified when dealing with a greater number of periods.

When characterising the aggregation of assets, it should be noted that generally if there is a portfolio of N assets with a price of $P_1, \ldots, P_N$ respectively, the price of the portfolio is the sum of the number of shares of each asset acquired $(q_1, \ldots, q_N)$ multiplied by the price of each share, that is, the value of the portfolio is $q_1P_1 + \ldots + q_NP_N$. On the other hand, the profitability of the portfolio is the sum of the returns of each asset $(R_1, \ldots, R_N)$, each weighted by the proportion of wealth invested in the asset in question $(\lambda_1, \ldots, \lambda_N)$, that is, the total return is $\lambda_1R_1 + \ldots + \lambda_NR_N$. The aggregation of continuous yields cannot be calculated in the same way as gross yields; however, the formula for the aggregation of gross yields can be applied to continuous yields, although not in exactly the same way, which constitutes a great approximation.

The following example clearly demonstrates this. There are two assets A and B, which today are worth €10 and €20 per share respectively, and tomorrow they will be worth (on average) €11 and €23. Their yields are thus $R_A = \frac{11-10}{10} = 0.1$ $R_B = \frac{23-20}{20} = 0.15$ or, equally, for every euro invested, a profit of €0.10 and €0.15 is made respectively. If four shares are purchased from the first asset and three from the second, the portfolio will be worth €100 today and $4 \cdot 11 + 3 \cdot 23 = 113$ tomorrow; for this reason the return is $R_{Tot} = \frac{113-100}{100} = 0.13$.

However, it is not necessary to work with a fixed number of shares: if they are converted into percentages of wealth, it is understood that four A shares are worth €40 and three B shares are worth €60, in other words 60

Table 3.1 Aggregation

Variable rates	Coefficients	Formula
Price	Quantities	$q_1P_1 + \ldots + q_NP_N$
Returns	Proportions	$\lambda_1R_1 + \ldots + \lambda_NR_N$

% of our wealth has been invested in A and 40 % in B. Therefore, since for every euro invested in A an extra €0.10 is made and for every euro in B an extra €0.15 is made, with this investment strategy for every euro invested the exact same result will be achieved: $\frac{40}{100}0.1 + \frac{60}{100}0.15 = 0.13€$.

Table 3.1 summarises the results outlined above.

3.2 Probabilistic Model

Before proposing a model, the properties of the financial series will be observed and later studied as the intention is to replicate their features. Thus, a typical case, the STOXX Europe 600 index, can be seen in Figs. 3.1 and 3.2.

Figure 3.1 represents the closure data of the STOXX Europe 600 index between 4 January 2000 and 24 April 2015 and, as demonstrated, the values do not seem to correspond to those of a stable variable. However, in the case of the returns (continuous) with the same dates, Fig. 3.2 is reached, whereby the data is like that of stable interest data

There is a very important issue, reviewed in specialised literature, which will not be discussed in this book due to its complexity, and that is that there are periods of high volatility and periods of low volatility,[1] as seen in Fig. 3.2. Thus, in this book it will be assumed that continuous yield is a stable variable.

Based on the terminology in the previous section and the figures in this section, the problem will be presented in probabilistic terms: the variables with subscript 0 are known, but it is unclear what will happen at $t = 1$ and

[1] This fact is the basis of GARCH models.

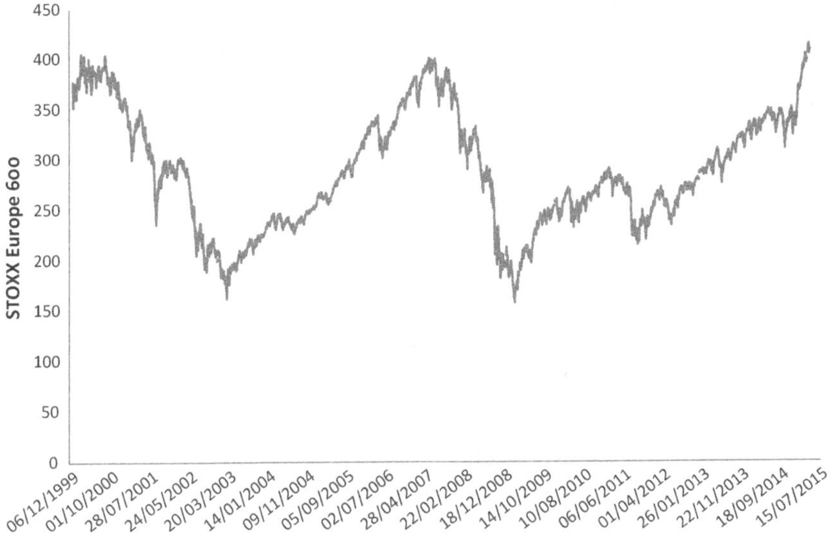

Fig. 3.1 STOXX Europe 600 (*Source*: Bloomberg)

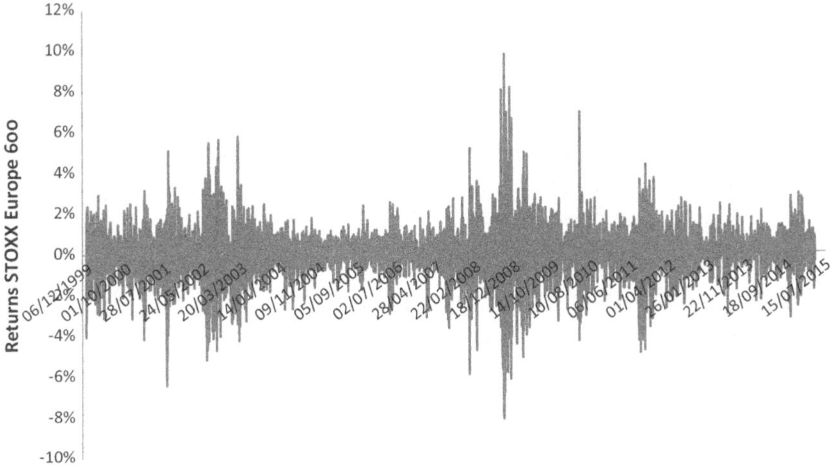

Fig. 3.2 Returns, STOXX Europe 600 (*Source*: Bloomberg)

thus P_1 is a random variable, as are r, $p_1$or R. Additionally, if it were possible to specify the probability distribution of any of these variables, it would be possible to obtain the others automatically.

The simplest and also the most commonly used model to characterise the probability distribution of these variables is to assume that continuous yield is a normal variable with an average of $\mu\Delta t$ and standard deviation $\sigma\sqrt{\Delta t}$ where Δt represents the time elapsed from the moment of investment $t = 0$, until the time when the value of the investment is measured, $t = 1$, in other words, continuous yield is distributed $r \equiv N\left(\mu\Delta t, \sigma\sqrt{\Delta t}\right)$. As demonstrated, the more time that passes between $t = 0$ and $t = 1$, the greater the standard deviation of probability distribution, which will have implications in terms of risk.

Another way to characterise this model is to say that $r = \mu\Delta t + \sigma\sqrt{\Delta t}$ ε where the variable ε is standard normal. Note that, since it is $r = p_1 - p_0$, this is the same as assuming the dynamic $p_1 = \mu\Delta t + p_0 + \sigma\sqrt{\Delta t}\varepsilon$, or generalised to more periods it is simply $p_{t+1} = \mu\Delta t + p_t + \sigma\sqrt{\Delta t}\varepsilon_t$, known as a random walk process, and that its simulation actually produces very similar graphs to that of the continuous yield of the STOXX Europe 600 presented previously.

As has just been noted, this model, where the price in logarithms tomorrow, p_{t+1}, is a random variable which has normal distribution, the average price today being p_t, plus a term, $\mu\Delta t$, which incorporates the fact that money tomorrow and money today are not equivalent and where appropriate, the risk of standard deviation $\sigma\sqrt{\Delta t}$, is the model used most frequently by both academics and investors. This is simply due to the great intuition behind it and the fact that in perfect markets all market information available at a given time is contained in the price. Regarding shares of assets without storage costs or convenience yields, the best, if not the only, option to characterise the probability distribution of the price tomorrow is to assume it is a probability distribution with the average price today altered by the factors mentioned previously plus a noise which represents the information received in the market between today and tomorrow which will change that price. Otherwise, if all the market information were not included in the price, it would mean that the asset would overvalued or undervalued because there would be information

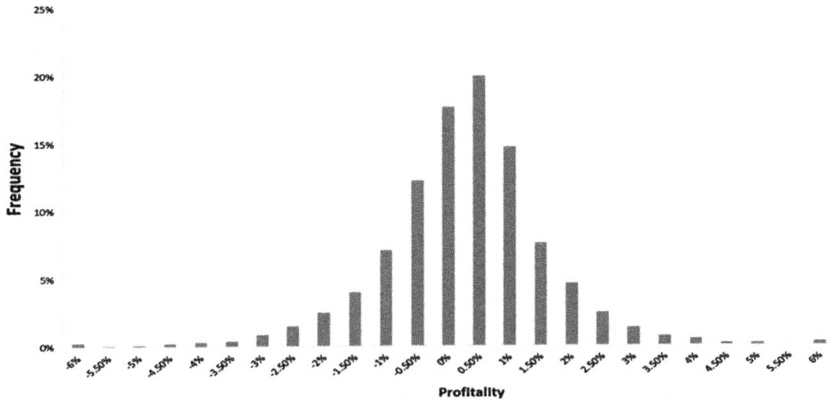

Fig. 3.3 Absolute frequency profitability (continuous) of the IBEX 35 (*Source*: Bloomberg)

that was not incorporated into the price. If this occurred and, for example, the asset were overvalued, agents that had the additional information would come to the stock market to sell at a price that, given this information, would be high, thus causing it to reduce to the level at which all information was incorporated. If the asset was undervalued, the opposite would occur.

An interesting question is to what extent the distribution, which can be considered to be stable, is really Gaussian. This is also a fact that can be tested empirically by observing the histogram of the continuous profitability of the IBEX 35 in Fig. 3.3.

Noting the previous figure (Fig. 3.3), it seems clear that normal distribution is a good approach; however, if standardised (the mean is subtracted and multiplied by the standard deviation to thereby obtain a probability distribution with zero mean and variance equal to one) it can be observed that the adjustment is far from perfect (Fig. 3.4).

Values where the theoretical distribution is lower and which therefore represent less probability are found both in the centre and at the ends. That is, the normal distribution has much more probability on the outskirts of its mean, not in the mean itself, and has "ends" which are much thinner, in other words, the actual distribution has excess kurtosis relative

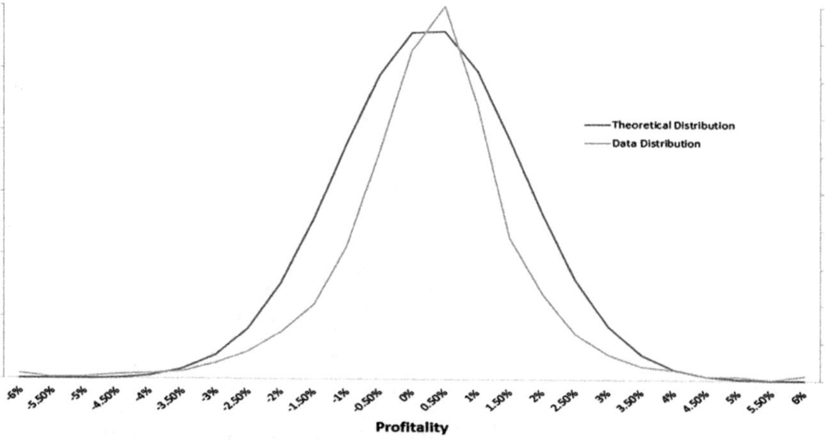

Fig. 3.4 IBEX Profitability (*Source*: Bloomberg)

to the normal,[2] which is known as the "thick ends" problem. The normal distribution implies that a catastrophic decline in the stock market can only occur once every 10,000 years, which is not very realistic. For all these reasons among others, it seems logical to think of using distributions with excess kurtosis, such as Student's t distributions or Lévy or Pareto distribution logarithms. Note that although these distributions are more complex than normal, in many applications they do not even cause operational problems. Therefore, from this point onwards this probabilistic model will be assumed for the one-dimensional case, assuming that ε is any random variable, the only requirement being that it is continuous and able to take values between $-\infty$ and $+\infty$; when normality is needed it will be analysed individually.

As is evident, once the probability distribution of p_1 is known, the probability distribution of P_1 should then be estimated. Equity risk is the risk that deals with uncertainty regarding future earnings due to changes in share price (not the logarithms). Thus, avoiding the problems of excess kurtosis mentioned previously, if it is assumed that the continuous yield follows a normal distribution, the price follows a log-normal distribution

[2] The kurtosis is a measurement of the probability at the ends.

with the same parameters as the normal that characterises the return multiplied by P_0. That is, if $r \sim N(\mu, \sigma)$, then since $r = \ln(P_1/P_0)$, then $P_1 \sim P_0$*Log-Normal(μ, σ).

Nothing has been said so far about how to estimate the parameters that characterise the aforementioned probability distributions: μ, σ, the correlation between random variables (ρ) in the case of having more than one asset and so on. The reason for this is that there are several types of estimates, one of which is calculated by using historical data, while another is inferred from the price of derivatives that have these as their underlying assets, as well as many more. Although estimation of these parameters is beyond the scope of this book, it may be noted that the parameter with the most problematic calculation is the correlation between assets. It is clear that the mean and standard deviation are relatively stable, and when they are unstable they aren't particularly difficult to characterise, as in the case of GARCH models. However, the correlation is extremely unstable and very sensitive to the economic cycle: in times of crisis it increases dramatically.

This section deals with the study of the probabilistic model from the viewpoint of equity risk, that is, the probabilistic model is adjusted to the share price but not always to the other variables that make up market risk (interest rates, exchange rates, commodity prices, etc.). Probabilistic models that best accommodate these variables will be dealt with in subsequent chapters; however, the other concepts that are addressed in this chapter will be applied as they are to the other risks which are encompassed in the market risk.

3.3 Value at Risk (VaR)

3.3.1 Concept

As indicated previously, equity risk is the uncertainty about future earnings resulting from changes in share prices. Thus, if considering the maximum risk of investing in equities, or in any market variable, the conclusion would be obvious: the maximum risk is the risk of losing everything, that is, the maximum risk is that at $t = 0$ a share has been bought at a price P_0 and at $t = 1$ the value of it is $P_1 = 0$. Obviously, this conclusion is useless because following this logic all shares have the same risk, which is clearly false. In order to measure the risk it is necessary to use a measure which allows us to distinguish the risk of different shares.

There are many ways to measure risk, but for the market in general and that of equities in particular, the most commonly used is the **value at risk** (VaR). By definition, the VaR is a measure of the maximum potential change that the value of a portfolio can suffer over a given time horizon and probability level. More specifically, assuming that the probability distribution of P_1 is known, which will be described in the following section, from this distribution a probability level α is fixed (it is usually fixed at 5 %, although in theory any can be used). Thus, the VaR is a P^* value, which can take the random variable P_1 such as $\text{Prob}(P_1 \leq P^*) = \alpha$ or equally $\text{Prob}(P_1 > P^*) = 1 - \alpha$. In other words, the VaR is a value (P^*) which can take the random variable P_1 in such a way that the probability of being below it is α; if dealing with a share it can be concluded that with a probability of $1 - \alpha$ its value will be at least P^*.

Measuring risk in this way avoids the problem outlined previously, whereby the minimum value is zero in every case, since the percentage α of the worst possible values of the portfolio is removed (i.e., $P_1 = 0$ will always be among these values) and then the minimum is calculated.

As seen in the previous definition, the VaR is a possible value that can be used to represent the portfolio, in which case it must have the same units as this portfolio. If the portfolio is in euros, the VaR will be as well. Additionally, it is necessary to emphasise that in the definition of VaR the time horizon, that is, the time difference between $t = 0$ and $t = 1$, is critical, as it is always the case that the longer the time horizon, the higher the variance of the aforementioned distribution, because there is more uncertainty.

This way of measuring risk is very well known, as it allows different shares to be differentiated by risk, that is, the VaR represents a maximum loss that is not the same in all shares, since the higher the σ is, the higher the VaR will be. It must also be noted that the definition of the VaR does not take into account the type of probability distribution P_1 in any way

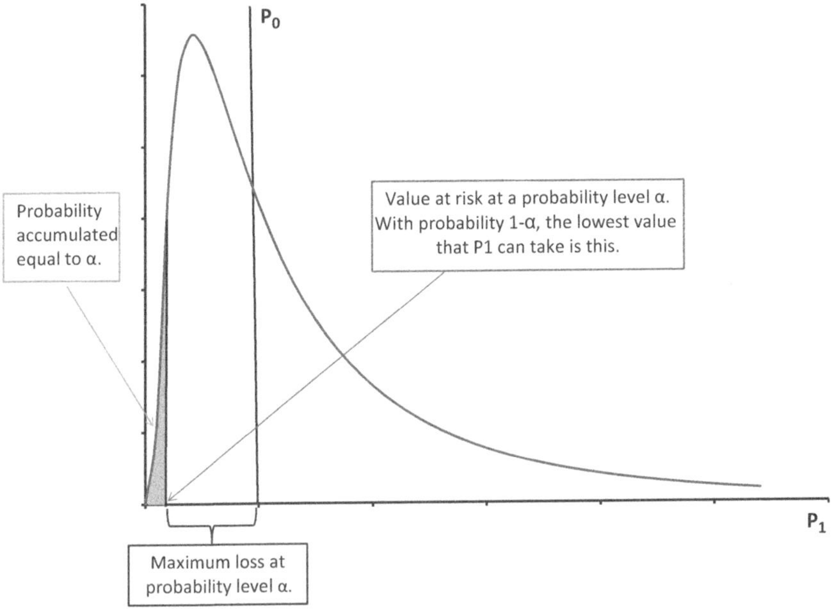

Fig. 3.5 VaR calculation (Author's own composition)

and, of course, it is not required to be a normal. Moreover, it is possible, as will be seen later, to calculate the VaR even if the probability distribution of P_1 is unknown. All that is required is that it exists and that it can be estimated in some way, that is, it is not necessary to know its parametric form explicitly or to adapt it to any known distribution. The calculation can be seen in Fig. 3.5.

As is evident from Figs. 3.6 and 3.7, the larger the σ is, the more likely it is that the P_1 values move away from their mean and therefore the greater the distance between the expected value of P_1 and the value of P^*, such that $\text{Prob}(P_1 \leq P^*) = \alpha$, and therefore the greater the risk will be.

Also note that in the definition of VaR it is stated explicitly that this is the value at a given time horizon, that is, the value at risk for a portfolio of shares with a time horizon of a year is not the same as that for two years. In the first case, the value at risk is greater, and therefore the loss is lower in the second case, or put another way, the greater the time horizon, the greater the standard deviation of probability distribution for a given value σ, as already discussed in the probabilistic model section.

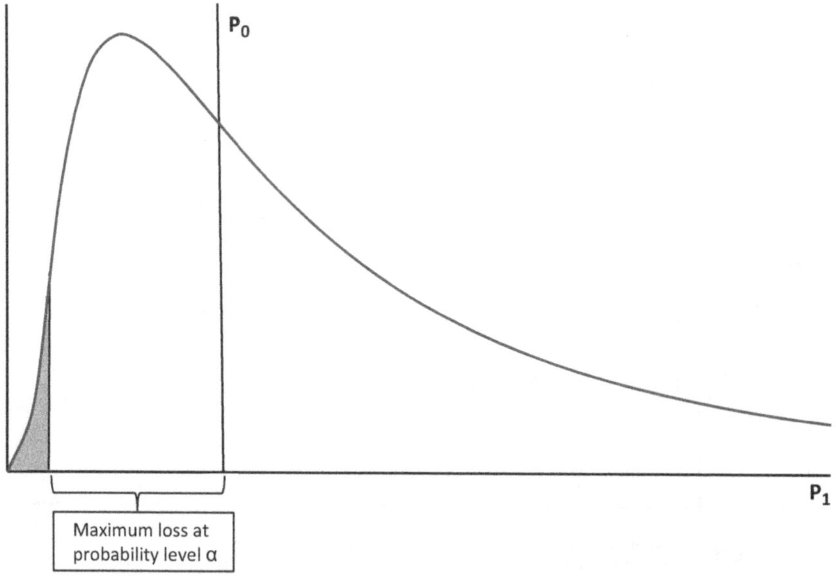

Fig. 3.6 Probability distribution with a high σ (Author's own composition)

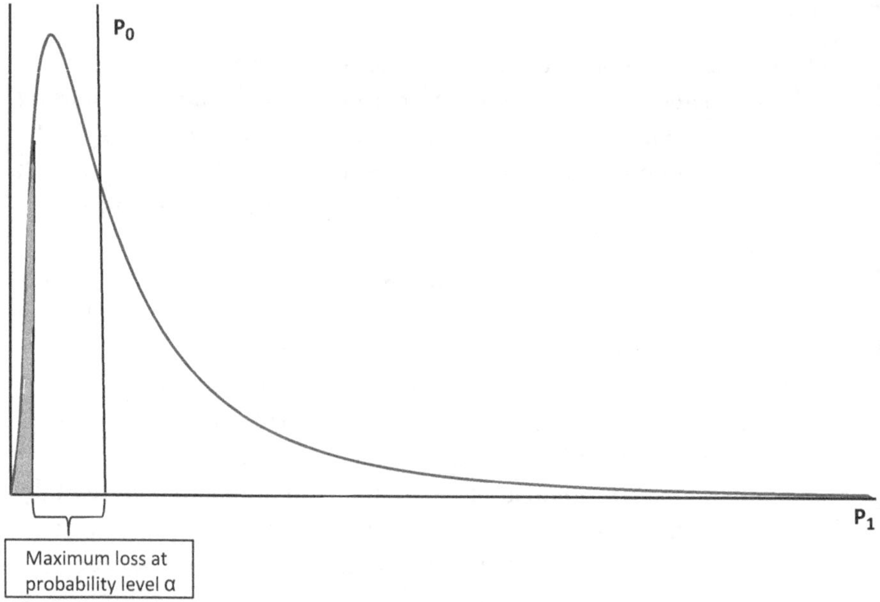

Fig. 3.7 Probability distribution with a low σ (Author's own composition)

3.3.2 Theoretical Calculation and Examples

If the probability distribution is known, the calculation of the VaR is straightforward, since if the probability distribution of p_1 is known, its distribution function $F()$ and the VaR calculation are known, that is, P^* can be calculated simply by considering $F(P^*) = \alpha$ and this equation can be solved explicitly by applying the opposite function $P^* = F^{-1}(\alpha)$.[3]

Imagine the price of a very risky share that provides high returns (of around 10 %) but also has potential for severe losses. Expressed mathematically following the probabilistic model presented previously, assume that the probability distribution of this share's continuous yield at a time horizon of one year is a normal which has an average of 10 % and a standard deviation of 20 %, that is, the profitability of this share follows the probabilistic model presented previously, $r = \mu\Delta t + \sigma\sqrt{\Delta t}\varepsilon$, with $\mu =$ 10 %, $\sigma =$ 20 % y $\Delta t = 1$. In this case the question is: what would the VaR be for profitability at a probability level of 5 %? And if the share price today is €80, what would the VaR be at 5 % for this price at a horizon of one year?

Regarding returns, the response is immediate, since it deals with a normal which has a 10 % average and a standard deviation of 20 %.[4] It can be observed in any table or spreadsheet that as long as exactly 5 % remains on the left of probability, the distribution value is −22.9 %, and therefore this −22.9 % is the value at risk of profitability.

Following the ideas discussed in the probabilistic model paragraph, the probability distribution of P_1 is the constant P_0, which in this case is $P_0 =$ €80, multiplied by a log-normal distribution of parameters $\mu =$ 10 % y $\sigma =$ 20 %.[5] As before, in any table or spreadsheet calculation it can be verified that the value of a probability distribution with these parameters that leaves 5 % of probability on the left is

[3] For the most common distributions, this investment function is implemented in virtually all programming languages and spreadsheets.

[4] It is evident that if the time horizon had been two years, the coefficient σ of the probability distributions would have been what in the probabilistic model is known as $\sigma\sqrt{\Delta t}$.

[5] As in the previous case, if the time frame had been two years, the coefficient σ of the probability distributions would have been what was called $\sigma\sqrt{\Delta t}$ in the probabilistic model.

0.7955, so the VaR of this share price at this time horizon is 0.795 * 80 = €63.62. In other words, at a one year horizon the maximum loss a share can suffer at a probability level of 5 % is 80 − 63.62 = €16.38.

In the same way, once you have the result for profitability it is also very easy to calculate the value at risk for the share price, since a continued profitability of −22.9 % equals a $1 + R = e^{-0.229} = 0.795$, which multiplied by the initial share price, P_0 = €80, gives the VaR of this share price at this time horizon, in this case 0.795 * 80 = €63.62.

As seen in the above calculations, VaR has the same units as the portfolio in question, that is, if the portfolio is formed by one or more assets with a certain value in euros, the VaR is also measured in euros since, as indicated above, the VaR is simply one possible value that the portfolio concerned could have and therefore it must have the same number of units. Additionally, this is a good example to demonstrate the importance of the time horizon due to the fact that at a one year horizon μ and σ are equal to 10 % and 20 % respectively. However, if the time horizon had been two years μ would have been 10 %*2 = 20 % and σ would have been $20\%*\sqrt{2} \approx 30\%$, which would have led to a higher VaR, as with a longer time horizon comes greater risk.

It has been possible to solve this example analytically, as normality has been assumed for continuous yield which is only an approximation and because the portfolio was formed by a single asset. Although normality is assumed in the continuous yield, it is clear that there is no closed analytical formula for the probability distribution of a portfolio consisting of two assets with correlated prices and log-normal distribution.

The only way to estimate the VaR of a portfolio consisting of two assets in the same way as in the previous example is to assume that the price, and not the profitability, is distributed normally, even if this is completely unrealistic. In any case, if it is assumed that the portfolio consists of two assets whose prices P^1 and P^2 at $t = 1$ are distributed by normal distribution paths with means μ_1 and μ_2, with standard deviations σ_1 and σ_2 with a correlation of ρ, it wouldn't be difficult to calculate the VaR analytically by simply acknowledging that the distribution of the total portfolio at $t =$ 1 is normal with mean $\mu_1 + \mu_2$ and standard deviation $\sqrt{\sigma_1^2 + \sigma_2^2 + \rho\sigma_1\sigma_2}$. As always, the value of a probability distribution that has these parameters and leaves the chosen probability level α on the left can be seen in any table or spreadsheet calculation.

If, instead of assuming normality for the price, normality had been assumed for profitability, it would have been possible to reach an analytical result, because although no analytical probability distribution characterising the probability distribution of the sum of two random log-normal variables is known, it is possible to characterise the probability distribution of the total investment return. If the price of each asset is distributed in the same way as a log-normal, profitability is distributed normally and, as noted previously, the portfolio return is simply the sum of the returns of its assets, weighted by the percentage of wealth that has been invested in each of them. For this reason, if the profitability of each of the two assets in question is distributed through normal distribution paths with means of μ_1 and μ_2 and with standard deviations of σ_1 and σ_2 with a correlation of ρ, it is clear that the probability distribution of portfolio returns is normal with an average of $\lambda_1\mu_1 + \lambda_2\mu_2$ and a standard deviation of $\sqrt{\lambda_1^2\sigma_1^2 + \lambda_2^2\sigma_2^2 + \lambda_1\lambda_2\rho\sigma_1\sigma_2}$, the percentage of wealth being λ_i invested in the asset i ($i = 1, 2$). And if the probability distribution of returns in $t = 1$ is normal, the probability distribution of the portfolio value at this date is known, namely log-normal, and therefore the VaR should then be calculated.

However, despite being able to calculate the VaR of a portfolio consisting of two or more assets with prices that have a log-normal probability distribution, there is the problem that the number of parameters required for the estimation is not proportional to the number of assets in the portfolio, but is proportional to this high squared number whereby the VaR calculation becomes heavier and more complex. This is a difficult problem to solve, as it is also evident when calculating VaR empirically through numerical simulation, and for this reason it is known as the "curse of dimensionality".

Finally, it should be noted that in the previous examples the VaR could be calculated analytically because the portfolios were all made up of linear exposures, but this is not always the case, as sometimes the exposures may be "option type". In these cases there is no option but to resort to calculating the VaR empirically.

3.3.3 Empirical VaR Calculation

As discussed in the previous section, when the probability distribution of P_1 is known it is not difficult to estimate the VaR. Unfortunately, this probability distribution is not easy to know, and the concept of value at risk can be used both to estimate the equity risk and to estimate many other types of market risk (derivatives, commodities, etc.) in which the distribution of P_1 cannot be characterised in a simple way, in most cases the assets are "option type" exposures.

In addition, when it comes to a portfolio that consists of more than one share, in theory it is possible to calculate the VaR; however, in practice it is very difficult due to the fact that the number of variance and correlation terms does not grow in proportion to the number of assets in the portfolio, but grows in a proportional manner to its square.

For all these reasons, the analytical method is often inapplicable and therefore alternatives must be found.

3.3.3.1 Numerical Simulation (Monte Carlo Experiment)

Of these existing alternatives to estimate market risk, possibly the most popular is numerical simulation, also known as the Monte Carlo experiment. This method is especially recommended when you have a probabilistic model for the underlying assets but not for the end result. In other words, when trying to calculate the VaR for an asset which is a derivative of a share and the probability distribution of the share is known at $t = 1$ (the P_1 is known), it is very likely that if the payments of this derivative are "option type" the probability distribution cannot be found analytically. Therefore, the only option is to use simulation to calculate its VaR. Additionally, in the case of equities it is possible to calculate the probability distribution P_1 when dealing with one share; however, when the portfolio consists of more than one share, it is possible to calculate the probability distribution P_1 of each share individually but it is virtually impossible to estimate the total VaR theoretically.

The phases of Monte Carlo simulation are:

a) **Generation of scenarios**: based on the probability distribution of each asset or underlying asset in the portfolio, as well as the correlations between each of them, random numbers are used to generate a large number of future price scenarios according to the probabilistic model that each one of the asset prices follows (for example, N scenarios are generated). Occasionally, as noted previously, it is easier to generate scenarios for price logarithms rather than for prices, as their probability distribution is simpler.
b) **Value of portfolio:** for each of these simulations the value of the portfolio is calculated. Thus N possible future values are available, one for each simulated scenario.
c) **Calculation of VaR:** once the value of the portfolio has been calculated in each scenario, the probability distribution can be estimated by simply putting the possible N values of the portfolio in ascending order, grouping them into intervals ("buckets") and assigning a defined probability to each of these intervals, such as the number of elements in the interval divided by N. Based on this empirical probability distribution the desired risk measure should then be calculated, which in this case is the VaR. Thus, the risk measurement desired, in this case the VaR, will simply be the item in the αN position when sorting the N values from lowest to highest.

By way of example, consider a portfolio consisting of two assets with returns distributed normally, or equivalently; its price logarithms are distributed through a normal following two separate random paths. The first is the process $p^1_{t=1} = \mu_1 + p^1_{t=0} + \varepsilon^1_{t=1}$, where $\varepsilon^1_{t=1}$ is distributed through a distribution $N(0, \sigma_1 * \Delta t)$ whereby $\mu_1 = 5\ \%$ and $\sigma_1 = 30\ \%$. The price of asset 1 at $t = 0$ is $P^1_{t=0} = €15$. The second follows the process $p^2_{t=1} = \mu_2 + p^2_{t=0} + \varepsilon^2_{t=1}$, where $\varepsilon^2_{t=1}$ is distributed by an $N(0, \sigma_2 * \Delta t)$ distribution where $\mu_2 = 7\ \%$ and $\sigma_2 = 40\ \%$. The price of asset 2 at $t - 0$ is $P^2_{t-0} = €20$. Additionally, it is assumed that the correlation between $\varepsilon^2_{t=1}$ and $\varepsilon^2_{t=1}$ is 50 % ($\rho = 50\ \%$) and for simplicity, the time horizon of one year will be ($\Delta t = 1$).

In order to calculate the VaR, many ${\varepsilon^1}_{t=1}$ and ${\varepsilon^2}_{t=1}$ scenarios should be produced through the generation of random numbers that follow a normal distribution and have the desired correlation. The simplest way to do this is to generate random uncorrelated numbers η^1 and η^2 that follow a probability distribution with mean zero ($\mu = 0$) and variance of one ($\sigma^2 = 1$) and then generate scenarios ${\varepsilon^1}_{t=1}$ and ${\varepsilon^2}_{t=1}$ from these variables.

Generating the ${\varepsilon^1}_{t=1}$ and ${\varepsilon^2}_{t=1}$ scenarios from η^1 and η^2 is simple and involves acknowledging that ${\varepsilon^1}_{t=1}$ and ${\varepsilon^2}_{t=1}$ defined as ${\varepsilon^1}_{t=1} = \sigma_1 * \eta^1$ and ${\varepsilon^2}_{t=1} = \sigma_2 * \left(\rho * \eta^1 + \sqrt{1 - \rho^2} * \eta^2\right)$ both follow a normal distribution, have zero mean, standard deviation σ_1 and σ_2 respectively and have a correlation of $\rho = 50\ \%$.

Once a number N of ${\varepsilon^1}_{t=1}$ and ${\varepsilon^2}_{t=1}$ scenarios have been generated from the prices at $t = 0$ (${P^1}_{t=0}$ and ${P^2}_{t=0}$), N price scenarios in $t = 1$ (${P^1}_{t=1}$ and ${P^2}_{t=1}$) should then be obtained by simply basing them on the price logarithms at $t = 0$ (${p^1}_{t=0} = \ln({P^1}_{t=0})$ and ${p^2}_{t=0} = \ln({P^2}_{t=0})$) and applying the probabilistic models that both price logarithms follow (${p^i}_{t=1} = \mu_i + {p^i}_{t=0} + {\varepsilon^i}_{t=1}$) to generate N scenarios of price logarithms (${p^1}_{t=1}$ and ${p^2}_{t=1}$) whereby the N price scenarios (${P^1}_{t=1} = \exp({p^1}_{t=1})$and ${P^2}_{t=1} = \exp({p^2}_{t=1})$) are immediately obtained. Using the N price scenarios, the N portfolio value scenarios are obtained $t = 1$ ($V_{t=1}$) by simply calculating $V_{t=1} = {P^1}_{t=1} + {P^2}_{t=1}$. Once these N scenarios of the portfolio value are obtained at $t = 1$, its probability distribution can be estimated by separating all possible values into sections and calculating the probability of each section as the number of observations in each divided by the number N of scenarios simulated (Figs. 3.8 and 3.9, Table 3.2).

The Excel workbook "Example VaR" discusses the development of this procedure and demonstrates that in this case the following values of probability distribution are obtained, as represented in Table 3.2 and Fig. 3.9.

Once you have the probability distribution of the portfolio value at $t = 1$, at a given probability level of, for example, 5 % the value at risk should then be calculated, which in this case is €22.40. In other words, at $t = 0$ €15 has been invested in the first asset and €20 in the second asset and, based on this probability distribution, at $t = 1$ the expected value obtained is equal to €39.70 (the €35 initially invested plus an increase due to the

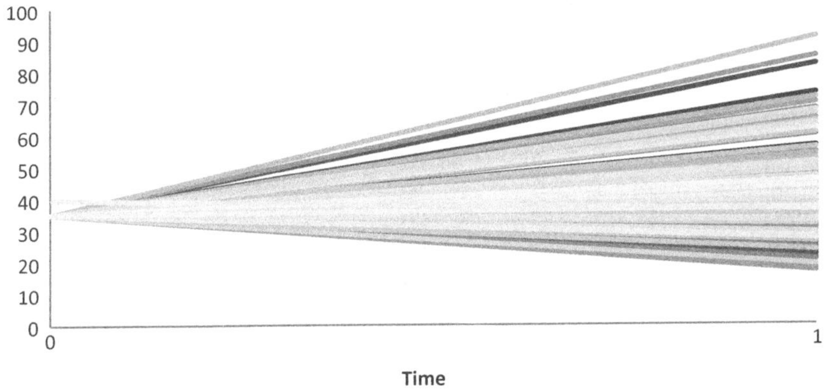

Fig. 3.8 Portfolio value (scenario simulation) (Author's own composition)

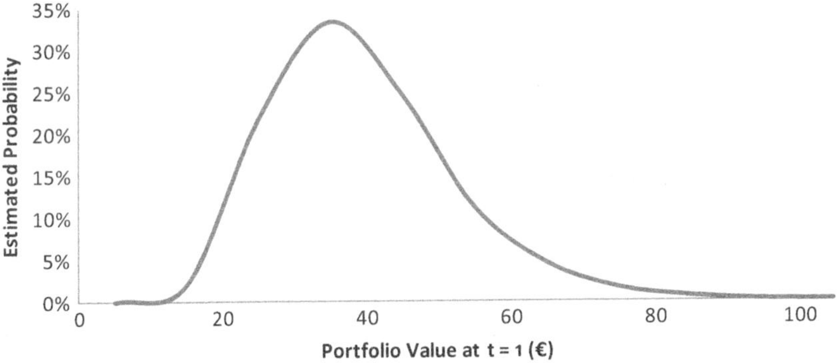

Fig. 3.9 Probability distribution of the portfolio value at $t = 1$ (Author's own composition)

fact that both μ_1 and μ_2 are positive) and a value at risk of €22.40. In this way, from the €35 invested at $t = 0$ or from the €39.70 of expected portfolio value at $t = 1$, excluding the 5 % of the sample corresponding to the worst probability level scenarios, in other words 5 % of the probability, the minimum value that the portfolio could have is €22.40.

Table 3.2 Estimated probability

Value of the portfolio at t=1(€)	Number of observations	Estimated probability
<10	1	0.01%
[10,20]	209	2.09%
[20,30]	2150	21.50%
[30,40]	3328	33.28%
[40,50]	2459	24.59%
[50,60]	1125	11.25%
[60,70]	463	4.63%
[70,80]	167	1.67%
[80,90]	63	0.63%
[90,100]	20	0.20%
<100	15	0.15%

As indicated, this does not mean that the value of the portfolio when at $t = 1$ cannot be less than this value—in fact it could be zero; it means that by eliminating 5 % of the sample corresponding to the worst scenarios shown, from the samples that are left the worst case scenario is that the portfolio is worth €22.40 at $t = 1$.

3.3.3.2 Historical Simulation

Another possibility is simulation using historical information. If sufficient data is available it may sometimes be preferable not to simulate prices, but instead to use their empirical distribution. The method is the same as in the previous section, but the values of the assets are not simulated and are instead taken from the time series. More specifically, steps (b) and (c) set out in the previous section remain unchanged, while step (a) is modified and instead of generating N future price scenarios, the price data of the time series is used. From this the differences between each share are calculated with the price delayed in time, the designated time horizon for estimating VaR. Based on P_0 and adding these variations, a potential price of P_1 can be generated for each of the variations calculated previously. By doing so, it is assumed that what was observed in the past will be repeated in the future. In this case, the time horizon also plays a crucial role because presumably, the longer the time horizon, the greater the changes in prices and the dispersion of probability distribution.

The main advantages of this procedure with respect to numerical simulation are that, in this case, a probabilistic model is not required for the probability distribution of future prices, as they are assumed to be the same as on previous occasions. It is also a directly interpretable methodology, since estimating by simulation could be more questionable because all simulation makes implicit assumptions about the probabilistic model. Finally, it should be noted that as it does not depend on parameters, it avoids the problem of the number of parameters growing with the square of the number of assets included in the portfolio (the "curse of dimensionality").

As for the disadvantages, it must be reiterated that the inference is limited by the amount of data, while in the case of simulation there is no limit to the number of simulations that can be made, that is, N can be as large as desired. Similarly it should be noted that this procedure does not take into account other factors or new issues that may arise (for example, it is not possible to determine whether some contributions come from one time cycle or another). Finally, it should be taken into account that without an underlying model, it is not possible to perceive the mistakes made or the reliability of the estimations, although this may be mitigated by comparing the results of different subsamples.

By way of example and in line with the previous section, we can consider the portfolio formed by one Telefónica stock (asset 1) and one Repsol stock (asset 2) acquired at $t = 0$ to estimate the value at risk at a time horizon of one year using historical simulation of the asset. In order to do this it is assumed, as in the previous example, that the price of asset 1 at $t = 0$ was $P^1_{t=0} =$ €15 while asset 2 is $P^2_{t=0} =$ €20.

Assuming you have quotes from both values from 22 January 1990 to 18 April 2012, 5,610 observations and have a time horizon of one year, the price variation of each asset is calculated at a horizon of one year. From this, N scenarios of prices at $t = 1$ ($P^1_{t=1}$ y $P^2_{t=1}$) are obtained (N being 5,610 − 250 due to the time elapsed) by simply adding the variations obtained previously to prices at $t = 0$ ($P^1_{t=0}$y $P^2_{t=0}$). Using the N scenarios of $P^1_{t=1}$ and $P^2_{t=1}$ (in the same way as in the previous examples) N scenarios of the portfolio values at $t = 1$ ($V_{t=1}$) are then

Table 3.3 Estimated probability

Value of the Portfolio at t=1 (€)	Number of observations	Estimated probability
<9	34	0.60%
[9,14]	83	1.50%
[19,14]	72	1.30%
[24,19]	215	4.00%
[29,24]	366	6.80%
[34,29]	649	12.10%
[39,34]	1835	34.20%
[44,39]	1315	24.50%
[49,44]	648	12.10%
[54,49]	142	2.60%
<54	1	0.00%

obtained using simply $V_{t=1} = P^1{}_{t=1} + P^2{}_{t=1}$. Following the same logic as before, once these N scenarios of the portfolio value at $t = 1$ have been obtained, its probability distribution can be estimated by separating all possible values into sections and calculating the probability of each segment as the number of observations in each divided by the number N of simulated scenarios.

The Excel workbook "Example VaR" includes the development of this procedure and indicates that the probability distribution values presented in Table 3.3 and Fig. 3.10 were obtained for this example.

Once the probability distribution of the portfolio value at $t = 1$ has been obtained at a given probability level of, for example, 5 %, the value at risk must then be calculated, which in this case is €21.70. That is, at $t = 0$ €15 was invested in asset 1 and €20 in asset 2, and based on this probability distribution at $t = 1$ its expected value is equal to €36.60 and a VaR of €21.70 is obtained.

3.3.3.3 Concrete Simulation Scenarios

The simulations proposed previously are very useful but lack the ability to adapt to specific scenarios that the analyst may want to study. For this reason, a third alternative is also proposed, known as a simulation scenario, in which specific values are assigned to prices to quantify the results

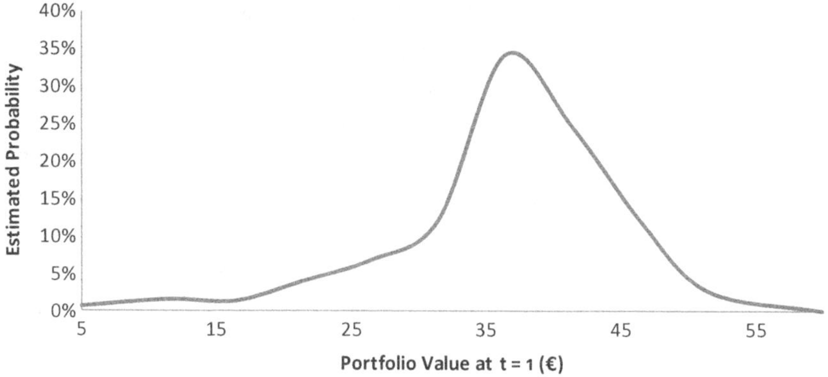

Fig. 3.10 Probability distribution of the portfolio value at $t = 1$ (Author's own composition)

in different chosen conditions. In other words, steps (b) and (c) set out in the previous sections remain unchanged, while step (a) is modified and N price data are taken according to the scenario defined and this proceeds in the same way for each scenario. These data can be simulated or taken from the series, while being restricted to those that meet the conditions set in the scenario in question or, conversely, can be set without following any established criteria, only to quantify what the returns would be.

The first thing to note is that the measurements used in this method are not exactly the same as in the previous methods because while the previous ones establish a more or less objective measurement of VaR, this approach answers the question "How much would the VaR be in these economic conditions?"

The main advantages of this operation are that it allows the estimations to be adjusted according to the working conditions and the interests of the client, and it is very easy to interpret as it avoids the "curse of dimensionality" referred to previously. On the other hand, the main disadvantage is that decisions regarding the establishment of scenarios are deeply subjective. In addition, there is no probabilistic model available, making it impossible to establish the probability of the proposed scenario.

By way of example and in line with the previous sections, simulation scenarios can be considered as a possible way to estimate the value at risk of a portfolio consisting of one share of Telefónica (asset 1) and one share of Repsol (asset 2) acquired at $t = 0$ at a time horizon of one year. In order to do this it is assumed, as in the previous example, that the price of asset one at $t = 0$ is $P^1_{t=0} =$ €15 while in asset two it is $P^2_{t=0} =$ €20.

In this case, the prices of both assets between the dates 22 January 1990 and 9 January 1996, equal to 1,496 observations, will be taken as a proposed scenario in order to see what would happen if both asset prices returned to the same levels as on the aforementioned dates. Thus, N ($N = 1{,}246$) $P^1_{t=1}$ and $P^2_{t=1}$ scenarios are obtained and with the N $P^1_{t=1}$ and $P^2_{t=1}$ scenarios, as always, the N scenarios of the portfolio value at $t = 1$ ($V_{t=1}$) are obtained by simply calculating $V_{t=1} = P^1_{t=1} + P^2_{t=1}$. Following the same logic as before, once these N scenarios of the portfolio value at $t = 1$ are obtained, the probability distribution can be estimated by grouping all possible values into sections and calculating the probability of each segment as the number of observations in each divided by the number N of simulated scenarios.

The Excel workbook "Example VaR" includes the development of this procedure and indicates that the probability distribution values presented in Table 3.4 and Fig. 3.11 were obtained for this example.

As can be seen in Fig. 3.11, in a scenario involving a much lower number of observations the probability distribution is more concentrated in the central sections, yielding a value at risk of €34.30, €35.80 being the average.

Table 3.4 Estimated probability

Value of the portfolio at $t = 1$ (€)	Number of observations	Estimated probability
<9	0	0.00%
[9,14]	0	0.00%
[19,14]	0	0.00%
[24,19]	0	0.00%
[29,24]	0	0.00%
[34,29]	229	18.40%
[39,34]	972	78.00%
[44,39]	45	3.60%
[49,44]	0	0.00%
[54,49]	0	0.00%
<54	0	0.00%

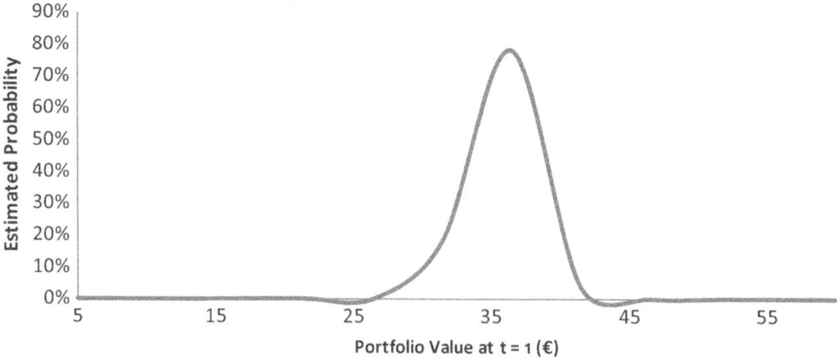

Fig. 3.11 Probability distribution of the portfolio value at $t = 1$ (Author's own composition)

Finally, it should be noted that in this case a method quoting historic assets between two dates has been chosen as a concrete scenario, but this need not always be the case. The specific scenario chosen may be the historic price of assets as well as some which are completely invented and inconsistent with the reality and history of the assets in the portfolio.

3.4 Incremental and Marginal Measures

3.4.1 General Ideas

A very useful tool in any kind of analysis is the use of incremental and marginal measures. An incremental measure is a comparison between two situations that can be arbitrarily close or distant. For example, if you have 50 shares of asset A and 100 of asset B and you come to have 90 shares of asset A and 180 shares of asset B, the question might be how to change the VaR, in other words to find the incremental VaR. A marginal measure is an incremental measure where the increase becomes infinitesimal and in mathematics it is a derivative. Continuing with the previous example, with 50 shares of asset A and 100 of Asset B, the marginal VaR relative to asset A would be the difference between the current VaR and the VaR corresponding to the portfolio whereby an additional infinitely small amount of money has been invested in shares of asset A.

Interestingly, an initial and a final position must always be specified for an incremental measure, while in the case of marginal measures only the initial situation must be specified. This has consequences since, in principle, incremental measures compare two situations and it should be clear that these are the two options to choose from, while marginal measures indicate which steps must be taken to achieve the desired results. More precisely, it can be said that marginal measures are useful because their denotation, and to a greater extent their magnitude, directly indicate which procedure should be followed to achieve certain results. This idea will be clarified by the following example:

Suppose that F represents the VaR of a portfolio with four assets A, B, C and D and therefore depends on the amounts invested in each. Now imagine that the four marginal VaRs are calculated and −0.5, 1, −4 and 3 are obtained respectively. Taking into account that the higher the VaR is, the lower the risk becomes, from these measures the following conclusions, among others, can be reached: increasing the position of assets A and C increases the risk, while doing so in assets B and D reduces risk. Furthermore, the reduction in risk arising from the position of D is three times that arising from asset B, meaning that for every euro invested in D to reduce the risk, three euros would need to be invested in B to obtain the same result. Similarly, the effect of lowering the risk due to asset B is twice that due to the increase in asset A, and therefore the position of A can be increased by a euro without increasing the risk, if fifty cents are invested in B.

Despite the previous explanations, it is very important to note the limitations of marginal measures due to the fact that these measures are local. In other words, they express what happens near a given point, that is, these measures, on being derivatives, are accurate when faced with infinitesimal changes, but as the changes become larger the results become increasingly inaccurate.[6] This phenomenon is more important when dealing with functions which are less linear, as in the linear case it is

[6] This phenomenon has the same basis as the convexity phenomenon in the case of credit risk.

non-existent, and it should be kept in mind at all times that the VaR is strongly non-linear. If you have a portfolio with 50 currency units (cu) in shares of asset A and 100 cu in shares of asset B, the marginal VaR of this portfolio can shed a great deal of light on what will happen if 50.1 cu are invested in asset A and 100.4 cu in asset B, but not on what will happen with a portfolio of 100 cu invested in each asset, for which the incremental VaR is required. This is because the distance between the points (50,100) and (100,100) is very large, even though the latter components are equal.

Such problems do not occur with incremental measures, but as stated previously, they provide no insight on how to modify the starting point because they only compare situations.

3.4.2 Formal Definition

This section will proceed to establish the formal definition of incremental and marginal measures. For each risk measurement, and in fact for any type of measurement, its marginal measure can be defined as the partial derivative with respect to the corresponding amount. Thus, the marginal VaR can be defined as the derivative of the VaR with respect to a specific asset, and its economic interpretation is, as previously stated, the variation of the VaR of a portfolio on increasing the amount invested in an asset, which may or may not be part of the initial portfolio, by an infinitesimal amount of money.

As explained in the definition, if you have a portfolio made up of assets A and B with a given VaR, it is possible to calculate its marginal VaR with respect to asset A and also with respect to asset B, but the marginal VaR with respect to any other asset (C, D, etc.) can also be calculated simply by applying the previous definition. It should also be noted that the marginal VaR depends not only on the asset in which an additional amount will be invested, but also on the original portfolio—in fact, it depends on the correlation between both the original portfolio and the new asset and can be negative if the correlation between them is also negative.

Finally, it must be mentioned here that while the VaR is in the same currency unit as that of the portfolio value in question, the marginal VaR has no units because it is the derivative of the VaR with respect to the price of a particular asset that can become a part of the portfolio and, therefore, has the same currency units.

Regarding the incremental VaR, it is defined as the difference between the VaR of two portfolios, the initial and final portfolios. This definition includes another similar measure, the component VaR, which is defined as the incremental VaR when the starting position does not have an asset and the final position does. More formally, if we consider a portfolio of N assets where $d_1,\ldots, d_N$ currency units are invested in assets $1,\ldots, N$ respectively, the VaR component of asset N is the VaR of a portfolio of N assets where $d_1,\ldots, d_N$ currency units are invested in assets $1,\ldots, N$ respectively, apart from the VaR of a portfolio of $N - 1$ assets, all assets of the previous portfolio but the last (asset N), where $d_1,\ldots, d_{N-1}$ currency units are invested in assets $1,\ldots, N - 1$ respectively.

The usefulness of this measure lies in the fact that if a company has $N - 1$ investment projects to which $d_1, \ldots, d_{N-1}$ monetary units are dedicated respectively and is able to invest in a new project, to which they intend to devote d_N currency units, the best way to ascertain the value of the investment and the benefits that the project could bring, in terms of risk, is to calculate the component VaR. The reason for this is that so far, the company's VaR is VaR $(d_1,\ldots, d_{N-1}, 0)$ while the new VaR would be VaR$(d_1,\ldots, d_N)$, so the difference between both is the component VaR. Thus, the component VaR measures the VaR variation owing to the new project and is a good tool to decide whether or not to go ahead with an investment; hence it is sometimes said that the component VaR is the contribution made by each component, or the element which changes the VaR on eliminating an asset.

Generalising this concept, these new incremental and marginal measures are very useful to understand why different companies take on different projects. While the expected return and VaR of an investment are independent of the company that made the investment, the marginal VaR and incremental VaR, and in this case the component VaR, depend on the portfolio of existing assets before investing and, thus, such an investment involves different risks for different companies.

Finally, it must be mentioned that the incremental VaR, and therefore that of the component, should then be determined simply by calculating the VaR of the initial portfolio and the final portfolio. However, the calculation of marginal measures is slightly more complicated, as it is based on the concept of a derivative. The easiest way to calculate this is to take two very close values and approximate the derivative using the formula $f'(x) \approx \frac{f(x+h)-f(x)}{h}$, or a formula which is closer to reality, $f'(x) \approx \frac{f(x+h)-f(x-h)}{2h}$.

3.5 VaR Applications

3.5.1 Relationship to Risk–Return Approach

When assessing an investment project it is very common to use the well-known risk–return approach. This methodology involves calculating the mathematical expectation of the portfolio return in the same way as standard deviation (called risk or volatility). In this way, given two possible investments with the same risk (standard deviation), the best investment is that with the greatest return (on average), while when the returns are the same (on average), the best option is the investment with less risk (standard deviation). If, on the contrary, both return and risk are different, the order is not defined and preference for one or the other depends on the risk aversion of the individual. In this section the relationship between the VaR and this approach will be studied.

It is not difficult to show that if a $\alpha < 50\%$ level is chosen (which is always the case) along with probability distributions that make certain assumptions (whereby normal distribution is always achieved), this results in the VaR increasing in mean and decreasing in variance. Thus, following the logic on which the risk–return approach is based, whereby investment projects with higher expected return and lower risk are chosen, on comparing the two projects it is better to choose the lowest "mean value – VaR," that is, the one with the lowest $E[P_1] - P^*$. In other words, if you compare project A with a "mean value – VaR" of 11 million and project B with a "mean value – VaR" of 10 million, it is evident that in the worst reasonable case one million less would be lost in B than in A. Of course, the expected return must also be considered.

3.5.2 Diversification and Hedging

As was seen in the previous examples, except in cases where the correlation is 100 % (perfect correlation), the risk, whether measured by VaR or virtually any other measurement, is not the sum of individual risks but something smaller; thus, combining several assets can reduce it. The reason for this is that when the correlation between two assets is below 100 % it is simply not possible for both to go always badly at the same time, but there is the possibility that while one goes badly the other goes well and the profits from one compensate for the losses of the other. For this reason, the accumulated risk is less than the sum of individual risk. This strategy is called diversification, to which the old saying "don't put all your eggs in one basket" can be applied, or in financial terms, "don't invest all your money in a single asset". Approaching the 100 % correlation scenarios in which the two assets move together is more likely, and the scenarios in which the loss of one is compensated for by the profits of another are less likely, therefore, when the correlation is close to reaching 100 % (the total risk tends to approach the sum of the individual risks). For this reason, the smaller the correlation between two assets, the greater the diversification and vice versa.

VaR measure considers that there is always diversification. The VaR of the final portfolio consisting of any two assets A and B, that is, P^*_{A+B} is greater than the sum of the VaRs of the two assets taken individually, P^*_A and P^*_B. This could also be expressed in another way, $P^*_{A+B} > P^*_A + P^*_B$.

It must also be noted that a diversified portfolio reduces the probability of large profits for the same reasons that it reduces the probability of large losses, that is, if the correlation is very low, the probability that the two assets provide large profits in unison is very small and therefore the probability of large profits in the entire portfolio is reduced.

A concept related to diversification is that of hedging. The idea is that some assets may move in opposite directions, or have a negative correlation, thus when one rises the chances are that the other will fall, at least in part. For example, it is well known that gold tends to rise in times of crisis, while stock indexes fall. Hedging is a strategy which uses the correlations between assets to reduce overall portfolio risk, that is, it doesn't just seek to make the total risk lower than the sum of the individual risks. What it really aims to do is ensure that when another asset is added to the portfolio its total risk reduces, not only that it becomes lower than the sum of the initial portfolio risk without the asset and the individual risk of the asset. Additionally, if after performing hedging the risk of the resulting portfolio proves to be zero, it is referred to as perfect hedging; otherwise it is known as imperfect hedging and residual risk remains in the portfolio.

In order for hedging to be perfect, meaning that when adding an additional asset to the original portfolio the resulting risk is zero, the correlation between the original and the asset portfolio must be −100 % since, in this way, when the value of the portfolio rises, the value of the asset falls. An example would be owning a share and a sell future on that title, since the correlation between the share and the future is −100 %: if the share price rises, the future price falls, as can be seen in Fig. 2.2 in Chap. 2. However, not only must the correlation be −100 %, but the portfolio is also required to be equally exposed to both. In the previous example, if instead of one future there are two, in spite of the fact that the correlation is −100 %, the hedging would not be perfect as in the entire portfolio the share risk is offset by one of the futures but the risk of the other future could not be offset by anything, and the total value of the entire portfolio consisting of the share and the two futures could not be known with certainty for another year.

At this point it seems legitimate to ask what the formal difference is between the concepts of diversification and hedging, or rather, the question might be: when does a strategy cease to be diversification and become hedging? The idea in both cases is to reduce the risk; in the first case it is understood that this is achieved by forming a portfolio which includes different assets, while in the second case the portfolio is based on assets with opposing price variations. There is no simple or specific answer to this question, but it could be said that whenever there is hedging there is also diversification, while diversification only involves hedging when the correlation is negative.

Formally it will be referred to as hedging as long as the VaR of the final portfolio consisting of an initial portfolio and any asset that is added to it, $P^*_{\text{Initial\_Porfolio + Asset}}$, is higher than the initial portfolio VaR$P^*_{\text{Initial_Portfolio}}$, that is, $P^*_{\text{Initial\_Porfolio + Asset}} > P^*_{\text{Initial\_Portfolio}}$. Moreover, diversification will be referred to even if the VaR of the final portfolio consisting of an initial portfolio and any asset that is added to it, $P^*_{\text{Initial\_Porfolio + Asset}}$, is lower than the VaR of the initial portfolio, $P^*_{\text{Initial\_Portfolio}}$, but it is higher than the sum of the VaR of the initial portfolio of assets plus the VaR of the added asset, that is, $P^*_{\text{Initial\_Porfolio + Asset}} > P^*_{\text{Initial\_Portfolio}} > P^*_{\text{Initial\_Portfolio}} + P^*_{\text{Asset}}$.

Marginal and incremental measures can be used to demonstrate variations in the risk when modifying the positions in a portfolio. In other words, when taking on a new project or investing in a new asset, a business must consider not only their return and their risk in isolation, but how they relate to other projects or assets in its portfolio, which implies that it is possible for a project to present an increased risk for one company and a decreased risk for another. Thus, if an asset with negative correlation with respect to the overall original portfolio is added to a given portfolio, the risk of the new portfolio is less than the original portfolio. However, at this point it is important to note that the negative correlation has to be relative to the overall portfolio and not with respect to a particular asset of it, because this may in fact be the case of adding an asset to a portfolio which has a correlation of −100 % with another specific asset from it and the risk of the entire portfolio increases due to the fact that the correlation with the overall portfolio is positive.

The following example can be studied to reinforce this concept, whereby the component VaR is used and it is possible for a project to be profitable for one company but not for another. Suppose a firm has invested in project A which has an expected profit of 100 million currency units with a deviation of 40, and there is another project, project B, which has an expected value of −5,000,000 cu with a deviation of 50 and the correlation between both projects is −0.8. Looked at in isolation, no company would ever undertake project B because on average they would lose money; however, if VaR is calculated using components, it can be concluded that the project in isolation has a VaR of 34 million cu but in conjunction with project B a VaR of 45 million cu is obtained.[7]

[7] Although not very realistic, to perform easily these calculations, normality has been assumed in all probability distributions. Assuming other types of probability distributions the results change although not what this example means.

Therefore, the VaR of component B is positive, with 11 million cu, so a company that is involved in project A may also take on project B, not based on the value of project B in itself but because it hedges the risk of A, or in other words, when A suffers losses, B makes profits.

On the other hand, given a portfolio with different assets, if perfect hedging is performed on each of them, as is evident, the risk is reduced to zero. However, this procedure has drawbacks, mainly because it is very expensive to hedge each asset and because there is not always hedging for all assets but usually only for the most liquid assets. Therefore, the best possible hedging is achieved by an asset or group of assets with the most negative correlation possible with the original portfolio, and the specific amount of assets chosen is crucial. Therefore, the optimal hedging ratio of a portfolio consisting of an asset or group of assets is defined as the extent to which this asset or group of assets incorporated into the original portfolio further reduce risk while taking into account the costs associated with hedging. The optimal hedging ratio of a portfolio in which one of its assets is a share of asset A with a sell future of this asset does not have to be −100 % but will be something different, and could be higher if the other assets are positively correlated with asset A, or less if this correlation is negative.

Finally, it is important to note that in both the concept of diversification and in that of hedging, and in all the other concepts discussed in this section, the key is in the correlation. Nevertheless, regarding diversification and hedging, caution must be taken and it must be kept in mind that the correlation between assets does not remain constant over time but varies. Additionally, it is shown that in times of economic crisis, the correlation between assets tends to approach 100 % very rapidly, which means that certain combinations of assets which in times of economic boom might seem to imply diversification, or even hedging, in times of crisis, when diversification or hedging is most needed, do not have the same effect. Therefore, when designing diversification or hedging strategies, care must be taken when estimating correlations, otherwise it could seem that the risk is lower than it is in reality, which leads to a false sense of security.

4

Multidimensional Market Risk

4.1 Basic Concepts

4.1.1 Cash Flow and Net Present Value

In Chap. 3 the market risk of an investment was studied from a one-dimensional perspective, that is, considering only two points in time: the moment when the investment is made, which involves buying a portfolio of shares, and the time at which its value is measured. The same concept can be used to study other types of investment when it is necessary to evaluate what will happen at various points in time after the investment has been made. For example, it could be used by a company that has the opportunity to carry out an investment project that will provide some payments, or cash flows (CF), over time but the amount to be obtained is uncertain. This is the case with any business project—opening a restaurant, building a factory, working a mine and so on—and the value of the project today depends on the expectations of these cash flows. This project value is known as "net present value" (NPV).

F.J. Población García, *Financial Risk Management*,
DOI 10.1007/978-3-319-41366-2_4

These figures, as well as many others related to them, are subject to risk and this risk is likely to be measured with the same approach as in Chap. 3, that is, in these cases the risk can also be measured using a value at risk approach. The objective is the same: to discover the maximum loss that a particular cash flow, or the whole project (NPV), could suffer in terms of expected value at a given probability level.

In this respect, the mathematical approach is essentially identical although the two cases deal with different things: there is a value (cash flow, net present value, etc.) which evolves over time and follows a certain probability distribution. Therefore, the aim is to obtain a summarised measure of this value, which will be a random variable and a value P^* representing the minimum value of this quantity at a probability level of α whereby anything below this value is considered an unexpected loss. The higher the value of P^*, the more favourable the investment is considered to be.

Regarding the notation, CF_t is used to represent the cash flows and NPV_t to represent net present value. The remaining notation is the same as in the previous section except that the time variable can now take more than two values, something which has not been seen here previously.

It is essential to note, as will be seen later, that the probabilistic models are different; however, we must not lose sight of the fact that the main ideas are virtually identical. Note that in this case, as there is more than one period, the time "t" variable can take more values than in Chap. 3.

4.1.2 Multi-Period Measures Concept and Classification

When the result of a particular investment must be evaluated over more than one period, when measuring its yield or risk, a way must be found to summarise all the information in a single number.

The specific method used to summarise depends on the measure being considered, but in the case of profits, the expected value of this quantity itself already provides a measure of profit arising from it. In terms of risk, there are measures for each of these quantities: for cash flows there is the CFaR (cash flow at risk), for the net present value there is the NPVaR (net present value at risk), for earnings per share there is the EPSAR (earning per share at risk) and so on.

The logic behind these risk measures is identical in all cases and equal to that of the VaR. The CFaR (NPVaR, EPSAR, etc.) is defined as the measure of the maximum potential change that cash flow (net present value, per share, etc.) being studied may suffer (it may be that of a particular project, a division, the entire company, etc.) at a time horizon and at a given probability level. Therefore, with these new risk measures the VaR definition becomes more generalised.

This generalisation of the concept of value at risk can be applied to a wide range of magnitudes; it can be applied to any type of balance sheet or the income statement of a company or any measure that represents the total or partial value of a company or investment project. However, as the study of these measures one to one may be repetitive, they will be separated into two groups: the measures without discount, where the maximum exponent is the CFaR; and measures with discount, where the maximum exponent will be the NPVaR. However, before proceeding to analyse each of these groups in detail, it is necessary to characterise the intertemporal dynamics the prices follow.

4.2 Probabilistic Models

As previously noted, this chapter focuses on the risk measurement of intertemporal magnitudes, or in other words, magnitudes which depend on observations made at different periods. Thus, the time dependence of the different variables must be taken into consideration, and for this reason several concepts must be introduced before proceeding further.

4.2.1 Time Series (Stochastic Processes)

The first concept to be introduced is the time series concept, since it will be useful in characterising price dynamics. More specifically, the theoretical models used to represent the price dynamics must be considered random variables with a temporal index. This type of variable is known as a stochastic process and studying them is one of the most important parts of Statistics. Sometimes they are also referred to as time series, although, strictly speaking, time series only describe values which are observed, while the stochastic process is the mechanism that generates them.

A general theory of stochastic processes will not be discussed here, as this can be found in specialist literature.[1] However, some general concepts and specific processes must be introduced, as they will be used later and they supplement those identified in Chap. 3. A stochastic process is a sequence of random variables indexed by a time index which usually has a notation of Y_t. In a stochastic process, a white noise is a process whereby all variables are independent, with zero mean and the same variance; if the value of this variance is one, this is known as a unitary white noise and is usually represented by Greek letters, such as ε_t.

Apart from white noise, a variety of other stochastic processes can be constructed, for example, the independent variable processes which come in the form of $Y_t = \mu + \sigma\sqrt{\Delta t}\varepsilon_t$ where $\sqrt{\Delta t}$ is the time that passes between "t" and " t + 1" and ε_t is unitary white noise, and therefore, although here the variables no longer have zero mean or unit variance, they remain independent of the μ average and standard deviation $\sigma\sqrt{\Delta t}$. As seen in the graph, the values are not consistent and oscillate around their mean with a given variance, in this case $\mu = 0\,, \sigma = 1 y \Delta t = 1$, that is, unitary white noise (Fig. 4.1).

As shown, this process has a perfect mean reversion, in other words, the same values tend to return to their mean immediately, as Y_t and Y_{t+1} are uncorrelated but have the same average.

Other well-known stochastic processes, discussed in Chap. 3, are random walks. When using this process, it is assumed that the variable in question follows the equation $Y_t = \mu + Y_{t-1} + \sigma\sqrt{\Delta t}\varepsilon_t$ whereby $\sqrt{\Delta t}$ is the time that passes between "t" and "t + 1" and ε_t is unitary white noise. This model assumes that the variable in the following period will take the same value as in this period plus a constant term and a noise measurement that reflects the magnitude of change and will be known in the following

[1] There are many manuals; Hamilton's book (1994) can be highlighted as a recommendation.

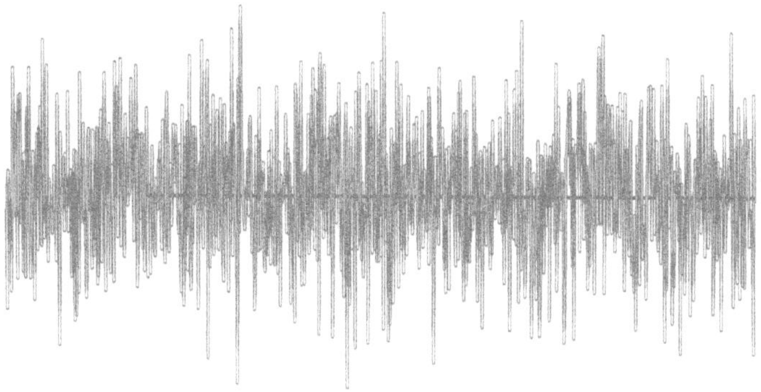

Fig. 4.1 Independent variable process (Author's own composition)

period. Thus, the difference in the value of this variable and the previous one is an independent variable $Y_t - Y_{t-1} = \mu + \sigma\sqrt{\Delta t}\varepsilon_t$, and therefore, it is stable. This type of stochastic process is very good at characterising the dynamics of financial series, such as shares, exchange rates or interest rates, in which it is certain that the variable in the next period will take the same value as the current variable with an additional constant factor reflecting the change in the value of money between two periods, as well as compensation for the risk taken and a noise term that represents the information that will reach the market during the time that passes between the two periods and causes price movements. These models assume that markets are perfect at all times, as all the information known to the market is reflected in the price, and therefore the correlation between the noise terms, ε_t, of any different time periods must be zero. Otherwise, it would mean that in a given period all existing information in the market is not incorporated in the price, as something is known about what will happen in the future that does not affect the price today.

In the following graph a random walk with $\mu = 0, \sigma = 1$ has been simulated and demonstrates that the range of values that can be taken by this variable is much higher and there is also no mean reversion (Fig. 4.2).

Unlike independent variable processes, the random walk is a process that does not involve mean reversion, as the value of Y_{t+1} is made up of Y_t with noise but without any imposition of returning to a long-term

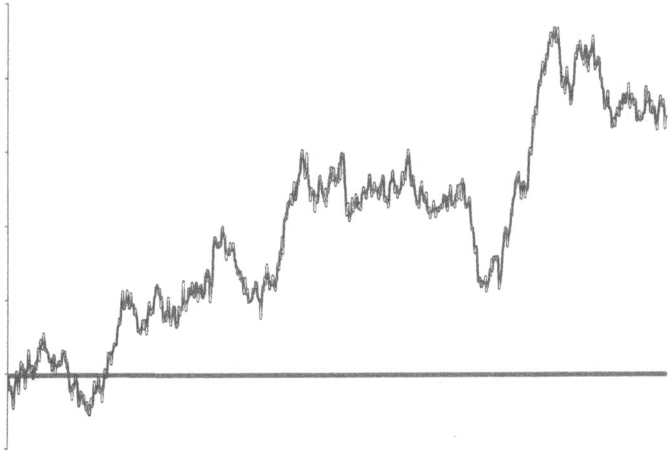

Fig. 4.2 Random walk (Author's own composition)

average, as can be seen in Fig. 4.2. Additionally, although it cannot be analysed in this book, in this process (random walk) the variance of Y_t grows linearly with t, as can be seen in the previous chart.

Between the two types of aforementioned stochastic processes—those that have perfect stability and mean reversion, in other words, models of independent variables, and the perfectly unstable type without mean reversion, also known as the random walk—there is a wide variety of stochastic processes, among which the autoregressive and moving average processes can be highlighted.

Autoregressive processes are stochastic processes in which it is assumed that the dynamics of the variable in question follow this equation $Y_t = \mu + \beta Y_{t-1} + \sigma\sqrt{\Delta t}\varepsilon_t$ or equivalently $Y_t - c = \beta(Y_{t-1} - c) + \sigma\sqrt{\Delta t}\varepsilon_t$, where $\sqrt{\Delta t}$ is the time between "t" and "t + 1" and ε_t is unitary white noise, c represents the long-term average of Y_t and the constant β, symbolising the process's degree of mean reversion, must be in the interval [0, 1].[2] As demonstrated, if the constant β is zero these processes become

[2] Even though they are known as autoregressive processes, those presented in this book are first-order autoregressive processes. In order to avoid lengthening the explanations unnecessarily, the other autoregressive processes are not mentioned.

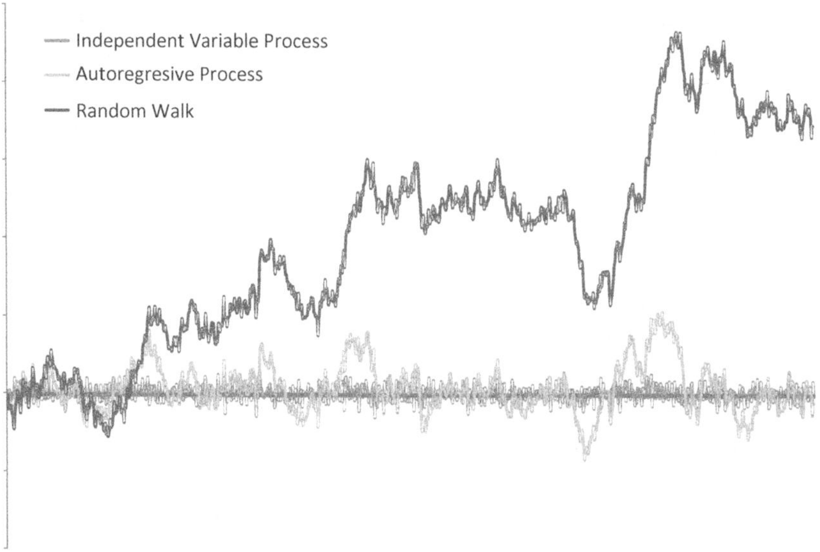

Fig. 4.3 Comparative processes (Author's own composition)

independent variable processes, while if it is equal to one the process in question is a random walk. For this reason, for an intermediate β which is neither zero nor one, the process will have stability and intermediate mean reversion between the independent variable process and random walk, as can be seen in Fig. 4.3.

In this type of process, it is assumed that there is a part of the Y_{t-1}variable, which grows as the value of the constant β becomes closer to zero, which passes to Y_t and, therefore, it is replaced by a long-term average which gives more stability to the process. However, as explained, this assumption is not compatible with the price dynamics in perfect markets since if the Y_t variable is above its long-term average "c" in the following period, it is more likely that $Y_{t+1} > Y_t$ and vice versa. Therefore, not all the information known at "t" is contained in Y_t, because if it were, nothing would be known about what may happen in the following period.

However, when the parameter β is larger, if the Y_t variable is used to characterise the price dynamics, this market imperfection reduces and therefore, in cases where the autoregressive process is used to characterise the price dynamics, it is often assumed, as in the case of the random walk, that the correlation between the noise terms (εt) of different periods must be zero.

It should also be indicated that if the Y_t variable is above its long-term average "c" in the following period, it is more likely that $Y_{t+1} > Y_t$ and vice versa, that is, the fact that there is a tendency to converge to this long-term average "c" is the reason for these processes presenting mean reversion, a trend which is more pronounced as the value of β approaches zero. Similarly, although it is beyond the scope of this book, the process will be more volatile and therefore the standard deviation of Y_t will grow with time "t" as the mean reversion decreases, or in other words as the value of β moves away from zero. So if $\beta = 1$ and the process is a random walk, the variance of Y_t will grow linearly with t.

Regarding moving average processes,[3] they can be described as stochastic processes in which it is assumed that the dynamics of the variable in question follow the equation $Y_t = \sigma\sqrt{\Delta t}\varepsilon_t + \beta\sigma\sqrt{\Delta t}\varepsilon_{t-1}$ where $\sqrt{\Delta t}$ is the time that passes between "t" and "$t + 1$" and ε_t is unitary white noise. As in the previous case and as demonstrated in Fig. 4.4, regarding stability and mean reversion, these processes are between independent variable processes and random walks.

4.2.2 Intertemporal Volatility and Correlation

The concept of volatility, within the quantitative finance discipline, can be defined in a precise manner but also with a great deal of complexity. Therefore, for the purposes of this book, volatility will not be defined in a specific way but will be determined by the degree of variability of the market variables. In this regard, note that in the models outlined previously and in every case without exception, volatility is constant over time, that is, all of these models assume that the degree of variability which the variables have remains the same over time.

---

[3] Even though they are known as moving average processes, this book only deals with moving average processes of the first order. In order to avoid extending this section unnecessarily, the remaining moving average processes do not feature here.

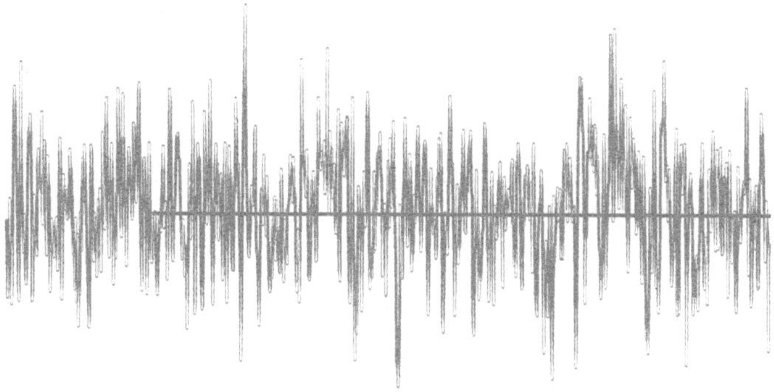

Fig. 4.4 Moving average process (Author's own composition)

In reality, market variables have different degrees of variability over time; thus, in theory, this type of model is only an approximation. For several years specialist literature has presented far more advanced models than those shown here, whereby volatility has the ability to change over time, which would have to be used in order to estimate risk more precisely. However, for simplicity only some of the aforementioned models will be included in this book.

One of the greatest challenges when characterising the dynamics of any market variable is to understand their intertemporal correlation structure. It must be reiterated that each of the models presented previously has a given intertemporal correlation structure. The independent variable process, as its name suggests, is defined as having no correlation between random variables at two given points in time, whereas in the case of a random walk, the correlation is very high. In the other two models, depending on the value assigned to their parameters, the correlation may be higher or lower.

However, as in the case of volatility, the actual intertemporal correlation structure of dynamic market variables is much more complex than that of the models mentioned previously which are, as indicated, very simple. Contrary to the case of volatility, there have been no manageable complexity models which deal with this problem in a precise manner. In any case, as noted with volatility, this book will only discuss the aforementioned models.

4.2.3 Temporal Aggregation and Considerations on Interest Rates

As previously stated, in a company or an investment project cash flow is produced in each period which, roughly speaking and without going into formal definitions, is the difference between income and expenses during that period. Additionally, the present value of the total cash flow is known as the net present value. Cash flows are the monetary values in the period in which they occur and are not affected by discount rates, whereas to calculate the NPV, cash flows are discounted and, therefore, in the case of studying NPV, interest rates are significant. Thus, in the NPV risk calculation the interest rate risk is also present.

As will be discussed later, interest rate risk management is complex; therefore, this chapter will assume that the interest rate is deterministic, that is, there is no interest rate risk and it is constant for the duration of the investment project or company in question. In other words, the term structure of interest rates will not be taken into account.

4.3 Risk Measures

4.3.1 Measures Without Discount: The CFaR

When it comes to cash flow, the discount factor does not apply because the cash flow is studied not as a present value but as a monetary amount at the time it is produced, and for this reason when studying it the value is considered the same regardless of when the payment is made, whether next year or in 20 years.

In turn, the CFaR refers to a specific cash flow, and thus it is relatively simple to estimate the risk measures associated with a variable with one cash flow, if the probability distribution associated with the cash flow, CF_T, is available, where T is the point in time when cash flow will be produced. It is often assumed, because it is what happens in reality, that the cash flow in question depends on market variables and when their probability distribution is known, it is possible to ascertain the probability distribution of the cash flow.

Therefore, if you have the probability distribution of the cash flow, the first thing that can be calculated is the expected value or mathematical expectation today ($t = 0$), with the information available to date (I_0), of the cash flow in question $E_t = 0$ [CF_T / I_0]. Once this expected value is known, the prediction of the cash flow is more accurate, and therefore this will be its market value at $t = 0$ if the discount is not taken into account.

However, this information changes over time, and therefore the market value may vary and consequently suffer a loss. In order to measure the risk associated with this, the CFaR can be calculated at a time horizon τ and a given probability level α. At the time τ, which must be $\tau \leq T$, the best prediction, and therefore the market value of the cash flow produced at T, will be $E_{t=\tau}[\ CF_T / I_\tau]$ which today, $t = 0$, is uncertain; however, it is possible to determine its probability distribution from the known probability distribution of CF_T. Once this probability distribution is known, the CFaR is simply this probability distribution point where the probability of this random variable taking this value or a lower value is α.

However, what can be and often is problematic is to determine the probability distribution of the future cash flow at a given time horizon. In the previous section, a number of probabilistic models were specified in an attempt to approximate this distribution, and in the next section the calculation itself will be studied.

Finally, strictly speaking the CFaR could be considered a one-dimensional risk measure, since it measures the risk of a cash flow that will occur on a specific future date in the same way as the VaR measures the portfolio risk at a specific time horizon. In spite of this, it is not common to study the CFaR of only one cash flow; however, as will be shown, the CFaRs of a set of cash flows are often studied simultaneously as they are often closely related; it is for this reason that the CFaR risk measure is studied in this chapter on multidimensional measures.

4.3.2 Measures with Discount: The NPVaR

Unlike in the case of cash flow, net present value is the aggregation of different cash flows discounted with an interest rate; therefore, in this case, to estimate the NPVaR, the probability distribution of all cash flows must be known, not only of one of them. Furthermore, it is necessary to know not only the probability distribution of these cash flows in isolation but also the relationship that exists between them; that is, the joint probability distribution of these variables must be known, and in particular their correlation.

By way of example, consider the case of an investment project or company which, from now until the time of its completion in the case of an investment project or liquidation in the case of a company, generates, at T_1, T_2, . . ., T_J, the cash flows CF_{T1}, CF_{T2}, . . ., CF_{TJ}, which depend on a number of market variables, and through the probability distribution of these variables the cash flows can be established.

Once the joint probability distribution of these cash flows is known, since the NPV is defined as $NPV = \frac{CF_{T_1}}{(1+r)^{T_1}} + \ldots + \frac{CF_{T_J}}{(1+r)^{T_J}}$, where r is the interest rate or discount, the first thing that can be estimated is the expected value, or mathematical expectation, of the NPV today, which is simply $E_{t=0}[NPV/I_0] = \frac{E_{t=0}[CF_1/I_0]}{(1+r)^{T_1}} + \ldots + \frac{E_{t=0}[CF_J/I_0]}{(1+r)^{T_J}}$ being I_0 the information available at time $t = 0$. In the same way as in the previous case, once this expected value is known, the best prediction of the cash flow is known, and therefore this would be its market value at $t = 0$.

However, as in the previous case, the information changes over time and therefore the market value may vary and suffer a loss. Consequently, to measure the associated risk the NPVaR can be calculated at a time horizon, τ, and given probability level (α). At time τ, which must be $\tau \leq T_N$, the best estimate, and therefore the market value of NPV, is $E_t = \tau$ [NPV/Iτ], which today ($t = 0$) is uncertain, but it is possible to determine the probability distribution if the joint probability distribution of cash flows is known. Once this probability distribution is known, the CFaR is merely this probability distribution at a point where the probability of this random variable taking this value or a lower value is α.

As in the previous case, the really complicated thing about the NPVaR estimation is adequately characterising the joint probability distribution of cash flows. Note that in this case it is necessary to know not only the probability distribution of each of the cash flows but also their joint distribution and, in particular, their correlation.

4.4 Calculation Methodology

Once the risk measures have been defined and all the elements have been taken into account in the previous sections, the only thing left to consider is their calculation. Firstly, the analytical resolution must be considered, followed by the numerical resolution; the latter will be the most used resolution due to the complexity of analytical resolution.

4.4.1 Analytical Estimation

If the probability distribution of a specific cash flow (CF_T) or the present value (NPV) is known, the estimation of CFaR or NPVaR can be carried out immediately by simply applying the concept of value at risk. However, as previously mentioned, the characterisation of these probability distributions is not straightforward, for several reasons. The first is that the cash flows, and thus the NPV, depend on market variables and it is not always easy to estimate their probability distribution, but also once the probability distribution of these macroeconomic variables is known, if the relationship between them and the cash flow is not linear but "option type", in most cases it is not possible to determine the probability distribution of the cash flow based on the probability distribution of the market variables.

Finally, it should be clarified that while the probability distributions of market variables may be known, and also the relationship between market variables and cash flow may be linear, there is the disadvantage that it is not always easy to determine the joint probability distribution, in particular the correlation. In addition, even if the joint probability distribution were known, with the exception of some probability distributions, the probability distribution of the sum of two random variables cannot be characterised even if each of them is known separately, which is of particular importance when dealing with the NPV.

Therefore, the analytical estimation of the CFaR and NPVaR can be achieved only very rarely and more so in the case of CFaR than in the case of NPVaR, where analytical calculations can only be carried out on very rare occasions. This section will present examples of calculating both the CFaR and the NPVaR, drawing particular attention to the conditions that must be met in order to perform the analytical calculation.

4.4.1.1 Example of Analytical Calculation of the CFaR

Suppose there is an investment project which at a future date "T" is expected to obtain a cash flow with log-normal distribution. For example, imagine an oil well which is expected to obtain a certain number of barrels "Q" in a given year. In this scenario, assuming for simplicity that all costs are paid at the beginning, when time "T" arrives, the cash flow obtained will be Q^*P_T, where P_T is the price of oil at time "T". It will also be assumed that the price of crude oil follows an autoregressive process as shown: $p_t = m + \beta p_{t-1} + \varepsilon_t$ where $p_t = \text{Ln}(P_t)$ and ε_t is a normal random variable with mean 0 and standard deviation σ; therefore it is assumed that Δt is equal to 1.[4]

With these assumptions it is possible to estimate analytically the CFaR at a probability level of α. In order to do this, the expected value of the cash flow from today ($t = 0$) must be $E_{t=0}[Q^* P_T/I_0] = Q^* E_{t=0}[P_T/I_0]$ and the logarithm price must follow an autoregressive process. Once the p_0 is known, $p_1 = m + \beta p_0 + \varepsilon_1$ must then be estimated, and once the p_1 is known, p_2 is found simply by applying the formula $p_2 = c + \rho p_1 + \varepsilon_2$ or equivalently: $p_2 = m + \beta m + \beta^2 p_0 + \rho\varepsilon_1 + \varepsilon_2$. Thus, by applying the formulas outlined above, the following result is obtained: $p_T = m\sum_{t=0}^{T}\beta^t + \beta^T p_0 + \sum_{t=0}^{T}\beta^t\varepsilon_t$ where p_T is a random

[4] As will be shown in subsequent chapters, the dynamics of commodity prices are more complex than a simple autoregressive process. However, for simplicity, this example will maintain this assumption.

variable normally distributed with a mean of $m\sum_{t=0}^{T}\beta^t + \beta^T p_0$ and a variance of $\frac{\beta^{T+1}-1}{\beta-1}\sigma^2$ and, therefore, P_T is distributed by a log-normal with these parameters.

Once the probability distribution of P_T is known, using a table or spreadsheet it is possible to obtain the value P_T, P_T^{α}, where the probability that P_T is less than P_T^{α} is "α". Finally, with P_T^{α} the CFaR calculation is straightforward because CFaR$= Q * P_T^{\alpha}$. In other words, once the probability distribution of P_T is known, the probability distribution of cash flow (CF $=$ Q*P_T) is calculated and since "Q" is constant, it can be observed that Q*P_T^{α} is the value of this probability distribution where the probability that the value of the cash flow is less than or equal to it is equal to "α".

As noted above, the CFaR of the different cash flows making up an investment project are closely related. As seen in this example, the probability distribution of the price at a given time "T_1" is closely related to the probability distribution of the same price at the time "T_2"; therefore, once the quantity at each moment in time is known, the probability distributions of the different cash flows that are incorporated in the price are closely related, and for this reason the CFaR of a particular cash flow is not studied in isolation but the CFaR of all cash flows are studied together.

Finally, note that the analytical estimation of the CFaR has been made possible because the probability distribution of cash flow was known and exposure was linear. However, this is not common because, as will be discussed later, it is not always easy to characterise the dynamics of the commodity prices or purchase/sale prices of inputs/outputs that make up the overall cash flow. In addition, it must be clarified that exposures to these prices are not always linear but may well be "option type". When quantities are also stochastic, it is extremely difficult to characterise the probability distribution of cash flow, even if the price distribution is known and exposure is linear. For this reason, in most cases the CFaR calculation must be performed through simulation.

4.4.1.2 The Analytical Estimation of NPVaR

The analytical calculation of NPVaR is more complex than that of CFaR, as in most cases the NPV incorporates more than one cash flow. For this reason, when the project consists of more than one cash flow, unless its probability distribution is normal, it is not possible to estimate the NPVaR in the same way as the CFaR. The only two simple and reasonable possibilities for an analytical NPVaR calculation is to assume that the cash flows are distributed normally or that the variation in percentage (equivalent to performance measurement) of the NPV is normal, and therefore the NPV is log-normally distributed.

In the case where the probability distribution of the various cash flows making up the project is normal, by definition, the probability distribution of the NPV is also normal, where mean is the sum of the mean and variance the sum of the variances corrected by correlation, as seen in previous examples. On the other hand, if normality is assumed in the percentage variation of NPV, as already indicated, the NPV will be distributed log-normally. As carried out in all the previous examples, once the probability distribution of the NPV has been calculated, the NPVaR can then be calculated using tables or spreadsheets.

Depending upon the underlying structure of the cash flows, the two previous assumptions will be more or less reasonable, but in any case they are no more than approximations. Additionally, in such simple examples as those expressed in the CFaR calculation in the previous paragraph, if the number of cash flows is greater than one, analytical calculation of the CFaR is no longer possible because it is not analytically feasible to characterise the probability distribution sum of two or more log-normals. In more complex examples, where cash flows are distributed through more sophisticated distributions or where cash flow is a product of "option type" exposure, the analytical calculation of the NPVaR is impossible and the only option is to simulate the calculation.

4.4.2 Numerical Estimation (Simulation)

Looking at the previous examples in detail, it is clear that the estimate of CFaR and NPVaR is linked to the fact that very restrictive conditions must be met, and that is why in most cases the calculation of these risk measures must be carried out numerically.

As in Chap. 3, among the existing alternatives probably the most popular is the numerical simulation or Monte Carlo experiment. This method is particularly suitable when you have a probabilistic model for market variables but not for the extent to which the risk is to be measured (CF, NPV, etc.).

The steps for simulation are very similar to those followed in Chap. 3:

a) **Generation of scenarios**: based on the time series model that guides the dynamics of each market variable affecting the magnitude whose risk we want to measure (CF, NPV, etc.), a large number of scenarios of the value of these variables is generated by random numbers in accordance with the time series process that each variable follows (for example, N scenarios are generated); this is done taking into account the correlations between them, if there is more than one market variable. As in Chap. 3, it is sometimes easier to generate scenarios for the logarithm of this variable's value rather than for the value itself.
b) **Assessment of the magnitude whose risk we want to measure**: for each of these simulations the value of the quantity whose risk we want to measure is calculated. Thus, there are N possible future values of the magnitude, one for each simulated scenario.
c) **Calculation of the risk measure:** once the portfolio has been valued in each scenario, we can estimate the probability distribution of the magnitude whose risk we want to measure by simply putting the N possible values of the portfolio in ascending order and separating them into intervals ("buckets"), and assigning to each of these intervals a probability defined as the number of elements in the range divided by N. From this empirical probability distribution the desired risk measure (the CFaR, the NPVaR, etc.) is then calculated. Thus, the desired

risk measure is simply the element that takes the place αN after sorting the N values from lowest to highest.

Continuing with the example of the CFaR calculation presented previously, it is assumed again that there is an investment project from which cash flows with log-normal distribution are expected at various future dates $T_1, \ldots, T_N$, for example, an oil well which is expected to get a certain number of barrels "Q" on the future dates outlined previously.[5] In this scenario, assuming for simplicity that all costs are covered initially, on each of the future dates, $T_1, \ldots, T_N$, the cash flow obtained will be $Q^* P_{Ti}$, where P_{Ti} are oil prices at time T_i. It will also be assumed that the price of oil follows an autoregressive process as follows: $p_t = m + \beta p_{t-1} + \varepsilon_t$ where $p_t = \mathrm{Ln}(P_t)$ and ε_t is a normal random variable with mean 0 and standard deviation σ, then as before, it is assumed that Δt is equal to 1. In this case, for numerical calculation specific values are assigned to the parameters. It is assumed that the cash flows are annual for 20 years $(T_1, \ldots, T_{20})$, that P_0 are \$100 per barrel (\$100/bbl) and the annual number of barrels is 100,000; also $\sigma = 30\%$, $m = 1$ and $\beta = 0.8$.

As in Chap. 3, to calculate the NPVaR and the CFaR, many scenarios should be generated for ε_t for $t = T_1, \ldots, T_{20}$ using random numbers that follow a normal distribution with mean zero and standard deviation $\sigma = 30\ \%$. The difference is that now, by construction, ε_t and ε_{t+1} will not correlate because in all the probability models presented previously it is assumed that the stochastic price variation between $t-1$ and t is independent of the stochastic variation between t and $t+1$. The reason is that this stochastic variation between two periods reflects the new information reaching the market between two given periods and was not known or even suspected in prior periods, and therefore it must be independent of the stochastic variation in the past. In order to generate this series $\{\varepsilon_t\}_{t=T_1,\cdots,T_N}$, the easiest way is to generate uncorrelated random numbers η_t that follow a probability distribution with zero mean and variance one and then generate scenarios ε_t from these variables simply by $\varepsilon_t = \sigma^* \eta_t$.

[5] For simplicity we will assume that in all cases the same number of barrels is obtained, but the problem would be equally easy to solve if the number of barrels obtained on each date was different, as long as these values were known and not random variables.

Once a number N of $\{\varepsilon_t\}_{t=T_1,\cdots,T_N}$ scenarios has been generated, from the price at $t = 0$ (P_0) N price scenarios at $T_1, \ldots, T_{20}$ are then generated from the probabilistic model that their logarithms follow ($p_t = m + \beta p_{t-1} + \varepsilon_t$), from which the N scenarios of prices in logarithms are generated $\{p_t\}_{t=T_1,\cdots,T_N}$, from which the N scenarios of the prices are then obtained. With the N scenarios of prices at times $T_1, \ldots, T_{20}$ N scenarios are obtained for each of the cash flows using simply $CF_t = Q^* P_t$ and N scenarios of the NPV by simply applying its definition ($NPV = \frac{CF_{T_1}}{(1+r)^{T_1}} + \ldots + \frac{CF_{T_J}}{(1+r)^{T_J}}$). Once these N scenarios are obtained for each of these financial figures, their probability distributions and risk measures can be estimated by simply grouping them into sections and estimating their probabilities in the same manner as in Chap. 3 (Fig. 4.5).

This development can be found in the Excel workbook "Example CFaR and NPVaR" and this demonstrates that for this example the following probability distribution for the NPV is obtained (Fig. 4.6, Table 4.1):

The probability distributions of each of the cash flows can also be estimated immediately; however, to avoid lengthening this example unnecessarily, only those corresponding to the cash flows for the first year and last year (year 20) are presented in Fig. 4.7.

As can be seen, the probability distribution of cash flow for year one is much less volatile than the cash flow for year 20. In turn, the probability distribution of a cash flow is closely related to that of the other flows. Finally, it should be noted that this chart very clearly shows that the probability distributions of cash flows are log-normal because in this simple example cash flow is defined as $CF_t = Q^* P_t$, where P_t is distributed log-normally. On the other hand, as can be seen in the graph above (Fig. 4.7), when the distribution of NPV is a combination of log-normals, its functional form is more indefinite.

Once the probability distributions of both the NPV and the CF have been calculated, their risk measures can then be calculated. For the NPV at a given probability level, of say 5 %, the NPVaR is around 125 million euros (M€) while the expected value of the NPV of this project is around €205M. Therefore, eliminating the 5 % worst-case scenarios, the maximum negative variation that the value of the project in question can suffer

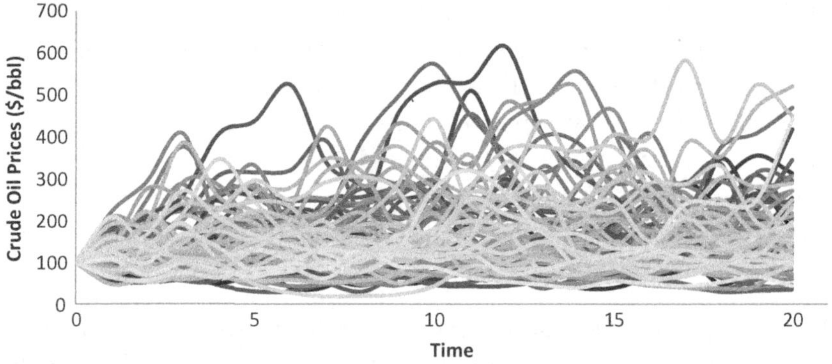

Fig. 4.5 Crude oil prices (simulation scenarios) (Author's own composition)

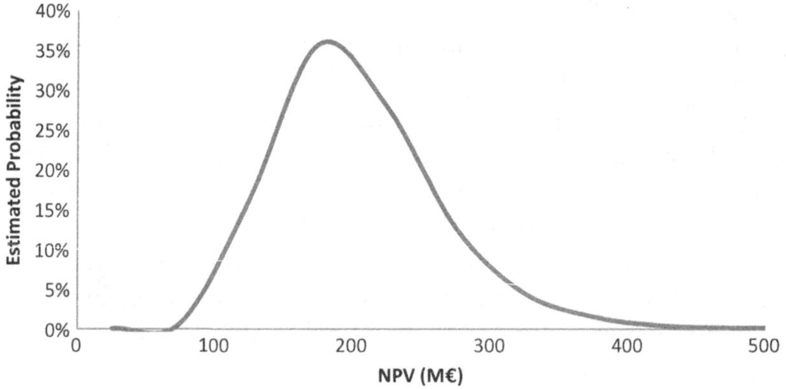

Fig. 4.6 Probability distribution of the NPV (Author's own composition)

is €80M. Thus, comparing the value of the investment to be made from the project and its expected NPV and NPVaR, a fairly accurate idea of its risk–return ratio can be obtained.

Each cash flow has a different probability distribution, and therefore their expected values and CFaR at the same probability level of 5 % are different, as shown in Table 4.2.

Table 4.1 Estimated probability (Author's own composition)

NPV (M€)	Number of observations	Estimated probability
<50	0	0.0%
[50, 100]	70	0.7%
[100, 150]	1616	16.2%
[150, 200]	3568	35.7%
[200, 250]	2797	28.0%
[250, 300]	1273	12.7%
[300, 350]	453	4.5%
[350, 400]	156	1.6%
[400, 450]	41	0.4%
[450, 500]	14	0.1%
<500	12	0.1%

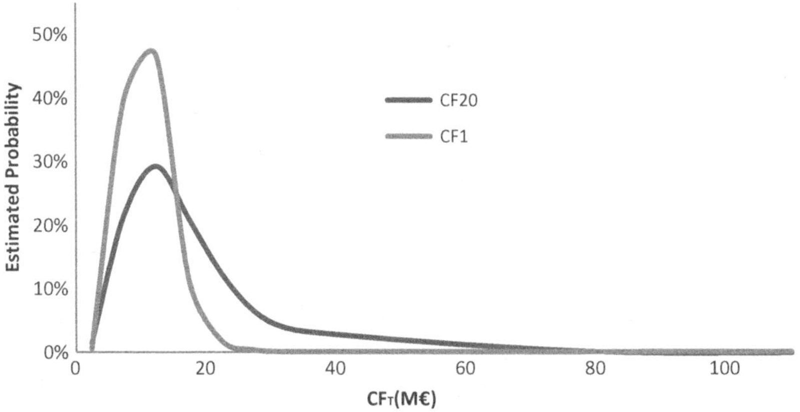

Fig. 4.7 Probability distribution of CF_T (Author's own composition)

The first thing to note from these results is that the expected value of the cash flows rises over time but at an increasingly slow rate, because $CF_t = Q^* P_t$, the amount Q being constant over time and the probabilistic model assumed for the price logarithm of crude oil shows mean reversion. Secondly, it is noteworthy that, despite this increase in the expected value, the CFaR remains at the same level between €6M and €6.5M, and therefore the maximum loss increases with time but, as in

Table 4.2 Maximum loss regarding expected value (5 %, M€) (Author's own composition)

	Expected value (M€)	CFaR (5%) (M€)	Maximum loss regarding expected value (5%) (M€)
CF1	11.3	6.6	4.7
CF2	12.3	6.1	6.2
CF3	13.2	5.9	7.3
CF4	13.9	6	7.9
CF5	14.5	5.9	8.5
CF6	15	6.1	8.9
CF7	15.3	6	9.3
CF8	15.7	6.2	9.4
CF9	15.9	6.3	9.6
CF10	16	6.3	9.8
CF11	16.1	6.3	9.8
CF12	16.2	6.3	9.9
CF13	16.4	6.4	10
CF14	16.4	6.3	10.1
CF15	16.5	6.4	10.1
CF16	16.5	6.4	10.1
CF17	16.5	6.4	10.2
CF18	16.6	6.6	10
CF19	16.7	6.6	10.1
CF20	16.8	6.5	10.3

the case of expected value, at an increasingly slower rate, also for the same reason.

As will be shown in later chapters, the price dynamics of commodities are more complex than a simple autoregressive process; in fact, in the case of oil, it is reasonable to assume that the price is the sum of a random walk plus an autoregressive process, and therefore the results obtained for the CFaR will be interpreted differently. In particular, if the μ of the random walk is greater than zero, then the expected value of the cash flows will grow over time as the price, on average, will increase due to this positive μ. Additionally, the maximum loss will also grow over time but now at the same rate; thus, in the long term, it is the dynamic random walk which is imposed.

The fact that commodity dynamics are more complex than a simple autoregressive process must also be highlighted, as this will mean the CFaR cannot be calculated analytically. However, by following the steps (a), (b) and (c) described previously, it is always possible to estimate the CFaR or NPVaR of any investment project, regardless of the underlying dynamics of market prices and other variables that may affect the cash flows.

Finally, to reiterate, as in Chap. 3 the use of this method is subject to knowing at least approximately the stochastic processes governing the dynamics of each of the market variables affecting the magnitude whose risk we want to measure, which is not always easy to achieve. However, if the time series governing the dynamics of these variables is not easy to characterise, as in Chap. 3, another type of simulation can be used: historical simulation and/or simulation scenarios.

4.4.3 Calculation Without an Explicit Model

Historical simulation can be carried out by simply observing the values that market variables took in previous years and then assuming that the behaviour is the same. This approach was described in Chap. 3 and the aforementioned advantages remain the same. However, in addition to the disadvantages already described for a period, it must be added that it is extremely questionable that the behaviour of all variables in all periods is the same, since for all practical purposes it is the equivalent of assuming the model of independent variables. In any case, this simulation method is best suited to when we do not know even approximately the time series model that governs the dynamics of market variable values that affect the magnitude with the risk to be measured.

Finally, there is simulation by scenario in which specific market variable values are assigned to quantify the results in different chosen conditions.

In order to avoid lengthening this description unnecessarily, examples of historical simulation and simulation scenarios will not be presented here. However, their development is very simple if based on the previous example of numerical simulation and the examples studied in Chap. 3.

4.5 Diversification and Hedging Considerations

Regarding incremental and marginal measures and their application to diversification and hedging, in this chapter it is important to highlight some concepts related to these marginal and incremental steps for the multi-period case.

As in Chap. 3, where it was indicated that it is possible to use the marginal VaR to see how risk changes by modifying the positions in a portfolio, the same can be said in the case of multi-period measures. The marginal CFaR, marginal NPVaR, or any of these risk measures can be used in their marginal form to see how the risk is modified by modifying the composition of the company's assets or investment project. However, this general comment has to be verified, as the first thing to be noted is that, depending on the measure used, it is possible for the risk to move in either direction by adding an asset, that is, it is possible that the CFaR of a cash flow increases and the NPVaR of an investment project or company decreases or vice versa, which means that the risk of a cash flow increases while the NPV of the investment decreases. In these cases it is the manager who has to decide which to prioritise in risk management, whether it is a cash flow, NPV or the magnitude in question whose risk we want to measure.

However, the same principle applies when undertaking a new project or investing in a new asset: a business should consider their return and risk not in isolation, but how it relates to other projects or assets in its portfolio. That means it is possible for a project to involve an increased risk for one company and for another a decreased risk. As in Chap. 3, it is feasible to undertake projects or invest in assets to hedge the risk; as noted, this also depends on the risk measure being used, as procedures that increase CFaR can decrease NPVaR and vice versa. An investment project or set of investment projects that make up a business can be referred to as optimal hedging when risk is reduced as much as possible and perfect hedging when the risk is zero. In line with Chap. 3, when discussing joint investment projects, it is not necessary to hedge each one individually, since investing in different projects already diversifies risk.

One problem that now arises with investment projects is indivisibility, which does not exist with the portfolios presented in Chap. 3. For example, if a company plans to open a new plant, from the standpoint of risk, the optimum could be to carry out 20 % of the investment, that is, 20 % of building a factory, which is impossible. While it is always possible to build the factory and keep the 20 % stake in it, this solution presents other agency-related problems. In any case, note that the problem of indivisibility appears in the case of non-financial investments as in the case of financial investments: although shares cannot be split, nominal prices are so small relative to the amounts typically handled by investors that they can be considered infinitely divisible.

5

Interest Rate Risk

5.1 Basic Concepts

When investing in bonds, it may seem that there is no risk, especially when purchasing a bond where the amount of money paid by each coupon and the bond face value are known. However, although the amount of the coupons and the repayment are known, the investor's final return can change for various reasons, mainly due to interest rate variation. With the exception of default risk, the price of the bond in question is simply $P = \frac{C}{(1+r)^{T_1}} + \ldots + \frac{C+N}{(1+r)^{T_J}}$ where C is the coupon, N is the face value, r is the interest rate (which in this case, for simplicity, is assumed to be the same in each maturity time) and $T_1, T_2, \ldots, T_J$ are the moments in time when the coupon and interest payment occur. Thus, if the interest rate changes, the price of the bond in question also varies, and the longer the payment period is, the greater the variation becomes.

The interest rate risk, which can be defined formally as a concept which deals with the uncertainty of future earnings resulting from changes in interest rates, generally occurs when the future behaviour of an interest rate is unknown and is manifested in two ways: the first, which was mentioned in the previous paragraph, is known as price risk and occurs

F.J. Población García, *Financial Risk Management*,
DOI 10.1007/978-3-319-41366-2_5

because when interest rates rise, the price of the bond, or the investment value in general, falls. The second is known as reinvestment risk because when interest rates fall, coupons and rebates are reinvested at lower rates.

Although this interest rate risk is the main risk when working with fixed income, there are others such as insolvency risk, liquidity risk and tax risk. Although these risks will be referred to here, they will be covered in greater depth later, as this chapter will focus on interest rate risk.

Before looking at interest rate risk in depth, the chapter will briefly review the various debt instruments, the different ways of characterising the interest rate, risk premium and the difference between real interest rates and nominal interest rates, which, in turn, will lead to a discussion on inflation risk.

5.1.1 Different Fixed-Income Instruments

The simplest debt instrument is known as a simple loan. A simple loan is a loan in which the lender gives the borrower a certain amount of money, called the principal, at a given time and the borrower returns it at a later date, called maturity, accompanied by some additional payments known as interest.

Another type of loan which is widely used in real life is the fixed payment loan or fully amortised loan. In this type of operation the borrower receives an amount of money from the lender today and repays the debt through a sequence of identical payments over time. The mortgage loan is the best known example.

The coupon bond is also well known since with this instrument the lender lends money, the bond value, and the borrower pays some interest, the coupon, every year of the loan except the last, in which interest is paid plus the face value of the bond which may coincide with the nominal value, although it is not required to do so. Coupon bonds are identified by three characteristics: the issuer, which could be public administration (central, regional, local government, etc.), a company (public or private) and so on; the maturity, which can range from short-term (from three months to one year) to long-term (more than a year); and the coupon rate of the bond, which is simply the ratio between the interest paid annually and the face value of the bond and which can be referred to as fixed, if the same payment is made in every period, or as variable, if the payment is tied to an index, such as Euribor.

This final category could include zero-coupon bonds or discount bonds. This bond returns its face value when it matures and at the beginning an amount that is less than the face value is paid for it; the difference is the return for the investor. In this way, between the start and the maturity the borrower does not pay the lender anything.

5.1.2 Different Ways of Characterising the Interest Rate

Unlike equities, where the share price is the equity value, fixed-income risk is measured through the interest rate, which obviously is not the bond value but is defined through bond value. As indicated above, the higher the interest rate, the lower the price of the bond and vice versa. For this reason, the interest rate can be defined in many ways.

The simplest way to define the interest rate is what is known as the simple interest rate. If working from a future cash flow, the simple interest rate (r^s) is defined from the value of this future flow when it occurs (VF), the flow value today (VP) and the time when the payment is made in the future (T) as follows: $\mathrm{VP} = \frac{\mathrm{VF}}{1+r^s*T}$. Due to its simplicity, this is the official interest rate used to characterise short-term interest rates in many countries. In particular, in Spain it is the official interest rate for Treasury bills.

Although very simple, this definition lacks desirable properties when it comes to interest rates. The main drawback is that with the simple interest rate, the interest generated in previous periods is not taken into account when creating interest for the following period, which does not allow for a homogeneous comparison between interest rates in different time periods. In order to avoid this and other additional complications, we resort to the definition of compound interest rate (r^c), which in practice is the most frequently used and is: $\mathrm{VP} = \frac{\mathrm{VF}}{(1+r^c)^T}$. When the time is measured in years, this compound interest rate is sometimes known as the "annual percentage rate" (APR).

Although the compound interest rate already presents desirable properties and is the most widely used in practice, the continuous interest rate (r^{cc}) will also be defined because it is the easiest to deal with mathematically. Its definition is: $\mathrm{VP} = \mathrm{VF}{*}e^{-r^{cc}*T}$. Although it goes beyond the scope of this book, note that this interest rate definition is the easiest to deal with in practice and is closely related to what was said in the chapters on market risk regarding the prices in logarithms: everything is based on $e^{a} * e^{b} = e^{a+b}$.

As this book is about risk management and not financial mathematics, the remainder of this book refers to the compound interest rate, unless otherwise stated.

5.1.3 The Risk Premium

Figure 5.1 shows the matured yields from different categories of long-term bonds between 28 January 2002 and 25 October 2012.

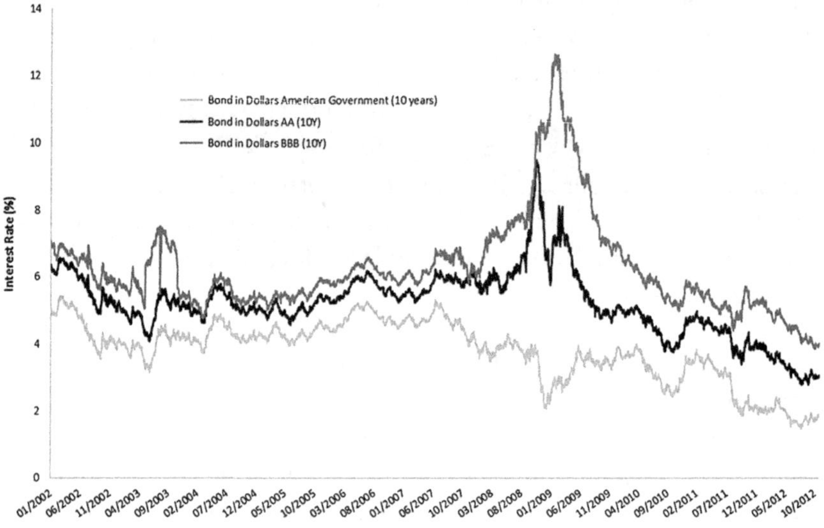

Fig. 5.1 Bonds interest rate (Data source: Bloomberg; Author's own composition)

At first glance two very important facts are clearly visible: the first is that on a given date interest rates of different bonds with the same maturity are also different; secondly, it is quite clear that these differences between interest rates, also known as credit "spreads", vary over time. Considering what has been discussed previously, the question arises as to why this is observed.

The first possible answer is that this is a consequence of the fact that these bonds have credit risk. As will be shown, credit risk is the risk that the bond issuer is unable to repay its interest and principal. In this sense, the probability of a company that suffers big losses in a given period of time repaying the bonds is much lower than the probability of company with great profits doing so. US government bonds have been considered traditionally as assets without default risk because the federal government can always raise taxes or print more money to repay them. However, in 1995 and 1996, the US Treasury threatened to default, causing bond rates to rise. In any case, bonds with no default risk are called risk-free bonds, and the difference between the interest rate of a risk-free bond and the interest rate of a bond with risk is called the risk premium (spread) of the bond with risk. The risk premium indicates how much additional interest must be offered to investors through the bond to compensate for the credit risk.

From the above, it can be concluded that a bond with a default risk has a positive risk premium and that an increased default risk also increases the risk premium. As will be discussed in later chapters, since the default risk is so important when determining the risk premium, there are credit rating agencies (Moody's, S&P, etc.) that assign ratings to companies (AA, BBB, etc.) according to their default risk. Returning to Fig. 5.1, it can now be explained why solvent government bonds have a lower interest rate than corporate bonds: corporate bonds have default risk while government bonds do not. Therefore, as the corporate bonds with a rating of BBB have a higher default risk than AA, the interest rate of AA bonds is lower than BBB-rated bonds. This line of reasoning also helps explain why the risk premium of BBB bonds suddenly increases in times of economic uncertainty, as it did from 2009 to 2010, because in these periods the credit risk increases and therefore the risk premium also rises.

Another attribute of a bond that has an impact on the interest rate is its liquidity, that is, the possibility of it becoming money. As economic theory states and as is evident, if everything else remains constant, the more liquid an asset is, the greater the demand is and therefore the higher the price is. Government bonds are the most liquid bonds in the market due to the large volume of debt issued by governments today; in addition, they can be bought and sold in many markets and transaction costs are low. By contrast, corporate bonds are a lot less liquid because there is no company that has the ability to issue as much debt as the government, and therefore the costs of having to sell them if an emergency occurs are greater. Therefore, it can be concluded that the risk premium reflects differences not only in default risk but also in liquidity.

Returning to Fig. 5.1, it can be said that all the most obvious facts have been explained. However, although not shown in the figure, it is well known that the behaviour of US municipal bonds relative to the country's government bonds is different. It is known that municipal bonds are not risk-free bonds, since during the Great Depression and also more recently many of them defaulted, and yet it is curious that during the last 50 years these bonds have had lower interest rates than government bonds. The reason for this is that municipal bonds are exempt from paying federal taxes, which implies that taxation is another essential factor when analysing an investment project.

5.1.4 Interest Rate Risk and Inflation

Inflation has not been taken into account in the interest rates discussed so far, which are known as nominal interest rates; these are different from the real interest rates. Real interest rates are obtained by simply subtracting the expected changes in the price level, that is, changes in inflation, from the nominal rates. For this reason, real interest rates better reflect the true cost of borrowing because they take into account not only money revaluation but also the revaluation of goods in the economy. That is to say, the nominal interest rates only show the change in the value of money between two periods but do not demonstrate how this variation is related to the value of other goods in the economy. In other words, nominal interest rates do not provide information on the change in purchasing power, while real interest rates do.

Real interest rates are defined more accurately through the Fisher equation: $r_N = r_R + \pi^e$ where r_N is the nominal interest rate, r_R is the real interest rate and π^e is the expected inflation.

Real interest rates are useful in the extent to which they can calculate the present value in real terms, that is, in terms of the value of future goods and services. That is, the nominal interest rate reflects the revaluation of money based on the price of current goods and services, if this money is invested in a specific financial instrument while, on the contrary, the real interest rate shows the revaluation in terms of future goods and services.

When real interest rates are low, there is great incentive to borrow and little to lend, and when real interest rates are high, there is a great incentive to lend and little to borrow. The real interest rate, not the nominal interest rate, indicates the true cost of borrowing, which is very important. For example, in the USA in the 1970s nominal interest rates were very high while real interest rates were very low or even negative, which could have led to confusion because by only observing the interest rates in nominal terms, it could be inferred that borrowing would be a bad deal, as nominal interest rates were around 15 %. However, on studying the interest rates in real terms, this is clearly false because although the interest to pay is high, the prices have also greatly increased, inflation is high, and therefore the purchasing power achieved with such high nominal interest is not much higher but actually even lower than at the beginning. Therefore, it is not such a bad idea to borrow and buy goods today because in the future they will be revalued, in some cases at a rate higher than the interest on the debt. In other words, lending is not as profitable a business as it might at first seem because when debt is repaid with interest, purchasing power may have dropped.

Although, after everything that has been discussed, it seems clear that it is more reasonable to work with real interest rates than with nominal interest rates, in practice investors always work with nominal interest rates. The reason for this is that estimating the expected inflation is a problem when trying to calculate the real interest rates. At present the nominal market interest rates are known for all maturities, but the inflation that will occur in each of them is not known, thus today there are nominal interest rates and estimates of the real interest rates calculated with the expected inflation for each term. The problem arises because estimating the inflation is very complex and generally the estimates are unreliable, and in turn the real interest rate estimates are as well. This concept can be referred to as inflation risk.

5.2 The Term Structure of Interest Rates

As already noted, various factors such as default risk, liquidity and taxes affect the price of bonds and, at the same time, interest rates. However, the most important factor influencing interest rates is that of the bond maturities. Bonds with identical risk, liquidity and taxes may have very different interest rates due to the fact that the time until maturity is not the same.

Thus, the graph presenting the interest rates of different bonds with the same risk, liquidity and tax but different maturities is known as the yield curve or term structure of interest rates (TSIR). More formally, the TSIR can be defined as the function relating interest rates to terms until the securities mature for bonds with similar credit ratings. Obviously, for each level of credit rating there is a curve of different rates, and thus the worse the credit rating is, the higher the interest rates are and vice versa.

The term structure of interest rates can be defined with different types of bond that have very different payment structures, but for consistency the TSIR is normally created with the interest rates of zero-coupon bonds. Thus, TSIRs that are created in this way are homogeneous and unless otherwise stated, from here onwards the TSIR will refer to its zero-coupon bonds.

Figure 5.2 shows the zero-coupon yield curve of government debt in Spain on three specific dates.

When the yield curve rises, short-term rates are lower than long-term rates; when it is flat, short-term and long-term rates are equal; and when it falls, short-term rates are higher than long-term rates. Moreover, as can be seen in Fig. 5.3, other shapes can be achieved (for example, rising at the beginning and falling at the end).

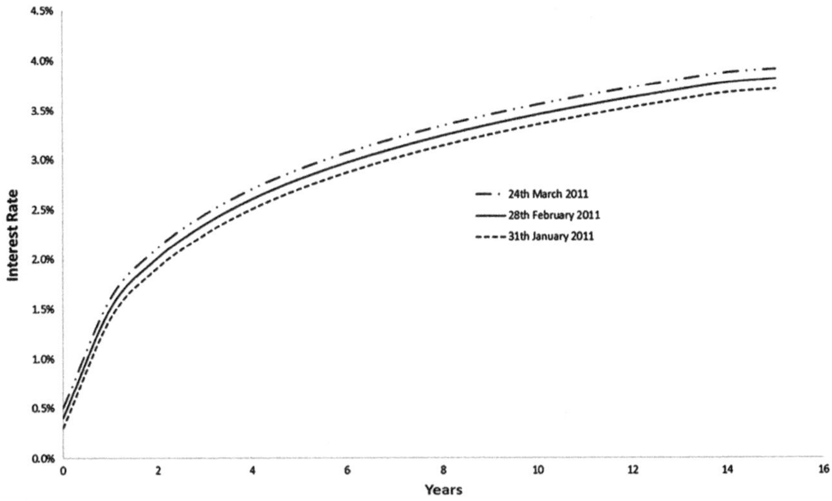

Fig. 5.2 Zero-coupon curve government debt in Spain (Data source: Bloomberg; Author's own composition)

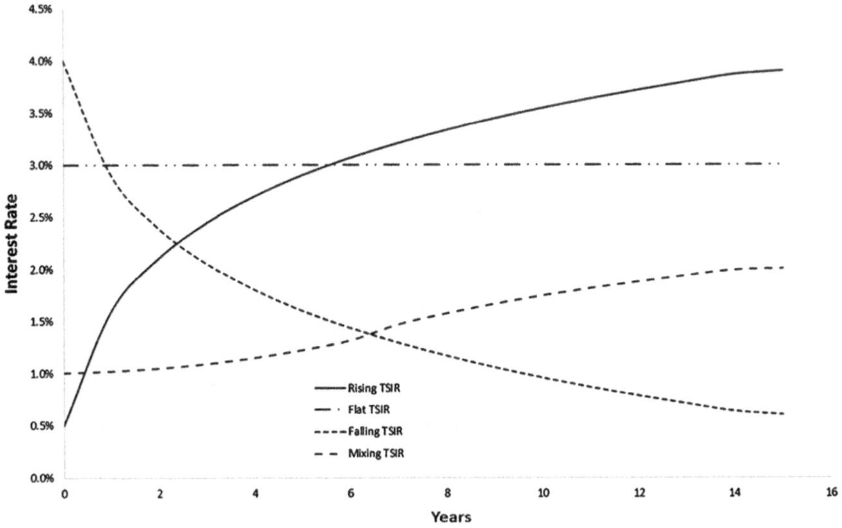

Fig. 5.3 Zero-coupon curve (Author's own composition)

5.2.1 Term Structure Theories of Interest Rates

Detailed study of the TSIR is very complex because each interest rate for each of the many bond price terms has a particular dynamic but is closely related to the dynamics of the other interest rates. Moreover, apart from having an interest rate based on each maturity, as will be discussed later, there is an interest rate for each issuer with its own dynamics but also closely related to the other interest rates at different maturities and from different issuers. Finally, note that interest rates are closely related to exchange rates.

For the reasons detailed above, a coherent characterisation of the general dynamics of interest rates and particularly its TSIR far exceeds the scope of this book and therefore will not be discussed. Regarding the TSIR, some brief points about its dynamics will be outlined. Specifically, the question we will try to answer is: why does the yield curve generally rise but sometimes take other forms?

As well as explaining why the yield curve assumes a certain form or another, at this level a good TSIR theory is considered to be one that explains the following three facts:

a) Interest rates on bonds of different maturities tend to move in the same direction (if one rises, all of them rise; if one falls, all of them fall).
b) When short-term interest rates are low, the yield curve is likely to rise, whereas when short-term interest rates are high, the yield curve is likely to decrease.
c) The yield curve almost always rises.

As only three events must be explained, instead of outlining a coherent and well-grounded financial theory of interest rates, three qualitative theories will be presented in an attempt to shed some light on the subject. In particular, note that there are three main theories to explain the behaviour of the TSIR, that is, the relationship between such rates at different maturities: the expectations theory, the segmentation theory and the liquidity premium theory (or the preferred habitat theory). The expectations theory explains the first two events, while the segmentation theory explains the third. For this reason, fusing both theories brings us to the third (liquidity premium theory) which manages to explain all three events.

The expectations theory of the TSIR is based on the following (obvious) statement: the interest rates of a long-term bond are equal to the average expected short-term interest rates over the life of the bond. In other words, if short-term interest rates are expected to rise, long-term interest rates today will be higher than short-term interest rates. The key assumption behind this is that bond buyers do not prefer bonds according to their terms, but if a bond has a lower expected return than another at a different maturity, they will purchase the bond with the highest expected return; this means that bonds at different maturities are perfect substitutes.

Under this assumption, the following investment strategies are equivalent: buying a one-year bond and after this period buying another one-year bond or buying a two-year bond. Therefore, if the strategies are equivalent, the profitability of both must be the same. The profitability of the first one is: $(1 + r_{0,1})\ (1 + r_{1,1}^{e}) - 1 = r_{0,1} + r_{1,1}^{e} + r_{0,1} * r_{1,1}^{e}$, where $r_{0,1}$, is the interest rate today ($t = 0$) of the one-year bond while $r_{1,1}^{e}$ is the interest rate that one-year bonds are expected to have within a year ($t = 1$). The yield of the second is $(1 + r_{0,2})^2 - 1 = 2r_{0,2} + (r_{0,2})^2$ where r_{02} is the interest rate of the bond today in two years.

Equating the return of both strategies and assuming for simplicity that both $r_{0,1} * r_{1,1}^{e}$ and $(r_{0,2})^2$ are zero, because the interest rates are usually around 2–5 % and therefore $(5\ \%)^2 = 0.25\ \%$ which is much lower than 5 %, it is calculated that $r_{0,1} + r_{1,1}^{e} = 2r_{0,2}$ or equally $r_{0,2} = \frac{r_{0,1} + r_{1,1}^{e}}{2}$. The interest rate of the zero-coupon bond in two years should be equal to the average interest rate of the zero-coupon bond in one year and the interest rate that the one-year zero-coupon bond is expected to have within a year. The reasoning is identical with longer maturity bonds.

The expectancy theory is an elegant theory that gives us an explanation of why the term structure of interest rates changes over time. When the yield curve increases, the expectancy theory tells us that short-term interest rates are expected to rise in the future, as easily demonstrated from what has been seen so far: if $r_{0,2} > r_{0,1}$, then $r_{1,1}^{e}$ must be greater than $r_{0,1}$ and thus $r_{0,2} = \frac{r_{0,1}+r^e_{1,1}}{2}$. This implies that the interest rate of one-year bonds is expected to rise within a year. By the same reasoning, if the yield curve falls, short-term rates are expected to fall in the next year.

This theory explains fact (a), which states that interest rates of bonds with different maturities tend to move in the same direction. The reason is that historically it has been observed that when short-term interest rates rise, they are expected to continue rising in the future. If short-term rates rise, they will be expected to continue rising and for this reason, as long-term rates are the average between short-term rates and their expectations, when short-term rates and their expectations rise, long-term rates also rise. Therefore, if short-term rates rise, long-term rates also rise and vice versa, and for this reason the rates move together, that is, if short-term rates move in one direction, long-term rates move in the same direction.

In addition, this expectancy theory explains fact (b), which states that when short-term interest rates are low, the yield curve is likely to increase, whereas when short-term interest rates are high, the yield curve is likely to fall. The reason is that historically, when short-term interest rates are low, the market expects them to rise and, therefore, following the same reasoning as before, which is that ${r_{1t+1}}^e > r_{1t}$ so $r_{2t} > r_{1t}$ when short-term interest rates are low, the yield curve rises and, by the same reasoning, when short-term interest rates are high, the yield curve falls.

The expectancy theory is an attractive theory because it gives us a simple explanation for the behaviour of the yield curve but it has one drawback: it fails to account for fact (c), which states that the yield curve usually rises. Following the logic of this theory, if the yield curve usually rises, then generally short-term interest rates are expected to rise in the future; however, it is noted that in practice short-term interest rates are equally likely to fall as they are to rise, and therefore the probability of the curve rising should be equal to the probability of it falling, which contradicts fact (c).

As its name suggests, the segmentation theory of the TSIR assumes that the markets of different maturity bonds are completely segmented and separated. The price and the interest rate of a bond with a given maturity is determined by the intersection of the supply curve and the demand curve for that bond, and these curves for a bond with a given maturity have nothing to do with the supply and demand curves for another bond with a different maturity. For this reason, in this theory the key assumption is that bonds at different maturities are not substitutes for each other, which is why the change in interest rates of a bond at a given maturity does not affect the interest rate of bonds with a different maturity. This theory is the extreme opposite of the segmentation theory, in which it was assumed that bonds at different maturities are perfect substitutes.

According to this theory, bonds with different maturities are not substitutes for each other, as investors have very strong preferences for certain types of bonds as opposed to others and therefore each investor looks for bonds with the maturity that interests them. An investor that needs to recover their money in the short term will invest in bonds maturing shortly, while if they want to invest in paying for their children's education they will focus on long-term maturities.

On the other hand, considering the fact that investors are risk averse and, therefore, prefer short-term investments, the segmentation theory can explain fact (c), which states that the yield curve rises. As indicated, the reason is that the demand for short-term bonds is usually higher than for long-term bonds and thus, having less demand, the price of the long-term bond will be less than that of the short-term bond. However, the short-term interest rates will be lower than the long-term rates and consequently the yield curve tends to rise.

Although this theory can explain fact (c), it fails when attempting to explain facts (a) and (b). As there is no relationship between bonds with one maturity and bonds with another if some interest rates move in one direction, there is no reason for all the others to move in the same direction and vice versa (fact a). In the same way, there is also no reason to apply fact (b), which states that if short-term rates are low, the yield curve rises and if they are high, it falls.

The liquidity premium theory of the TSIR assumes that the interest rate of a long-term bond is the average of the short-term interest rate and of its expectations over the life of the long-term bond plus a liquidity premium which is determined by supply and demand in the long-term bond. This theory assumes that bonds of different maturities are substitutes, although not perfect substitutes, because changes in interest rates of a bond at one maturity affect those of other bond maturities. However, it also allows for the fact that some investors prefer bonds of one maturity instead of bonds of another.

Investors generally prefer short-term bonds because they have less interest rate risk and, therefore, long-term bonds offer a positive liquidity premium to increase the demand for them. As a result of this theory, we have something similar to what was seen in the expectations theory but with an added liquidity premium: $r_{0,n} = \frac{r_{0,1}+r^e_{1,1}+r^e_{2,1}+\cdots+r^e_{n,1}}{n} + \lambda_{0,n}$ where r_{1t} is the interest rate in a year, $r_{1,1}{}^e$, is the annual interest rate expected in a year, $r_{2,1}{}^e$ is the annual interest rate expected in two years . . . and,. . . y $\lambda_{0,n}$, n is the liquidity premium today ($t = 0$) for the bond which matures in "n" years.

In turn, it is assumed that this liquidity premium is always positive and grows with "n" and because of this premium the resulting yield curve tends to rise and to do so more steeply than that derived from the expectations theory.

The preferred habitat theory is very similar to the liquidity premium theory and is based on a less direct approach to modifying the expectation theory, but it comes to the same conclusions. This theory assumes that investors have a preference for one type of bond as opposed to others—they prefer short-term bonds to long-term bonds—but it also assumes that if they notice differences between short-term and long-term rates, they may also want to buy long-term bonds for the extra return these provide. This leads to an equation like that expressed previously and, of course, also leads to the same conclusion.

This liquidity premium theory (or preferred habitat theory) is consistent with the three empirical facts discussed previously. In regards to fact (a) it can be said that, as in the expectations theory, when short-term interest rates rise, the expectations of short-term rates do too; then long-term rates rise and, therefore, interest rates tend to move in the same direction.

It also explains why the yield curve tends to rise when short-term rates are low and fall when they are high, that is, fact (b). As in the expectations theory, when short-term rates are low, they are expected to rise and when they are high, they are expected to fall; for this reason, when short-term rates are low, long-term rates are high—a rising curve, whereas when short-term rates are high, long-term rates are low—a decreasing curve.

Unlike the expectations theory, the liquidity premium theory and the preferred habitat theory may also explain fact (c), which states that the yield curve usually rises. The reason for this is the liquidity premium, which is always positive and increases with the maturity of the bond. Even if short-term interest rates are expected to remain constant, due to the liquidity premium, the long-term rates will outweigh the short-term rates and will rise according to their maturity.

At this point, the question might arise regarding how these theories can explain the fact that the yield curve sometimes decreases. The answer is easy: this occurs when expectations that short-term rates will fall are so great that their decreasing effect on long-term rates exceeds the effect of the liquidity premium.

Another attractive conclusion of the liquidity premium theory is that the market prediction of future short-term rates can be deduced from the shape of the yield curve: if the yield curve rises with a large slope, it can be concluded that the market expects a rise in short-term rates in the future, whereas if the yield curve rises with a moderate slope, it shows that the market expects short-term rates to remain more or less stable (with very slight increases or decreases). Conversely, if the yield curve is flat, moderate decreases in short-term rates are expected while if it falls, large declines are expected in these short-term rates.

5.2.2 The Implicit Interest Rate, the Forward Interest Rate and IRR

As in most markets, including in the case of interest rates, there are spot rates and forward rates. The spot interest rate, $r_{0,n}$, is the annual cash goal of a simple operation in which a price P_0 is paid and is repaid within n years obtaining a value of P_n, that is, $P_0 = \frac{P_n}{\left(1+r_{0,n}\right)^n}$, while the term interest rate or forward rate, $r^e_{t,T}$, is the interest rate at a given maturity, "T", which it is expected to have within a time "t".

Accordingly, given the close relationship between interest rates, the implicit interest rate, $r^i_{t,T}$, is also defined as the rate that is implicit between two spot rates, particularly between the spot rate maturing at

"t" and the spot rate maturing at "$T + t$". In other words, $r_{t,T}^{i}$ is defined such that: $(1 + r_{0,T+t}) = (1 + r_{0,t}) * (1 + r_{t,T}^{i})$.

If the dynamics of the TSIR were defined by the expectations theory, it is evident that the forward interest rate and the implicit rate would be the same. However, considering the theory which best fits the dynamics of the TSIR is the liquidity premium, the implicit interest rate will always be higher than the forward interest rate, as the risk premium is always positive. As this risk premium increases in line with the maturity, the greater the maturity is, the greater the difference between the implicit interest rate and future interest rate will be.

Finally, and to finish characterising the interest rate, a concept known as the internal rate of return (IRR) must be defined. Once the TSIR for a level of risk is known, the price of a payment structure similar to the TSIR risk should then be calculated by simply discounting each expected payment at the initial time with the interest rate of the corresponding TSIR: $P = \frac{\text{Payment}_1}{\left(1+r_{0,T_1}\right)^{T_1}} + \ldots + \frac{\text{Payment}_n}{\left(1+r_{0,T_n}\right)^{T_n}}$, "payment" being the payment expected to occur in each of the $T_1, T_2, \ldots, T_n$ periods. Thus, for a given payment structure, the IRR, "r", is defined as the discount rate such that $P = \frac{\text{Payment}_1}{(1+r)^{T_1}} + \ldots + \frac{\text{Payment}_n}{(1+r)^{T_n}}$, that is, the internal rate of an investment is simply the geometric average of expected future returns from that investment.

For a given payment structure, this rate "r" (IRR) financially equals the price paid and the profits made, which is why it is the interest rate that the market assigns to these securities or equivalently the internal point at which this operation occurs.

5.3 Duration

5.3.1 Simple or Macaulay Duration and Modified Duration

The interest rate risk is defined as uncertainty about future earnings as a result of changes in the market interest rate. The impact of this risk can be seen in two ways; firstly, it changes the market value of future payments—the higher the interest rates are, the lower the value of future payments discounted today; and secondly, it changes monetary flows which depend on the interest rate (as in the case of bonds). In general, a priori it cannot be claimed that a rise or fall in interest rates affects the value of the investment in one way or another. Only if cash flows do not depend on interest rates can it be claimed that the interest rate only affects future payment discounts and therefore the higher the interest rate is, the lower the value of investment is and vice versa.

This is a market risk and is therefore susceptible to being measured in the same way as any other market risk, that is, using the same methodology as the value at risk. This issue will be addressed in subsequent sections; however, given the complexity of characterising the dynamics of all interest rates on market products adequately and consistently, before moving on to this issue other more simple and operational concepts to measure and manage interest rate risk will be introduced.

If you have an investment and its value, P_0, is determined by the present value of its future cash flows, Q_t, discounted at its IRR, r, that is, $P_0 = \frac{Q_1}{1+r} + \frac{Q_2}{(1+r)^2} + \ldots + \frac{Q_n}{(1+r)^n}$, a variation in r causes a variation in P_0 that is higher or lower depending on its sensitivity. The easiest way to estimate the effect that a change in r has on P_0, and therefore the interest rate risk of P_0, is to resort to calculating the corresponding derivative, $\mathrm{d}P_0/\mathrm{d}r$, which to use comparatively must be expressed in proportional terms with respect to P_0: $\frac{1}{P_0}\frac{\mathrm{d}P_0}{\mathrm{d}r}$.

Assuming that Q_t does not depend on the interest rate, to calculate the derivative we obtain: $\frac{1}{P_0}\frac{\mathrm{d}P_0}{\mathrm{d}r} = -\frac{\frac{1}{P_0}\sum_{i=1}^{n} t\frac{Q_t}{(1+r)^t}}{1+r}$, an expression that coincides, except for the symbol, with what is known as modified duration (D^*), $D^* = -\frac{1}{P_0}\frac{\mathrm{d}P_0}{\mathrm{d}r}$, which explains that the duration is taken as a good measure of sensitivity and, therefore, risk. However, before delving into the concept of modified duration, the notion of simple duration will be dealt with.

Simple duration or Macaulay duration is a weighted average because it is the average of the different terms or maturities in which the financial transaction will generate a cash flow where the weight is the present value of the cash flow corresponding to that period. Assuming a flat term structure, that is, that interest rates at different maturities are equal and, in turn, equal to the IRR,[1] $D = \frac{\sum_{t=1}^{n} t \frac{Q_t}{(1+r)^t}}{\sum_{t=1}^{n} \frac{Q_t}{(1+r)^t}} = \frac{1}{P_0} \sum_{t=1}^{n} t \frac{Q_t}{(1+r)^t}$ where D is the duration, t is the time period in which the flow occurs, n is the deadline and Q_t is the flow at time t. The duration is a time average so its unit is the time, usually years, and is a measure that tells us the time when a payment should be made to replace all the flows of the operation by just one equivalent if desired.

As is the case for the asset price, the concept of duration is also influenced by changes in its components. Thus, if there are two bonds which have all the same characteristics apart from the coupon, the one with the larger coupon will have the shortest duration. Similarly, given two bonds with all the same characteristics apart from the frequency of coupon payment, the one which has greater frequency will have a shorter duration. Finally, when there are changes in the IRR of a bond, the duration varies in the same way as the price, that is, the higher the IRR is, the lower the price and shorter the duration will be and vice versa.

If duration and the aforementioned modified duration are compared, it can be observed that when Q_t does not depend on the interest rate, if the duration is divided by $(1 + r)$, the modified duration is obtained as shown: $D^* = D/(1 + r)$. For this reason, if Q_t does not depend on the interest rate, the simple duration is virtually the same as the modified duration which, except for the symbol, is the derivative of P_0 with respect to r, that is, the percentage change in the value of the asset when there are variations of one percentage point in the interest rate $D^* = -\frac{1}{P_0} \frac{dP_0}{dr} = \frac{\frac{1}{P_0} \sum_{i=1}^{n} t \frac{Q_t}{(1+r)^t}}{1+r}$.

[1] If the interest rates at different maturities are not equal, in the definition of duration each flow should be discounted by the interest rate of the term in which it occurs.

A priori, the two very different concepts of duration (a time average) and modified duration (the price sensitivity to the interest rate) are so similar in this case because if Q_t does not depend on the interest rate, P_0 will be more sensitive to the interest rate the later the payments are made. Since Q_t does not depend on the interest rate, the only relationship between the price and the interest rate is that which is established through discount, $1/(1 + r)^T$, which, as is evident, is more sensitive to the interest rate the greater the term T is. The longer the duration is, that is, the longer the average payment term is, the higher the sensitivity of P_0 is to interest rate, that is, the modified duration.

Note that the value of the duration and modified duration is always positive, but when used as a measure of sensitivity they must be interpreted in a negative sense: as a variation in the asset value in contrast to the variation in interest rates. Thus, if the asset value is $P(r)$ for an interest rate r, using the concept of modified duration it is possible to estimate the value of the asset if the interest rate undergoes a change of Δr by simply using the Taylor expansion: $P(r + \Delta r) = P(r) + \mathrm{d}P(r)/\mathrm{d}r * \Delta r + \ldots\ldots$, avoiding second order or higher yields terms: $P(r + \Delta r) - P(r) = \Delta P = \mathrm{d}P(r)/\mathrm{d}r * \Delta r$ o, equivalently: $\frac{P(r+\Delta r)-P(r)}{P(r)} = \frac{\Delta P(r)}{P(r)} = \frac{1}{P(r)} \frac{\mathrm{d}P(r)}{\mathrm{d}r} \Delta r = -D^{*} * \Delta r$ and finally: $P(r + \Delta r) = P(r) - D^{*} * P(r) * \Delta r$.

5.3.2 Convexity

The concept of duration can be used to predict the variation of the bond price when there are changes in the interest rate, as just shown. Like that of the investment value, P_0, the duration depends on the interest rate. For this reason, the duration of an investment calculated for a given interest rate, such as (r_0), is not useful for understanding the percentage change in asset values when there are variations of one percentage point in the interest rate and the initial interest rate is different (r_1). As shown in the following graph, the duration of a bond when the interest rate is 1 % is not equal to the duration when the interest rate is 8 %. At a higher interest rate, the duration will be shorter, so at an interest rate of 8 %, the duration of the bond will be shorter. This phenomenon is called convexity (Fig. 5.4).

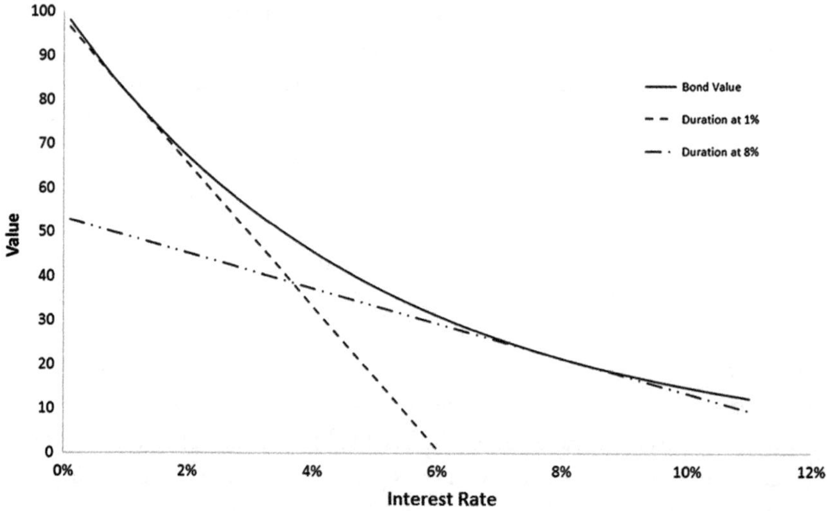

Fig. 5.4 Convexity (Author's own composition)

The sensitivity measurement that the modified duration provides is only accurate for small changes in the interest rate since, as has been shown, it is really a derivative and this only measures the effect of infinitesimal variations. Equivalently, the phenomenon of convexity can be understood as the difference between the actual price and the estimated price with the modified duration, in other words, the price variation is not explained by the modified duration. When r has a large variation, there is then a significant deviation between the actual price and the price estimated with the modified duration, as shown in Fig. 5.5.

The convexity of a bond has a positive effect, as it always benefits the investor, that is, when profitability falls, the bond price increases more than the price estimated with the duration, while when the profitability rises, the price of the bond falls below the estimated price. Likewise, it is not difficult to ascertain and, in fact, it can be inferred from the previous figures that profitability reductions have greater convexity effects than increases.

In any case, whether interest rates rise or fall, if the variation is large, the modified duration alone cannot estimate the actual variation that the price

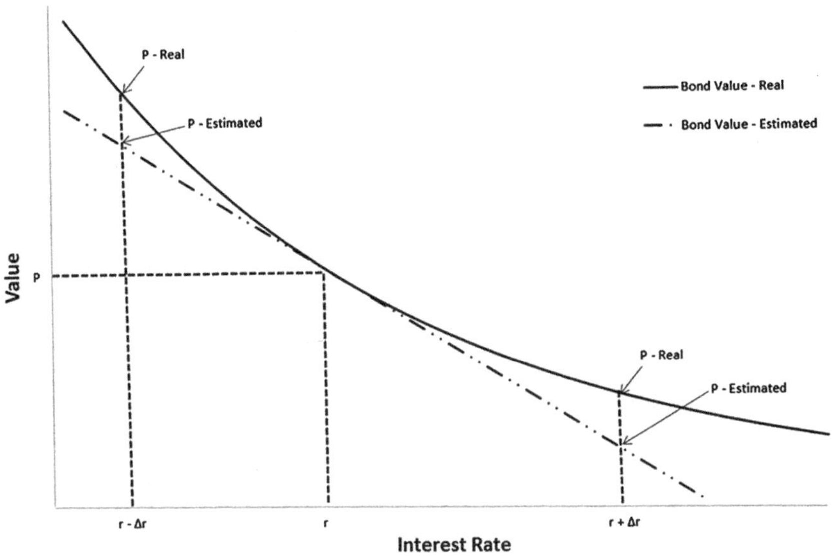

Fig. 5.5 Convexity (Author's own composition)

suffers and, for this reason, a correction for this convexity phenomenon must be included. As before, the best way to do this is by using the Taylor development but also considering the second order terms: $P(r + \Delta r) = P(r) + \mathrm{d}P(r)/\mathrm{d}r * \Delta r + (1/2) * \mathrm{d}^2P(r)/\mathrm{d}r^2 * (\Delta r)^2$. Working in the same way as before, $\frac{\Delta P(r)}{P(r)} = -D^* * \Delta r + \frac{1}{2} * \frac{1}{P(r)} * \frac{\mathrm{d}^2 P(r)}{\mathrm{d}r^2} * (\Delta r)^2$ is obtained and in the same way as $D^* * \Delta r$ is the first order correction term, the term $\frac{1}{2} * \frac{1}{P(r)} * \frac{\mathrm{d}^2 P(r)}{\mathrm{d}r^2} * (\Delta r)^2$ is the second order correction term and is known as convexity correction (CCC). The term $\frac{\mathrm{d}^2 P(r)}{\mathrm{d}r^2}$, which if Q_t is not dependent on r is expressed as $\frac{\mathrm{d}^2 P(r)}{\mathrm{d}r^2} = \frac{\sum_{i=1}^{n} t(t+1) \frac{Q_t}{(1+r)^t}}{(1+r)^2}$, is known as absolute convexity (C), while the term $\frac{1}{P(r)} * \frac{\mathrm{d}^2 P(r)}{\mathrm{d}r^2} = \frac{C}{P(r)}$ is called corrected convexity (CC).

5.3.3 Portfolio Immunisation

Traditionally, fixed-income investors have sought to ensure a steady income. This type of investor is usually averse to risk, preferring a more or less fixed flow of income. However, as is being considered throughout this chapter, the interest rate risk can be very important, especially as it affects long-term investments through the risk of bond prices and short-term investments through the reinvestment risk. With regard to price risk, if, for example, there is a zero-coupon bond with a 30-year maturity and the interest rate during this term goes from 3 % to 4 %, the loss of bond value will be around 25 %, a much higher loss than usually occurs in other markets, such as the equity market. Losses can also reach similar values with reinvestment risk.

Thus, portfolio immunisation is a technique that seeks to guarantee the initial yield of the portfolio regardless of the evolution of interest rates over the investment horizon. It is, therefore, a technique that immunises the portfolio from adverse changes in interest rates, and the key to this process is the concept of duration discussed previously.

Suppose an investor is faced with a future payment in a number of years and to this end decides to create a fixed-income bond portfolio by acquiring bonds with different maturities and payment structures. Naturally, the value of the portfolio will increase over time depending on the profitability at each moment, due to the received flows, bond coupons, nominal matured and so on that it obtains. For simplicity, assume there is a unique bond with ten years remaining until its maturity, it has a 5 % coupon, an 8.1-year duration and 0.75 convexity. Similarly, also for simplicity, assume that the TSIR is flat, that is, all interest rates at different maturities are equal and have a value of 5 %.

Profits made from the portfolio just formed by the investor come from three sources: the continued receipt of coupons (and if the portfolio was made up of more bonds with shorter maturities, the nominal charged at their maturity), the reinvestment of those coupons and any variation in the market price of the securities that make up the portfolio. Of these three sources, the receipt of coupons, or in some cases nominal values, is fixed, as the investor has the right to collect these profits assuming they are bonds without credit risk.[2] The second source does generate variations in the final outcome of the portfolio, because reinvestment rates of coupons may vary when market interest rates vary; this is the reinvestment risk previously stated. And, finally, any change in market interest rates will have an immediate effect on the price of the bond and therefore on the valuation of the investor's portfolio, that is, this third source is subject to the price risk designated previously.

Now suppose that market interest rates, 5 %, remained constant throughout the life of the bond; due to the coupons received, the value of the portfolio would increase at a constant rate until maturity. If one million euros were invested initially, then the value at the end of the investment would be 1.62 million euros.

If, instead, it is assumed that when the bonds have just been bought, market interest rates fall from 5 % to 3 % for the entire TSIR and remain constant until the maturity of the portfolio, the effect on the price is immediate: the price rises from the initial one million euros to 1.17 million euros. However, although the value of the portfolio is initially greater, the flows received during that time will be reinvested at a lower rate and the portfolio value in ten years will be 1.57 million. The same calculations can be performed if, after forming the portfolio, the returns increase to 7 %. In this case the initial value of the portfolio is 0.86 million euros but as the flows received now are reinvested at a higher rate, after ten years the value of the portfolio will be 1.69 million euros.

Analysing all this information raises the question: is the effect of changes in profits on the portfolio valuation offset at any point by the effect of changes in the reinvestment rate on flows? As shown in Fig. 5.6, the answer is that there is a point in time (the duration) at which the value of the portfolio is the same in each of the three cases discusssed previously. Moreover, the value is the same regardless of the variation occurring in interest rates. At this point in time (duration) the price effect and the reinvestment effect cancel each other out, which would also have been achieved if the investor had purchased zero-coupon bonds maturing at

[2] The credit risk in bonds will be discussed in the credit risk section.

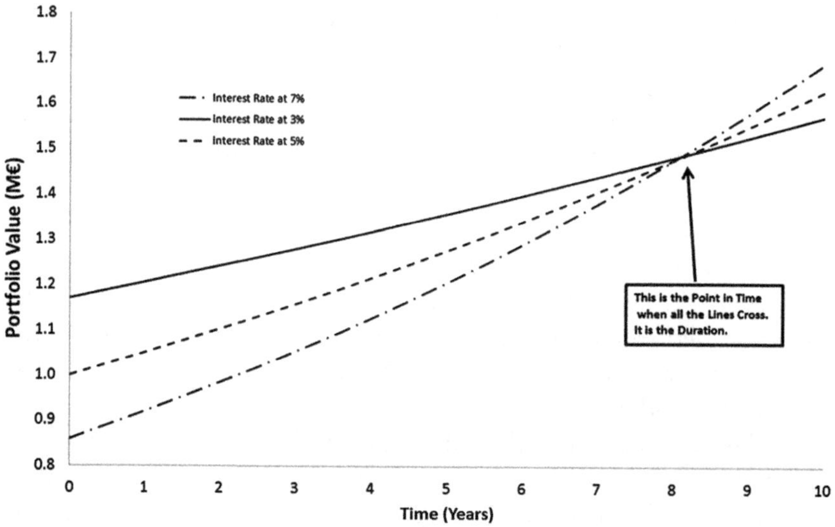

Fig. 5.6 Portfolio immunisation (Author's own composition)

their investment horizon (duration), since they also guarantee the initial yield at maturity, as they do not have interim payments.

Duration is a measure that indicates when the payment should be made in order to replace all the flows of the operation with one equivalent; therefore, regardless of the evolution of market interest rates and the returns required in the portfolio, the cumulative value of this will be the same. Therefore, at a term that matches the duration of the portfolio, it behaves like a zero-coupon bond whose nominal is the value of the portfolio at that point.

In accordance with the information presented so far, to immunise a fixed-income portfolio and prevent changes in market returns affecting their profitability, that is, to fully hedge its interest rate risk, a portfolio must be formed where the initial rate of return, IRR, is the preference with a duration matching the desired investment horizon. This is what is known as the immunisation theorem portfolio and is the work of Reddington.

It must not be forgotten that this works as long as the TSIR is flat and changes in interest rates are parallel. More generally, where the yield curve is not flat and changes in interest rates are not parallel, immunisation can also be achieved but with more elaborate strategies where its own convexity must be taken into account. The only problem lies in the fact that these more elaborate strategies require periodic adjustments to the portfolio,[3] which generates transaction costs and also does not eliminate 100 % of its risk.

5.4 The VaR for Fixed Income

The interest rate risk is a particular type of market risk and can be measured with the same criteria as the general market risk and, in particular, equity risk. Specifically, by applying the definition of value at risk (VaR) to a fixed-income portfolio it can be stated that the VaR is a measure of the maximum potential change that the value of a portfolio can suffer, in this case a fixed-income portfolio, at a time horizon and at a given probability level, due to changes in interest rates.

The difficulty with using the VaR in a fixed-income portfolio is not so much in its definition, which is a direct application of the general definition of value at risk, but rather in the fact that characterising the dynamics of interest rates is very complex, for two main reasons: the wide range of products and the close relationship that exists between them.

In this sense, even though characterising this dynamic is complex and exceeds the scope of this book, some general principles will be established. The first is that by studying the interest rate at a particular term, as seen in the graph in Sect. 5.1.3., (Fig. 5.1) dynamics of mean reversion are evident, that is, to characterise the dynamics of the interest rate at a given term the best model of those presented in this book is the autoregressive process, thus ruling out processes such as random walk because, as shown in the figure, interest rates, whatever the maturity, are in a stable interval most of the time. Fig. 5.1 shows that the government

[3] As will be discussed in later chapters, such hedging strategies are known as dynamic hedging.

bond over ten years is always between 1 % and 6 % throughout the period.

The main reason for the interest rate dynamics presenting mean reversion is that what is bought or sold is not the interest rate but the bond, and when this bond matures, unless there are credit risk issues, it pays for the nominal—nothing more and nothing less. This is why its price before maturity fluctuates around this value, leading to a fluctuation in the interest rate which in turn involves the movement of mean reversion.

However, although there are stochastic processes that characterise interest rate dynamics at a given maturity reasonably well, it is difficult to coherently characterise the joint dynamics of interest rates at different maturities. In these cases, it is normally assumed that all TSIR variability is given by a certain number of stochastic factors. Thus, the dynamics of each of the interest rates at each term is defined using these stochastic factors, establishing the relationship between the different dynamics. Once this definition has been obtained, the parameters of these stochastic factors are set so that the dynamics of the theoretical model are as close as possible to the actual dynamics observed using statistical techniques such as maximum likelihood.

There are many simple approaches in this regard. One of them is based on the work of Black et al. (1990) in which it is assumed that the implicit interest rates between period t and period $t + 1$, where Δt is the time between period t and period $t + 1$, have the following dynamics: $\ln(r_{t,t+1}{}^{\tau+1}) = \ln(r_{t,t+1}{}^{\tau}) + \theta(t)\Delta\tau + \sigma\varepsilon_\tau$, being τ *today*, $\Delta\tau$ the time between τ and $\tau + 1$, and ε_τ a random variable that is distributed by a normal with mean zero and variance one, independent of $\varepsilon_{\tau*}$ for all τ and τ^*. As demonstrated, this dynamic depends on the moment in time (τ) that occurs and the time until maturity (t). The value of these implicit interest rates varies as time (τ) passes and also according to maturity (t), because at any given time the implicit rate between one year and one year and one month and between ten years and ten years and one month is not the same. Thus, as in the other stochastic processes for market variables, over time the value of the implicit rate, which is the market variable in this case, varies in a non-perfectly predictable way mainly due to $\varepsilon_{\tau,}$ but also in this case the dynamics of the implicit rate are different depending on the term and are not the same at different maturities.

Thus, from the current TSIR and if possible those from the past, the parameters σ and $\theta(t)$ are estimated and the theoretical model is adapted as much as possible to the actual data. Once the parameters have been estimated, by numerical simulation, in the same way as in the examples presented previously, the VaR can be calculated.

While there are many simple approaches, the one presented here is based on a single factor because, as can be seen, at each point in time τ there is only one source of uncertainty which is $\varepsilon\tau$. However, although it is beyond the scope of the book, there are more sophisticated approaches based on several factors.

Given the complexity of this dynamic, as established in previous chapters, a particularly interesting option would be to estimate the VaR using historical simulation. In this case, historical simulation is especially useful since it does not require any probabilistic model, which greatly simplifies the calculation.

At the same time, it must also be highlighted that for the interest rate dynamics of a TSIR of risky bonds, it is necessary to simulate the risk-free interest rate and the risk premium, which also varies over time, together. The risk-free rate and the premium could be calculated separately, which introduces more complexity into the already complex problem of coherently characterising interest rate dynamics.

Finally, it should be mentioned that when the net present value at risk (NPVaR) calculation was discussed, a constant interest rate was assumed for simplicity; however, as it is being considered in this chapter, although with difficulty, it is possible to characterise the interest rate dynamics and incorporate them when estimating the NPVaR, which will provide more accurate estimates although they are also more complex.

5.5 Interest Rate Derivatives

Although techniques used to hedge interest rate risk such as portfolio immunisation have already been discussed, this last section of the chapter will briefly present some considerations on interest rate derivatives used to hedge this risk.

5.5.1 Interest Rate Futures

Interest rate futures are based on fixed financial assets whose price depends on the interest rate. One of the fundamental rules in finance, especially in negotiating with fixed-income assets, is that when profits rise, the prices of these assets fall and when profits fall, the price of fixed-income assets rises. Therefore the investor who takes a long position on a future regarding interest rates agrees to purchase a fixed-income financial asset at a specified price on a future date, and what this investor expects is that the interest rate will fall, because when it does the price of fixed-income bonds will rise and the investor will be obliged to buy the asset at a price below its market price. Moreover, the seller of a future regarding interest rates is counting on the fact that they will rise, so that the price of the underlying asset falls.

Interest rate futures are typically implemented through what is known as the notional bond, which is a fictional government bond that exists because of the impossibility of creating a financial future for each of the maturities of the government bonds issued. In the Spanish market this notional bond has a ten-year maturity, pays a coupon of 4 %, the contract nominal is 100,000 euros and is listed as a percentage of the par value. Similarly, months of negotiation are on a quarterly cycle and the date is the third Wednesday of the expiration month, and the minimum fluctuation is a basic point, that is, ten euros. This contract has delivery obligations, and using this future involves a more complex problem. To better understand this concept, suppose a contract is signed for one of these futures at a price of 88.75 % and its final price is 88 %. The difference is 75 basis points, which is the equivalent of 750 euros made by the seller and lost by the buyer, but on the date of its maturity the seller is obliged to hand the notional bond over to the buyer knowing that this bond does not exist. For this reason, a list of deliverable bonds is presented, or what is the same, a set of Treasury bonds with characteristics closely resembling those of the notional bond which the seller of futures can choose to deliver. As these are not a perfect replica of the notional bond, a multiplier is attached next to each bond which converts the notional bond into a replica of each one. This multiplier is called a conversion factor (CF). The seller studies the bonds on the list offered to them and selects the bond to be given to the buyer; however, in order for this bond to be given it must be purchased in the market first and at its market price. The seller observes the bond prices on the list and chooses the one which minimises the loss. This chosen bond is known as the cheapest to deliver.

These interest rate futures enable interest rate hedging, though not perfectly as bond risk is not hedged specifically, but a general provision is made. For this reason, in the following sections another way to hedge interest rate risk using derivatives will be discussed.

5.5.2 Forward Rate Agreement (FRA) and Interest Rate Swap (IRS)

As discussed in the previous subsection the future interest rate risk hedges long-term, that is, ten-year, interest rates. In the same way, there was at one time the short-term interest rate future, which was a future on the Euribor. However, it was discontinued in Spain due to its scarce trading volume. The closest existing contract is the forward rate agreement (FRA), which is a commitment between two parties who agree on a fixed interest rate to be paid by a theoretical deposit with a specific maturity on a future date. On the date the contract is signed, the fixed rate is established along with the date when the theoretical deposit transfer begins.

At maturity, the seller will pay the buyer the difference if the current interest rate, that is, the variable—which in this case is Euribor —exceeds the agreed interest rate. If, however, the current interest rate is less than the rate taken as a reference, the buyer will pay the seller. For example, a business (the buyer) which expects to be in debt within six months and wants to ensure that the interest rate on that date will remain the same as the current rate of 12 % can subscribe to a bank (the seller) an FRA, whereby six months from then the seller will pay the buyer the market interest rate, that is, Euribor, while the buyer will pay the seller 12 %. Thus, in this example the company ensures that the interest rate of this particular borrowing operation will be 12 % because on the one hand, Euribor will be paid for the debt operation but in turn, Euribor will be received in exchange for the 12 % paid to the bank, so they will pay 12 % net regardless of the developments in Euribor.

An interest rate swap (IRS) is an agreement between two parties whereby each agrees to make periodic payments to the other on certain future dates in such a way that one of them is interested in receiving or paying a variable interest rate while the other party is interested in receiving or paying a fixed rate. As in the FRA, the fixed-rate payer must make payments based on a specified fixed interest rate, while the variable-rate payer must make payments based on a variable interest rate, such as the Euribor. As in the FRA, such payments are calculated based on a theoretical nominal amount and settlements are calculated based on the differences established between the reference rates, such as the Euribor, and the rates fixed in the contract.

It should then be verified that this contract is a set of FRAs with identical interest rates and successive settlement dates, since it is a specially designed contract for those cases in which it is expected that the rate trend maintains a certain line in the mean and long term.

5.5.3 Cap, Floor and Collar

As indicated at the beginning of the chapter, interest rates affect the value of the investment in two ways: through discounts and through flows when they depend on interest rates. Portfolio immunisation hedges the entire interest rate risk, the risk which is affected by discounts and the risk which is affected by flows. However, it is sometimes desirable to hedge the cash flow risk and not the value of the investment, and for this reason the bond investor may sometimes be interested in hedging the interest rate risk included in the cash flows and not the total interest rate risk that affects the price. For example, imagine an investor who purchases a bond which pays a coupon linked to Euribor; in this case, putting credit risk, liquidity and tax considerations aside, it is easy to demonstrate that the value of the bond matches its nominal. Thus, it seems clear that hedging would not be necessary for the risk of bond price variation due to interest rates; however, due to the structure of this bond, the coupons that were to be received in the future are not known with certainty because they vary with the Euribor.

For this reason, sometimes the opposite of what happened with portfolio immunisation is desirable: to hedge the interest rate risk of flows only, that is, coupons, not the total value of the bond, which in this case is its price. In these cases, it must be remembered that only a portion of the risk is being hedged and the bond price will vary when interest rates vary, so interest rate risk will not be hedged. This same problem occurs if the cash flows of a project are hedged rather than its net present value.

To hedge the interest rate risk of flows only, that is, coupons, generally interest rate derivatives are used, among the most common of which are "Caps", "Floors" and "Collars".

A "Cap" is nothing more than a call option (purchased by the bond issuer who pays the market interest rate as a coupon, in this case the Euribor, and sold by the buyer of that bond) which causes the issuer's final payment, that is, the buyer's final bond collection, to be no more than a given interest rate, the exercise price, or "strike", of the option. Thus, with the Cap the bond issuer is guaranteed not to pay more than a certain interest rate. The case may arise, and in fact it does, that the person buying the Cap is not the bond issuer or the person selling is not actually the buyer, because both the buyer and the seller are speculators (Fig. 5.7).

Similarly, a "Floor" is nothing more than a put option (sold by the bond issuer who pays the market interest rate as a coupon, in this case the Euribor, and purchased by the buyer of this bond) which causes the issuer's final payment or the buyer's final bond collection to be a minimum determined interest rate, the exercise price or "strike", of the option. Thus, with the Floor the bond buyer ensures that they receive a minimum specified interest rate (Fig. 5.8).

The "Collar" is simply a combination of a Cap and a Floor and therefore hedges both the bond issuer, who is guaranteed to pay no

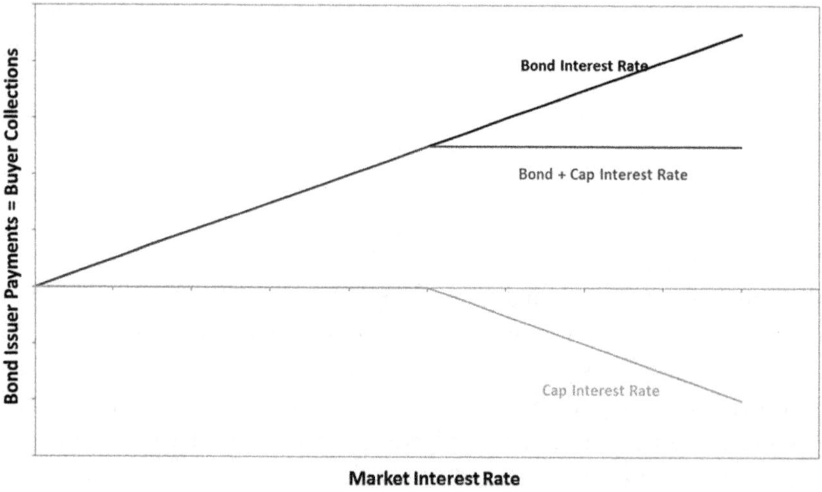

Fig. 5.7 Cap (Author's own composition)

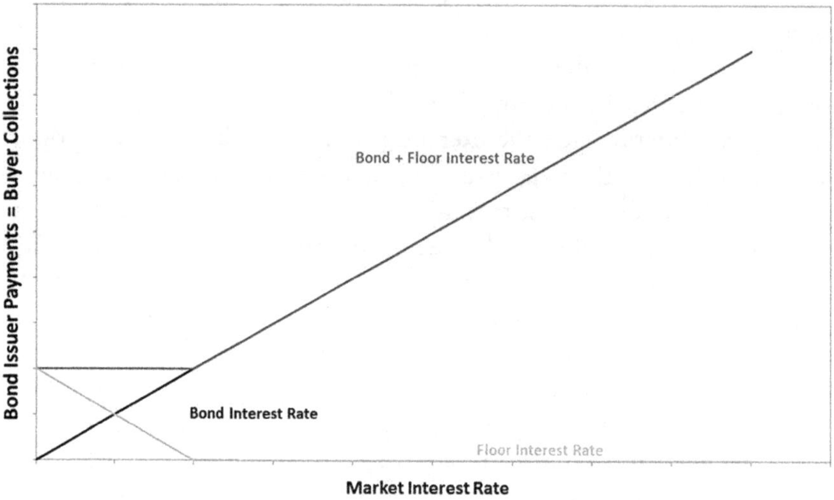

Fig. 5.8 Floor (Author's own composition)

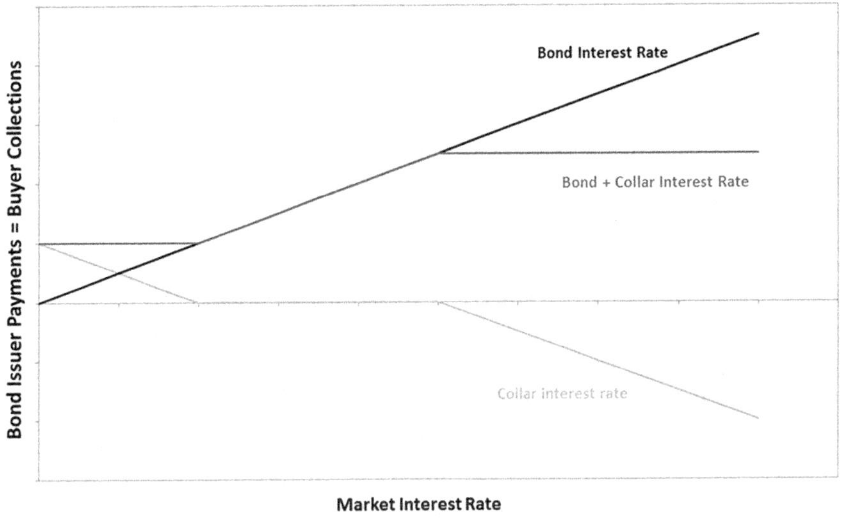

Fig. 5.9 Collar (Author's own composition)

more than a maximum price, and the buyer, who is guaranteed to receive no less than a minimum price (Fig. 5.9).

Valuing these derivatives is a very complex task, since unlike in the case of equities, the dynamics of interest rates are very complex, as is the quantification and hedging of interest rate risk.

5.6 Structured Bonds

As will be shown in the discussion of credit risk, in recent years a complex type of bond has appeared which is aimed at transferring risk to the market through a securitisation process of certain financial assets (mortgages, credit card receivables, auto loans, etc.). This process allows financial institutions to remove certain illiquid assets from their balance sheets as well as providing investors with access to diversified asset classes. Common examples of assets created through this securitisation process, known as structured bonds, include ABS, CDO, MBS and CMS, among others.

An asset-backed security (ABS) is a security which is created by pooling non-mortgage assets and is then resold to investors. The pool of assets is typically a group of illiquid assets which are difficult to sell individually. Therefore, pooling the assets into financial instruments allows them to be sold to investors. The pools of underlying assets can include payments from auto loans, royalty payments and so on. The securitisation process of asset-backed securities is handled by an institution called a special purpose vehicle (SPV) that creates and sells the securities and uses the proceeds from the sale to pay back the institution (typically a bank) that originated the underlying assets. Over time, market practice developed more sophisticated names for securities issued via the securitisation of specific assets, such as mortgages or debt, leaving the name ABS for the plain vanilla securitisation of low-risk bonds.

Collateralised debt obligations (CDOs) are a type of ABS; however, they differ in the type of pool of underlying assets used to create them. Specifically, CDOs are obligations backed by a set of debt assets, such as credit card debt.

Mortgage-backed securities (MBS) are bonds that are backed by pools of mortgages loans, such as mortgage papers, house papers or land and property papers.

A collateralised mortgage obligation (CMO) is a more complicated version of the MBS. Specifically, CMOs are multi-class bonds backed by a pool of mortgage pass-through or mortgages loans. CMOs may be collateralised by either mortgage pass-through securities or mortgage loans, or a combination of them.

6

Exchange Rate Risk

6.1 Basic Concepts

Corporations conduct business in an increasingly global international context; in fact, the major national companies have evolved in recent years to become large companies worldwide. There are some examples of this in Spain such as Telefónica, Santander Bank, BBVA, Repsol, Iberdrola and so on, but globally the examples are countless. In the financial sector there are numerous commercial banks and investment banks that have been large not only in their home country but worldwide for decades, such as Citibank, Bank of America, Barclays, HSBC, BNP, Deutsche Bank and Unicredito; in the telecommunications sector the same can be said of Vodafone, BT, France Telecom and others; in the oil sector there are also representatives of many nationalities, such as Total, Exxon, BP, Shell, Chevron and ENI; and in the same way the examples of major companies in all sectors of the economy would fill many pages.

For this reason the stakeholders of these large corporations, that is, individuals or firms that are interested in these corporations, such as shareholders, creditors, customers, suppliers, tax collectors and so on, are no longer purely national but have become international. Similarly,

F.J. Población García, *Financial Risk Management*,
DOI 10.1007/978-3-319-41366-2_6

in these large firms neither the results nor the assets or liabilities are generated exclusively or mainly in the country where the main office is based.

Clearly, this fact must be taken into account when managing the risk of such corporations; for example, in the mid-1980s US companies were less competitive with respect to foreign competitors, while in the 1990s and 2000s their competitiveness increased. Under these circumstances the question arises: is this fact related to the standard of US managers during these 30 years, or in other words, were the managers of American companies in the 1980s worse than in the following decades? The answer is obviously no. US companies were less competitive at that time because in the 1980s the dollar was worth more compared with foreign currencies and therefore American products were more expensive when expressed in terms of other currencies. In the decades that followed, the dollar began to lose value compared with other currencies and American products became more competitive.

In this sense, we define the exchange rate risk as the degree of uncertainty that exists about future net returns to be obtained by making an investment due to changes in the value of foreign currencies. It refers to the volatility that exchange rates may suffer when they are floating and to the risk of devaluation when exchange rates are fixed.

6.1.1 Exchange Rate Markets

As is well known, most countries have their own currency, so when two agents from different countries do business, inevitably one currency is exchanged for another. The price of one currency denominated in terms of another currency is called the exchange rate. Similarly, the international financial market where currencies or bank deposits denominated in the currency of other countries are bought and sold is called the exchange rate market. As is evident, it is in these markets where the exchange rate is determined, and as can be seen in the following figures, they are very volatile (Figs. 6.1, 6.2, and 6.3).

As seen in the figures, the euro went from being worth \$0.80 to \$1.60, that is, twice as much in just eight years, from 2000 to 2008, which does

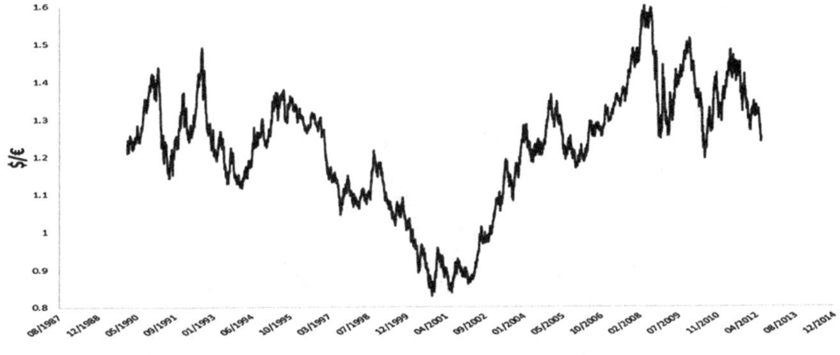

Fig. 6.1 Exchange rate $/€ (Data source: Bloomberg; Author's own composition)

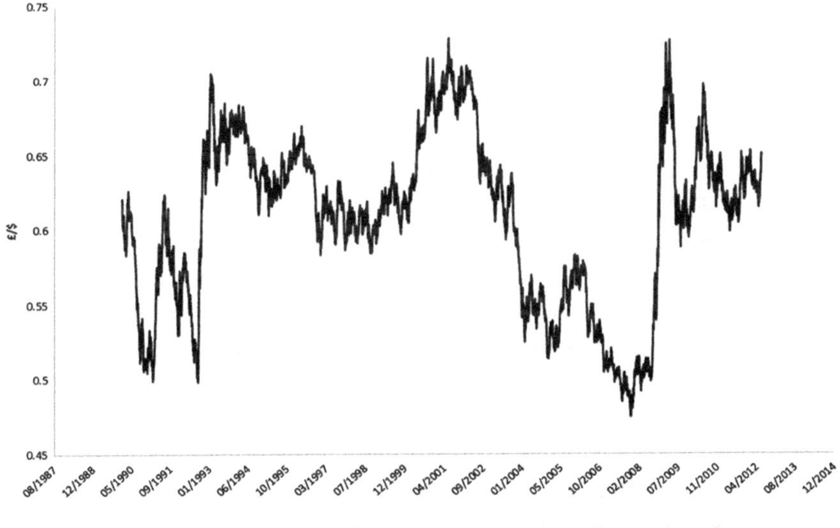

Fig. 6.2 Exchange rate £/€ (Data source: Bloomberg; Author's own composition)

not often happen for other types of assets such as fixed income. The case of the pound or the yen is even clearer: one dollar went from a value of a little more than £0.45 to just over £0.70 in one year (from 2008 to 2009),

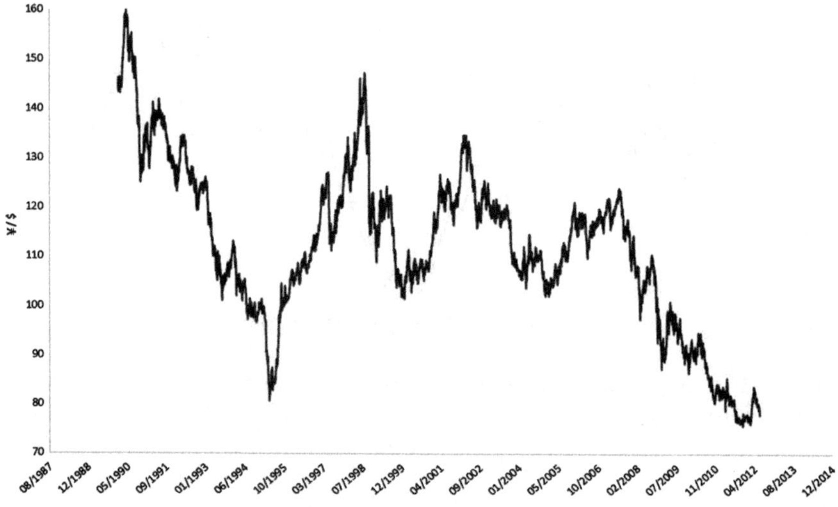

Fig. 6.3 Exchange rate ¥/$ (Data source: Bloomberg; Author's own composition)

while a dollar went from being worth more than 120 yen to just over 70 from 2008 to present.

As in most markets, in exchange rate markets there are two main types of transactions: spot transactions are the most predominant, whereby bank deposits denominated in different currencies are exchanged almost instantly (within two days); and forward transactions are transactions whereby the parties agree to exchange bank deposits denominated in different currencies on a future date at a given exchange rate defined today.

Therefore, in exchange rate markets there is always a spot exchange rate which corresponds to the exchange of bank deposits carried out at the time, and one forward exchange rate per term corresponding to the exchange of future deposits agreed today at an exchange rate defined today. Similarly, when a currency increases in value, it is worth more compared with other currencies and is said to appreciate, whereas when a currency drops in value, it is worth less compared with other currencies and is said to depreciate. As previously indicated, exchange rates are important because they affect the relative price of domestic and foreign products, that is, when the currency of a country appreciates, the property of this country becomes more expensive abroad and foreign goods become cheaper in this country, whereas when a country's currency depreciates, the assets of this country become cheaper abroad and foreign goods become more expensive in this country.

Note that the exchange rate market is not a centralised market like a stock exchange, rather it is an OTC (over-the-counter) market in which there are a hundred "dealers", almost all of which are banks, which agree to buy and sell deposits at rates that are set at each moment. As these "dealers" are in constant contact, the market is very efficient and, in fact, for practical purposes, it works like a centralised market. Subsequently, each participant in this market, typically a bank, has a retail market which changes the currency at market rates plus a commission.

In exchange rate markets it is not coins and notes that are exchanged but denominated bank deposits in different currencies and the volume of these markets is huge, exceeding one trillion dollars daily, and usually exceeding one million dollars in each individual operation.

6.1.2 Types of Exposure with Exchange Rate Risk

Regarding the exchange rate risk, three types of exposures should be distinguished: transaction exposure, economic exposure and accounting exposure. Transaction exposure refers to possible profit variation or, in other words, the risk derived from exchange rate variation that can occur in a particular transaction of a company, usually an international transaction. This case focuses purely on the exchange rate risk of a particular transaction without taking anything else into account.

Considering all the transactions of a company and also the location of the business and denomination currency of their liabilities, the economic exposure of the company to the exchange rate can and should be calculated. In this case, the economic exposure of any of the company's results, such as revenue, gross profit, gross income and so on, is defined as the possible variation of this result, that is, the risk arising from changes in the exchange rate.

Obviously, taking into account all the transactions combined, economic exposure arising from a transaction can be very different from the isolated exposure that this transaction has to the exchange rate. Here we can apply the same ideas as those used to deal with marginal and incremental measures relating to market risk, in the sense that one transaction can affect the economic exposure of two different companies in different ways. It is possible that for one company it makes sense in terms of risk to carry out a transaction, while for their competitors in the market it does not.

As in previous chapters, diversification and hedging can be discussed in relation to this topic. Diversification occurs when the correlation between an individual transaction and the rest of this company's transactions is not 100 %, which involves the risk of the portfolio consisting of all the initial transactions plus the additional transaction being less than the sum of the risk that all the initial transactions of the portfolio have separately plus the individual transaction. However, hedging occurs when the risk of the portfolio consisting of all the initial transactions plus the additional transaction is less than the risk of the portfolio consisting of all the initial transactions.

However, these are not the only exposures to be taken into account when managing the exchange rate risk in a company. In this case, as in many others, the accounting factor can become crucial. The accounting standard establishes general principles that require some balance amounts to be updated at market exchange rates, while others must remain constant when there are exchange rate variations except when their updated value at market rates is lower than their accounting value, in which case the asset must be depreciated. Accordingly, the accounting exposure to the exchange rate of any income statement line or any aggregate balance amount such as assets, liabilities, property value, capital, borrowings and so on can be, and usually are, substantially different from the economic exposure of the company, which is a problem because financial statements are the only source of information transmitted to the market. The "real" exposure is economic exposure, however, for market agents (analysts, investors, etc.), these financial statements are their main source of information.

6.2 Denomination Currency Versus Exposure Currency

In order to calculate exposures to exchange rate accurately, the difference between the concepts of denomination currency and exposure currency must be clearly understood. As a first rough definition, the denomination currency of a product or service globally, in a particular country or economic environment can be described as the currency in which receipts and payments for these products or services are carried out globally, in a particular country or economic environment. However, the exposure currency of the same product or service is the "natural" currency for their receipts and payments.

A better understanding of the difference between denomination currency and exposure currency requires further investigation. The laws of most countries state that the currency is the one issued by its central bank and that this is the only payment method accepted in transactions within that country. Therefore, the denomination currency of the goods and services which are exchanged in a given country is the currency issued by the central bank of this country. In the USA the denomination currency is the US dollar, in the eurozone the EU denomination currency is the euro, in the UK it is the pound sterling and so on.

In order to understand exactly what the exposure currency is, imagine a product that is not produced in a given country and is therefore imported in its entirety. In this case, the denomination currency is a currency issued by the central bank of the country importing the product. However, the foreign supplier of the product usually requires payment to be made in their currency and not in the currency of that country and, therefore, if the price of the product in the foreign currency is stable, the price of the product expressed in domestic currency fluctuates with the exchange rate. Therefore, in this case the exposure currency ("natural" currency) of this asset is the currency of the foreign country where it is produced.

More specifically, suppose there is a product that is produced and consumed almost exclusively in the USA. In the USA the price of this product is denominated in dollars. Assume also that the price of this product in the USA is very stable and the only variation comes from the annual inflation update. Specifically, assume that the price of this product in the USA was \$20 from January 1990 to October 1997, \$22 from November 1997 to July 2005 and \$24 from August 2005 to June 2012. Finally, suppose that a country in the eurozone, such as Spain, chose to import this asset.

As already indicated, in Spain the denomination currency of this product is the euro. However, the supplier of the product in the United States requires the exported product to be paid for in dollars at the same rate that it has in the United States and, consequently, the price of the product expressed in euros fluctuates with changes in the €/\$ exchange rate.

As shown in Fig. 6.4, the €/\$ exchange rate is very volatile; therefore, the retailers of the product in Spain will have to change its price in euros with some frequency in order to ensure that they are able to pay the US provider in dollars without much exchange rate risk. For this reason, as seen in Figs. 6.5 and 6.6, the price of the product in the United States

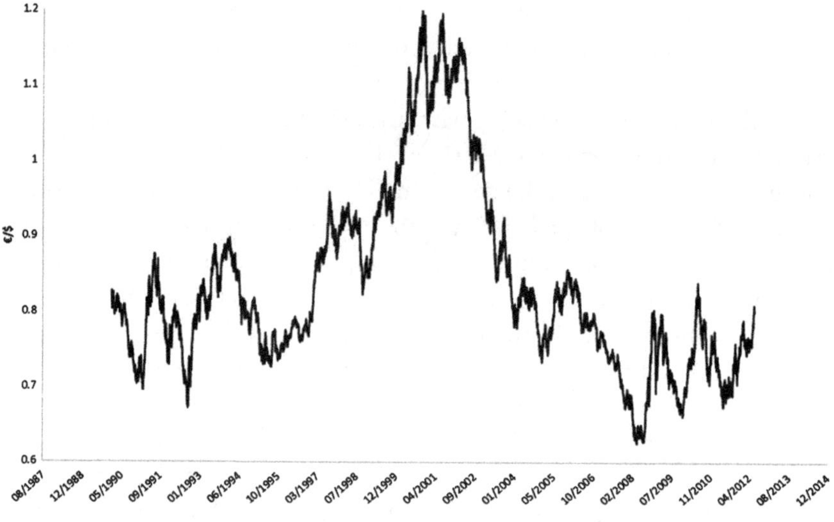

Fig. 6.4 Exchange rate €/\$ (Data source: Bloomberg; Author's own composition)

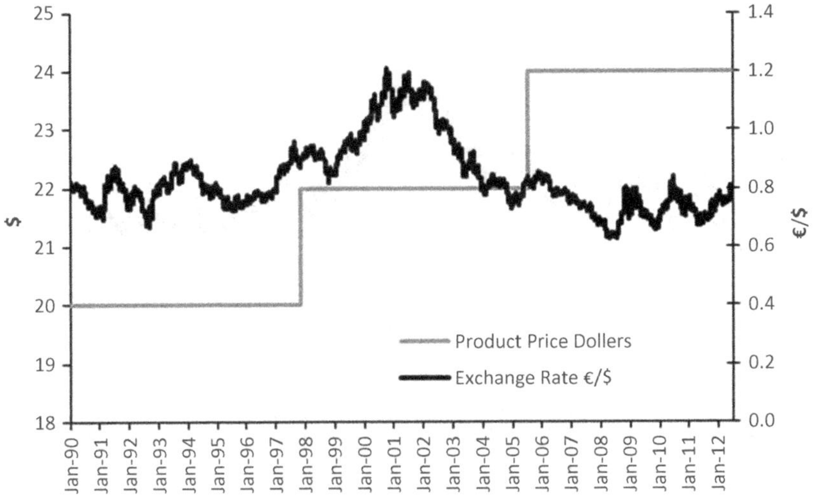

Fig. 6.5 Comparison of €/$ exchange rate and product price in $ (Data source: Bloomberg; Author's own composition)

denominated in dollars is stable, that is, does not fluctuate with the exchange rate €/$, while its price in Spain, which is denominated in euros, is not stable but rather fluctuates in much the same way as the exchange rate €/$.

Consequently, the consumer of this product in Spain, despite paying in euros (the denomination currency), is exposed to the €/$ exchange rate. In Spain the denomination currency of the imported product is the euro and the exposure currency is the dollar, which is the natural currency for payments of this product.

Following the logic of the example, it can be concluded that the exposure currency of a product is one in which the price of the product does not vary in response to variations in the exchange rate. In the above example, when the product was being produced and consumed entirely in the USA, its price in dollars did not vary in response to changes in the $/€ exchange rate, while the price of the product in euros is very sensitive and varies widely when there are changes in the $/€ exchange rate.

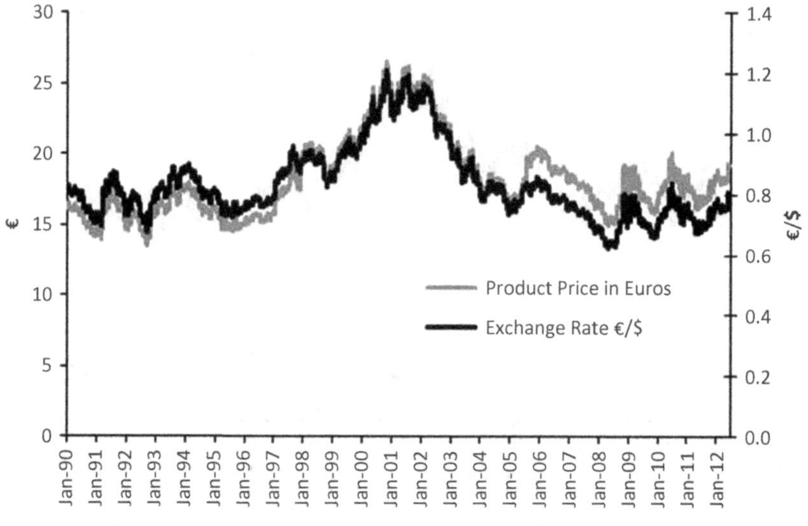

Fig. 6.6 Comparison of €/$ exchange rate and product price in € (Data source: Bloomberg; Author's own composition)

6.2.1 Estimation of Exposure Currency

The example above is a simple case in which it was assumed that there was only one exposure currency and the prices were stable in this currency. But these two assumptions are not always realised in practice, especially in the case of goods that are consumed in many parts of the world where there are restrictions on their production and/or transportation. For example, hydrocarbons are produced and consumed worldwide but cannot be produced according to the desired amount. Instead, the quantity of the product depends on the amount discovered and its transport costs, especially in cases such as natural gas. Similarly, agricultural products are produced and consumed worldwide and their production depends on external factors such as weather, well-established production cycles and transport costs.

For this reason, in this section a technique that can be used to determine, at least approximately, the exposure currency or currencies of a particular product will be analysed. This explanation will be based on a real example to better establish the relevant concepts. It is well known that the denomination currency of oil in almost all parts of the world is the US dollar since in all oil markets, regardless of where they are located, it is priced in dollars. The question then may be asked: is the exposure currency in oil prices the dollar?

It is not easy to answer this question because oil is produced and consumed worldwide. Its price varies depending on the change in established reserves, the discovery of new deposits, the agreements reached by the OPEC countries, the variation in the country risk of the producer countries, the economic cycle of the consumer countries and so on. However, to answer this question, the logic remains the same and the exposure currency will be the one in which the price does not vary with changes in the exchange rate.

As in the previous example, a graphical analysis can be useful here because it shows the price variations in a currency over time and the exchange rate variations over time. In this way, the relationship between the two can be studied. Figs. 6.7 and 6.8 show the evolution of the price of oil in dollars per barrel ($/bbl) and €/bbl compared to the exchange rate.

As can be seen in the graphs, in the years 2000–2003 (solid circle) there was a less noticeable increase in the oil price in $/bbl than in €/bbl, in a context of dollar appreciation (the scale can be misleading, but in €/bbl the price went from being under €20/bbl to over €40/bbl, while in $/bbl

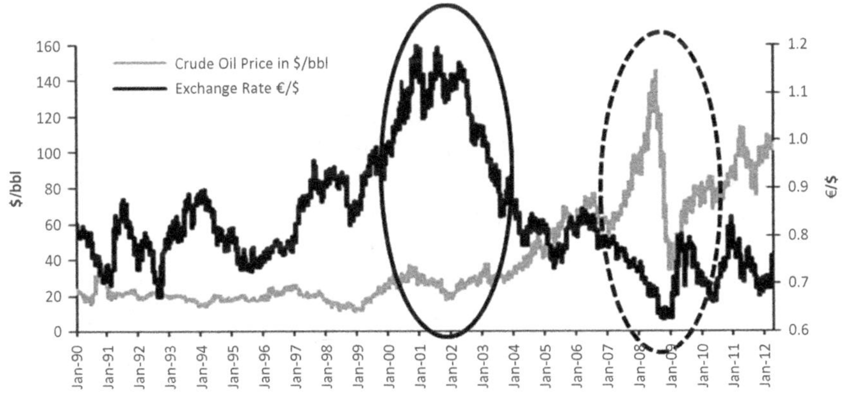

Fig. 6.7 Comparison of crude oil price in $/bbl and €/$ exchange rate (Data source: Bloomberg; Author's own composition)

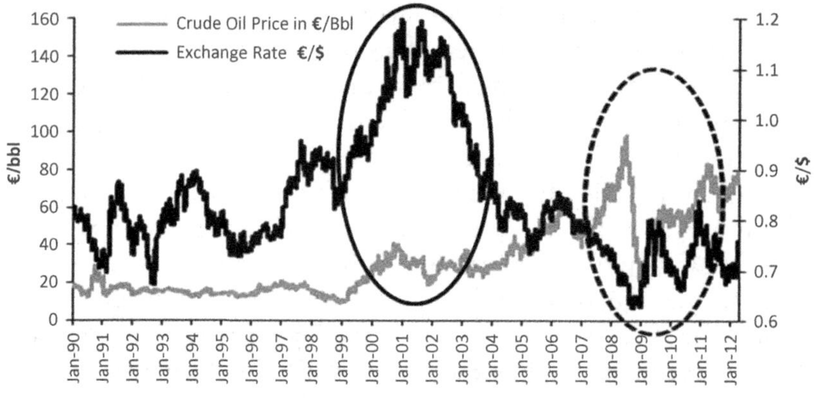

Fig. 6.8 Comparison of crude oil price in €/bbl and €/$ exchange rate (Data source: Bloomberg; Author's own composition)

the price had a similar level initially but barely reached $30/bbl). Following the logic of the previous example, it seems that at that time the exposure currency was the dollar. However, in the years 2009–2011 (dotted circle) the price of crude oil increased in both currencies, with a far greater increase in dollars coinciding with an appreciation of the euro against the dollar. In this case, it appears that the exposure currency of crude oil at least at this time was the euro, since there were fewer variations when there were changes in the exchange rate.

Repeating this graph with the oil price in $/bbl and Argentine pesos/bbl, as seen in Figs. 6.9 and 6.10, the conclusion is quite different because while the price of crude oil in $/bbl has no connection with the exchange rate $/Argentine peso, oil prices in Argentine pesos/bbl are closely related to the exchange rate $/Argentine peso. Specifically, in 2002, when the dollar suddenly became worth three Argentine pesos as opposed to one previously, the oil price in Argentine pesos/bbl tripled while in $/bbl it remained unchanged.

From this graphical analysis, it can be concluded that the dollar and the euro appear to be oil exposure currencies while the Argentine peso does not. Deeper statistical studies, which are beyond the scope of this book, show that there is not just one exposure currency of crude oil but a

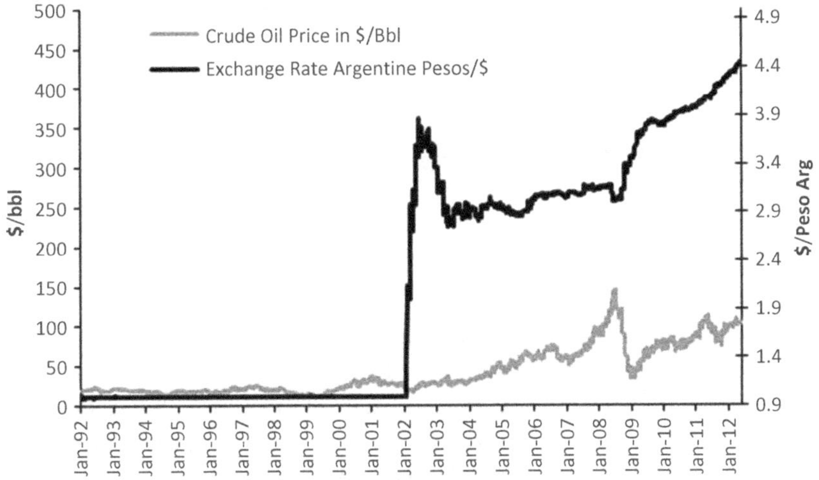

Fig. 6.9 Comparison of crude oil price in $/bbl and Argentine pesos/$ exchange rate (Data source: Bloomberg; Author's own composition)

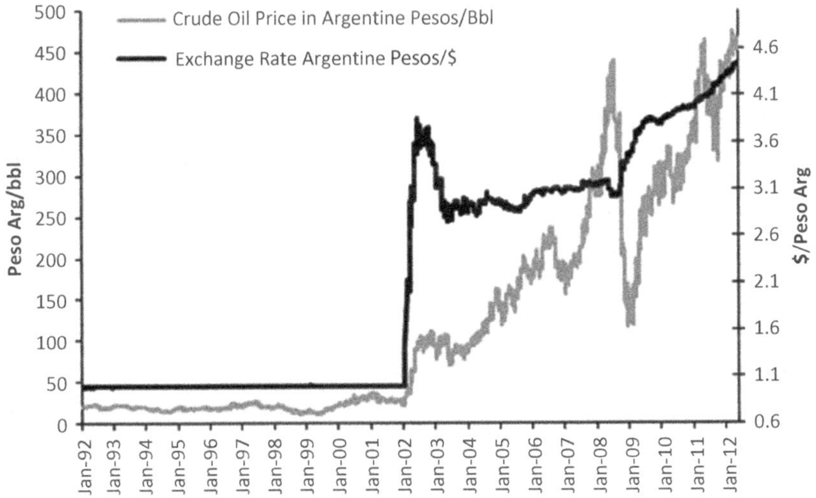

Fig. 6.10 Comparison of crude oil price in Argentine pesos/bbl and Argentine pesos/$ exchange rate (Data source: Bloomberg; Author's own composition)

combination of several, of which the dollar and the euro stand out, the dollar weighted at around 60 % and the euro weighted at around 40 %.

6.3 VaR in the Exchange Rate

In the same way as the interest rate risk, the exchange rate risk is a particular type of market risk and, therefore, it can be measured with the same criteria as the general market risk and, in particular, equity risk which was studied previously. Specifically, applying the definition of value at risk (VaR) to the exchange rate risk of a portfolio, VaR can be described as a measure of the maximum potential change that the value of a portfolio may suffer over a time horizon and at a given probability level, in this case due to changes in exchange rates.

The dynamics of the exchange rate are not as complex as those of the interest rate; however, we must consider that there are hardly any products exclusively at risk of the exchange rate. There is usually another type of market risk, like interest rate risk or equity risk, as well as the exchange rate risk and so on. In these cases, the primary complication lies in establishing the joint dynamics of all the risks, especially if this involves the interest rate risk.

It is important to note that not all exchange rates are equal; the exchange rate of the currencies of two Organisation for Economic Co-operation and Development (OECD) countries is not the same as that of two currencies of developing countries. Also note that even within OECD countries, the dynamics of exchange rates do not necessarily have to be the same. In this sense, of the stochastic processes presented throughout this book, perhaps the most suitable is the random walk because the dynamics of the exchange rate follow the same logic as the price of equities, that is, the quote today contains all the information that is available in the market and, therefore, the best prediction of the price tomorrow is the price today plus a noise that reflects the information coming into the market between today and tomorrow.

That said, some exchange rates may have mean reversion and in these cases, of the stochastic processes presented in this book, the most appropriate would be the autoregressive process. There are various statistical tests beyond the scope of this book that are used to test whether the autoregressive process is more appropriate than the random walk to characterise the dynamics of a particular exchange rate.[1] In any case, it should be noted that when the constant β in the autoregressive process tends to one, this process behaves in the same way as a random walk.

It must also be emphasised that, like many macroeconomic variables, the exchange rate sometimes suffers what is known as a structural change, which refers to a situation in which a country's currency is devalued at any given time after suffering a crisis or for some other reason, resulting in a sudden change in the exchange rate quote inconsistent with the dynamics seen up to that point. This is very difficult to characterise using the simple stochastic processes presented in this book.

As established in Chap. 5, a particularly attractive option for estimating the VaR is to use historical simulation, as it does not require any probabilistic model which simplifies the calculation.

6.4 Exchange Rate Derivatives

In the same way as in other markets, the exchange rate is agreed upon using both spots and futures, with parties agreeing to exchange currency in the future at a rate that is fixed today.

In these markets there is a very popular type of product known as a cross currency swap rate (CCRS), which can be defined as a commitment between two parties whereby one pays the other an amount in a currency at various specific points in time in return for another amount in a different currency, that is, both parties agree to regularly exchange one currency for another at a rate that is fixed today. The usefulness of this product lies in the fact that, with increasing globalisation, many companies regularly obtain cash flows in foreign currencies, and in order to avoid being exposed to exchange rate risk they sign a contract with the CCRS in order to guarantee an established exchange rate.

[1] These tests are the unit root tests, such as the Johansen test.

6.5 Exchange Rate Hedging under Uncertainty in Cash Flows

As indicated in Chap. 1, in a world without hedging costs, a company would ideally hedge the risks they do not know how to manage and not those that they can manage; for this reason, many international companies would like to hedge the exchange rate risk of their results, since the company in question is normally able to manage the inherent risk of running the business but not the exchange rate risk. The problem arises because, in many cases, when the future cash flows coming in and going out are not known with certainty, exchange rate risk hedging is difficult because it is not possible to ascertain the exact amount to be hedged; therefore, there will always be a residual risk, in addition to accounting issues that may arise.

As discussed in previous chapters, a hedging strategy may be referred to as hedge accounting at a given time and cease to be so shortly thereafter. In the case of cash flow hedging, this can happen very easily if the cash flow that actually occurs is significantly different from the expected cash flow that was hedged. At that point the hedging strategy ceases to be "highly effective", and from that moment the asset being hedged must be rated as a permanent investment which does not vary in value when there are changes in the exchange rate, while the hedging instrument must be rated in the market and, therefore, any changes in its value must go through results, which can cause great volatility in the results. For this reason, there is no specific answer to the question of whether to hedge the exchange rate risk under uncertainty in the cash flows. It all depends on the volatility of the cash flows and their structure in relation to the criteria of the accounting standards.

However, despite the difficulty of hedging the exchange rate risk, some general guidelines can be given regarding the uncertainty of future cash flows: when permitted by the accounting standards, a minimum can be hedged assuming the future cash flow will never be less than this minimum. In this case, although the accounting risk persists, it is much lower than it was in the beginning. Under certain circumstances, usually when the amount is fixed, the accounting standard allows a portion of future income or payments to be hedged against the exchange rate risk; the payment or collection of a coupon, for example, is one of these cases.

6.6 Relationship between Interest Rate and Exchange Rate

There is a very close relationship between interest rates and exchange rates. This relationship is known as covered exchange rate parity. The logic behind this relationship lies in the fact that the following investments must have the same result: (a) investing a euro in buying a one-year European bond and (b) changing the euro for a dollar today, investing the dollar in US bonds today and agreeing on a future exchange rate today to change the dollars back to euros after one year. Otherwise, money could be made without risk, which is not possible in a perfect market. Based on this logic, covered exchange rate parity, which is a mathematical relationship, is estimated (Fig. 6.11).

On the one hand, there is the interest rate of the one-year European bond, $r_€$, which is the return of the first investment alternative, that is, one euro invested in a European bond with rents $1 + r_€$ in a year.

On the other hand, the euro can be changed into dollars at the spot exchange rate, that is, TC_{Spot}_€/\$, and TC_{Spot}_€/\$ dollars are obtained which can be used to invest in the one-year US bond which offers a yield of $r_\$$. After this time the value of the investment is TC_{Spot}_€/\$$*(1 + r_\$)$ dollars. Thus, as TC_{Spot}_€/\$ and $r_\$$ are known today, the number of

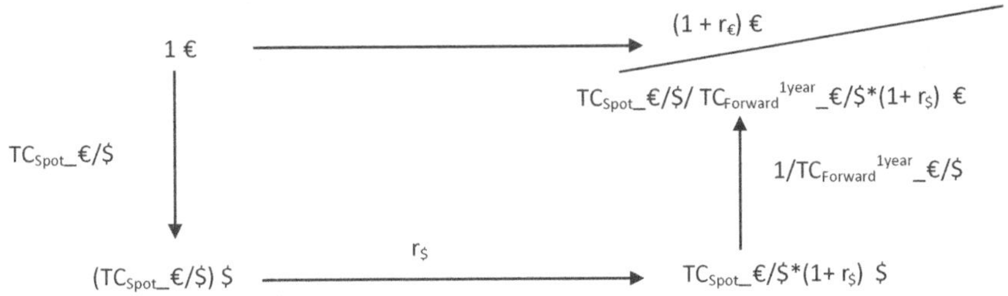

Fig. 6.11 Relationship between interest rate and exchange rate (Author's own composition)

dollars to be obtained in one year is also known, which is TC_{Spot}_€/\$*(1 + $r_\$$) dollars, and therefore a future exchange rate can now be agreed upon in order to convert these dollars to euros in a year at an exchange rate that is fixed today, $TC_{Forward}{}^{1year}$_€/\$. Thus, one euro invested in this second income strategy within a year will definitely be: $\frac{TC_{Spot}\_€/\$}{TC^{1año}_{Forward}\_€/\$}(1 + r_\$)$, an amount of money already in euros.

In short, there are two investment alternatives in which the following results would definitely be obtained in a year by investing one euro today:

a) 1 + $r_€$ euros, if the first of the investment strategies is followed.
b) $\frac{TC_{Spot}\_€/\$}{TC^{1año}_{Forward}\_€/\$}(1 + r_\$)$ euros, if the second of the investment strategies is followed.

At this point, the key is to understand that neither of the strategies is at risk, therefore if one will make more profits than the other all investors, both European and American, would invest in this one and short-sell the other, thus altering the exchange rate. That is, if the first investment strategy was more profitable than the second, all investors would invest in the European bond, selling or sometimes short-selling, the US bond. In particular, US investors would invest in the European bond, changing their dollars for euros, and equally no investor would change their euros for dollars, which would entail an increase in the spot exchange rate, TC_{Spot}_€/\$. On the other hand, if all investors demanded European bonds and there was no demand for US bonds, the price of European bonds would rise while that of US bonds would decline, so $r_€$ would decline and $r_\$$ would increase. In turn, US investors would change the euros obtained into dollars using the first of the strategies and $TC_{Forward}$ ^{1year}_€/\$ would decrease. Therefore, the profitability of the second investment strategy would increase while that of the first would decrease, and this would continue happening until it reached a point where both investment strategies had the same returns.

On the other hand, if the second strategy offered higher returns, exactly the opposite would happen, so the returns of the first of these strategies would increase, while those of the second would decrease. Therefore, on balance $1 + r_{€} = \frac{TC_{\text{Spot}\_€/\$}}{TC^{\text{1año}}_{\text{Forward}\_€/\$}}(1 + r_{\$})$ would be achieved, or equivalently $\frac{TC^{\text{1año}}_{\text{Forward}\_€/\$}}{TC_{\text{Spot}\_€/\$}} r_{€} = r_{\$} - \frac{TC^{\text{1año}}_{\text{Forward}\_€/\$} - TC_{\text{Spot}\_€/\$}}{TC_{\text{Spot}\_€/\$}}$, a relationship which is known as covered exchange rate parity.

7

Price Risk in Commodities

7.1 Basic Concepts

Equity risk, interest rate risk and exchange rate risk have already been discussed, but this chapter examines commodity price risk. The commodity price risk deals with uncertainty about future earnings resulting from changes in commodity prices.

As is well known, all production processes require "inputs" or commodities which are transformed into other products through industrial techniques. These products may well be the commodities of another production process to be sold in the retail market. In this case, when the product is sold in the final retail market, its price is set by marketing strategies that are beyond the scope of this book. Conversely, commodities are generally used by various companies, industries and sectors that produce different products which are usually sold in organised wholesale markets, for example the Chicago Mercantile Exchange. These commodities always have a market price and therefore, when dealing with them, the investor is subject to the commodity price risk defined in the previous paragraph.

The share price fits very naturally into the definition of a random walk, as it follows the principle that at any given moment in time all

F.J. Población García, *Financial Risk Management*,
DOI 10.1007/978-3-319-41366-2_7

information is incorporated in the price, and therefore the best prediction of the price tomorrow will be the price today plus a noise which represents the information that enters the market between today and tomorrow. Therefore, when dealing with the commodity price risk, a first approach could be to equate it to equity market risk and apply the same principles. The problem is that this would not be suitable because commodities have two features that shares do not: storage costs and convenience yield. These two features of commodities cause prices to behave in a specific way that is reflected in the way the prices of their associated derivatives behave, especially the price of futures at different maturities, that is, the forward curve, which in some cases presents phenomena as distinct as seasonality.

7.1.1 Storage Costs

At present, the shares of a company are electronic entries in value markets and/or depositary entities and thus, except for administration and custody costs, which are not usually material, they incur no costs. Of course, the owner of the shares is subject to market risk and if the market price rises, they make profits while if it falls, they lose profits, but under no circumstances must they bear any cost. It is, therefore, reasonable to assume that at any given point in time all the information is incorporated into the price and, consequently, the best prediction of the price tomorrow will be the price today plus a noise which represents the information that will enter the market between today and tomorrow. Otherwise, if all the market information is not included in the price, it will mean that the asset is overvalued or undervalued because there is information that is not incorporated in the price. If, for example, the asset is overvalued, agents that have the additional information will come to the market to sell at a price that, given this additional information, is high, lowering the price to the level at which all the information is incorporated. If the asset is undervalued, the opposite will happen.

In the case of commodities this is no longer true, because if a certain amount of a commodity is acquired, it must be assumed that there is a storage cost until the time it is used in the production process or until it is sold, if its purchase was a speculative purchase. Therefore, in this case it is no longer reasonable to assume that all information is incorporated in the spot price, but it can be incorporated into the future price. It is even less reasonable to assume the best prediction of the price tomorrow is the price today plus a noise that reflects the information that enters the market between today and tomorrow. Now, it is no longer true that if market information is not incorporated in the spot price, agents act in the spot market. If the commodity is acquired, its storage costs must be incurred. As will be shown, characterising the dynamics of commodity prices is more complex than in the case of shares.

Finally, it must be emphasised that these storage costs do not just refer to the cost of renting the storage for the product but include other costs as well, such as storage to prevent theft; security if the product is flammable or potentially dangerous; and maintenance costs, such as refrigerators, in cases where the commodity is perishable. In this regard, note that although discussed in more detail when dealing with the regulatory or legal risk, over time the extent of legal requirements when storing commodities has increased significantly, resulting in a rise in storage costs. As is well known, more and more security measures are required to prevent theft if the commodity is valuable, and even more so if the commodity is flammable or potentially hazardous to public health. These mandatory security measures are becoming increasingly expensive, as are maintenance costs for perishable commodities.

7.1.2 Convenience Yield

From the previous description of storage costs, it could be considered ideal to acquire commodities just before using them in order to avoid these costs. This is not the case, however, since there is another factor to be considered that has the opposite effect of storage costs: convenience yield. The formal definition of the convenience yield is the value that the owner of a commodity assigns to it by physically owning it instead of having a firm agreement for its future purchase.

In order to explain this concept in more depth the following example can be given: imagine a refinery which constantly uses oil to produce refined products such as petrol and diesel. This refinery, like all refineries in the world, constantly has crude oil stored in stock and due to storage costs, which as mentioned could become high, another option may be considered: the possibility of eliminating their oil stock and buying it through term contracts, acquiring the oil to be refined when it is needed.

Obviously, this procedure eliminates storage costs and brings profits to the company. However, it is not without its drawbacks. The main difficulty is that in the event of a disruption in supplies, the refinery would have to stop production and so incur costs, for example of turning the machinery on and off, which in heavy industries can be prohibitive. The legal costs of interrupting the supply and breaching trade agreements must also be considered. In addition, the missed opportunity to make profits due to being unable to meet extraordinary and urgent orders as a result of not having the necessary commodity cannot be ignored.

Therefore, as the refinery in the example physically owns oil instead of having future purchase agreements, it will make a profit, which is called a convenience yield. Obviously, the ideal level of oil for the example refinery to have in stock is determined by considering both storage costs and convenience yield. There are many other examples of this in other industrial companies in different sectors, and a convenience yield can always be found. The convenience yield is the profit the owner makes as a result of physically possessing the commodity.

7.1.3 The Forward Curve

Considering everything mentioned previously, the dynamics of commodity prices are much more complicated than those of other assets such as shares. The following sections will explore how to characterise them. However, it is first necessary to present in this subsection a short analysis of future commodity prices and to address the problem of seasonality.

Firstly, the concept of a forward curve must be defined: the forward curve is the curve formed by the different prices of futures at different maturities. If there is a graph in which the x-axis is the maturity of the futures and the y-axis is the price of the futures, the forward curve is the curve that would be drawn by joining the points of the futures at different maturities.

It has been shown in previous chapters that in the case of equities at $t = 0$, the price of the future that matures at T is simply the spot price of the underlying asset, S_0, updated with the interest rate of the riskless bond, r, in other words: $F_{0,T} = S_0e^{rT}$. If this were not the case, money could be made without risk and it would be possible to implement arbitrage strategies. If $F_{0,T} > S_0e^{rT}$, investors would borrow at $t = 0$ the amount S_0, acquire a share and take a short position on the future that matures at T to deliver the share at the time T and obtain $F_{0,T}$, while what is owed for what was borrowed is S_0e^{rT}, which by hypothesis is less than $F_{0,T}$, thus obtaining a profit without risk. As all investors act in this way, or in other words, as all investors would buy shares at $t = 0$ while at the same time taking short positions on the future which matures at T, the spot price, S_0, would rise and future price $F_{0,T}$, would fall until $F_{0,T} = S_0e^{rT}$. If, however, $F_{0,T} < S_0e^{rT}$, the procedure that investors would follow to make money without risk would be the opposite: at $t = 0$ they would sell shares, obtaining S_0 per share, which would be invested in the riskless bond, and they would take a long position on the future that matures at T to obtain at T an amount of money S_0e^{rT}. This amount, in theory, would be higher than the amount they would have to pay to get back the share and, therefore, they would make a profit without risk. Proceeding in this way, selling shares at $t = 0$ while simultaneously taking a long position on the future that matures at T, the stock price, S_0, would fall while that of the future, $F_{0,T}$, would rise until $F_{0,T} = S_0e^{rT}$. For this reason, the forward curve which is formed by the $F_{0,T}$ when T varies, in the case of equities, except for dividends, is a line with slope "r", as $F_{0,T} = S_0e^{rT}$.

In the case of commodities, this relationship has no reason to remain this way and, in fact, it almost never does due to the factors studied previously: storage costs and convenience yield, factors which have opposite effects. Thus, at certain times $F_{0,T} > S_0e^{rT}$ may be and actually is observed in the market, while at other times the opposite occurs, $F_{0,T} < S_0e^{rT}$. In cases where $F_{0,T} > S_0e^{rT}$, the arbitrage strategy described above could not be performed because if a given amount of a commodity is acquired at $t = 0$, storage costs should also be considered and, depending on these costs, this situation could and does arise. Similarly, in cases where $F_{0,T} < S_0e^{rT}$, it is not possible to implement this aforementioned stock trading strategy as the market agents who own the commodities do not want to sell and take a long position on the future due to the convenience yield, that is, due to the value of keeping them.

Therefore, in the market there are times when the spot price is higher than that of the futures forward curve, and times when it is lower. In addition, there are situations in which the future prices for short maturities are higher or lower than the spot price, while for long maturities the relationship is reversed. In all cases, the key lies in the relationship between storage costs and convenience yield, a relationship which changes over time and with the maturity of the futures, as both the storage costs and the convenience yield are variables which change the value over time due to many factors such as the level of use of warehouses, the probability of disruption and so on.

By definition, it is said that when $F_{0,T} < S_0$ the forward curve is in backwardation, while when $F_{0,T} > S_0$ the forward curve is in contango. Figure 7.1 demonstrates that for the same commodity, in this case crude oil, due to the variability of storage costs and the convenience yield, at certain times the curve is in backwardation, while at others it is in contango.

7.1.4 Seasonality

The price of commodities, like that of any other asset, is always defined by the intersection of a supply curve and a demand curve which do not remain static over time and, therefore, the price also varies. What sets some commodities apart from other assets like shares is that in some cases these supply and demand curves can move in time with a seasonal component. For example, fuel for heating is in greater demand in winter than in summer, while the supply of certain agricultural products, such as wheat, barley and so on, is higher in summer than in winter.

For this reason, with certain commodities, either because storage costs are very high, as in the case of natural gas, or for any other reason, the supply cannot keep up with the demand and the prices of these products have a clear seasonal component, as can be seen in Fig. 7.2 for the case of natural gas.

Finally, as seen in Fig. 7.2, it should be noted that in some cases this seasonal component can represent a high percentage of the price. For example, both the future and the spot prices for natural gas on the date

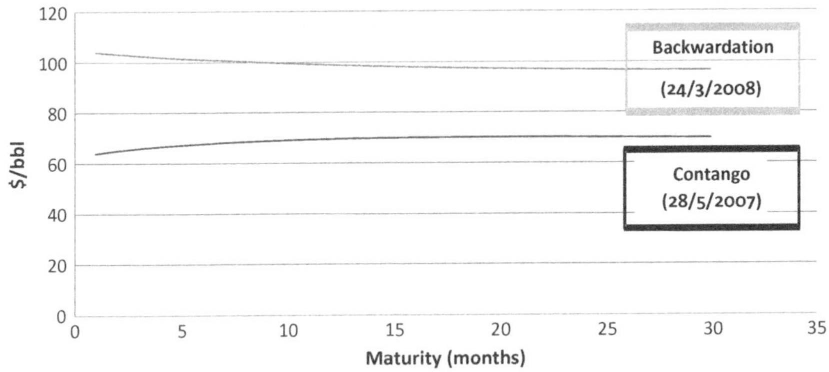

Fig. 7.1 Crude oil forward curve (Data source: Bloomberg; Author's own composition)

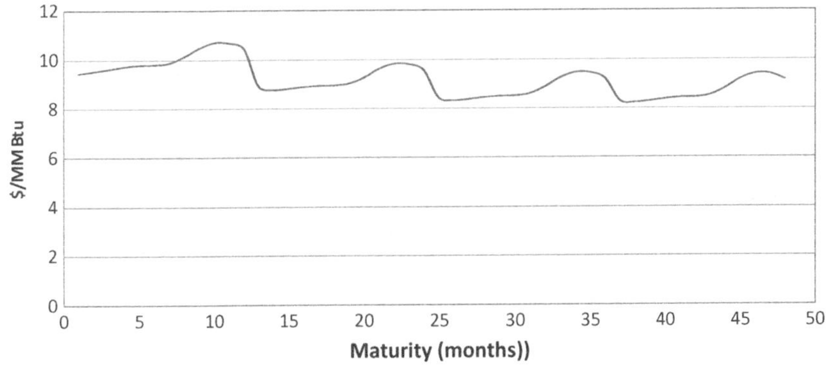

Fig. 7.2 Natural gas forward curve (Data source: Bloomberg; Author's own composition)

shown on the graph were between \$8 and \$10/MMBtu, while the seasonal component, that is, the difference between the winter and summer price, was between \$2 and \$3/MMBtu, which represents roughly 25–30 % of the total price. On other dates, the seasonal component of natural gas was able to reach 40–50 % of the total price, while in other commodities this percentage can be much higher.

7.2 Commodity Price Dynamics

All the factors presented in the previous section lead to the conclusion that the dynamics of commodity prices are very complex and, therefore, it is very difficult to quantify and hedge their risk.

7.2.1 Mean Reversion

One of the most striking features of the price dynamics of many commodities is that they have some degree of mean reversion. The reason for this degree of mean reversion is that production costs in general, and for mining in particular, are not constant and, therefore, many productive basins will be profitable depending on the price; here the price will have a decisive role in the availability of the supply, which does not occur with other types of assets.

For example, in the gold market or that of any metal there are many mines and mining areas from which raw materials can be extracted, but not all have the same extraction costs. Consequently, if the price rises, many unprofitable mines become profitable and, thus, extraction—that is, supply—increases, which has a downward effect on prices. Conversely, if the price drops, many of the mines currently in production are no longer profitable, thus the supply is reduced, causing a rise in prices. In both cases, whether the price increases or decreases, there are market forces that push it towards a hypothetical long-term average. If the price increases, these forces push it down, while if it decreases, they push it up. Given the above, it can be concluded that, unlike share prices, commodity prices usually have some degree of mean reversion, as is shown in the following graphs. The prices of certain commodities can be compared with the share prices of certain companies engaged in the commodity sector in question and whose outcome definitively and directly depends on them (Figs. 7.3, 7.4, and 7.5).

As can be seen in Figs. 7.6 and 7.7, both the price of gold and the price of oil show a clear mean reversion tendency, which does not happen in the

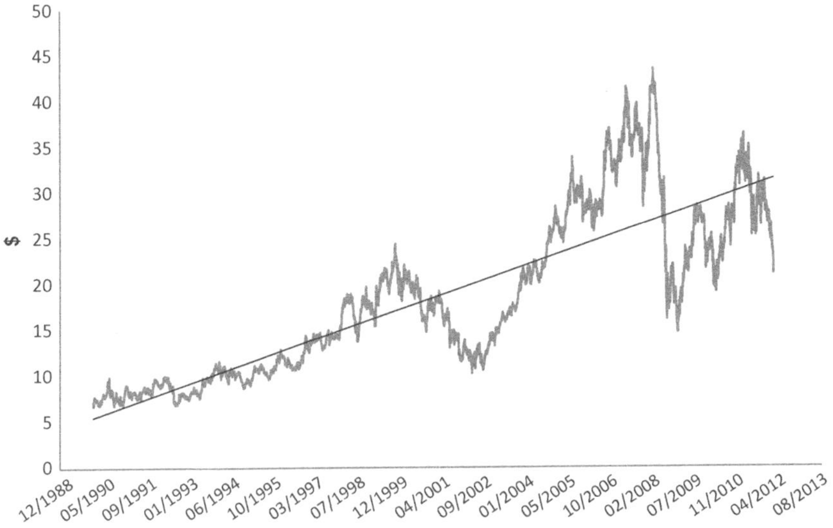

Fig. 7.3 Repsol (Data source: Bloomberg; Author's own composition)

price of companies whose outcome depends definitively and directly on these commodities. In these cases, there is clearly an increasing trend.

However, as can also be seen in the figures, although it is true that commodity prices have some mean reversion, it is no less true that mean reversion is usually not the only trend observed. Its dynamics are complex and are not always possible to characterise using stochastic processes of pure mean reversion, as in the case of the autoregressive process. This is because the movements of the supply and demand curves are guided not only by prices but by other factors as well, such as geopolitical issues, the discovery of new deposits or mines, the discovery of substitutes and so on.

7.2.2 Factorial Models

As noted, stochastic processes such as random walk are not ideal for characterising the price dynamics of commodities, as they are not able to incorporate the mean reversion tendency that these prices have to a greater or lesser extent. In addition, given the complexity of these price

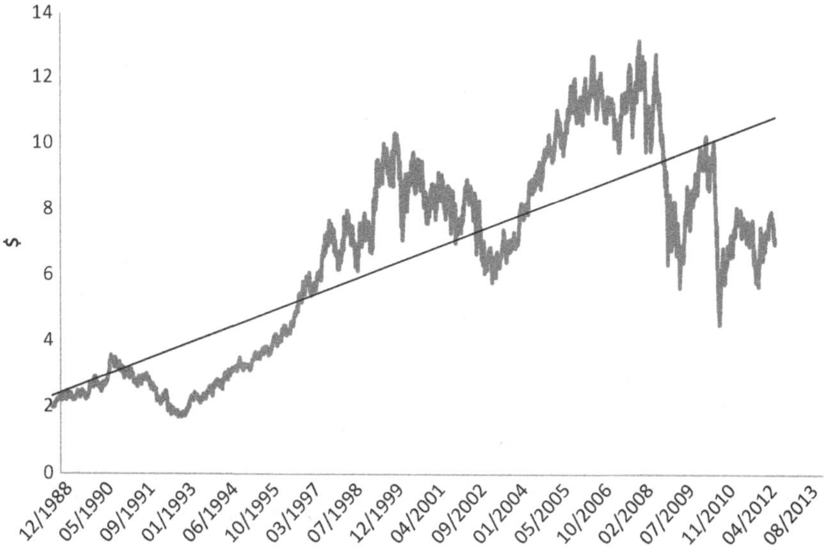

Fig. 7.4 BP (Data source: Bloomberg; Author's own composition)

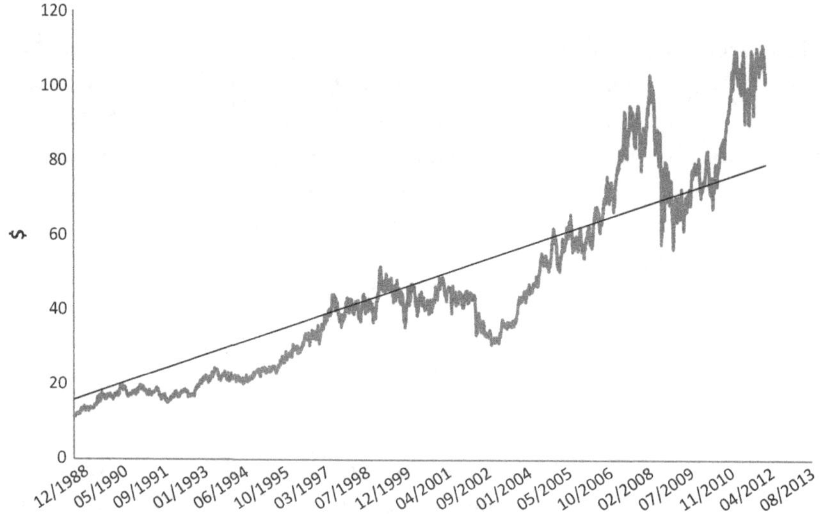

Fig. 7.5 Chevron (Data source: Bloomberg; Author's own composition)

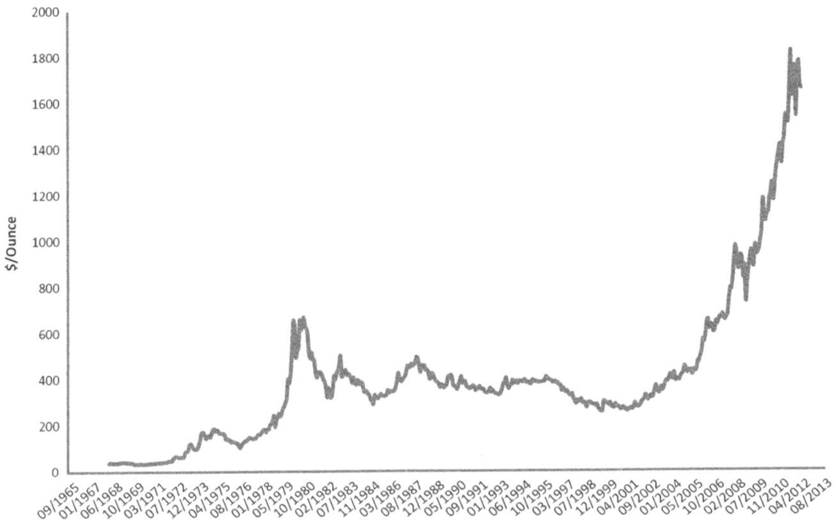

Fig. 7.6 Gold price (Data source: Bloomberg; Author's own composition)

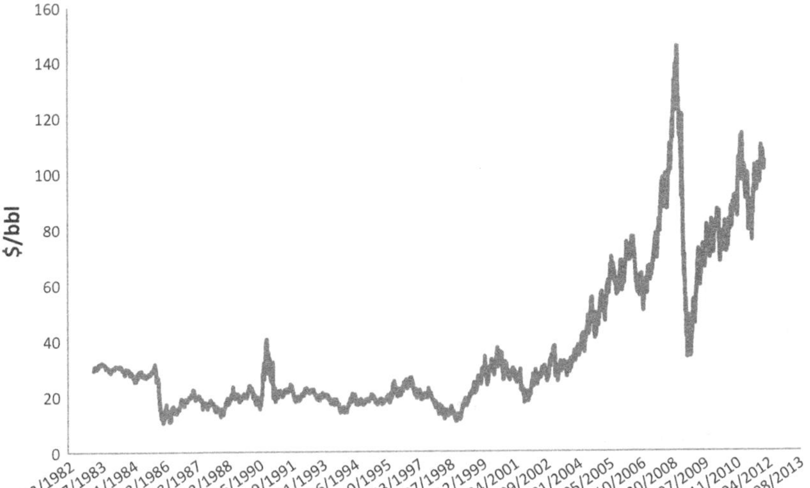

Fig. 7.7 Crude oil (WTI) price (Data source: Bloomberg; Author's own composition)

dynamics, a simple mean reversion process is not the most suitable way to characterise them. For this reason, several models are used in specialised literature to characterise the dynamics of commodities, models in which it is assumed that the commodity price, or the logarithm of the commodity price, is the sum of several factors, hence the name factorial models. The dynamics of these factors are characterised by simple stochastic processes like those presented in previous chapters.

Although a thorough review of the literature is beyond the scope of this book, it can be concluded that a model which fits reasonably well with the price dynamics of many commodities is Schwartz–Smith's two-factor model (2000): this model assumes that the price of the commodity in question, $p_t = \ln(P_t)$, is the sum of two factors, one long-term (ξ_t) and another short-term (χ_t), $p_t = \chi_t + \xi_t$. It also assumes that the long-term factor follows a random walk process, that is, $\xi_t = \mu + \xi_{t-1} + \sigma\sqrt{\Delta t}\varepsilon_t$, where ε_t is white noise, while the short-term factor is characterised by an autoregressive process with a long-term average equal to zero, that is, $\chi_t = \beta\chi_{t-1} + \sigma\sqrt{\Delta t}\eta_t$ where η_t is white noise.

As the autoregressive process has its long-term average equal to zero, in the short term this factor will take a certain value but in the long term it will converge to its long-term average, which is zero. Thus, what this model implicitly assumes is that the price dynamics of commodities in the long term are governed by the same principles as other assets, such as equities, while in the short term there is a mean reversion component whose persistence depends on the parameter β.

This model characterises the price dynamics of commodities in a very reasonable manner. However, it presents one problem regarding the use of simple models: the estimation of parameters. Assuming price dynamics are characterised by a stochastic process, for example a random walk, the estimation of the parameters of this process can be performed simply by making a comparison. The data series estimated using the model, which in this case is the random walk, is compared with the data series of prices actually observed and any adjustment measure, such as the mean square error, is minimised. The problem with models of more than one factor is that these so-called factors are not actually observed; rather, what is observed is the sum of them, which is the price. It is therefore not possible to estimate the parameters of these processes directly and more elaborate processes, such as the Kalman filter methodology, must be used to estimate these parameters based on the futures price quotations.

7.3 VaR Calculation for Commodities

As with the interest rate and exchange rate risk, the commodity price risk is a particular type of market risk and, therefore, it is likely to be measured with the same criteria as market risk in general and equity risk in particular. Specifically, applying the definition of value at risk (VaR) to the price risk of a commodity portfolio, it could be claimed that the VaR is a measure of the maximum potential change that the value of a portfolio may suffer over a time horizon and at a given probability level, in this case due to changes in the commodity prices.

The difference here, with respect to the aforementioned considerations on estimating the VaR in a portfolio of equities, is the fact that the dynamics of commodity prices are rather more complex than in the case of equities. However, like other market variables (equity, interest rate, exchange rate, etc.), once their dynamics have been characterised, the process of estimating the risk measures studied previously (VaR, CFaR, NPVaR, etc.) is identical in all cases.

7.4 Risk Management in Commodities

As stated above, commodities are not electronic assets and therefore they involve storage costs; moreover, they should be available at a particular moment during the production process (convenience yield). Therefore, as in the case of measuring, risk management in commodities is something that presents some idiosyncratic characteristics that should be taken into account.

Due to diversification and other issues, at times commodities are especially appealing for investors, and under these circumstances commodity price volatility can increase sharply. For example, during 2007 and 2008 commodity demand and, consequently, prices rose significantly not only for oil, but also for many other commodities like aluminium, copper, steel and iron ore. This increase in price and demand created market uncertainty and highlighted a lack of resources on a global scale.

Moreover, the geopolitical risk facing commodity firms is significant and takes many forms, as will be shown in relation to country risk. However, it can be assumed that a key risk variable for firms that face commodity risk comes from their relations with governments and the degree of uncertainty around regulatory frameworks. Nevertheless, as will be discussed in the following chapters, these risks arise not only in underdeveloped countries but also in Organisation for Economic Co-operation and Development (OECD) countries; more specifically, risks related to government policies on some technologies, such as nuclear and renewable resources and carbon emissions, can also be involved, which has a critical impact on investment decisions in the sector. That is one of the reasons, along with the fact that commodity projects tend to be very capital-intensive, that production sharing agreements are signed between commodity firms.

Strategies for managing commodity risk vary significantly across companies based on their risk appetite. They range from acceptance, through hedging with derivatives, to more sophisticated approaches such as vertical integration. The most common ones will be briefly described here.

A simple strategy to manage commodity price risk is to pass it on to end customers. Companies that can do this without negatively affecting sales have no exposure to commodity risk; however, in practice some level of price elasticity is naturally at play in markets.

Beyond accepting commodity risk or raising prices to accommodate cost increases, many companies manage commodity risk through entering into fixed price contracts of different lengths directly with suppliers. This is advantageous since it is the simplest way to fix input prices; however, this simplicity may be outweighed by higher costs and less flexibility.

As will be shown in Chap. 8, often the most flexible and efficient mechanism for managing commodity risk is to use derivative instruments to hedge underlying commodity price exposures.

Up to this point, all the approaches that we have presented for managing commodity price risk have the common theme of transferring risk to a third party: the customer (margin), the supplier (fixing price) or a financial institution (hedging). In addition to these approaches, a range of other alternatives which rely less on risk transfer or mitigation and more on a broader suite of responses can be considered, for example, many industry models have combined resources, processing and market capabilities through vertical integration. Although vertical integration may not be the most efficient way to mitigate commodity risk, it can be effective. Moreover, many of the strategies discussed above are focused on mitigating volatility in the short term (e.g., hedging), whereas vertical integration has the advantage of permanently reducing commodity risk exposures.

8

Market Risk Hedging

8.1 Basic Concepts

8.1.1 Hedging Costs and Profits

The issue of market risk management has been addressed throughout this book, particularly in the section related to market risk, and ways of hedging this risk have been discussed. However, this concept has been studied alongside other considerations, noting that different portfolios have different risks, and some ideas have been introduced as to how to modify a portfolio to vary its risk. Nevertheless, the discussion has not been systematic and derivative assets have barely been mentioned. For this reason, this chapter will delve deeper into the subject.

Firstly, it is important to remember that hedging is a concept related to risk management and involves taking positions that develop in the opposite way to the assets at risk. As indicated in Chap. 1, one of the aims of hedging is to reduce the costs associated with "financial distress": the direct and indirect costs associated with default and bankruptcy and the cost of missed opportunities as a result of being unable to cope with potentially profitable investment projects. However, also following the

F.J. Población García, *Financial Risk Management*,
DOI 10.1007/978-3-319-41366-2_8

logic of Chap. 1, the reduction of these undesirable effects is not attained for free, as hedges also have associated costs and difficulties: brokerage costs ("bid–ask spreads", commission, etc.), counterparty risk in hedging instruments, administration costs, and accounting control and impact. The manager's task is to deal with the "trade-off" between the costs which are protected by the hedge and the costs of hedging itself, based on the client's needs.

Elaborating on this idea, as mentioned in Chap. 1, in theory the risk aversion of the investor should not be relevant for this analysis because the investor can manage the risk of their portfolio. A complete and efficient market should provide them with the tools to choose the combination of risk and return that best suits their needs. The manager could limit themselves to choosing the appropriate instruments and any choice of return and risk would be possible, in particular zero risk.

However, this theory is not entirely correct due to agency problems, that is, the shareholders, and especially the minority shareholders, do not have the same information about the risk of the company as the managers have. Similarly, the costs of hedging are not the same for large corporations as they are for small shareholders; in fact, the size of some hedging instruments makes them prohibitive for the small investor.

Another factor to consider when hedging is competition. There are sectors in which it is accepted that the prices of goods and services fluctuate when the price of commodities fluctuates, thus without hedging the margin of the company is more or less constant, whereas if some type of hedging is carried out, all that is achieved is more variability in the margins.

Moreover, within the framework of competition, it is important to remember that while hedging increases the result in certain situations, it reduces it in others. For example, if the investor has an oil deposit and they decide to hedge against a possible fall in oil prices, if the price of oil does in fact fall, the value of the hedge increases. However, if the price of oil increases, the value of the hedge falls and thus the overall result of the company is lower than that of a competitor who decided not to hedge.

Additionally, it must not be forgotten that as well as reducing the risk, hedging also reduces profitability. Regardless of the type of hedging that is carried out, if the overall risk is zero, the total return must be no more than that of the riskless bond, otherwise investors would no longer demand the riskless bond and instead there would be a greater demand for instruments providing a combined riskless return higher than that of the riskless bond. If this were the case, the risk-free bond yields would rise, while those of the other instruments would fall until a balance was reached.

This process is independent of the type of hedging implemented—natural hedges, with futures, with swaps, with options and the like. With certain hedges, as in the case of futures, the final price is fixed regardless of future price developments, while with other hedges, as in the case of options, one party only has rights and the other only has obligations. If the risk is reduced to the same extent in both cases, the returns are also reduced to the same extent, due to either an immovable price or a premium paid initially.

8.1.2 The Residual Risk

A perfect hedge is one in which the risk is completely eliminated; perfect hedges are rare, however, and therefore the study of risk hedging is the study of how to reduce the risk as much as possible. In most cases hedging is imperfect and, consequently, a residual risk remains.

One reason for this is that the asset whose price is to be hedged may not be an exact match for the underlying asset of the derivative that is to be used as a hedge. Note that in markets there are futures and options in Repsol and Banco Santander but not in Cepsa or Banco Popular, thus it is not unusual to hedge the market risk of Cepsa or Banco Popular shares with futures whose underlying asset is Repsol or Banco Santander. Equally, it is not always known exactly when it will be possible to buy or sell an asset. However, the derivative asset used as a hedge has a price and a fixed and immovable term. In turn, the amount of the underlying asset in a derivative is fixed and does not always correspond to the amount of assets to be bought or sold.

Finally, note that in many situations not only can uncertainty be included in the price but it can also be included in the quantity or the term. For example, if an investor wants to sell an asset but does not know at what point, it must be taken into account that the market only offers derivative assets that have prices with fixed and immovable maturities. Similarly, if the amount of the underlying asset to be bought or sold is unknown, it must be kept in mind that the market only offers derivatives with fixed amounts.

For these reasons, there is usually a residual risk after performing hedging. Therefore, hedging instruments with an underlying asset, a term and a quantity are chosen to ensure that the residual risk is as minimal as possible. In other words, the ideal hedge has a value that varies in the most similar way possible to the asset being hedged, although just in the opposite direction. Specifically, the most desirable hedges are those that ensure the change in value of the asset to be hedged and the value of the hedging instrument have the most negative correlation possible and similar volatilities.

8.2 Types of Hedging

The way in which a procedure is established with respect to hedging is called a hedging strategy. Three different criteria will be used to classify the types of strategies: the objectives to be achieved, the instruments to be used and the best way to achieve the objectives. There are two types of objectives to be achieved through hedging:

- **Short hedging (short position):** this is an operation which is performed to protect the value of an investment that the investor currently owns. For example, if the investor has a share, they run the risk that its price may decrease. Therefore, to hedge this risk in some way a seller position is taken to ensure that what is lost in the share is gained in the hedge and vice versa.
- **Long hedging (long position):** this type of hedging is used in situations where the investor anticipates an asset that must be purchased in the future. In this case the risk is that the asset price may increase and consequently, by taking a long position, the investor fixes the purchase prices of assets.

This distinction between the objectives to be achieved is fundamental, since it refers to the aims or the reasons "why" hedging is performed. Regarding the instruments to be used, hedging can be divided into:

- **Natural hedging:** hedging which is carried out through purchasing and selling processes in the spot market.
- **Hedging using derivative assets:** this type of hedging requires the introduction of the derivative assets that were presented in previous chapters, futures and options, as well as other derivative assets: exotic options, swaps, swaptions and so on.

Regarding the procedure, or "how" this can be achieved, two types of hedging can be distinguished.

- **Static hedging**: when the same position is maintained throughout the entire time horizon.
- **Dynamic hedging**: when the position varies with the value of the asset and the hedging instrument with some changing rules that are established at the beginning of this process; otherwise, the strategy could not be considered as hedging and would have to be considered as speculative.

In previous chapters, when the term hedging was mentioned, it referred to static hedging. The static strategy and the dynamic strategy are two conflicting strategies which will now be discussed in more detail. The best way to reduce the residual risk with static hedges is to find a combination of instruments whereby the correlation between the portfolio to be hedged and the hedging instruments is as negative as possible and the volatilities are similar.

However, the problem with static hedges is that a combination of hedging instruments with the desired characteristics is not always found. Equally, hedging costs are proportional to the number of assets used, and therefore even if the combination of desired assets is found, hedging can prove to be very expensive. Additionally, correlations and volatilities of assets change over time; while it is true that changes are not usually radical, they can become relevant when measuring the efficiency of hedging. An *ex ante* hedging strategy which, calculated using volatilities and historical correlations, is expected to work reasonably well, *ex post* can be very inefficient due to variations in volatilities and correlations. Finally, note that there is evidence that asset correlation is much higher in times of recession than in times of expansion.

As a result, sophisticated investors are turning to dynamic hedging to reduce their risk. When dynamic hedging is performed, the position on the hedging instrument changes with the value of the portfolio to be hedged and the hedging instrument. However, the hedging strategy is defined at the start of the process and is never changed; otherwise, it would be a speculative strategy trying to take advantage of market movements assuming a risk for their own benefit. When the hedging process begins, the position of the hedging instrument is clearly defined based on the value of the portfolio to be hedged and the hedging instrument. Therefore, when dynamic hedging is performed, the position of the hedging instrument must vary over time so that, although dependent on the value of the portfolio to be hedged and the hedging instrument, it is determined from the start of the process.

The idea behind dynamic hedging is that the value of the portfolio to be hedged does not vary in a linear fashion with the value of the assets that comprise it. In these cases, static hedging is not usually very effective because a certain value of the portfolio to be hedged requires a certain amount of hedging instruments. If the value of the portfolio changes, the amount of hedging instruments required also changes. The concept behind this is very similar to that of convexity.

The following example explains the concept in greater depth: suppose an investor has a portfolio consisting exclusively of a "call" on a particular underlying asset whose price at any time "t" is S_t. As explained in previous chapters, the value of the "call" and therefore of the portfolio is: $S_t{*}N(d_1) - e^{-rT}{*}K{*}N(d_2)$, where d_1 and d_2 depend on S_t. Equally, for simplicity the case of equity securities will be considered, whereby $E[S_T] = e^{rT}{*}S_t$.

Obviously, in this case the relationship between the value of the portfolio to be hedged and the value of S_t is not linear. Thus, if the investor wants to hedge the value of the portfolio with the underlying asset of the option (S_t), static hedging is not a good idea because through static hedging a short position would be taken on a certain quantity (Q) of the underlying asset and the value of hedging at each point in time "t" will be $-Q^*S_t$, while the value of the portfolio will be $S_t{}^*N(d_1) - e^{-rT*}K^*N(d_2)$. Therefore, as the value of the portfolio to be hedged does not depend linearly on S_t, variations in the value of it will never be completely offset by changes in the value of the hedge. In the same way, the further away S_t is from its initial value, the higher the residual risk of the hedging strategy will be.

In these cases, dynamic hedging is much more effective.[1] At the start of the hedge it is specified that the strategy will involve taking a short position at all times on a given quantity of the underlying asset of the option. This amount will vary over time with the value of the underlying asset of the option and at all times will be: $Q_t = N(d_1) - e^{-rT*}K^*N(d_2)/S_t$. As is to be expected, this hedging strategy implies that the position on the hedging instrument must be updated periodically so that this amount is always Q_t.

By definition, when dynamic hedging is carried out, the position on the hedging instrument must be updated with a certain frequency—daily, weekly and so on. However, as this update cannot be carried out continuously, there is always some residual risk, although it is substantially lower than that of static hedging. In order to decide upon the ideal update frequency, a cost–benefit analysis must be used, since the more frequently updates are carried out, the less residual risk there will be but the higher the costs will be.

Finally, it should be noted that while dynamic hedging is certainly much more effective than static hedging, besides the well-known additional costs involved, having to update the position with a certain frequency involves additional risks. These include operational risks that result in the possibility of error in performance, and liquidity risks arising from the fact that in the future the situation may change and it may no longer be possible to update the position, even if there is more than enough liquidity in the instruments to update the position today.

[1] This dynamic hedging is called a delta-hedge.

8.3 Hedging Instruments

8.3.1 Derivative Assets

Natural hedges are conceptually the simplest type. However, they do not have sufficient flexibility for most of the necessary applications and thus, considering profitability, risk and cost, it is not always ideal to hedge a long position by selling in the market or a short position by anticipating a purchase. For this reason, it is often best to carry out hedging using derivative assets.

By definition, a derivative asset is a financial instrument whose payment structure depends on another asset or portfolio of assets, which is called the underlying asset. Sometimes they are referred to as derivative products rather than assets.[2]

The use of derivatives has abundant advantages over natural hedges: faster deployment, lower transaction costs, the possibility to maintain the structure of the position in the spot market and the possibility to design a fixed payment structure (maximum earnings, minimum prices, etc.) which is essentially chosen by the client.

Although the payments are the same, depending on where they are created there are two types of derivatives: "exchange-trade derivatives" or "listed derivatives", which are highly standardised contracts and are publicly traded in derivative markets; and over-the-counter (OTC) derivatives, which are agreed between private agents and do not appear in any financial market. The terms of a contract of this type are virtually free and are tailored to the clients, meaning they are usually more complex than traded derivatives. Technically, embedded derivatives, which will be discussed later, are OTC derivatives.

As discussed in previous chapters, the value of futures and forwards (the only difference between futures and forwards is that futures are "listed derivatives" whereas forwards are OTC derivatives) varies linearly with the value of the underlying asset, and for this reason they can be used to hedge portfolios with linear exposures to certain assets. However, there isn't a

---

[2] The two expressions are equivalent for all purposes.

future for every underlying asset in the market, as there are only futures for the most liquid assets and for certain indexes (IBEX 35, Euro Stoxx 50, S&P 500, etc.). In the event that there is no future for a given underlying asset, the strategy is to find futures with an underlying asset whose price has a very high correlation with the underlying asset to be hedged and, in this case, the hedging relationship must no longer involve having a future for each asset to be hedged.

It has also been shown in previous chapters that the value of options varies in a non-linear way with the value of the underlying asset, and therefore they can be used to hedge portfolios with non-linear exposures to certain assets. Similarly, hedging with options compensates for losses that occur in the portfolio. However, unlike the case of futures, it is not necessary to forgo any extra profits that may eventually arise. Hedging with options is more expensive than with futures as it involves the payment of a premium, and due to this payment, however hedging is performed, a certain reduction of risk involves the same reduction of profitability, either by renouncing possible gains (with futures) or paying a premium (with options).

8.3.1.1 Payment System Design

Derivatives are particularly useful when creating payment schemes; as they are extremely flexible, a huge variety of structures can be designed using "put" and "call" options, futures, risk-free bonds and the underlying asset itself. This allows strategies to be designed at the client's discretion, limiting losses and allowing more risk in some regions than in others.

Before payment systems can be constructed, the main elements must be characterised. The first is the underlying asset (a financial asset, cash flow or investment project) which produces a payment S_T, which is random at each future time T. The second is the insurance asset which provides a payment of 1 in all situations; thus its price is e^{-r}, where r is the interest rate. The third and fourth elements are the "call" option and "put" option defined above. The fifth is the future or forward, which is the same in terms of payments. The interesting question is not about the previously studied future or the options themselves, but about how to use them to design payment schemes. One answer is that assets are not independent, but can quite often be designed depending on others.

In order to explain this concept in greater depth, some examples will be presented here, some of which have already been discussed in previous chapters. Buying a forward is the same as buying a call option and selling a put option with the same strike price K.

Buying a call option produces maturity payments $\begin{cases} 0, & S_T < K \\ S_T - K, & S_T \geq K \end{cases}$,
and selling a put has the same maturity payment as buying it but the process is reversed: $(-1) \cdot \begin{cases} K - S_T, & S_T < K \\ 0, & S_T \geq K \end{cases}$ I.e. $\begin{cases} S_T - K, & S_T < K \\ 0, & S_T \geq K \end{cases}$.

Thus, it is clear that whatever the value of S_T, the maturity payments of this structure are identical to the payments of a future or forward, hence today they must undoubtedly have the same value.

If the investor has a portfolio with one asset and wants to hedge it with a future, the risk is completely hedged in the sense that it is no longer possible to suffer a loss; however, it is no longer possible to make a profit either. If their goal is to eliminate the risk of loss, a put option can be acquired with strike price K, maintaining the position in the underlying asset. By doing this the investor ensures that whatever the value of S_T, the minimum payment is K, as shown in Fig. 8.1, where K was taken to equal 2. The risk of this asset having a high value does not really need to be hedged.

Now assume that the underlying asset represents the price of a product and that two parties agree on its purchase and sale at a given time at the market price at that time. Both parties are interested in moderating the risk: the buyer does not want the price to be very high, while the seller seeks to ensure a minimum price. It is therefore possible to agree to pay not the market price, but a derivative of it. To do this, a put with strike price K_1 is added to the underlying asset to limit the payment in the region where the market price of the underlying asset is low. In addition, taking a short position on a call with a strike price of K_2, $K_1 < K_2$, limits the

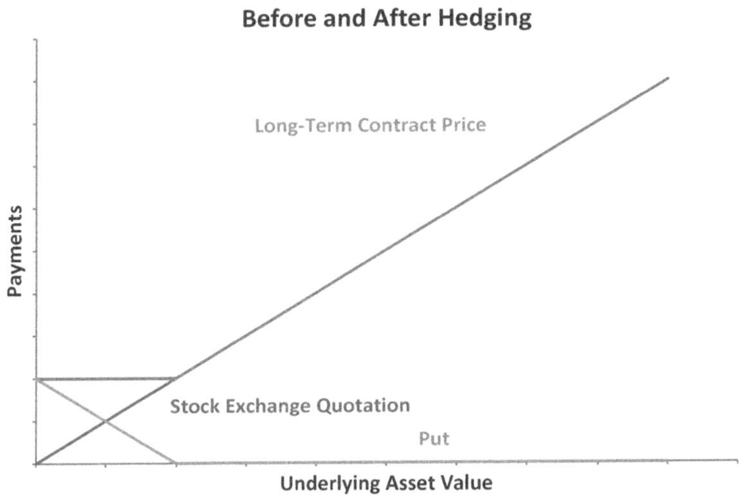

Fig. 8.1 Put hedging

payment to the region in which the market price of the underlying asset is high.

The first thing to note is that there are two strike prices and, consequently, there are three intervals in the underlying market price, that is, values lower than K_1, values between K_1 and K_2 and values greater than K_2. Remember that put, call and underlying asset payments, depending on the underlying assets, are $\begin{cases} K_1 - S_T, & S_T < K_1 \\ 0, & S_T \geq K_1 \end{cases}$ for the put, $\begin{cases} 0, & S_T < K_2 \\ S_T - K_2, & S_T \geq K_2 \end{cases}$ for the call and S_T for the underlying asset. However, it must be taken into account that in this payment structure the position on the call is a selling position, so its payments are those of the call but reversed, that is, $\begin{cases} 0, & S_T < K_2 \\ K_2 - S_T, & S_T \geq K_2 \end{cases}$.

The payment structure before and after hedging is shown by combining all these payments in Fig. 8.2:

Such structures where payments have both upper and lower limits are known as "collars".

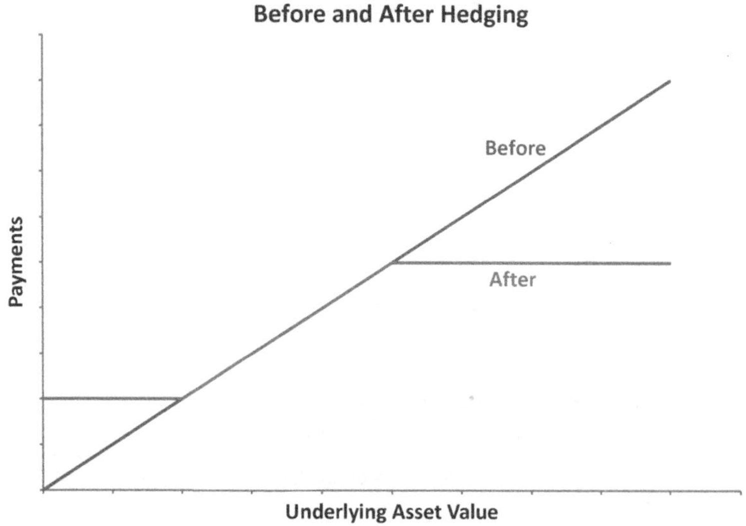

Fig. 8.2 Collar (put and call) hedging

8.3.1.2 Derivative Asset Valuation

Derivative asset valuation is possibly the most active and complex branch of Finance, as well as the one with the most mathematical content. Therefore, this book only deals with the basic ideas and the simplest tools superficially to give an idea of how it is performed. For simplicity, this subsection will focus exclusively on European options, although the ideas presented can be applied to all types of derivative assets.

Essentially, any ideas on the valuation of assets (derivative or not) rest on the principle of a lack of arbitrary trading, which can be stated simply as follows: "If two assets always produce the same payments, then the two assets must have the same price". If this were not the case, there would be an "arbitrage opportunity" as it is known in the terminology of the field, that is, the possibility to make a risk-free profit. For example, if Repsol shares are worth €20 per share in London and €21 per share in Madrid, this means that a million shares can be bought in London and sold in Madrid, making one million euros with absolutely no risk. Now, if this were possible, all investors would implement the same strategy, so the London shares would rise due to an influx of sellers, while in Madrid they would fall for the opposite reason and thus prices would be equalised in both places.

Although it may seem strange, arbitrage opportunities do exist and are constantly appearing in the market, yet the differences in prices are usually very small and they last for a very short time because they are instantly exploited by large investment firms which typically detect them automatically using sophisticated computer programs.

As far as this book is concerned, it can be concluded from the above that to calculate the value of a derivative asset, that is, to estimate its market price, the following actions are performed: its payment structure at maturity is estimated, the relationship between this payment structure and a combination of known assets is verified and, if they correspond, the price of the derivative asset is expressed as a combination of the prices of the other assets.

For example, if a long position is taken on a future, $S_T - K$ is collected at maturity, a payment which can be replicated by buying a share and selling K bonds short. Specifically, the future with strike prices equal to €20 pays the buyer $S_T - 20$ at maturity. Thus, this long position on the future is equivalent to buying a share and selling 20 bonds. If the share is worth €19 today and the riskless bond €0.90, due to the discount, the forward price must be $19 - 0.9{*}20 = €1$ because if not, there would be arbitrage possibilities.

A more sophisticated example, which is in fact one of the basic results of the valuation theory of derivative assets, is as follows: the price of a call and a put with the same strike price on the same underlying asset are not independent and one value can be obtained from another because, although a put presents payments at maturity of $\begin{cases} K - S_T, & S_T < K \\ 0, & S_T \geq K \end{cases}$ while call payments take the form $\begin{cases} 0, & S_T < K \\ S_T - K, & S_T \geq K \end{cases}$, which are apparently very different, if $K - S_T$ is added to call values in the S_T range the same payment structure as a put is obtained. Risk-free bonds are used to obtain K at maturity; K risk-free bonds with a value of e^{-r} per bond must be purchased today, while to obtain $-S_T$ at maturity the underlying asset must be sold now provided it does not present storage costs or convenience yield. This result can be formalised as follows: "A put is equivalent to buying a call with the same strike price, buying *K*risk-less bonds and selling an underlying share short", a result which is known as put–call parity. By the principle of the absence of arbitrage, a put must be worth the same as a call, minus the value of the underlying asset, plus the value of K units of the risk-free asset, which in this case is Ke^{-r}.

Following similar reasoning, although of a complexity beyond the scope of this book, the price, or premium, of a call and a put can be estimated from the safe asset and the underlying asset, provided it does not present storage costs or convenience yield. The result of this estimation is the Black–Scholes formula presented in Chap. 2.

It should also be noted that, as in the case of the "call" and "put" on assets without storage costs or convenience yield, it is often possible to find a closed formula for the value of the position on a particular derivative based on the principle of the absence of arbitrage opportunities. However, in other cases this is not possible and the value of the derivative can only be estimated by numerical methods.

In any case, whether or not it can be estimated by a closed formula, the price of a derivative is the sum of two values:

- **Intrinsic value**: collections/payments that would occur if the maturity of the derivative was at present.
- **Time value**: extra value that a derivative has due to the fact that over time collections/payments may increase.

In derivatives with linear payment functions (as in the case of futures), the time value is zero and thus, over time, collections/payments are equally as likely to increase as to decrease. These cases are symmetrical and the investor is equally as likely to lose money as they are to make profits, because neither party has more rights or obligations than the other. However, in the case of derivatives with non-linear payment functions, as in the case of options, the time value is always greater than zero and it is more likely that the collections/payments increase over time because one party only has rights and the other only has obligations. This time value of derivatives with non-linear payment systems is what is sometimes very difficult to assess. Figures 8.3 and 8.4 show the price,

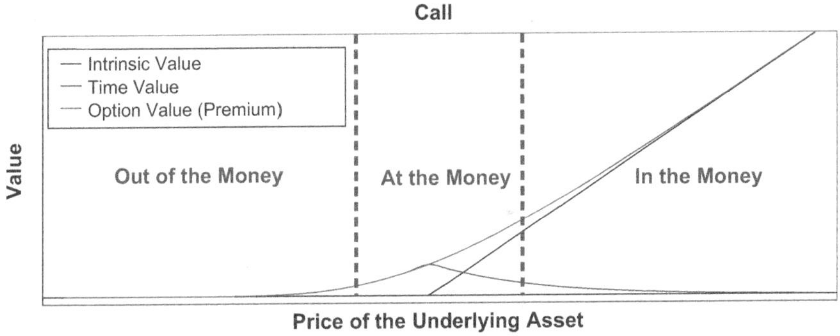

Fig. 8.3 Call

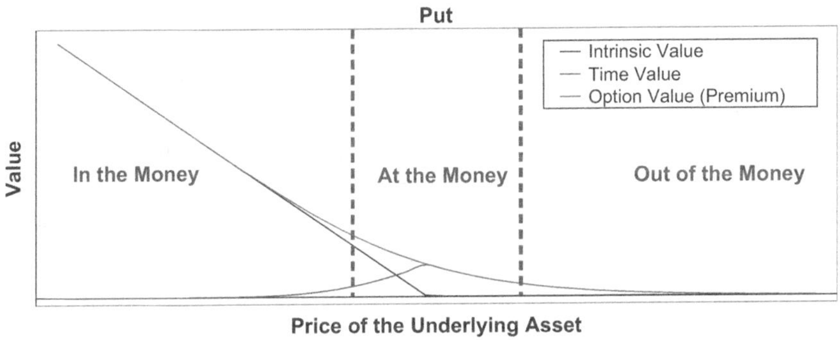

Fig. 8.4 Put

premium, of a "call" and a "put" divided into its intrinsic value and its time value depending on the value of the underlying asset.

As shown in Figs. 8.3 and 8.4, the time value is higher when the underlying asset price is equal to the strike price of the option and tends to zero when the two prices differ substantially. The reason for this is that when the underlying asset price is equal to the strike price, the intrinsic value of the option is zero. As in these cases the option gives the right to buy or sell something according to its value, this right is worth nothing; in turn, it is highly likely for the underlying asset price to evolve over time in such a way that the option becomes valuable. In the event that the price does not develop in this way and the opposite occurs, losses are limited and the value of the "option" is zero, since the party that only has rights does not exercise the option. This is the asymmetry that gives rise to the time value of the option. In these cases, when the underlying asset price is equal to the strike price, the option is said to be "at the money".

Conversely, when the price of the underlying asset and the strike differ substantially, the time value is low when the option premium is virtually the same as its intrinsic value. When the strike price differs greatly from the underlying asset price, the underlying asset price must vary greatly for the aforementioned asymmetry to occur. In these cases, when the option value is very close to zero, the option is said to be "out of the money", whereas when the option is valuable it is said to be "in the money". When the call is in the money, the underlying asset price is well above the strike price, and thus, if the price of the underlying asset rises, the option is worth more, while if it falls it is worth less. There is no asymmetry here whatsoever and the option premium is practically equal to its intrinsic value. In the same way, if the call is out of the money, the underlying asset price is well below the strike and whether the underlying asset price rises or falls, the option value hardly changes and is zero in all cases; there is also a lack of asymmetry here. For this reason, there is no time value when the option premium and the intrinsic value are the same and equal to zero.

8.3.1.3 Risk Management in Derivatives

Strictly speaking, a derivative cannot be considered a financial asset since the saver does not make their savings available to the investor through a derivative, but rather two agents in the economy mutually transfer risk. In any case, when an investor takes a position on a derivative, this position is subject to risk, especially market risk. By definition, market risk is the uncertainty about future earnings resulting from changes in market conditions, and any position on a derivative changes value as a result of changes in market conditions.

When dealing with risk in derivative positions, a particular type of market risk is likely to be measured with the same criteria as general market risk, and equity risk in particular, as discussed previously. Specifically, applying the definition of value at risk (VaR), for risk in positions on portfolio derivatives it can be claimed that the VaR is a measure of the maximum potential change that the value of a portfolio can suffer over a time horizon and at a given probability level, in this case due to changes in market variables that affect the value of the derivative positions.

The peculiarity here is that the change in value of the position on the derivative is produced by the variation in the value of the underlying asset and this in turn may be affected by market variables. In this case there is an additional step which was presented in the case of equities when estimating the VaR, as the value of the derivative must be calculated for each scenario. In other words, when estimating the VaR in a portfolio of equities, the noise is simulated and from this the share price is simulated, and with these simulations the VaR of the portfolio is estimated. In order to estimate the VaR another step must be introduced, whereby for each simulation of the underlying asset price the value of the position on this derivative must be estimated, and this estimate can sometimes be complex. Additionally, the value of the derivative can sometimes only be estimated by numerical procedures, which adds an additional complication to the estimation of its risk.

However, although the estimate may be complex, the rationale behind it is exactly the same as that discussed for equities.

8.3.2 Embedded Derivatives

Derivative assets are not only traded in financial markets; there are also clauses in commercial contracts that work for all purposes as if they were derivative assets. For example, when an oil or mining company makes a discovery, the exploitation usually takes more than 30 years and typically requires a large initial investment. In order to ensure that the initial investment is recovered, long-term purchase–sale contracts are usually implemented, and to ensure that in 20 years the transaction takes place at market prices, the prices of these contracts are usually linked to international prices. In the same way, utility and transport companies want to ensure supply for long periods of time, and in general all companies are interested in having stable relationships with their suppliers and customers, so it is common to sign long-term agreements and link them to indexes to ensure that at the time of payment no large deviations from market prices have occurred over the years.

However, linking price indexes involves taking on a risk, because it is not known how these indexes will evolve and, obviously, it is in the interest of companies to reduce risk in general. These long-term contracts may include clauses that limit the maximum price to be paid or the minimum price to be received; in particular, companies that make a large initial investment such as oil, power, mining, construction and the like generally impose a minimum price to be received in the contract to ensure they recover this major investment. On the other hand, companies that buy supplies, such as electricity distributors or large supermarket chains, although keen to guarantee supply for long periods of time, cannot afford more than a certain price, thus they usually impose a maximum price to be paid in the contract. For this reason, the price formula of these long-term contracts is usually linked to a stock ticker but with clauses that guarantee a certain minimum and maximum price. Regardless of its legal origin, a payment that depends on an index is a derivative; in fact, as will be shown below, a payment with a minimum and maximum price can be specified in terms of put and call options. For this reason, these clauses are known as embedded derivatives and, strictly speaking, fall into the category of OTC derivatives.

Formally, an embedded derivative is defined as a payment structure dependent on an underlying asset which is specified in a commercial contract. Clearly this definition is the same as that used for regular derivatives; the only difference is where the derivative is found. Figure 8.5 shows an example of an embedded derivative and, as can be seen, it makes no difference if it occurs as a result of a commercial contract or a derivative market. In both cases, this type of scheme is a typical derivative, called a "collar", and can only be achieved by a combination of buying and selling options.

A simple contract that can be replicated with "calls" and "puts" has been shown, but in fact a great variety of embedded derivatives can be found in commercial contracts: swaps, exotic options, swaptions and so on. The problem with embedded derivatives is their specification; due to the complexity of commercial contracts, which usually contain several hundred pages, it is not surprising that the detection of embedded

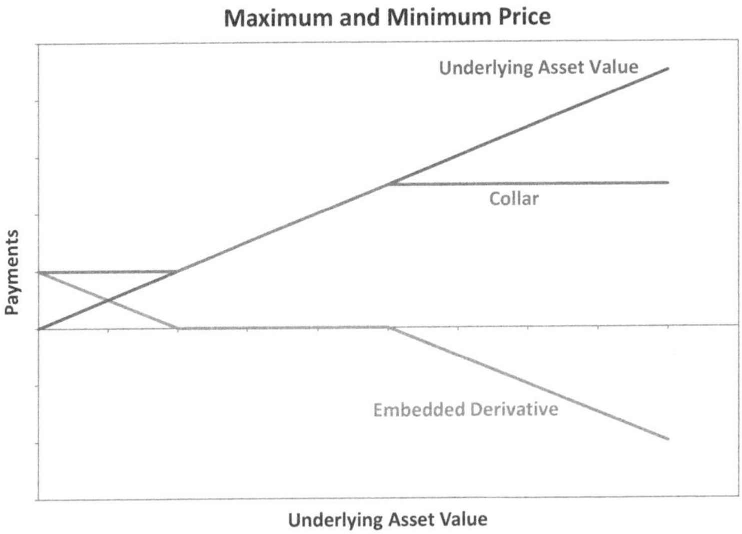

Fig. 8.5 Collar hedging

derivatives may prove to be very complex. The fact that they are difficult to detect often causes them to go unnoticed by managers of industrial enterprises. This does not generally occur with financial derivatives because, as they have market prices, they are much more visible.

Sometimes value cannot be given to those clauses, and even if it is, it is usually quite general without assigning their market value, despite the fact that identical financial derivatives are traded in the market. If, for example, the price of oil is $70/bbl, all managers are aware of the market value ("premium") of a call on a barrel of crude oil with a strike price of $110/bbl or a put on a barrel of oil with a strike of $30/bbl. However, most managers attribute the same value to the maximum and minimum price clause, since both are the same "distance" from the market price. As the price of oil is $70/bbl, most managers tend to think that a maximum price clause of $110(70 + 40)/bbl is equivalent to a minimum price clause of $30(70 − 40)/bbl, as both are $40/bbl from the market price. However, financial theory states that the value of a call and the value of a put are not equal because it is clear that when payments are not restricted, under the same conditions the value of the call exceeds the value of the put, and therefore for both clauses to have the same value the distance between the maximum price and the market price must be greater than that between the minimum price and the market price.

8.4 Hedge Accounting

8.4.1 General Issues

As discussed in previous chapters, the two main accounting regulations are:

- FAS (Federal Accounting Standards), which are in force in the USA.
- IAS (International Accounting Standards), which are in force in all other Organisation for Economic Co-operation and Development (OECD) countries.

Except for slight differences, which may be of great importance in certain cases, both laws are virtually identical and, for this reason, this book will follow the regulation of the IAS, knowing that everything established here is still valid in terms of the FAS.

8.4.1.1 Held-to-Maturity Investment Accounting

In paragraph 11 of IAS 32 it is stated that: "A financial instrument is a contract that simultaneously gives rise to a financial asset of one entity and a financial liability or equity instrument of another entity". In turn, this paragraph establishes that a financial asset is "any asset that is: cash, an equity instrument of another entity, a contractual right or a contract that will or may be 'settled in the entities' own equity instruments".

Thus, paragraph 43 of IAS 39 states that: "When a financial asset or financial liability is recognised initially, an entity shall measure it at its fair value plus, in the case of a financial asset or financial liability not at fair value through profit or loss, transaction costs that are directly attributable to the acquisition or issue of the financial asset or financial liability".

Paragraph 45 states that: "for the purpose of measuring a financial asset after initial recognition, this Standard classifies financial assets into the following four categories: financial assets at fair value through profit or loss, held-to-maturity investments, loans and receivables and available-for-sale financial assets", while Article 9 states that "held-to-maturity investments are non-derivative financial assets with fixed or determinable payments and fixed maturity that an entity has the positive intention and ability to hold to maturity". Finally, paragraph 46 of IAS 39 states that: "After initial recognition, an entity shall measure financial assets, including derivatives that are assets, at their fair values . . . except: . . . held-to-maturity investments which shall be measured at amortised cost".

In other words, an investment that the company intends to hold to maturity should be recorded at its initial value, taking depreciation into account. If a company invests in any one asset, accounting rules require this asset to be recorded at its market value in each period, unless it is an investment that they intend to manage and not to sell, in which case this investment is required to be recorded at its redemption net acquisition value.

The objective of the balance of a company is to reflect the value of its assets and liabilities as carefully and accurately as possible, and consequently the accounting regulations stipulate that all assets are recorded at their market value. Held-to-maturity investments are an exception to this rule and are required to be recorded at their acquisition cost, mainly due to accounting prudence, so that the value of the asset is stable rather than suffering large variations from one period to another. If the investment is to be maintained until maturity, in principle, it will not be sold and the gain or loss will not materialise.

8.4.1.2 Derivative Accounting

As has just been noted, paragraph 46 of IAS 39 states that in each period derivatives should be recorded at their market value, which presents a problem: if a derivative is contracted in order to hedge the risk associated with an investment that the investor intends to hold until maturity, it is recorded as a permanent investment and, although this hedge is perfect from a financial standpoint, financial statements may create large distortions.

However, to avoid such situations, IAS 39 states that if there is a hedging relationship between a hedging instrument, usually a derivative, and a hedged item as described in paragraphs 85–88 and in paragraphs GA102 to GA104 of the appendix, accounting for the gain or loss of the hedging instrument and the hedged item shall follow the provisions established in paragraphs 89 to 102 of the Standards. Specifically, paragraph 88 states that for a hedging relationship to be considered as account hedging the following five conditions must be met:

a) At the beginning of the hedge there must be a formal description and documentation supporting this description, as well as the objectives of the organisation in terms of risk management and the strategy to perform hedging. This documentation must clearly identify the hedging instrument, the asset to be hedged, the nature of the risk to be hedged and how the entity plans to assess the effectiveness of the hedge.
b) Hedging is expected to be "highly effective".
c) In the case of a "cash flow hedge", there should be almost complete certainty that cash flows will be produced.
d) The effectiveness of hedging must be measured in a "reliable" way. This definition will not be described here; suffice to say that the accounting standard defines very clearly what is considered reliable and what is not.
e) In addition, being highly effective in its initial definition is not enough. The effectiveness of hedging until now and whether it is expected to remain effective until completion is verified in each accounting period report.

As stated in paragraph AG105 of IAS 39, hedging is recognised as highly effective if the following two conditions are met:

a) At the beginning and in subsequent periods, hedging is expected to be highly effective in offsetting changes in the "fair value" or the "cash flows" attributable to the risk to be hedged during the designated period. The fact that it is expected to be highly effective can be demonstrated in several ways, one of which is the comparison between past changes in the "fair value" or the "cash flows" attributable to this hedging instrument risk and the asset to be hedged; another way of demonstrating this is when there is a high correlation between the "fair value" or the "cash flows" of the asset to be hedged and the hedging instrument.

b) The actual result of hedging must be in the range of 80–125 % in at least each result presentation period. For example, if the hedging instrument makes a loss of 120 monetary units and the asset to be hedged makes a profit of 100 monetary units, the actual outcome of hedging will be 120/100 = 120 % or 100/120 = 83 % and therefore, if the first condition is met, it can be concluded that hedging is highly effective.

For a hedging instrument to be designated as hedge accounting on an asset, it must first be demonstrated that at the beginning and throughout the life of the hedge it is expected to be highly effective, which is demonstrated by establishing a high correlation in the historical value of both or verifying that in the past their values varied in unison; and secondly that for the duration of hedging, profits or losses of the asset to be hedged must be offset by the losses or profits of the hedging instrument at a rate that must be in the range of 80–125 %.

Similarly, paragraphs 46, 47, AG80 and AG81 of IAS 39 detail what is meant by measuring hedging reliably. To avoid going into too much detail, these paragraphs will not be repeated here; however, in short, they explain that where there is a market quotation, it is this quotation that must be used, unless it is considered to be unreliable for some reason, for example liquidity. If there is no market price or it is not reliable, the best estimate of this market value must be found, such as the last transaction, the value of similar assets, and so on.

In the event that a hedging relationship meets all the above conditions and may therefore be designated as hedge accounting, the accounting of the hedging instrument and of the asset to be hedged is different depending on the type of hedging, as will be discussed in the next section. Basically, in all cases it is stated that the hedging instrument, which is generally a derivative, is recorded at a fair value, that is, its market value, in the same way as the asset to be hedged which, although it is classified in accounting terms as a held-to-maturity investment, is also priced at a fair value. The ineffective portion of hedging is shown in the results and has to be minimal for hedging to still qualify as hedge accounting.

The big risk of signing a hedging contract for an asset which is considered to be a held-to-maturity investment on the balance sheet is that at the beginning or during the hedging period the definition of hedge accounting may not be adhered to. As a consequence, in the financial statements of the company the asset to be hedged may be recorded at its acquisition value, while the hedging instrument may be recorded at its market value, which would cause large variations in value. These variations must be shown in results, although they are offset economically, at least in part, by the change in the value of the asset to be hedged.

The main reason why hedging, which from an economic-financial perspective makes perfect sense, cannot be classified as hedge accounting from an accounting perspective is that it does not meet the requirement of being highly effective. This condition of being highly effective as established is very reasonable and seemingly easy to comply with; however, in the actual operation of a company compliance may be very difficult, since it is not always possible to find a hedging instrument with exactly the same characteristics as the asset to be hedged and which can ensure full compliance with the conditions established previously.

For example, it can be acknowledged that, in general, all refineries keep a certain number of litres of fuel (petrol, diesel, kerosene, asphalts, etc.) in storage, so as to avoid problems if there is a cut in the supply. Thus, if the aim is to hedge the market risk of these reserves, derivative assets with underlying assets of each of these products should be found, which is not conceptually difficult. The problem arises in organised markets (stock exchanges) where there are only derivatives of crude oil, petrol and in some cases diesel, but not of kerosene and certainly not of other products such as asphalt. Outside organised markets, in OTC markets it is possible to find counterparties willing to offer derivative contracts on these types of products,[3] but due to their liquidity, this contract is offered at a very high cost (i.e., commission, bid–ask spread, etc.).

To avoid paying the costs described above, since there is a high correlation between the price of petrol and that of kerosene, hedging the reserves of kerosene with a derivative on petrol could be considered. Based on the definition of highly effective hedging, initially this derivative may be designated as hedge accounting of kerosene reserves, since it easily fulfils the requirements established in the first condition to be highly effective. Nevertheless, over time it could happen, and in fact it often does, that the prices of petrol and kerosene become momentarily more distant and, in this particular time period, the requirements established in the second condition are not met. In this case, automatically, the changes in the value of the derivative on petrol could not be offset by the changes in the value of kerosene reserves and would have to be shown in the results. Given the magnitude of reserves, changes in the real value of kerosene reserves and therefore of the derivative on petrol, they could become an appreciable amount, and this would produce significant distortions in the financial statements (balance sheets and income statements) of the refinery period after period.

8.4.2 Types of Hedge Accounting

If there is a hedging relationship between a hedging instrument and a hedged item as described in paragraphs 85–88 and paragraphs GA102–GA104 in Appendix A, recording the profit or loss of the hedging instrument and the hedged item will follow what was established in paragraphs 89–102 of IAS 39. In this regard, these paragraphs state that there are three kinds of hedging relationships:

a) **Fair value hedge**: the hedging of the exposure to changes in the fair value of recognised assets or liabilities or unrecognised firm

---

[3] OTC markets are markets in which each agent searches for their counterpart and there are no standard contracts, as with stock exchanges. Thus, contracts are designed by the parties and everything can be negotiated.

commitments, as well as hedging of an identified portion of such assets, liabilities or firm commitments, which is attributable to a particular risk and could affect the profit or loss in that period.

b) **Cash flow hedge**: the hedging of exposure to variation in cash flows which is attributable to a particular risk associated with a recognised asset or liability, such as all or some of the future interest payments of a variable interest rate debt or a highly probable forecast transaction, which could affect the profit or loss of that period.

c) **Net investment hedge**: as defined in IAS 21, this is the hedging of exposure to the net value of an investment abroad.

If a fair value hedge meets the requirements of paragraph 88 during the period, it is recorded as follows (paragraph 89):

- The profit or loss made from remeasuring the hedging instrument at a fair value, in the case of a derivative which is a hedging instrument, is recognised in the result of the period.
- The profit or loss on the hedged item attributable to the hedged risk adjusts the amount of the hedged item in books and is recognised in the result of that period. This applies even if the hedged item is recorded as a held-to-maturity investment.

When a cash flow hedge meets the conditions in paragraph 88 during the period, it is recorded as follows (paragraph 95):

- The portion of the profit or loss made on the hedging instrument which has been determined to be a highly effective hedge is recognised directly in equity through the statement of equity changes.
- The ineffective portion of the profit or loss on the hedging instrument is recognised in the result of the period.

Net investment hedges are recorded in a similar way to cash flow hedges (paragraph 102):

- The portion of the profit or loss made on the hedging instrument that has been designated as highly effective hedging is recognised directly in equity.
- The ineffective portion is recognised in the result of the period.

8.4.3 Embedded Derivatives Accounting

As previously indicated, unlike conventional hedging instruments, embedded derivatives appear within business contracts and often are not easily detected. Similarly, the accounting treatment of these assets is different.

In IAS 39, paragraph 10 defines the embedded derivative as the component of a hybrid instrument that also includes a non-derivative in such a way that part of the cash flows of the combined instrument would vary in the same way as a financial derivative. In other words, whenever there is a clause in a commercial contract that somehow modifies the price of the product subject to purchase or sale, making it different to its market price, there is an embedded derivative. In a more concise way, if the payment system is not linear, there is an embedded derivative. It should be noted that there cannot be derivatives if there is no underlying asset, hence embedded derivatives can only exist if there are, either nationally or internationally, market prices for the product subject to purchase or sale.

Paragraph 11 of IAS 39 states that in certain circumstances almost all embedded derivatives are achieved; basically, if their economic and risk characteristics do not match those of the original contract but they correspond to the definition of a financial derivative, an embedded derivative must be separated from its original contract and recorded in the same way as any financial derivative. This type of accounting causes the embedded derivatives to be a potential source of risk because, as in other types of hedging, it is possible for the original contract to be part of a held-to-maturity investment, while the embedded derivative cannot be recorded in this way. In this case, the first will remain stable, and the second, like any other financial derivative that does not qualify as hedge accounting, must be updated in each accounting report.

As with other types of derivatives, such situations can be avoided if the contract is designed to ensure that the embedded derivative meets the conditions for hedge accounting. Of course, it is not always possible to design the contract in this way, particularly if the pricing formula of the purchase–sale contract is not "appropriate" to value the product subject to purchase and sale, that is, if the contract states that the price of the product exchanged does not reflect its market value.

Part III

Credit Risk

9

Credit Risk: Measurement

9.1 Basic Concepts

As stated at the beginning of this book, risk can be defined as the degree of uncertainty about future net earnings which can take various forms, one of which is credit risk. In recent years, especially given the international financial crisis, credit risk has become one of the main challenges in risk management.

More formally, it can be concluded that credit risk arises from the possibility that borrowers, bond issuers or counterparties in derivative transactions will not meet their obligations. In addition, the very formal definition is as follows: credit risk is defined as the possibility of losses arising from the counterparty's total or partial failure to meet their contractual obligations in terms of the total amount or the due date. The main consequence of this is the replacement cost of the relinquished cash flows.

As credit exposure has increased, so has the need for sophisticated techniques to measure and manage credit risk. However, before starting to develop the various techniques for measuring credit risk, it is necessary

---

Electronic Supplementary Material: The online version of this article (DOI 10.1007/978-3-319-41366-2_9) contains supplementary material, which is available to authorized users.

F.J. Población García, *Financial Risk Management*,
DOI 10.1007/978-3-319-41366-2_9

to understand the main cause of credit risk, credit events or default and the relationship between credit risk and other risks, primarily market risk.

9.1.1 Credit Risk Versus Market Risk

The credit event is a dichotomous phenomenon, as it may or may not occur; this is the main difference between credit risk and market risk, where risk originates from market variables, generally prices, which can take a continuum of values, usually between zero and infinity. For this reason, as will be seen in this chapter, the study of credit risk will be very different from that of market risk.

By way of example and to clarify a situation where the difference between credit risk and market risk is not so obvious, consider a transaction where a trader buys one million pounds in bank A with a payment to be made in a month at an exchange rate that is fixed today and is the current two-day exchange rate which, more specifically, is $1.50/GBP. If after this month the exchange rate changes and falls to $1.40/GBP, the trader buys $1.50/GBP which is worth $1.40/GBP in the market, and therefore the trader's loss is ($1.50/GBP – $1.40/GBP)*1,000,000 GBP = $100,000, a loss which is caused by market risk. If, instead, the exchange rate rises to $1.60/GBP and, at the time of the payment to bank A, the bank files for bankruptcy and therefore cannot meet its obligations, the "trader" in the example has to buy pounds at another bank at an exchange rate of $1.60/GBP, a higher rate than that negotiated with bank A, which generates a loss of ($1.60/GBP – $1.50/GBP) 1,000,000 GBP = $100,000 as a result of credit risk.

As demonstrated by this simple example, credit risk is a longer-term risk than market risk, as prices of market variables change constantly, while bankruptcy in companies or defaults by individuals do not occur as often. It is also immediately ascertained that legalities are not important in the case of market risk but are crucial in the case of credit risk, as concepts like "bankruptcy" are legal terms.

9.1.2 The Credit Event

Before beginning to study credit risk, it is necessary to have a better understanding of credit events, as this concept is not as straightforward as it might at first seem. The credit rating agency Standard & Poor's defines default as the first time any financial obligation is breached, except when unpaid interest occurs within the grace period. While this is perhaps the most intuitive definition of the credit event, it is not the only one. The International Swaps and Derivatives Association (ISDA) defines the following as credit events:

- **Bankruptcy**: a situation that involves (1) dissolution of the entity that has the obligation; (2) insolvency or inability to pay the debt; (3) assignment of receivables; (4) the institution of bankruptcy proceedings; (5) appointment from the Judicial Administration; (6) substantial seizure of assets by third parties.
- **Failure to pay**: failure of the debtor to make the payments which take place after the grace period and are above a certain amount.
- **Obligation/cross default**: an additional default which occurs as a result of the inability to pay in any other similar obligation.
- **Obligation/cross acceleration**: an additional default which occurs as a result of the inability to pay in any other similar obligation which involves the obligation immediately becoming a lawsuit.
- **Repudiation/moratorium**: the counterparty rejects or challenges the validity of the obligation.
- **Restructuring**: waiver, postponement or rescheduling of the obligation under less favourable initial conditions.

Similarly, Banco de España (Spanish Central Bank)'s Accounting Circular (4/2004) states that credit institutions must classify any loans that are granted in accordance with the following categories:

- **Normal risk**: includes all debt instruments and contingent risks that do not meet the requirements to be classified into other categories. In turn, the operations in this category are subdivided into the following risk classes: negligible risk, low risk, medium-low risk, medium risk, medium-high risk and high risk. In this category it is necessary to identify operations that merit special monitoring, defined as those with small weaknesses, which do not require greater hedging than that established for normal risk operations, but for which special monitoring by the entity is advisable.

- **Substandard risk**: includes all debt instruments and contingent risks which do not meet the criteria to be individually classified as doubtful or failed but which have weaknesses that could entail losses greater than hedging for the entity due to the deterioration of risks being specially monitored.
- **Doubtful risk due to customer default**: includes the total amount of debt instruments, regardless of the holder and the security, which have some matured amount from the principal, interest or fees agreed contractually over three months ago, unless it is appropriate to classify them as failed; and contingent risks where the collateral loan has entered into arrears.
- **Doubtful risk for reasons other than customer default**: Includes debt instruments, whether matured or not, which do not meet the requirements to be classified as failed or doubtful due to customer default but which raise reasonable doubts as to their full repayment (principal and interest) in the contractually agreed terms. It also includes contingent risks and contingent commitments which are not classified as doubtful due to customer default, where payment by the institution is likely but recovery is doubtful.
- **Failed risk**: This category includes the number of debt securities, whether matured or not, whose recovery is considered remote after an individual analysis, leading to the termination of this financial asset contract. Unless proven otherwise, this category includes all debits, excluding amounts hedged with enough effective safeguards, which were incurred by creditors who have been declared bankrupt, have declared or will declare the liquidation phase or are suffering from a noticeable and unrecoverable deterioration of solvency. Balance transactions which are classified as doubtful due to arrears dating back more than four years are also included here.

As is evident, the ISDA and the Banco de España's Accounting Circular provide different definitions of the credit event; for this reason, in the case of credit risk the first thing that should be clearly established is what is meant by the term credit event.

9.1.2.1 Default Definition in Banking Regulation

In current banking regulation (CRR, or Capital Requirements Regulation (Article 178)) it is established that:

"A default shall be considered to have occurred with regard to a particular obligor when either or both of the following have taken place:

(a) The institution considers that the obligor is unlikely to pay its credit obligations to the institution, the parent undertaking or any of its subsidiaries in full, without recourse by the institution to actions such as realising security;
(b) the obligor is past due more than 90 days on any material credit obligation to the institution, the parent undertaking or any of its subsidiaries. Competent authorities may replace the 90 days with 180 days for exposures secured by residential or SME commercial real estate in the retail exposure class, as well as exposures to public sector entities). The 180 days shall not apply for the purposes of Article 127".

Based on the above definition it is easy to calculate default rates for a specific portfolio over a specific period of time. As a general rule we can say that a default rate is the number of defaulted creditors during this period of time divided by the number of creditors in the portfolio. However, we must consider that some loans can mature before the end of the period and other loans can be granted after the beginning of the period. In those cases we have to assess the creditors once they are included in the sample and they can default.

Consequently, retail loans that have been granted in the final three months of the period have zero weight because they cannot default. In other words, loans that are active and can default in the whole period should have a weight equal to one and loans that mature before the end of the period or that are granted after the beginning of the period should have a weight equal to the time within the period that they are active and can default divided by the period of time.

9.2 Measuring Credit Risk

With regard to credit risk, credit institutions are subject to regulations which require them to keep a percentage of capital to hedge this credit risk. Other companies, although they are not subject to special regulation, are also exposed to credit risk, and therefore the measurement and management of credit risk is fundamental in both banks and non-banks to maintain capital gains and price stability.

The distribution of credit risk can be understood as a process that involves the following variables:

- **Default** is the credit event; it is a discrete state and occurs with a certain probability, known as probability of default (PD).
- **Loss given default (LGD)** represents the percentage of loss after default. For example, if the recovery rate after default is 30 %, the LGD value is 70 %.
- **Exposure at default (EAD)** is the economic value of the loan at the time of the breach.

Once these three values have been characterised, measurements related to credit risk can be performed. For example, if there is a portfolio of homogeneous credit operations and their PD, EAD and LGD are known, it is clear that the expected loss of this portfolio is PD * LGD * EAD. If the probability distributions of each of these parameters are also known or assumed, the unexpected loss in certain adverse scenarios can be estimated. In any case, before going on to discuss these concepts, PD, LGD and EAD must be characterised in more detail.

9.2.1 Probability of Default (PD)

As noted earlier, the credit event is a dichotomous phenomenon: either it is breached or it is not. The first factor to consider when characterising credit risk is the likelihood of this phenomenon occurring, that is, the probability of default.

Regarding the probability of default, one of the first considerations should be the fact that it depends on the term, and of course the longer term, the greater the probability of default. This implies that for a given operation, the probability of default occurring in the next year is less than the probability of this happening in the next two years, which should be taken into account when estimating this probability. When the probability of default is studied, the desired term should be noted initially. This could be a short term, for example the following month, or a long term, such as the entire life of the transaction.

Among the techniques that have been developed to estimate the probability of default, the three most important are: estimates calculated using historical data, those calculated using bond prices and those calculated using share prices and volatilities. Techniques have also been developed to estimate the probability of default using credit derivatives; however, their substrate is comparable to that of the bond and/or share price method and, for this reason, in order to avoid lengthening this section unnecessarily, this will not be discussed in this book.

9.2.1.1 Estimates from Historical Data (Credit Scoring/Rating)

Edward Altman pioneered the use of financial ratios to predict the failure of companies; in 1968 he developed the algorithm known as Z-score or Z-Altman Score which involves estimating the probability of default based on financial ratios. Specifically, based on the following ratios: working capital/sales (X_1), retained earnings/assets (X_2), earnings before interest and taxes/assets (X_3), capital market value/liability book value (X_4) and sales/assets (X_5), Altman established the benchmark (Z-score) $Z - 1.2X_1 + 1.4X_2 + 3.3X_3 + 0.6X_4 + 0.999X_5$ which determines the probability of default. Specifically, Altman's study concluded that if $Z > 3$, default is unlikely; if $2.7 < Z < 3$, vigilance is required; if $1.8 < Z < 2.7$, there is a moderate chance of default; and if $Z < 1.8$, there is a high probability of default.

The development started by Altman has evolved into credit scoring/rating models which assign a probability of default depending on the characteristics of the borrower and the loan transaction in question. There are several ways of doing this, but the most common is by using multinomial models and, in particular, logit or probit models. These models are based on the fact that, as noted above, the default phenomenon is dichotomous (either there is a default or not) and stochastic (today it is impossible to know with certainty whether or not there will be a default in the future). It is, therefore, natural to define a random variable, "B", which takes the value 1 if it defaults and 0 if the opposite happens, where PD is the probability of default. Obviously, "B" is distributed binomially:

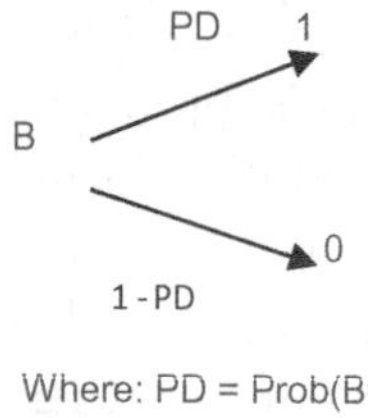

Where: PD = Prob(B = 1)

As indicated, multinomial models are the standard way of characterising PD based on several variables which are, simply, the characteristics of the borrower and the loan transaction in question. In these models a random variable or an unobservable latent factor, "y", is defined in such a way that if "y" is greater than zero, there will be a default, whereas if it is less than zero, no default will occur. It is also assumed that "y" is as follows: $y = \beta_1 x_1 + \cdots + \beta_n x_n + \varepsilon$ where $x_1, \ldots, x_n$ represents these variables, which in the case of a borrower could be their level of income, age, marital status and so on, while for a loan transaction the variables could be the existence of guarantees, the term, the amount and so forth. The ε variable is a random variable representing the characteristics of the borrower and the loan transaction not included in the above variables, and therefore it is also known as the error term. The coefficients

$\beta_1, \ldots, \beta_n$, which are unknown, are a measure of how these variables affect the unobservable latent factor "y".

From the above it can be concluded that:

$$PD = Prob(B = 1) = Prob(y > 0) = Prob(\varepsilon > -\beta_1 x_1 - \cdots - \beta_n x_n)$$

If ε is now assumed to be a random variable with a probability distribution, it can be concluded that: $PD = Prob(\varepsilon > -\beta_1 x_1 - \cdots - \beta_n x_n) = 1 - F(-\beta_1 x_1 - \cdots - \beta_n x_n)$, where $F(.)$ is the cumulative distribution function of ε. Thus, if it is assumed that ε is distributed normally, the model is called a "probit" model, whereas if it is assumed to be distributed logistically, the model is called a "logit" model.

The maximum likelihood method is used to estimate the β coefficients: where N is the number of transactions in the sample, $x_1{}^i, \ldots, x_n{}^i$ represents the variables associated with the transaction "i", $i = 1, \ldots, N$ and N_1 represents the number of these operations that have defaulted in the sampling period. The logarithmic maximum likelihood function for all these borrowers is:

$$LMV = \sum_{i=1}^{N_1} \log\left[F\left(-\beta_1 x_1^i - \cdots - \beta_n x_n^i\right)\right] + \sum_{i=N_1}^{N} \log[1 - F(-\beta_1 x_{1i} - \cdots - \beta_n x_n^i)]$$ [1,2]

An estimation of coefficients $\beta_1, \ldots, \beta_n$ is obtained by maximising this function. With this estimate a score for each borrower is defined as follows: $Score_i = \beta_1 x_1^i + \cdots + \beta_n x_n^i$. By construction, the more negative the score is, the less likely the operation is to default and, of course, as noted above, the outcome of this process depends on the term, that is, the results produced when the probability of default is characterised in the short term differ from the results produced when it is characterised in the long term. In other words, for each term the estimates of the coefficients $\beta_1, \ldots, \beta_n$ will be different.

---

[1] This is the standard likelihood function for binomial variables.

[2] For clarity in the expression, the LMV function has been written in its simplest form. When considering operations that begin and end at different times, which may or may not be within the sample period, the expression of the function is complicated.

In "Ejemplo Probit.xlsx" we have two examples. In sheet "Coin" we have a very simple example of calculating the probability of getting "C" in flipping a coin. In cell "C4" we have this probability whereas in cell "C5" we have the probability of getting "X" (the opposite one). We have flipped the coin ten times and in column "E" we have the results ("C" or "X"), whereas in column "F" we have the occurrence probability (cell "C4" in case of "C" and cell "C5" in case of "X"). Finally, in cell "I4" we have the whole sample occurrence probability (likelihood function).

Using Excel "Solver" function we can maximize "I4" (likelihood function) modifying "C4" (the probability). If we modify column E and, for example, we include a lot of "C"s, the probability of "C" will grow because we are looking for the parameter with which the occurrence has the maximum probability.

In sheet "Probit" we have created a scoring/rating system. We have four variables: age, marital status (a dummy variable which is 1 if married and 0 if single), employment status (a dummy variable which is 1 if employed and 0 if unemployed) and income. Consequently, we have five coefficients: β_0, β_1, β_2, β_3 and β_4. These coefficients are in cells "D2" through "D6".

We have ten borrowers whose characteristics are in rows 9 through 18; in columns "C" through "F" we have the variables; in column "G" we have the default status, which is the equivalent of column "E" in sheet "Coin"; and in column "H" we have the scoring, which, as noted earlier, is:

$$\text{Score}_i = \beta_1 x_1^i + \cdots + \beta_n x_n^i.$$

In column "I" we have the PD which, as stated before, is:

$$\text{PD} = \text{Prob}(\varepsilon > -\beta_1 x_1 - \cdots - \beta_n x_n) = 1 - N(-\beta_1 x_1 - \cdots - \beta_n x_n)$$

In column "J" we have the probability of occurrence of the event (default in some cases and non-default in others), which is equivalent to column "F" in "Coin" sheet. Finally, in cell "L11" we have the probability of occurrence of the event for the whole sample, in other words, the likelihood function. Again, using the Excel "Solver" function we can maximize cell "L11" (likelihood function) modifying cells "D2:D6" (beta coefficients).

As expected, we have coefficients that lead to a situation in which defaulted borrowers are the ones with higher default probabilities (see red cells), which is the main purpose of the exercise. Consequently, if default behaviour in my portfolio is similar to default behaviour in my construction sample, I can assign reliable default probabilities based on my scoring. If we modify borrowers' characteristics or default status, we will get different beta coefficients.

By construction, the more negative the score, the less likely the operation is to default. Of course, as noted above, the outcome of this process depends on the term, that is, the results produced when the probability of default is characterised in the short term differ from the results produced when it is characterised in the long term; that is, for each term estimates of the coefficients $\beta_1, \ldots, \beta_n$ will be different.

Based on this score, the operations can be distributed into homogeneous groups. These homogeneous groups are simply credit rating levels. It must also be noted that when operation features are more important in the transaction (warranty, term, amount, etc.), as in the case of mortgage loans, the credit worthiness is called "scoring", whereas when the most important characteristics are those of the borrower, as in the case of corporate loans, it is called credit "rating". Therefore, agencies which assess credit worthiness are called "credit rating agencies" since they assign credit ratings to companies, not to their specific operations.

Table 9.1 shows the long-term ratings classifications provided by rating agencies such as Moody's, Standard and Poor's, Fitch and others.

More specifically, for the investment grade the following is established:

- AAA: companies with better credit quality, reliability and stability.
- AA: companies with high credit quality and with a slightly higher risk than AAA.
- A: the economic situation can have a financial effect on companies with this rating.
- BBB: medium-sized companies with a satisfactory situation at present.

Table 9.1 Grades

Grade	Moody's	Standard & Poor's, Fitch	Meaning
Investment grade	Aaa	AAA	Maximum creditworthiness
	Aa1	AA+	Very high creditworthiness
	Aa2	AA	
	Aa3	AA−	
	A1	A+	High creditworthiness
	A2	A	
	A3	A−	
	Baa1	BBB+	Good creditworthiness
	Baa2	BBB	
	Baa3	BBB−	
Speculative grade	Ba1	BB+	Speculative
	Ba2	BB	
	Ba3	BB−	
	B1	B+	Highly speculative
	B2	B	
	B3	B−	
	Caa	CCC	High risk of default
	Ca	CC	
	C	C	
	D	D	Default

Data sources: https://www.moodys.com/ and https://www.standardandpoors.com; Author's own composition

While for the speculative grade, the following is established:

- BB: companies more likely to be affected by changes in the economy.
- B: companies whose financial situation varies considerably.
- CCC: companies which are currently vulnerable and dependent on favourable economic conditions to meet their commitments.
- CC: highly vulnerable companies.
- C: highly vulnerable companies which may be bankrupt or default on payments but continue to meet the obligations.

Similarly, credit rating agencies issue short-term ratings, as shown in Table 9.2.

It should also be noted that the objective of agencies when issuing a rating is for it to remain unchanged in the short term and to vary only

Table 9.2 Short-term ratings

Moody's	Fitch	Standard & Poor's	Meaning
Prime – 1	F1	A – 1	Maximum creditworthiness
Prime – 2	F2	A – 2	Good creditworthiness
Prime – 3	F3	A – 3	Adequate creditworthiness
	B	B	Speculative
	C	C	High default risk
	D	D	Default

Data sources: https://www.moodys.com/ and https://www.standardandpoors.com; Author's own composition

when there is reason to believe that there has been a change in the solvency of the company.

At this point it should be noted that the above works quite well for relatively large samples of transactions that have a significant probability of default. The problem arises in small samples or operations with little probability of default, as in the case of transactions with large companies. However, a possible solution is to simplify the calculation of the probability of default by assuming a transition matrix for rating migrations. Migration is a discrete process that involves changes in the rating from one period to another; thus, the transition matrix expresses the rating change probability conditional on the rating at the start of the period. It is generally assumed that the changes follow a Markov process, that is, the changes between states are independent from one period to the next.

For example, in Table 9.3 a simple transition matrix is shown for four states, where state D represents default.

Regarding the company in year 0 in category B, the company may default in year 1 with probability $P(D_1/B_0) = 3$ %. Calculating the probability of default in year 2 becomes difficult, since there are many ways in which default can occur: from year 0 to year 1 it may have been able to move from B to A and in year 2 from A to D, or having stayed in B from year 0 to 1 it may move from B to D from year 1 to 2 and so on. Therefore, the total probability is 0 $P(D_2/B_0) = P(D_2/A_1)^*P(A_1/B_0) + P(D_2/B_1)^*P(B_1/B_0) + P(D_2/C_1)^*P(C_1/B_0) = 0.00^*0.02 + 0.03^*0.93 + 0.23^*0.02 = 3.25$ %. Thus, the cumulative probability of default in two

Table 9.3 Rating transition probability matrix (Author's own composition)

Rating transition probability matrix					
	Final state				
Initial state	A	B	C	D	Total probability
A	0.97	0.03	0.00	0.00	1.00
B	0.02	0.93	0.02	0.03	1.00
C	0.01	0.12	0.64	0.23	1.00
D	0	0	0	1.00	1.00

years for a borrower with a "*B*" rating is 3 % + 3.25 % = 6.25 %. The same logic applies in subsequent years.

Consequently, when the sample is reduced or the probability of default is low, the information contained in the transition matrix can be used to estimate the probabilities of default reliably.

Banks' Regulatory Requirements for PD Calculation

Banks' regulatory requirements (the Basel Accords) for PD calculation can be based on credit rating methodology using internal models (IRB, or internal ratings based) and, specifically, in CRR (Article 180) it is established that "...institutions shall estimate PDs by obligor grade from long run averages of one-year default rates...". Consequently, it is clearly established that the period of time for calculating PDs is one year and that these PDs have to be "long-run" averages; in other words, these PDs should reflect the default probability not just for a particular year but for a long-term period average.

Therefore, even though the length of time to be considered is not specifically established, it is clear that it must include at least one complete business cycle. Moreover, there must be a balance between "good years" and "bad years" for it to be considered a "long-run" average.

A very common problem within the world financial system in 2005–2006 when Basel II and, consequently, internal models started to be applied was the fact that institutions didn't have default rates for "crisis times" and they had to estimate them based on macroeconomic data. In order to do that, one possibility is to incorporate macroeconomic variables

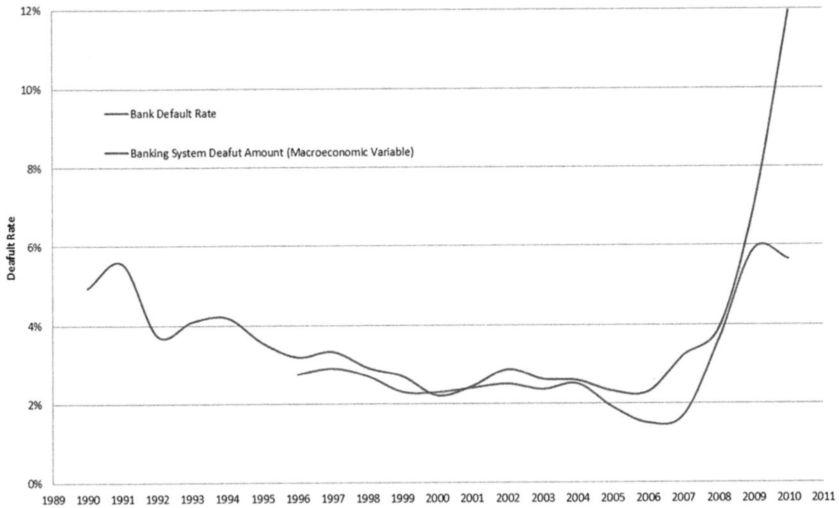

Fig. 9.1 Long-run PD (Author's own composition)

(GDP, banking system default amount, unemployment rate, etc.) in ratings/scorings; however, this is not a good idea because macroeconomic variables are correlated with the rest of the variables and have less predictive power than the rest, which leads to parameter estimation problems.

Consequently, the objective is to get rating levels as through-the-cycle as possible. In doing so, banks establish a relationship between default rates estimated during times in which there is data and a macroeconomic variable. Let's say, for example, that we have a portfolio of default rates and macroeconomic variables like those in Fig. 9.1.

This relationship allows default rates to be estimated in periods in which we have no database on the value of the macroeconomic variable during these periods. As stated above, since there are credit rating/scoring levels, we could establish a relationship between each rating/scoring level and the macroeconomic variable; however, as not all rating level default rates follow the same dynamics, it is not always possible to establish a clear relationship between rating level default rates and macroeconomic variables.

Consequently, the most common way of proceeding is to establish a relationship between the whole portfolio default rate (which is known as central tendency) and the macroeconomic variable. After establishing this relationship between central tendency and the macroeconomic variable, the effects can then be split among the rating levels. In doing so, Bayes' theorem is the most commonly used technique.

Broadly speaking, there are two basic sets of procedures to establish these relationships: procedures which establish linear relationships and procedures based on the Merton model. Procedures which establish linear relationships are the classic ones: linear regression (LSE, or least squares estimation), average ratios and the like.

Since the Merton model is the methodology used in Basel II, many institutions use procedures based on this. In the Merton model, for each scoring/rating level a y_h variable is defined. For example, if y_h is higher than zero, we have default. y_h is defined as:

$$y_h = \beta_0^* I_h + v_h + \varepsilon_h$$

where I_h is the average rating in this rating level, v_h is the systemic factor and ε_h is the error term.

It is assumed that the systemic factor can be defined as:

$$v_h = \beta_1^* x_1^* + \cdots + \beta_n^* x_n^* + w_h$$

where x's variables are macroeconomic variables and w_h is the error term.

Following a similar maximum likelihood procedure to the one used in the multinomial model calibration, we can estimate β coefficients.

Continuing with the previous example, based on linear relationships or the Merton model we can estimate default rates as shown in Fig. 9.2.

The average of the default rates from the data (blue line) from 1996 to 2010 is 2.86 %. However, taking into account estimates from 1990 to 1995 to include "bad years" in the sample as well (green line), the average is 2.94 %.

In Excel file "Ejemplo Ajuste a Ciclo" we have the above example using linear regressions. In sheets TC, cells from "M4" to "M5" we have the

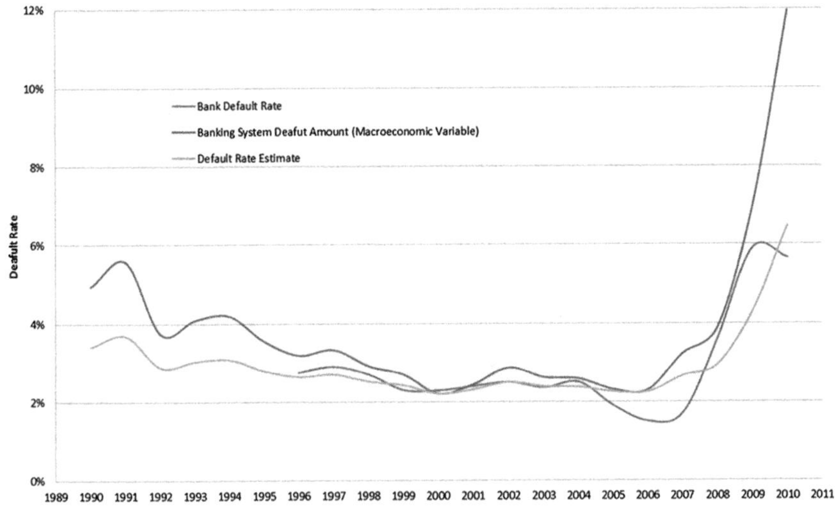

Fig. 9.2 Long-run PD (Author's own composition)

linear regression alpha and beta coefficients. To measure the goodness of fit we have in cell "P4" the R2 coefficient, in this case 77 %, which is not a bad goodness of fit.

Once we have the central tendency, as stated above, using Bayes' theorem or something equivalent, we can translate this change in central tendency level from 2.86 % to 2.94 % to each rating/scoring level. Bayes' theorem is stated mathematically as the following equation:

$$P(A \mid \mathrm{B}) = \frac{P(\mathrm{A})P(B \mid \mathrm{A})}{P(B)}$$

where A and B are events; $P(A)$ and $P(B)$ are the probabilities of A and B occurring independently of each other; $P(A \mid B)$, a conditional probability, is the probability of observing event A given that B is true; and $P(B \mid A)$ is the probability of observing event B given that A is true.

Applying Bayes' theorem to our problem we can see that:

$$P(\text{Default}/\text{Rating Bucket}_i) = \frac{P(\text{Default})P(\text{Rating Bucket}_i/\text{Default})}{P(\text{Rating Bucket}_i)}$$

In the above formula, $P(\text{Default}/\text{Rating Bucket}_i)$ is what we want to calculate, which is the PD for each rating bucket, $P(\text{Default})$ is the central tendency PD calculated before, $P(\text{Rating Bucket}_i/\text{Default})$ is the percentage of defaults in each bucket in the construction sample, and $P(\text{Rating Bucket}_i)$ is the probability in each bucket, which is:

$$\begin{aligned} P(\text{Rating Bucket}_i) = {} & P(\text{Default})P(\text{Rating Bucket}_i/\text{Default}) \\ & + P(\text{Non} - \text{Default})P(\text{Rating Bucket}_i/\text{Non} - \text{Default}) \end{aligned}$$

Consequently:

$$P(\text{Default}/\text{Rating Bucket}_i) = \frac{P(\text{Default})P(\text{Rating Bucket}_i/\text{Default})}{P(\text{Default})P(\text{Rating Bucket}_i/\text{Default}) + P(\text{Non}-\text{Default})P(\text{Rating Bucket}_i/\text{Non}-\text{Default})}$$

In sheet Bayes in Excel file "Ejemplo Ajuste a Ciclo" we have an example of this. As can be seen, each bucket PD (*P*(Default/RatingBucketi)) is not the same as each bucket default rate because the portfolio PD must be the long-run average PD.

Once we have defined the buckets, regulations obligate banks to prove that this process provides a significant differentiation of risk and, as result, provides buckets which are sufficiently homogeneous. In order to do that, the most used methodology is the one which proposes the following statistical test:

$$\begin{aligned} H_0 &: p_1 - p_2 = \Delta \\ H_1 &: p_1 - p_2 > \Delta \end{aligned}$$

In this case Δ is 0, p_1 is the ratio between bad loans and the total in rating level t_1, and p_2 is the ratio between bad loans and the total in rating level t_2. We can also define q_1 as the ratio between good loans and the total in rating level t_1 $(= 1 - p_1)$ and q_2 as the ratio between good loans and the total in bucket t_2 $(= 1 - p_2)$.

The statistical test which tells us if there are significant differences between default rates in buckets t_1 and t_2 is:

$$\frac{(\widehat{p_1} - \widehat{p_2}) - \Delta}{\sqrt{\frac{\widehat{p_1}\widehat{q_1}}{n_1} + \frac{\widehat{p_2}\widehat{q_2}}{n_2}}} = Z_{\text{exp}} \cong N(0,1)$$

The numerator is the average of the difference between the default rates in both buckets, whereas the denominator is the variance. In other words, the statistical test says that if the average of the difference, divided by its variance, is high enough, we can say that default rates in both rating classes are different and, consequently, we can provide a significant differentiation of risk.

With the former statistical test we reject the null hypothesis H_0 if $Z_{\text{exp}} > z_{1\_\alpha}$. In the case of $N(0,1)$, if $\alpha = 5\ \%$ then $z_{95\%} = 1.65$. As stated above, the statistical test applied to two consecutive rating classes, at a 95 % confidence level, tells us whether the default probability of these two rating classes is different.

9.2.1.2 Estimates from Bond Prices

The estimate of the probability of default established in the previous section is based on historical data and therefore is not without its limitations, mainly the fact that the future probability of default does not necessarily coincide with the historical probability observed. The alternative to solve this problem is to use models based on market prices which allow more accurate and up-to-date measurements, since financial markets have access to a large amount of information. Default rates can be obtained from the market prices of securities affected by default, such as corporate bonds and stocks. Each of these alternatives will be studied both in this section and in the next.

As mentioned in previous chapters, the fact that corporate bonds present default risk causes the interest rate on these bonds to exceed that of government bonds which have traditionally been viewed as risk-free bonds, implying that a corporate bond has a yield (r^*) greater than a risk-free bond (r). Therefore, the probability of default of a company can be estimated from the bond prices issued. In order to do so, it must be initially assumed that the only reason to sell a bond at a lower price than a bond which is similar but risk-free is the possibility of default, which is a very reasonable assumption in markets with sufficient liquidity. However, if the corporate bond market is not very liquid, this assumption is not very reasonable and, as a result, this method of estimation will not be very reliable.

In order to demonstrate that the probability of default can be obtained from the bond price, consider the example of a bond which makes a single payment of \$100 within a period of time. As discussed in previous chapters, the market return r^* can be obtained from the market price P^* as follows: $P^* = \frac{100\$}{(1+r^*)}$. Moreover, bond payments can be defined by a simple default process, as shown in the following graph:

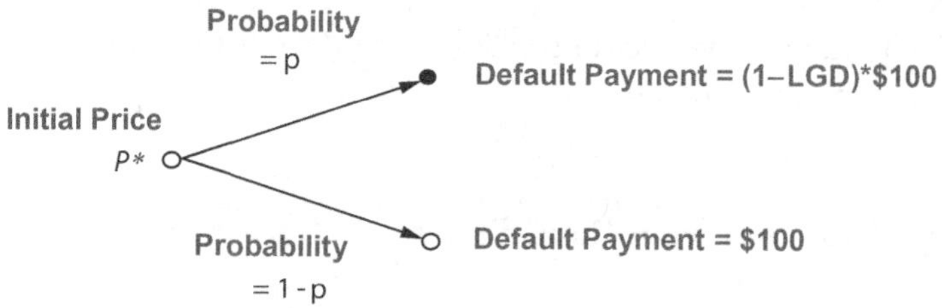

Where 1 − LGD is the rate of recovery. Defining "PD" as the probability of default over the period, assuming risk neutrality, the bond price must be the mathematical expectation of the values in the two states discounted at the risk-free rate. Hence:

$$P^* = \frac{100\$}{(1+r^*)} = \left[\frac{100\$}{(1+r)}\right]*(1-\text{PD}) + \left[\frac{(1-\text{LGD})*100\$}{(1+r)}\right]*\text{PD}$$

Thus, there is clear evidence that: $(1+r) = (1+r^*)(1 - \text{PD} * \text{LGD})$ and therefore: $\text{PD} = \frac{1}{\text{LGD}}\left[1 - \frac{(1+r)}{(1+r^*)}\right]$. Simplifying this expression by removing the second order terms, the following is obtained: $r^* \approx r + \text{PD} * \text{LGD}$, an equation which demonstrates that the credit spread, that is, $r^* - r$, is equal to the PD multiplied by the expected loss after the default, that is, the severity (LGD).

This result can be generalised by relaxing the assumption of a single period and payment date. Maintaining a single payment date but introducing multiple periods, the above expression becomes: $P* = \frac{100\$}{(1+r*)^T} = \left[\frac{100\$}{(1+r)^T}\right] * (1 - \text{PD})^T + \left[\frac{(1-\text{LGD}) * 100\$}{(1+r)^T}\right] * \left[1 - (1 - \text{PD})^T\right]$, which can be rewritten as $(1 + r)^T = (1 + r^*)^T\{(1 - \text{PD})^T + (1 - \text{LGD})[1 - (1 - \text{PD})^T]\}$, an expression which can be used to obtain the probability of default.

When there are multiple maturities, they can be used to calculate default probabilities at different horizons and in doing so, a structure of default probabilities is obtained from zero-coupon bonds. When coupon bonds are used, the calculation is more complex but its fundamentals are the same as those explained here. For example, suppose a corporate bond has an approximate yield of 200 basis points (2 %) over the same risk-free bond and the expected recovery rate is 40 %. Then, the owner of the bond expects to lose 200 basis points per year in case of default and, as a consequence, given the recovery rate, this implies that an estimate of the conditional annual default rate (h) where there has not been a prior default is $h = \frac{\text{spread}}{\text{LGD}} = \frac{0.02}{1-0.4} = 3.33\%$.

Extending the calculation to a bond that pays a periodic coupon, the probability of default can be obtained by calculating the value of the expected loss today depending on the rate of default. In order to do this, assume that the corporate bond in question lasts five years and pays a coupon of 6 % per annum, payable semi-annually, and has a continuous internal rate of return (IRR) of 7 % per annum. Since the spread is 200 basis points, a similar risk-free bond has a IRR of 5 % per annum. These returns imply that bond prices are \$95.34 for the corporate bond and \$104.09 for the risk-free bond.[3] Hence, the difference between the price of the risk-free bond and the corporate bond over the five years is \$104.09 − \$95.34 = \$8.75.

Assuming that the annual probability of default is constant (PD); that default can only occur just before the following dates: 0.5, 1.5, 2.5, 3.5 and 4.5 years; that the nominal of the bond is \$100; that in all periods in case of default the amount recovered is \$40; and that the risk-free rate for

[3] Since both bonds have similar characteristics, except for profitability, the price of the bond today is calculated by discounting (continuously) payments during the five years (taking into account that the coupon is paid semi-annually, \$3 twice per year) to the corresponding returns rate for each bond (5 % for the risk-free bond and 7 % for the corporate bond).

Table 9.4 Expected loss of default (Author's own composition)

Year	Probability of default	Amount recovered ($)	Risk-free amount ($)	Loss ($)	Discount factor	Present value of the expected loss ($)
0.5	PD	40	106.73	66.73	0.9753	65.08*PD
1.5	PD	40	105.97	65.97	0.9277	61.20*PD
2.5	PD	40	105.17	65.17	0.8825	57.52*PD
3.5	PD	40	104.34	64.34	0.8395	54.01*PD
4.5	PD	40	103.46	63.46	0.7985	50.67*PD
Total						288.48*PD

all maturities is 5 %, the expected loss of default can be calculated in terms of PD, as shown in Table 9.4.

In order to calculate what in the table is called risk-free value, the coupons remaining to maturity are discounted. They are $3 coupons paid twice a year (6 % per year) and in the last year the nominal value is also taken into account: $100 plus $3 of the coupon. The loss is simply the risk-free value minus the amount recovered, while what is called the present value of the expected loss is the loss multiplied by the discount factor, a factor which, providing they are continuous yields, is the number e raised to the risk-free yield multiplied by the time.

Equating the value obtained from the expected loss ($ 288.48*PD) to the differential value between the price of the corporate bond and the risk-free bond as previously calculated ($8.75), the annual probability of default is calculated to be $Q = 3.03$ %. The calculation assumes that the probability of default is the same every year and that default can only occur twice a year, but the analysis can be extended to cases where default can occur more frequently.

Before concluding this section it should be noted that the probabilities of default obtained from the price of corporate bonds as just studied are probabilities with risk neutrality, that is, they assume that investors are neutral to risk, while the probabilities obtained from historical data in the previous section are real probabilities. In other words, in the methodology proposed in this section it is assumed that investors are risk neutral, which is not always true, and as a result probabilities obtained in this way may differ somewhat from those obtained from historical data. Similarly, the results obtained with these approaches may differ for other reasons, such as the fact that corporate bonds are less liquid than government bonds, which are considered to be risk-free, and investors require extra compensation.

9.2.1.3 Estimates from Share Prices and Volatility

The approach based on bond prices is useful when there is an adequate sample of data. However, this rarely happens because many countries do not have developed corporate bond markets and, therefore, these bonds are not very liquid. In addition, many companies do not have outstanding bonds listed publicly. As a result, it is sometimes convenient to use share prices as the basis for default models, since they are available for a large number of companies and tend to be more liquid than bond prices.

In 1974, Merton proposed a model where the value of the company's shares is an option on the company's assets. For simplicity, imagine that the company has a zero-coupon bond that matures at "T", where V_0 is the value of the company's assets, tangible and intangible, today and V_T is the value of these assets at a future date "T". Equally, E_0 and E_T represent the value of the company's shares today and at time "T", while D denotes the value of the debt to be paid at "T". Finally, σ_V and σ_E are the volatility of the assets and shares respectively.

If $V_T < D$, in theory, the company will declare bankruptcy at T and the value of the shares will be zero. If, instead, $V_T > D$, the company must pay the debt at T, and therefore the value of the shares at maturity will be $V_T - D$. Thus, the Merton model defines the value of the shares at the time of maturity as $E_T = \max(V_T - D, 0)$, an equation which demonstrates that the value of the company's shares is a call option on the value of the assets with a strike price equal to the debt replacement value. Applying the Black–Scholes option pricing formula, the value of the shares today can be expressed as $E_0 = V_0 N(d_1) - De^{-rT} N(d_2)$, where N(d) is the cumulative distribution function for the normal distribution $d_1 = \frac{\ln\left(V_0/D\right) + \left(r + \sigma_v^2/2\right)T}{\sigma_v\sqrt{T}}$ and $d_2 - d_1 - \sigma_V\sqrt{T}$. As is to be expected, the value of the debt today is $V_0 - E_0$. Although beyond the scope of this book, following the Black–Scholes

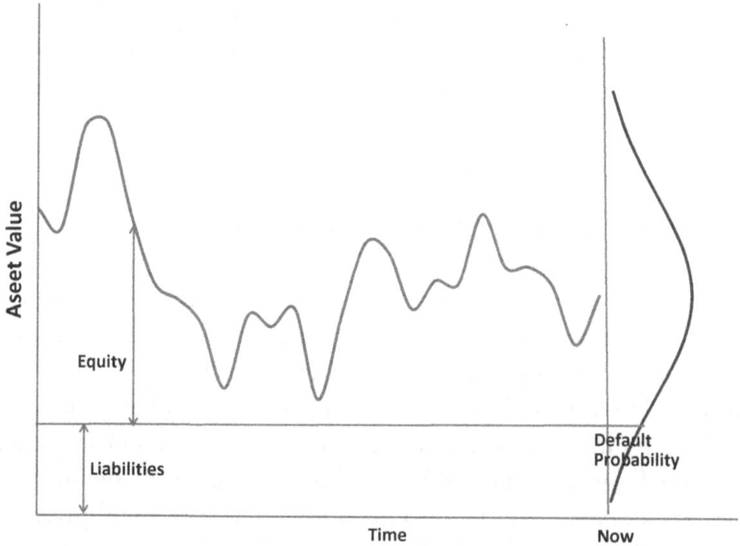

Fig. 9.3 Asset value (Author's own composition)

logic, it is not very difficult to prove that the risk-neutral probability of the company defaulting is $N(-d_2)$, that is, PD $= N(-d_2)$.

Thus, with the procedure outlined above, it seems easier to estimate the probability of default; however, in order to perform this calculation V_0 and σ_V must be known, but they are not directly observable. However, if the company is listed in the stock market, E_0 can be observed in each period and therefore σ_E can also be estimated. Similarly, using a result from the stochastic calculation it can be demonstrated that $\sigma_E E_0 = \frac{\partial E}{\partial V}\sigma_v V_0$, or equivalently $\sigma_E E_0 = N(d_1)\sigma_v V_0$ and, with the latter equation and the Black–Scholes equation,[4] the values of V_0 and σ_V can be found from E_0 and σ_E. The explanations above are summarised in Fig. 9.3.

[4] To solve non-linear equations with the form $F(X,Y) = 0$ *y* $G(X,Y) = 0$, the "Solver" function can be used in Excel to find the values of X and Y which minimise $[F(X,Y)^2 + G(X,Y)^2]$.

However, in practice the default is much more complex than the graph indicates and can even occur at an intermediate stage of the target date. For this reason, the distance-to-default measurement, which is simply the number of standard deviations in which the price of the asset must change to reach default in T years and is calculated from the expression $\frac{\ln(V_0)-\ln(D)+\left(r-\sigma_v^2/2\right)T}{\sigma_v\sqrt{T}}$, has been developed to describe the output of the Merton model.

This Merton approach has several advantages: the first is that, as mentioned, it uses share prices rather than bond prices. It also takes into account the fact that the correlation in share prices may generate correlations in the default rate, making them much easier to measure than in other circumstances. The main disadvantage is that they cannot be used to assess sovereign credit risk, since governments have no share price, which is a problem for credit derivatives where most of the market depends on government risks. Additionally, assuming a capital structure and constant business risk, it is too restrictive and it cannot be forgotten that, as in the case of bond prices, probabilities obtained in this way are risk neutral.

9.2.2 Loss Given Default (LGD)

Credit risk is associated with the possibility of the borrower failing to meet their obligations, thus causing a loss for the lender. It is for this reason that the probability of default was studied in the previous section: it is a measure of the possibility of the credit event, that is, default, occurring. However, this is not the only variable required to measure credit risk, as the loss is not always the same whenever default occurs but will be higher or lower depending on various factors, such as the borrower rating, the degree of debt subordination, the warranty, the business cycle and so on. This is the concept to be studied in this section: the loss given default, LGD, also known as severity. As is evident, the recovery or recovery rate on a defaulted loan is the opposite of the LGD, that is: recovery rate = 100 % − LGD.

The formal definition of the LGD is the loss that occurs on a taxable instrument subject to credit risk once the default has occurred. As has just been noted, the LGD is specific to each instrument as it is influenced by several factors:

- **Type of borrower**: individuals are accountable for their debts with all their assets, while firms have limited liability, that is, neither the directors nor the shareholders of the firm respond to the debts of the company with their assets. For this reason, when an individual defaults on a credit event, the subsequent treatment and management of this arrears process is different from when a corporation defaults and thus, while all other characteristics remain identical, the LGD of an individual is different from that of a company.
- **Guarantees**: in certain loans, in order to reduce the probability of default and also to ensure that if the loan defaults the recovery rate is higher, a collateral or guarantee is introduced so that in the event of default it can be executed by the lender. In this sense, the ideal scenario is for this collateral to have the lowest possible relation to the credit in question, and thus its value will not be lower than it was at the time when the contract was signed if default occurs at a later period. Obviously, the mere existence of the guarantee implies a lower LGD, and the higher the value of this collateral and the less associated it is with credit, the more effective it is and, consequently, the lower the LGD will be.
- **Degree of debt subordination**: when a borrower issues debt, this may be issued in various forms, that is, a borrower may have a debt with a lender in which there is collateral and another debt with another lender in which there is no collateral. Similarly, the degree of debt subordination can be established. For example, the lender may offer favourable terms, if the borrower issues debt for the first time and agrees that if they issue new debt, in the event of default, this new debt must be paid off after the first has been satisfied; thus, in these cases, an order of priority or degree of debt subordination is established. This is very common in cases where the borrower is a firm. The standard categories of this order of priority are: "Senior Secured", "Senior Unsecured", "Senior Subordinated", "Subordinated" and "Junior Subordinated", where "Senior Secured" is the degree of subordination to receive payments first and "Junior Subordinated" is the degree of

subordination that is paid last. As is evident, the higher the degree of subordination, the greater the LGD will be and, therefore, the lower the recovery rate will be.

- **Time of business cycle:** as is well known, both the payment capacity of the borrower and the value of the collateral vary with the business cycle; therefore, when all other factors remain the same, the LGD will be higher in times of crisis than in times of economic prosperity.

When calculating the LGD, different criteria can be used. The most popular is known as "Gross LGD" in which the total losses incurred are divided by the EAD. When there is collateral, another possibility is to divide the losses by the portion of the EAD not hedged by the warranty, that is, by EAD – "Collateral Values", a criterion known as "Blanco LGD" which, as is evident, coincides with the Gross LGD in cases where there are no guarantees.

In any case, whichever criterion is used, the procedure followed to calculate the losses suffered and to establish the EAD must be clearly stated. The next section will deal with establishing the EAD, while this section will briefly discuss the criteria used to determine what is meant by loss. When defining loss (or recovery, which is the opposite) the first factor that should be considered is that of the discount, since default occurs on one date and recovery occurs on multiple future dates; thus, the amount recovered must be deducted from the time, or times, when it occurs until the date of default. Another consideration is the relative value of the guarantee if it is kept by the lender, that is, in cases where there is a default on a loan with collateral as a guarantee and this guarantee can be executed by the lender making them the owner of the collateral, a value must be assigned to this collateral to calculate the loss. The problem lies in assigning a value to this collateral when it is illiquid; moreover, in some cases such as housing which serves as collateral for mortgage loans, the collateral can be considered to have a market price in times of prosperity, while in times of crisis more defaults occur, and therefore when the lender acquires more properties, market liquidity evaporates. Thus it is extremely difficult to assign a market value to this collateral and obtain a reliable estimate of the LGD.

Another important consideration in LGD calculation is the definition of recovery cycles. When doing this, concepts such as cure rates and recurrence have critical importance. Finally, in calculating LGD the lost delay interest and administration costs must be taken into account and, in some cases, can represent a considerable amount of money.

In the case of cure rates and recovery cycles, PD and LGD calculations should be coherent. In this respect, if in PD calculation we consider that we need one year to regard a loan as cured, and consequently we acknowledge the same default if one loan defaulted twice in a year, we should consider the same LGD recovery cycle if one loan defaulted twice in a year. In other words, if due to the cure rates definition we increase (reduce) PD, LGD will go down (up).

9.2.2.1 Banks' Regulatory Requirements for LGD Calculation

Banks' regulatory requirements for LGD calculation can be based on internal models (IRB). Under the foundation approach (F-IRB), Basel Accords, fixed LGD ratios are prescribed for certain classes of unsecured exposures: senior claims on corporates, sovereigns and banks not secured by recognised collateral attract a 45 % LGD, whereas all subordinated claims on corporates, sovereigns and banks attract a 75 % LGD.

The effective loss given default (LGD*) applicable to a collateralised transaction can be expressed as:

$$LGD^* = LGD\frac{*}{E}$$

Under the advance approach (A-IRB) and for the retail portfolio under the foundation approach (F-IRB), the bank itself determines the appropriate loss given default to be applied to each exposure, on the basis of robust data and analysis. Thus, as stated above, a bank using internal LGD estimates for capital purposes might be able to differentiate LGD values on the basis of a wider set of transaction characteristics (e.g., product type, wider range of collateral types, loan-to-value, etc.) as well as borrower characteristics. Moreover, a bank wishing to use its own estimates of LGD will need to demonstrate to a supervisor that it can meet minimum requirements pertinent to the integrity and reliability of these estimates.

Basel Accords establishes that banks and other financial institutions are recommended to calculate "downturn LGD" (downturn loss given default), which it is defined as the loss occurring during a "downturn" in a business cycle for regulatory purposes.

The calculation of LGD (or Downturn LGD) poses significant challenges to modellers and practitioners. Final resolutions of defaults can take many years and final losses, and hence final LGD, cannot be calculated until all of this information is available. The most problematic issues in defining downturn conditions are, as stated above, the collateral value determination and risk premium calculation (discount rate).

In determining the collateral value in mortgage loans we must take into account housing price evolution in an economic area and use this information to make conservative assumptions. In the case of the discount rate, we should start from the risk-free rate and then country risk premium and portfolio risk premium should be added. In the eurozone the risk-free rate is the German bond with maturity closer to that of the defaulted loans in the portfolio. The country risk premium is the difference between the risk-free rate and each country bond, whereas the portfolio risk premium is the difference between the country bond interest rate and the interest rate associated with portfolio risk.

Current regulation also recommends that banks calculate LGD work-out and long-run LGD. LGD work-out is the realised LGD for a particular year/portfolio, whereas the Long-run LGD concept is similar to the PD long-run average; it is a long-run average LGD for a complete business cycle. Although banks calculate LGD work-out and Long-run LGD, as we will discuss later, they are not used in minimum capital requirement calculations.

The last LGD concept that will be dealt with here is the best estimate LGD (BELGD), which is the LGD for defaulted assets. It is well known that the longer the default period, the higher the LGD, and consequently the two main drivers in calculating the BELGD are the amount of time that the loan has been in default and the amount of money already recovered. Accordingly, based on the past default history, it is common to calculate a BELGD for each combination of time in default and money already recovered.

Moreover, since we need to calculate expected losses and capital requirements, in some cases two BELGDs are needed: the BELGD and the downturn BELGD. As before, in the case of Downturn BELGD calculations the idea is to put more stress on collateral value and discount rates. However, from a theoretical point of view, there is one main difference between defaulted and non-defaulted assets in this respect: non-defaulted assets should have a low expected loss (provisions) and a higher unexpected loss (capital requirements) because they are performing, whereas defaulted assets should have a high expected loss (provisions) and a much lower unexpected loss (capital requirements) since they are non-performing.

Finally, we will discuss how LGD for mortgage loans is calculated. In the case of a defaulted mortgage loan, the recovery cycle can finish in two very different ways: non-confiscation (friendly end) and confiscation. In the first case, the borrower receives money to continue repaying the mortgage loan, whereas in the second case the bank confiscates the collateral. The LGD in each of these two cases is very different: while in the first case the LGD is close to zero, in the second case the LGD is significantly relevant. Consequently, the standard method for calculating LGD for mortgage loans is by calculating: LGD in case of "non-confiscation"" (LGD^{NC}), LGD in case of "confiscation" (LGD^{C}) and "confiscation" probability (P^{C}). These three factors can be used in the following calculation:

$$\mathrm{LGD} = P^C * \mathrm{LGD}^C + \left(1 - P^C\right) * \mathrm{LGD}^{\mathrm{NC}}$$

Moreover, in the case of LGD for mortgage loans, loan-to-value (LTV) is a crucial driver and an LGD must be calculated for each LTV bucket. In other words, the three factors must be calculated (LGD in case of "non-confiscation", LGD in case of "confiscation" and "confiscation" probability) for each LTV bucket.

9.2.3 Exposure at Default (EAD)

After studying the PD and LGD, the only concept that remains to be analysed in order to measure credit risk is the exposure at default (EAD), an exposure which is very easy to measure in normal loans, as it is simply the difference between the amount that the creditor lent initially minus the amount paid by the borrower before default. However, there are types of loans in which this does not occur: if additional quantities are available to the borrower at the expense of the lender after credit is granted, these loans are known as revolving loans.

In these revolving loans, such as credit accounts or credit cards, as long as the borrower meets certain fairly standard conditions, such as not having defaulted on any loan and not exceeding a limit, additional funds up to a certain limit may be available without having to apply for approval. Therefore, the amount currently available to the borrower is usually less than the amount available at the time of default. Therefore, in these cases, based on the amount currently available, the further provisions that will be available at the time of default must be estimated in some way, if it occurs.

This can be estimated in many ways but the most common is through the so-called CCF (or credit conversion factor), defined as the available portion, that is, the portion below the limit not currently available, which is estimated to be available until the time of default. Once the CCF has been estimated, the EAD = Current Exposure + CCF*Limit not currently available, so CCF = [EAD – Current Exposure]/Limit not currently available = [EAD – Current Exposure]/[Limit – Current Exposure].

Another possibility, especially helpful in a portfolio with a low limit which is not currently available, is the K-factor, defined as the portion, that is, the portion below the total limit, which is estimated to be available until the time of default. In this case, once the K-factor has been estimated, the EAD = K*Limit.

As in the case of the PD and the LGD, the EAD, or the CCF, is different at certain times of the business cycle. It is higher in times of crisis than in times of prosperity and, for this reason, these parameters can be estimated in different scenarios which will lead to different estimates of loss, as will be discussed in the next section.

9.2.3.1 Banks' Regulatory Requirements for EAD Calculation

The calculation of EAD is different when using the foundation and advanced approach. While in the foundation approach (F-IRB) the calculation of EAD is guided by the regulators, in the advanced approach (A-IRB) banks enjoy greater flexibility in how they calculate EAD.

Under F-IRB EAD is calculated taking account of the underlying asset, forward valuation, facility type and commitment details. This value does not reflect guarantees, collateral or security (i.e., it ignores credit risk mitigation techniques, with the exception of on-balance sheet netting where the effect of netting is included in EAD). For on-balance sheet transactions, EAD is identical to the nominal amount of exposure. On-balance sheet netting of loans and deposits from a bank to a corporate counterparty is permitted to reduce the estimate of EAD under certain conditions. For off-balance sheet items, there are two broad types which the IRB approach needs to address: transactions with uncertain future drawdown, such as commitments and revolving credits, and over-the-counter (OTC) foreign exchange, interest rate and equity derivative contracts.

Under A-IRB, the bank itself determines how the appropriate EAD is to be applied to each exposure. A bank using internal EAD estimates for capital purposes might be able to differentiate EAD values on the basis of a wider set of transaction characteristics (e.g., product type) as well as borrower characteristics. These values would be expected to represent a conservative view of long-run averages, although banks would be free to use more conservative estimates.

EAD is the only parameter which the bank can influence in advance by predefining limits on credit approvals for certain PD/LGD combinations. In active agreements, the bank can also impose limits by agreeing on additional covenants.

9.3 Expected Loss Versus Unexpected Loss

Once PD, LGD and EAD, or CCF which is the same, are known, it is very easy to calculate the loss which, on average, is expected to be obtained through the credit risk for a loan, by simply multiplying the parameters: Loss = PD*LGD*EAD.

The problem lies in the fact that these parameters are unknown, must be estimated, and also vary in time depending on various factors such as the business cycle; therefore, when estimating the future loss due to credit risk which, on average, will be obtained with a loan or with a portfolio of homogeneous loans, the question that immediately arises is: in what scenario? That is, if a loan or portfolio of homogeneous loans is available today and the aim is to estimate its possible future loss, the predicted future scenario must first be established.

In this sense, if the aim is to measure the average loss in a mid-range scenario, a scenario which is not anticipated as being either good or bad, using historical data which covers different times of the business cycle would be sufficient, while if the aim is to measure the average loss in an adverse scenario, data from adverse moments of the cycle must be used and, in addition, as noted in the case of the LGD, special care should be taken in choosing discount rates. Obviously, they cannot all be risk-free rates, but instead they must be increased with a risk premium. Similarly, when considering the value of awarded collateral, special care must be taken to assign a value that reflects its possible value in times of crisis, when there are no reliable market prices due to a lack of liquidity.

Similarly, in the credit risk environment, especially in the field of banking regulation, the concepts of expected loss and unexpected loss are defined. The concept of expected loss corresponds to an average loss that can be expected at a given time and is therefore different depending on where it is in the cycle, but given a point in the business cycle, what is expected to be lost is the definition of loss (loss = PD * LGD * EAD) calculating the parameters according to the circumstances of the business cycle they are in. The unexpected loss can also be defined for a given

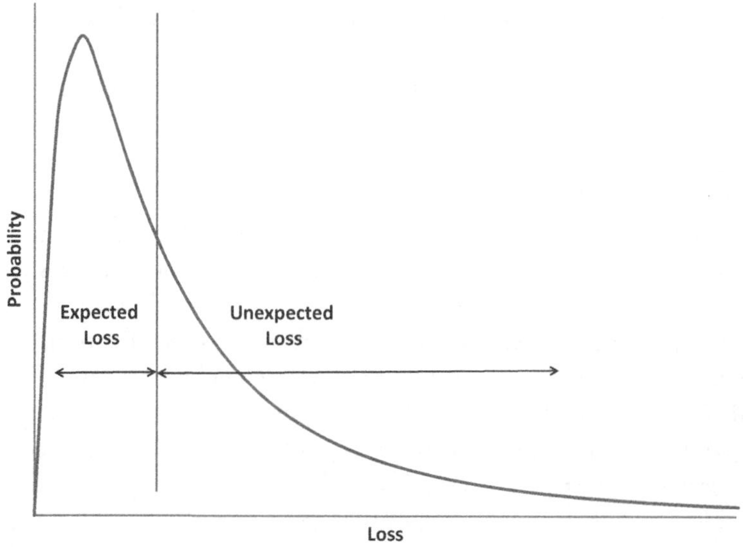

Fig. 9.4 Probability (Author's own composition)

point in the business cycle as the loss that will occur if the economic environment suddenly becomes much more adverse than reasonably expected, that is, the concept of unexpected loss in the credit risk environment corresponds to the concept of value at risk (VaR) for market risk. In other words, given an economic environment for a loan or portfolio of loans, the expected loss can be estimated by estimating the parameters in conditions that reflect the economic environment, but the unexpected loss can also be defined as the loss in a situation where a stress is added to the current situation, which implies that the losses must be greater, as shown in Fig. 9.4.

As shown in Fig. 9.4, the probability of the unexpected loss occurring is far less than the expected loss. In the same way, the unexpected loss can be estimated from the expected loss by simply stressing the calculation of the parameters (PD, LGD and EAD).

10

Credit Risk: Validation

10.1 Basic Concepts

Chapter 9 discussed the most common techniques used to measure credit risk. This chapter will introduce the validation procedures which should be used to establish whether or not the credit risk measurement is reliable.

The term validation is defined in the context of credit risk as follows: once a scoring/rating system and/or mathematical/statistical models for parameter (probability of default (PD), loss given default (LGD) and exposure at default (EAD)) calculation have been developed, validation should include monitoring of model performance and stability; review of model relationships; and testing of model outputs against outcomes.

Quantitative validation fulfils all validation procedures in which statistical indicators are calculated and interpreted on the basis of an observed data set. In contrast, qualitative validation comprises the primary task of ensuring applicability and the correct application of the quantitative methods in practice. These two aspects of validation complement each other.

F.J. Población García, *Financial Risk Management*,
DOI 10.1007/978-3-319-41366-2_10

10.2 Qualitative Validation

Qualitative validation is mostly focused on qualitative model design and data quality analysis. Qualitative model design refers to the qualitative applicability of the model to the purpose for which it is applied. In statistical models, data quality stands out as a goodness-of-fit criterion even during model development. Moreover, a comprehensive data set is an essential prerequisite for quantitative validation.

In this context, a number of aspects must be considered: Data sources, data available, completeness of the data set, representativeness of the sample, data cleanse and so on.

10.3 Quantitative Validation

10.3.1 Discriminatory Power

10.3.1.1 Rating/Scoring Systems: Probability of Default (PD)

The term "discriminatory power" refers to the capacity of a scoring/rating model to differentiate between good and bad cases. In this context, the categories good and bad refer to whether a credit default occurs (bad) or does not occur (good) over the forecasting horizon after the scoring/rating system has classified the case.

An example of a rating model with 12 classes is presented here; however, the procedures can also be applied to any other scale, even to individual score values. At the same time, it is necessary to note that statistical fluctuations predominate in a small number of cases per class observed, and thus it may not be possible to generate meaningful results (Table 10.1, Fig. 10.1).

In the example shown in Table 10.1 and Fig. 10.1, the default rate (i.e., the proportion of bad cases) for each rating class increases progressively from class 1 to class 10, therefore the underlying rating system is able to classify

Table 10.1 Rating class comparison (Author's own composition)

Rating class	Number good cases	Number of defaults	Total	Proportion of cases per rating class	Default per rating class
1	35	0	35	0.2%	0.0%
2	546	1	547	2.7%	0.2%
3	1102	4	1106	5.4%	0.4%
4	1985	12	1997	9.8%	0.6%
5	2158	24	2182	10.7%	1.1%
6	4589	64	4653	22.9%	1.4%
7	3567	74	3641	17.9%	2.0%
8	2552	71	2623	12.9%	2.7%
9	1598	55	1653	8.1%	3.3%
10	1037	48	1085	5.3%	4.4%
11	436	37	473	2.3%	7.8%
12	325	42	367	1.8%	11.4%
All classes	19,930	432	20,362	100.0%	2.1%

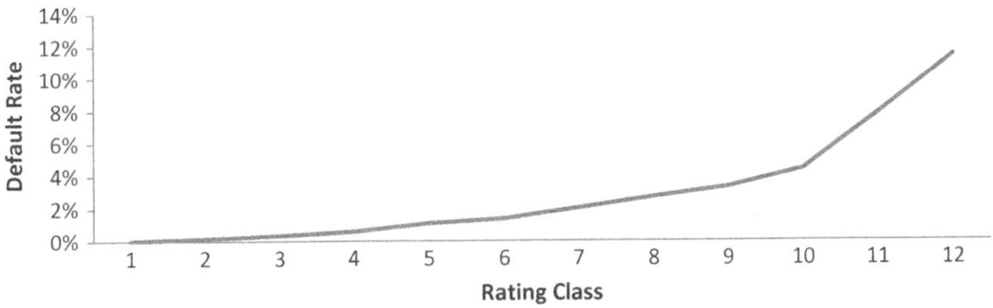

Fig. 10.1 Default per rating class (Author's own composition)

cases by default probability. Nevertheless, let's describe the methods and indicators used to quantify the discriminatory power of rating models.

The density functions and the cumulative frequencies of good cases and defaults shown in Table 10.2 and Figs. 10.2 and 10.3 serve as the starting point for calculating discriminatory power.

The density functions show a considerable difference between good cases and defaults. The cumulative frequencies show that approximately 70 % of the good cases, but only 40 % of the defaults, belong to rating classes 1 to 7. On the other hand, 30 % of the defaults but only 9 % of the

Table 10.2 Rating class comparison (Author's own composition)

Rating class	Density function for good cases	Density function for defaults	Cumulative frequency good cases (%)	Cumulative frequency defaults (%)	Cumulative frequency total (%)
1	0.2%	0.0%	0.2%	0.0%	0.2%
2	2.7%	0.2%	2.9%	0.2%	2.9%
3	5.5%	0.9%	8.4%	1.2%	8.3%
4	10.0%	2.8%	18.4%	3.9%	18.1%
5	10.8%	5.6%	29.2%	9.5%	28.8%
6	23.0%	14.8%	52.3%	24.3%	51.7%
7	17.9%	17.1%	70.2%	41.4%	69.5%
8	12.8%	16.4%	83.0%	57.9%	82.4%
9	8.0%	12.7%	91.0%	70.6%	90.5%
10	5.2%	11.1%	96.2%	81.7%	95.9%
11	2.2%	8.6%	98.4%	90.3%	98.2%
12	1.6%	9.7%	100.0%	100.0%	100.0%
All classes	100.0%	100.0%			

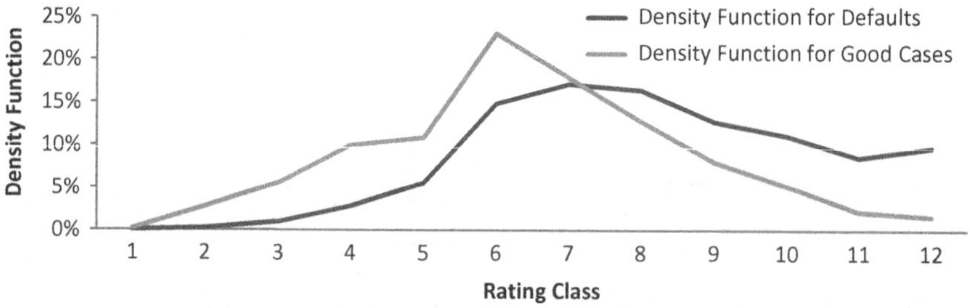

Fig. 10.2 Density functions (Author's own composition)

good cases can be found in classes 9 to 12. Here it is clear that the cumulative probability of defaults is greater than that of the good cases for almost all rating classes when the classes are arranged in order from bad to good.

α and β errors can be defined based on density functions, while credit approval can be based on scoring/rating classes. If the scoring/rating class is lower than a predefined cut-off value, the credit application is rejected,

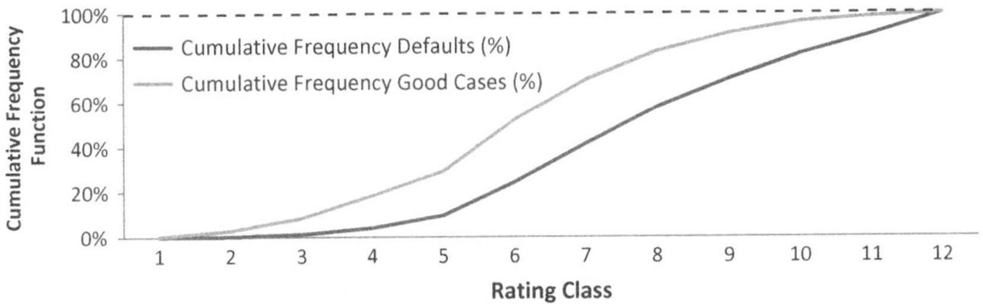

Fig. 10.3 Cumulative frequency functions (Author's own composition)

whereas if the rating class is higher than that value, the credit application is approved. In this context, α and β errors can be defined as follows:[1]

- **α error (type 1 error):** A case which is not rejected despite default.
- **β error (type 2 error):** A case which is rejected despite being good.

In practice, α errors cause damage due to credit defaults, whereas β errors cause comparatively less damage in the form of lost business. Consequently it is important to define the cut-off value with due attention to the costs of each type of error.

ROC Curve

One common way of describing the discriminatory power of rating procedures is the receiver operating characteristic (ROC) curve, which is constructed by plotting the cumulative frequencies of defaults as points on the y-axis and the cumulative frequencies of good cases along the x-axis. In Fig. 10.4 we have:

A perfect scoring/rating procedure would classify all actual defaults in the worst rating class, and therefore the ROC curve of the ideal procedure would run vertically from the lower left point (0%, 0%) upwards to point (0%, 100%) and from there to the right to point (100%, 100%). The

[1] Usually, α and β errors are indicated not as absolute numbers but as percentages.

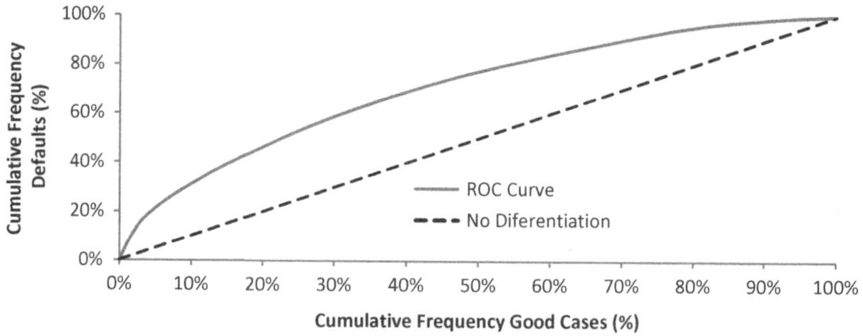

Fig. 10.4 ROC curve (Author's own composition)

x and y values of the ROC curve are always equal if the frequency distributions of good and bad cases are identical (non-differentiation case); consequently, the ROC curve for a scoring/rating procedure which cannot distinguish between good and bad cases will run along the diagonal.

Taking all the above into consideration, it is possible to define the AUC (area under curve) as the area under the ROC curve. It is a graphic measure of a scoring/rating procedure's discriminatory power derived from the ROC curve. The higher the AUC value, the higher the discriminatory power of the rating model, and it is clear that in perfect scoring/rating models the AUC = 1, whereas for models which cannot differentiate between good and bad cases the AUC = 1/2. Values where the AUC < 1/2 are possible but indicate that the rating system in question classifies, at least partly, in the wrong order.

Although the AUC measure is a very useful tool in measuring discriminatory power, it is a one-dimensional measure of discriminatory power, and crucial information on the shape of the ROC curve and the properties of the scoring/rating model examined is lost in the calculation of this value. Therefore, when two different rating models using the same sample are compared on the basis of AUC alone, it is not immediately clear which of the procedures is better in terms of performance, which is particularly true when the ROC curves intersect. In practice, the procedure which shows a steeper curve in the worse range of scores/ratings would be preferable because fewer errors occur at the same level of β error in this range.

Another similar one-dimensional measure of discriminatory power which can be derived from the ROC curve is the Pietra Index. In geometric terms, the Pietra Index is defined as twice the area of the largest triangle which can be drawn between the diagonal and the ROC curve. In the case of a concave ROC curve, the area of this triangle can also be calculated as the product of the diagonal's length and the largest distance between the ROC curve and the diagonal. The Pietra Index can take on values between 0 (non-differentiating scoring/rating system) and 1 (perfect scoring/rating system). As can be demonstrated, it is also possible to understand the Pietra Index as the maximum difference between the cumulative frequency distributions of good cases and defaults.

$$\text{Pietra Index} = \max\left\{F^{\text{good}}{}_{\text{cum}} - F^{\text{good}}{}_{\text{cum}}\right\}$$

Understanding the Pietra Index as the maximum difference between the cumulative frequency distributions for the score/rating values of good cases and defaults makes it possible to perform the Kolmogorov–Smirnov test (KS test) for two independent samples.

The null hypothesis tested in the KS test is: "The score distributions of good cases and defaults are identical". This hypothesis is rejected at level q if the Pietra Index equals or exceeds the following value (D):

$$D = \frac{D_q}{\sqrt{Np(1-p)}}$$

where N denotes the number of cases in the sample examined and p refers to the observed default rate. The values D_q for the individual significance levels (q) are shown in Table 10.3.

Table 10.3 Individual significance (Author's own composition)

q	20%	15%	10%	5%	1%	0.10%
Dq	1.07	1.14	1.22	1.36	1.63	1.95

If the Pietra Index >= D, significant differences exist between the score values of good and bad cases.

CAP Curve

Another form of representation which is similar to the ROC curve is the cumulative accuracy profiles (CAP) curve, in which the cumulative frequencies of all cases are on the x-axis instead of the cumulative frequencies of the good cases alone. The ROC and CAP curves contain the same information, a fact which manifests itself in the associated discriminatory power measures (AUC for the ROC curve, Gini coefficient for the CAP curve).

A perfect rating procedure would classify all defaults (and only those cases) in the worst rating class. This rating class would then contain the precise share PD of all cases, with PD equalling the observed default rate in the sample examined (Fig. 10.5).

For a perfect scoring/rating system, the CAP curve would thus run from point (0,0) to point (PD,1) and from there to point (1,1). Therefore, a triangular area in the upper left corner of the graph cannot be reached by the CAP curve. As stated above, one geometrical measure of discriminatory power from the CAP curve is the Gini coefficient.

The Gini coefficient is calculated as the ratio between the area encircled by the CAP curve and the diagonal for the scoring/rating system and the

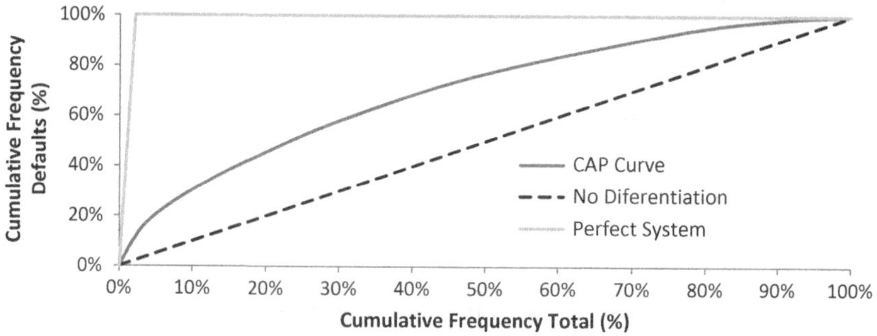

Fig. 10.5 Cap curve (Author's own composition)

corresponding area in a perfect scoring/rating system. As stated above, the information contained in the summary measures of discriminatory power derived from the CAP and ROC curves is equivalent since Gini coefficient = 2*AUC − 1.

10.3.1.2 LGD and EAD

A power curve on model level or a cumulative LGD accuracy ratio (CLAR) on bucket level can be used to test the discriminatory power in LGD. A power curve for loss given default (LGD) is similar to the ROC curve for PD since it is constructed by ranking from high to low all predicted losses at default (LGD times EAD). On the x-axis the cumulative percentage of observations is stated and on the y-axis the cumulative percentage of observed losses at default is stated. Then, based on Fig. 10.6, the power curve ratio is calculated by $B/(A + B)$.

A different measure is used to test the discriminatory power on a bucket level for LGD; this measure is called the "cumulative LGD accuracy ratio". In order to calculate the CLAR, observed LGDs are ordered from high to low; from these ordered LGDs the first X values are selected, where X is the number of values in the highest LGD bucket. From these X values the number of observations out of the highest LGD bucket is counted. The total number of observations minus the observations out of the highest LGD bucket is divided by the total number of observations,

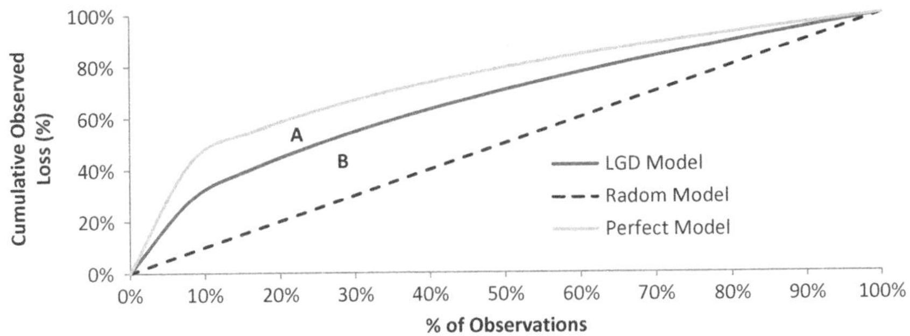

Fig. 10.6 Power curve (Author's own composition)

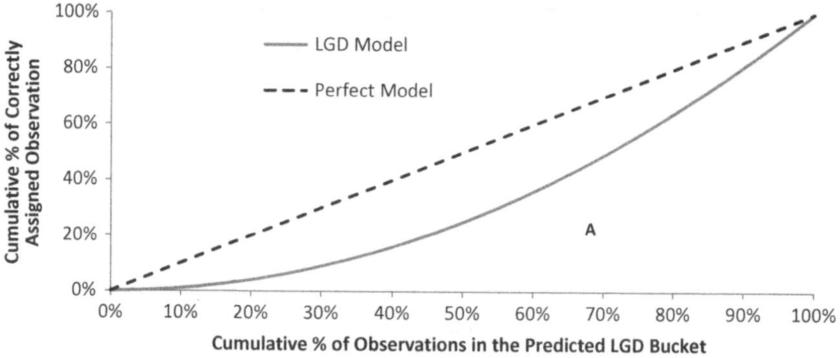

Fig. 10.7 LGD model and perfect model comparison (Author's own composition)

and this is repeated on a cumulative basis for each LGD bucket to obtain the CLAR.

The CLAR in Fig. 10.7 is twice the area under the curve (A).

Similar procedures can be used for exposure at default (EAD).

10.3.2 Parameters

10.3.2.1 Predictive Power: Back-Testing

PD

Chapter 9 dealt with how to assign probabilities of default to scoring/rating systems. The quality of this assignment depends on how the default probabilities predicted by the scoring/rating model match the default rates actually realised. Therefore, reviewing the calibration of a rating model is frequently referred to as back-testing. Similar logic applies to the other parameters (LGD and EAD).

Realised default rates will deviate from estimated ones and thus validation procedures need to examine whether the deviation is considerable and should lead to a review of the model, or whether they can be attributed to statistical noise. In order to do that we should focus on the significance of deviations and the monotony of PDs with regards to "risk".

The average quadratic deviation of the default rate forecast for each of the samples examined from the rate realised in that case (1 for default, 0 for no default) is known as the Brier Score:

$$\mathrm{BS} = \frac{1}{N}\sum_{n=1}^{N}\left(p_n^{\text{forecast}} - y_n\right)^2 \text{where } y_n \begin{cases} 1 \text{ for default in } n \\ 0 \text{ for default in n} \end{cases}$$

It is clear that the lower the Brier Score, the better the calibration of the scoring/rating model; however, it is necessary to develop indicators to show how well the scoring/rating system estimates the PD parameter. In general, two assumptions can be made: assumption of uncorrelated default events and assumption of default correlation. Default correlations which are not equal to zero have the effect of strengthening fluctuations in default probabilities; consequently, the tolerance ranges for the deviation of realised default rates from estimated values may therefore be substantially larger when default correlations are taken into account.

As expected, empirical studies show that default events are generally not uncorrelated, and typical values of default correlations range between 0.5 % and 3 %. However, taking the above statement into consideration, it is sometimes necessary to review the calibration under the initial assumption of uncorrelated default events in order to ensure conservative estimates. Nevertheless, this could lead to more frequent recalibration of the scoring/rating model, which can have negative effects on the model's stability over time. Therefore, in some cases, it could be necessary to determine at least the approximate extent to which default correlations influence PD estimates.

The statistical test used here checks the null hypothesis "The forecast default probability in a rating class is correct" against the alternative hypothesis "The forecast default probability is incorrect" using the data available for back-testing. One simple test for the calibration of default rates under the assumption of uncorrelated default events uses standard normal distribution and states that:

- If $\left(p_c^{\text{observed}} - p_c^{\text{forecast}}\right) > \phi^{-1}(q)\sqrt{\frac{p_c^{\text{forecast}}\left(1-p_c^{\text{forecast}}\right)}{N_c}}$, the default rate in class c is significantly underestimated at the confidence level q.
- If $\left(p_c^{\text{observed}} - p_c^{\text{forecast}}\right) < \phi^{-1}(q)\sqrt{\frac{p_c^{\text{forecast}}\left(1-p_c^{\text{forecast}}\right)}{N_c}}$, the default rate in class c is significantly overestimated at the confidence level q.
- If $\left|p_c^{\text{observed}} - p_c^{\text{forecast}}\right| > \phi^{-1}\left(\frac{q+1}{2}\right)\sqrt{\frac{p_c^{\text{forecast}}\left(1-p_c^{\text{forecast}}\right)}{N_c}}$, the default rate in class c is significantly mis-estimated at confidence level q.

In the formulas above, ϕ^{-1} denotes the inverse cumulative distribution function for the standard normal distribution, N_c stands for the number of cases in rating class c and p_c refers to the default rate.

When discussing credit ratings/scorings, it was stated that when the sample is reduced or the probability of default is low, the information contained in the transition matrix can be used to estimate the probabilities of default reliably. In general, the methods applied for default probabilities can also be used to back-test the transition matrix. However, there are two essential differences in this procedure: back-testing transition matrices involves simultaneous testing of a far larger number of probabilities, and transition probability changes during back-testing.

LGD and EAD

Testing the predictive power involves comparing loss at default and LGD. There are several measures for doing so; one of them, the loss shortfall (LS), indicates how much lower the loss at default is than was predicted:

$$\text{Loss Shortfall} = 1 - \frac{\sum_{i=1}^{N}(LGD_i * EAD_i)}{\sum_{i=1}^{N}(\text{OLGD}_i * EAD_i)}$$

where OLGD is the observed LGD and LGD is the predicted LGD. The model tests conservatism because the model is only accepted if the observed loss is lower than the predicted loss. The predictive power of the

LGD model is considered to be low if LS is above zero and below −0.20, whereas it is high if LS is between −0.10 and zero. Between −0.20 and −0.10 the predictive power of the LGD model is considered to be medium.

The mean absolute deviation (MAD) is the absolute difference between the observed loss (OLGD) and the predicted loss (LGD) and it is calculated as:

$$\text{MAD} = \frac{\sum_{i=1}^{N} |\text{OLGD}_i - LGD_i| * EAD_i}{\sum_{i=1}^{N} EAD_i}$$

The predictive power of the LGD model is regarded as low if MAD is above 20 %, whereas it is high if MAD is below 10 %. Between 10 % and 20 % the predictive power of the LGD model is considered to be medium.

The LS compares the total loss levels while the MAD measures the average difference per facility. As for PD, the LGD predictions on model and bucket level can be tested by constructing a confidence interval around the predictions.

Similar procedures can be used for EAD.

10.3.2.2 Benchmarking

In quantitative validation it is necessary to recognise the difference between back-testing and benchmarking. Back-testing refers to validation on the basis of a bank's in-house data, that is, this term refers to a comparison of forecast and realised parameters (PD, LGD and EAD) in the bank's credit portfolio.

In contrast, benchmarking refers to validation on the basis of outside data; in particular, this term describes the comparison between the bank's parameters (PD, LGD and EAD) and other banks' parameters for a similar credit portfolio.

In terms of method and content, back-testing and benchmarking involve the same procedures. However, the results of the two procedures are interpreted differently in terms of scope and orientation. That means that both quantitative validation methods should complement each other in the quantitative validation process.

For example, on the one hand, poor results in the bank's own data set primarily indicate weaknesses in the model used for parameter calculation and should prompt the development of a new or revised model. However, sound results from back-testing alone do not provide a reliable indication of a model's goodness of fit compared to other models. On the other hand, poor results using external reference data may indicate structural differences between the data sets used for development and benchmarking. This is especially true when the model performance is comparatively high in back-testing.

11

Credit Risk Management

11.1 Basic Concepts

As noted in previous chapters, the measurement and therefore the management of credit risk are much more complex than those of market risk. One of the fundamental reasons credit risk is difficult to manage is that, unlike market risk, it is based on a discontinuous phenomenon: either it defaults or it does not. Additionally, in the event of default, it is not easy to determine the probability distribution of the loss and, as discussed, in some cases it is also difficult to determine the exposure to default. Another reason for this is that legal elements are critical in this type of risk, which is not the case with market risk.

As a result of this complexity, until very recently the only way to manage this risk was to take provisions on an expected loss of the portfolio (i.e., to recognise it as a loss) and also to provide capital allocation to deal with unexpected losses. At present, it is also possible to manage credit risk

Electronic Supplementary Material: The online version of this article (DOI 10.1007/978-3-319-41366-2_11) contains supplementary material, which is available to authorized users.

F.J. Población García, *Financial Risk Management*,
DOI 10.1007/978-3-319-41366-2_11

with derivatives, specifically with credit derivatives, where credit default swaps (CDS) are the most popular choice.

Credit institutions, whose primary business involves taking money from savings and lending it to investment, are subject to special regulation and strict supervision by the central bank in order to prevent the depositor from losing their money due to bankruptcy. In this sense, the principles of this strict regulation are based on the above points: taking provisions for expected loss and providing capital allocation.

11.2 Traditional Management

Traditionally, this risk has been managed by taking provisions for the expected loss and providing capital allocation for the unexpected loss, with both the provisions and the allocation being calculated based on the concepts of expected loss and unexpected loss discussed in previous chapters. Therefore, the provisions and the allocation are substantially different depending on the portfolio in question: they are higher in portfolios with higher risk and lower in portfolios with lower risk, and are measured using the risk parameters probability of default (PD), loss given default (LGD) and exposure at default (EAD) discussed previously.

Thus, the regulation of credit institutions requires credit risk to be measured by distinguishing between different types of exposures according to their characteristics. Specifically, the Basel Accords state that credit risk is made up of the following categories: central government, regional governments, public sector entities, multilateral development banks, international organisations, banks, companies, retailers, exposures to individuals or companies secured by residential or commercial real estate, default exposures, high-risk exposures, hedged bonds, securitisation positions, exposures to institutions and companies with short-term credit rating, exposures to collective investment schemes (CIS) and other exposures.

Although this book addresses risk from a general perspective and not from the specific point of view of a credit institution, this principle that credit risk differs depending on the type of exposure in question must be maintained. Following the same logic, it should be noted that credit institutions have significant exposure to nearly all the categories above, while an industrial company usually has exposure to business and retail categories; for this reason, these are the only two categories that will be discussed in this book.

11.2.1 Retail and Corporate Portfolios

11.2.1.1 The Retail Portfolio

The Basel Accords state that credit risk exposures which meet the following criteria should be included in the retail category:

- Exposures to individuals or small and medium-sized enterprises (SMEs).
- Parts of a business segment that have a high number of exposures with similar characteristics which are offered publicly and on a massive scale, resulting in diversification which substantially reduces the risks associated with such exposures.
- The total amount of debt incurred by the client or group of connected clients when the debt is repaid to the credit institution, including any default exposure, does not exceed one million euros.

In other words, an exposure that the credit institution has with an individual or an SME is considered a retail exposure provided that the credit institution has many exposures very similar to this one and which are equal to or less than one million euros. For the purposes of this book, a retail exposure to credit risk for a company can be considered to fit the same definition, except for the amount of one million euros which must be adjusted depending on the size of the company. There are many examples of such exposures in a company, such as a provider to small business that, as discussed, charges at 90, 120 or 180 days, a warehouse or utility company that allows the customer to pay using their loyalty card and so on.

Having defined retail exposure, it should be noted that these exposures are characterised by the fact that, as there are many very similar exposures, idiosyncratic risk is diversified and systemic risk remains, and therefore the uncertainty is generally lower than in other types of exposure where such diversification does not occur. In other words, when an industrial company, due to its activity, has a very large number of similar borrowers and maintains a small amount of exposure with each of them, this debt portfolio can be considered a retail portfolio. This portfolio will be characterised by the fact that, as there is less uncertainty, risk is easier to measure and manage than in other types of exposure because, according to statistics, roughly the same number of borrowers default (PD) in each period with a similar exposure (EAD) and also a similar loss given default (LGD). Thus, the expected loss can be estimated relatively easily and reliably where the unexpected loss is not excessively high due to diversification. It should also be noted that in this type of portfolio PD and LGD parameters are usually moderate, that is, not extreme, which further facilitates the process.

Therefore, in these portfolios it is very reasonable to take provisions for an amount equal to or slightly higher than the expected loss and to provide capital to hedge unexpected losses which are not excessively high because, as noted, there is some diversification.

Although risk in such exposures is easy to measure or manage because there is less uncertainty, this does not necessarily mean that this risk has to be lower than that of other exposures. In this regard it must be noted that, as a general rule, probability of default in such portfolios, although moderate, is usually higher in other types of portfolios, such as corporate portfolios, while uncertainty about the parameters is usually lower and therefore the expected loss is usually higher than in other types of portfolio, while the unexpected loss is usually lower.

11.2.1.2 The Corporate Portfolio

The Basel Accords state that the category of companies will include exposures to any kind of business, including individual entrepreneurs and non-profit companies, which cannot be included in any other category. Therefore, an exposure to companies cannot be considered retail exposure, that is, exposure to a borrower with a high debt or whose characteristics are not common to other credit risk exposures.

Unlike in the previous case, in this type of portfolio there is *no* diversification for any kind of risk and therefore the uncertainty is higher, while risk parameters, especially PD, are usually lower. It is for this reason that, in this case, the expected loss is usually less than in retail exposures while the unexpected loss is usually higher, and therefore in these portfolios it is not unusual to take provisions of a slightly higher amount than the expected loss, but generally lower than the provisions taken in the retail portfolio, also providing an amount of capital which, in general, will be higher than that provided for the retail portfolio.

Within this portfolio, depending on the characteristics of the loan—amount, existence of guarantees and so on, and the characteristics of the borrower—size, sector and so on, the amounts of these expected and unexpected losses, and therefore of the provisions and allocation, will be different. As a general rule, the greater the borrower is, the lower the PD is and the greater the LGD is.

11.2.2 Capital Requirements

Current regulation establishes minimum capital requirements for banks based on the above parameter calculation. Specifically, it states that minimum capital requirements are risk weighted assets (RWA) times 8 %.

$$\text{Minimum Capital Requirements} = 8\% * \text{RWA}$$

11.2.2.1 Non-defaulted Assets

In the case of non-defaulted assets for retail exposures it is established that:

$$\text{RW} = \left(\text{LGD} * N\left(\frac{1}{\sqrt{1-R}} * G(\text{PD}) + \sqrt{\frac{R}{1-R}} * G(0.999)\right) - \text{LGD} * \text{PD}\right) * 12.5 * 1.06$$

- The 12.5 factor is needed in order to cancel out the factor (8 %) which multiplies RWA to get minimum capital requirements.
- The 1.06 factor is a conservative factor established in regulation which is not related to risk parameters.
- N is the cumulative distribution function for a standard normal random variable.
- G is the inverse cumulative distribution function for a standard normal random variable.
- PD is the long-run average PD explained above.
- LGD is the downturn LGD (DLGD) explained above.
- R is the correlation factor.

Leaving aside the 12.5 and 1.06 factors, there are two elements inside the parentheses:

$$LGD * N\left(\frac{1}{\sqrt{1-R}} * G(PD) + \sqrt{\frac{R}{1-R}} * G(0.999)\right) - LGD * PD$$

The average PD multiplied by downturn LGD appears inside the red circle, whereas stressed PD (blue sub-circle) multiplied by downturn LGD is shown in the green circle. Thus, the green circle represents the maximum amount of loss that can occur (stressed PD and LGD), which is the sum of expected loss and unexpected loss (as will be discussed later).

However, the red circle is not the expected loss, since it is not the average PD multiplied by the average LGD. Nevertheless, in current regulation the red circle is defined as the expected loss and, consequently, RWA simply deals with unexpected loss.

To understand how the Basel Accords stress PD in the formula, we extend our multinomial model from Chap. 9 stating that for a particular borrower ("i"):

$$y_i = I_i + v_i + \varepsilon_i$$

Where, as before, $I_i = \beta_1 x_{1i} + \cdots + \beta_n x_{ni}$ is the scoring and ε_i is the error term of this particular borrower, v_i is the systemic factor which determines the correlation of borrower "*i*" and the rest of the borrowers in the sample and, consequently, $v_i \sim N(0, R_i)$ and $\varepsilon_i \sim N(0, 1 - R_i)$, R_i being the correlation of borrower "*i*" and the rest of the sample. Assuming R is constant among borrowers, conditioning a specific moment of the business cycle we have:

$$\text{PD} = \text{Prob}(y > 0/v_i) = \text{Prob}(\varepsilon > -I_i - v_i) = N\left(\frac{I_i + v_i}{\sqrt{1-R}}\right)$$

Going back to our formula, there are two elements to be found inside the blue circle, which is the cumulative distribution function for a standard normal random variable:

$$LGD * N\left(\frac{1}{\sqrt{1-R}} * G(PD) + \sqrt{\frac{R}{1-R}} * G(0.999)\right) - LGD * PD$$

The first element, the yellow circle, is $I_i/\sqrt{1-R}$, or, in other words, it is the PD average, since v_i is zero (no good and no bad moment in the business cycle). The second element, the red circle, is the PD under a very adverse scenario (PD = 99.9 %). The correlation is used as weight between both elements.

The higher the correlation, the higher the weight of PD = 99.9 %. It makes sense since we would like to ask for more capital (unexpected loss) if the borrowers default is more correlated. In the case of correlation equal to zero, capital is not needed since diversification leads unexpected loss equal to zero (Central Limit Theorem [CLT]).

In the Basel Accords, for retail exposures R is defined as:

$$R = 0.03 * \frac{1 - e^{-35*\text{PD}}}{1 - e^{-35}} + 0.16 * \left(1 - \frac{1 - e^{-35*\text{PD}}}{1 - e^{-35}}\right)$$

The higher the PD, the lower the R and vice versa.

For corporates the Basel Accords establish that RWA are:

$$\mathrm{RW} = \left(\mathrm{LGD} * N\left(\frac{1}{\sqrt{1-R}} * G(\mathrm{PD}) + \sqrt{\frac{R}{1-R}} * G(0.999)\right) - \mathrm{LGD} * \mathrm{PD}\right) * \frac{1 + (M - 2.5) * b}{1 - 1.5 * b} 12.5 * 1.06$$

This formula is similar to the one for retail but with some additional elements:

- M is the maturity factor.
- b is the maturity adjustment factor, which is defined as:

$$b = (0.11852 - 0.05478 * \ln(\mathrm{PD}))^2$$

- The correlation factor is now:

$$R = 0.12 * \frac{1 - e^{-50 * \mathrm{PD}}}{1 - e^{-50}} + 0.24 * \left(1 - \frac{1 - e^{-50 * \mathrm{PD}}}{1 - e^{-50}}\right)$$

- And, finally, this correlation factor formula can change under some circumstances.

To conclude, it is interesting to note that the RWA formula is convex, and consequently it is not the same to calculate capital loan by loan as it is to calculate it at a portfolio level. Since the Basel Accords establish that capital has to be calculated loan by loan, it is not possible to calculate it using the aggregate portfolio.

11.3 Hedging with Derivatives

Traditional credit risk management is based on recognising that a loss will occur and the only difficulty lies in measuring the amount that will be lost in the most reliable way possible; however, it does not deal with how to avoid or at least minimise the amount in any way. For this reason, as in the case of market risk, in recent years products have been developed to try to minimise this loss or at least contain it; these products are credit derivatives.

In finance, a credit derivative refers to any one of "various instruments and techniques designed to separate and then transfer the credit risk" or the risk of a corporate or sovereign borrower defaulting, transferring it to an entity other than the lender or debt holder. There are two main kinds of credit derivatives: unfunded and funded credit derivatives.

An unfunded credit derivative is one where credit protection is bought and sold between bilateral counterparties without the protection seller having to pay money upfront or at any given time during the life of the deal unless an event of default occurs. In other words, an unfunded credit derivative is a bilateral contract between two parties, where each party is responsible for making its own payments by contract without recourse to other assets.

The most popular type of unfunded credit derivative is the credit default swap, but there are many others including "constant maturity credit default swap" (CMCDS), "total return swap," "credit default swaption," "first to default credit default swap," "portfolio credit default swap," "credit spread option" and so on.

A funded credit derivative is a credit derivative which is entered into by a financial institution or a special purpose vehicle (SPV) and payments under the credit derivative are funded using securitisation techniques, such that a debt obligation is issued by the financial institution or SPV to support these obligations. In other words, a funded credit derivative involves the protection seller (the party that assumes the credit risk) making an initial payment that is used to settle any potential credit events. (The protection buyer, however, may still be exposed to the credit risk of the protection seller itself, which is known as counterparty risk.)

Funded credit derivative products include products like "credit-linked note" (CLN), "synthetic collateralised debt obligation" (CDO), "constant proportion debt obligation" (CPDO) and "synthetic constant proportion portfolio insurance" (synthetic CPPI).

Many of these products are over-the-counter (OTC) traded products tailored to the two contracting parties, and in most of them the International Swaps and Derivatives Association (ISDA) provides model contracts.[1]

The CDS has become the keystone product of the credit derivatives market and, broadly speaking, it represents one-third of the credit derivatives market. A CDS is a credit derivative which is implemented through a swap contract on a particular credit instrument, usually a bond or a loan, where the buyer of the swap makes a series of periodic payments, called the spread, to the seller and in exchange is paid an amount of money if the title that serves as the underlying asset to the contract is unpaid at maturity or the issuer defaults. The product has many variations, including the possibility of having a basket or portfolio of reference entities, although fundamentally the principles remain the same.

These swaps are issued on the underlying assets specified, which are loans or debt securities, such as obligations or a private or public bond. In addition, the organisation or company which issues the underlying securities is named as the reference entity. As with all kind of swaps, settlement may be performed either as physical settlement, where the buyer gives the bonds to the seller and the seller pays the buyer the fixed amount, or alternatively, as cash settlement, whereby the seller only pays the buyer the loss of the value of the securities.

The main theoretical purpose of credit default swaps is to serve as insurance so that the holder of a debt security is hedged from possible credit risk, basically default; in order to do this, they go to a CDS seller who is paid an annual premium. In case of default, the seller responds by paying the security's face value to the holder. However, although a CDS is similar to an insurance policy, it has one significant difference: the buyer of the CDS is not required to be at real risk of debt purchase. Insurance is

[1] More details about OTC products and ISDA are provided in Chap. 12.

based on something that is owned by the insured party, but a CDS can also be contracted on an asset that is not owned by the person who contracts the CDS. This type of CDS carried out on an asset that is not owned by the person contracting it is known as "naked" and, in fact, it is the equivalent of making a bet. In this case, the purpose of the operation is speculation on the evolution of the underlying asset, and there may even be the paradox that more credit default swaps are issued than there are existing titles, such as in a case in which 1,000 bonds were issued, but there were 20,000 CDSs on those bonds.

In the same way, although credit default swaps have some elements in common with insurance transactions, they are not regulated like the insurance business and thus it is not necessary for the selling entities to meet any of the solvency standards for the insurance activity, although there is a greater risk of default than in insurance contracts regulated as such. Note that there is no regulation of these operations in most countries. It should also be noted here that CDSs have become a focus of attention during the current financial crisis after being used as instruments of a speculative attack on public debt in some countries such as Greece in 2010; they were also responsible for the decline of the American company American International Group (AIG) in 2008. For this reason, the European Parliament banned "naked" CDSs from 1 December 2011.

In addition to funded credit derivatives, credit linked notes should also be discussed (CLN). A credit linked note is a claim in which payments depend upon an event defined by negotiations between the parties to the note (which may be a default, a change in credit spread or a rating change). In practice a CLN combines a credit default swap with a regular note (with coupon, maturity, redemption). Normally, a CLN is purchased to hedge against possible downgrades or loan defaults. The classic CLN consists of a bond, issued by a well-rated borrower, packaged jointly with a CDS on a less creditworthy risk.

As stated above, other interesting funded credit derivative products include collateralised debt obligations (CDO), bonds issued against a mixed pool of assets; collateralised bond obligations (CBO), bonds issued against a pool of bond assets or other securities; and collateralised loan obligations (CLO), bonds issued against a pool of bank loans.

11.4 Stress Test

In order to finish this chapter about risk management, we are going to present the stress test tool, which help managers since it provide them with very useful information: how is the resilience of the bank under stress conditions. More concretely, the objective of the stress test is to provide supervisors, banks and other market participants with a common analytical framework to consistently compare and assess the resilience of banks and the banking system to shocks and to challenge the capital position of banks. The exercise is based on a common methodology, internally consistent and relevant scenarios, and a set of templates to capture starting point data and stress test results to allow a rigorous assessment of the banks in the sample.

In the context of credit risk, banks are required to translate the macroeconomic scenarios provided into the corresponding credit risk impact on both the capital available, that is, via impairments and thus the profit and loss (P&L), and the risk exposure amount for positions exposed to risks stemming from the default of counterparties.

Banks are requested to make use of their models but subject to a number of conservative constraints. These projections will be based on default and loss parameters (both point-in-time and regulatory) that will depend, amongst other factors, on the banks' business models, asset portfolio distribution and internal models. The estimation of impairments and translation to available capital requires the use of statistical methods and will include the following main steps: estimating starting values of the risk parameters, estimating the impact of the scenarios on the risk parameters and computing impairment flows as the basis for provisions that affect the P&L.

For the estimation of risk exposure amounts, banks should adhere to regulatory requirements based on stressed regulatory risk parameters. A classical assumption is that the balance sheet is held static as of the starting point of the exercise. Consistent with the static balance sheet assumption, banks are not permitted to replace defaulted assets; defaulted assets are moved into the defaulted assets stock, reducing non-defaulted assets and keeping total exposure constant. Furthermore, for the purpose of calculating exposures, it is assumed that no cures, charge-offs or write-offs take place within the three-year horizon of the exercise. Within the credit risk framework, the initial residual maturity is kept constant for all assets. This means that assets do not mature.

As a general principle banks should resort to data from internal models rather than accounting approximations:

- For internal ratings based (IRB) portfolios, banks are required to base their estimation of starting level point-in-time (pit) values on their approved internal parameter estimation models (PDpit and LGDpit).
- For standard (STA) banks or IRB banks which cannot extract starting level point-in-time parameters from their internal models for portfolios where there are no approved models in place, banks should use non-approved models to extract point-in-time parameters provided those models are regularly used in internal risk management and stress testing and the competent authority is satisfied with their use for the purpose of the stress test.
- For portfolios where no appropriate internal models are in use for estimating the starting level PDpit or LGDpit, banks are expected to approximate PiT PD and LGD starting values via default and loss rates (historically observed).

Satellite models are used to link risk level parameters with macro and financial factors to project the evolution of the bank balance sheet conditional on an adverse scenario; however, not all satellite models have the same goodness of fit. In Excel file "Ejemplo Satellite Models. xlsx" we have the default rate and we want to get PDpit. It is interesting to note in the sheet "Calculations" that not all goodness-of-fit results are the same and also that in one case (cell "N21") the sign in the estimate makes no sense. It is for this reason that the in-sample predictive ability is not the same in all cases, as can be seen in Fig. 11.1.

Jointly with the fact that macroeconomic variable projections do not have the same degree of stress, the differences in goodness of fit lead to very different projections, as can be seen in Fig. 11.2.

Moreover, even though the linear regression is a very simple and useful model, it has limitations since it relies on the following assumptions:

- **Weak exogeneity**. This essentially means that the predictor variables x can be treated as fixed values, rather than random variables. This

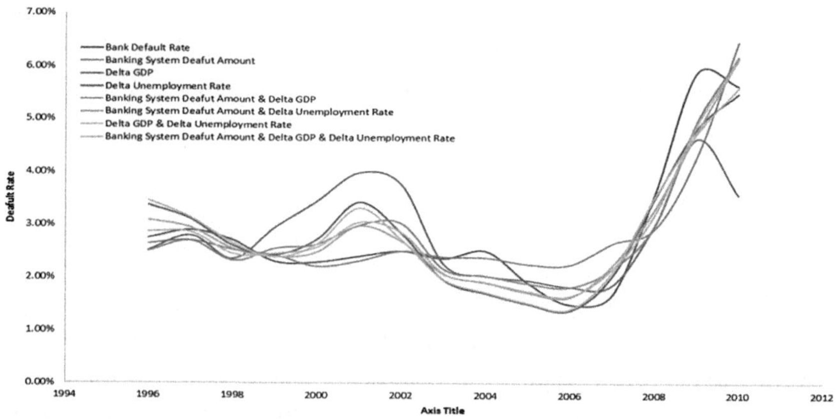

Fig. 11.1 Default rate—construction (Author's own composition)

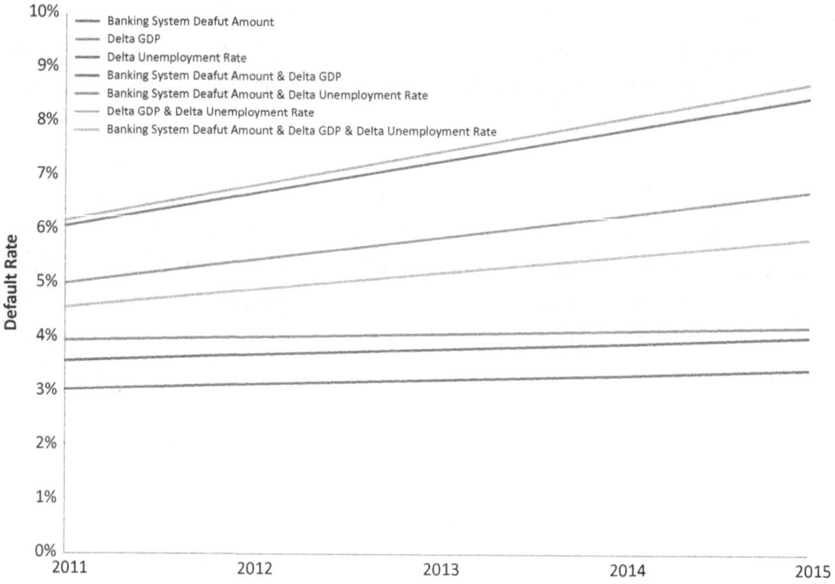

Fig. 11.2 Default rate—projections (Author's own composition)

means, for example, that predictor variables are assumed to be error-free, that is, not contaminated with measurement errors.

- **Linearity**. This means that the mean of the response variable is a linear combination of the parameters (regression coefficients) and the predictor variables.
- **Constant variance (homoscedasticity)**. This means that different response variables have the same variance in their errors, regardless of the values of the predictor variables.
- **Independence of errors**. This assumes that the errors of the response variables are uncorrelated with each other.
- **Lack of multicollinearity in the predictors**. For standard least squares estimation methods, the design matrix X must have full column rank p; otherwise, we have a condition known as multicollinearity in the predictor variables. This can be triggered by having two or more perfectly correlated predictor variables (e.g., if the same predictor variable is mistakenly given twice, either without transforming one of the copies or by transforming one of the copies linearly).

As a general rule, PiT parameters (PDs and LGDs) are portfolio level estimations, thus affected by PD/LGD grade migrations. Banks' methodologies must address this migration effect, taking into account the macroeconomic scenario. In the case of estimating a relationship between point-in-time parameters and the macroeconomic variables at the PD/LGD grade level and, consequently, obtaining parameters for each grade within a portfolio, the aggregate parameters are obtained directly as the weighted average of the respective buckets. In such cases, the exposure distribution among buckets must incorporate rating migrations linked to the macroeconomic scenario and consequently would in this case require the banks to calculate point-in-time migration matrices. The file "PIE example.xlsx" provides an example of this being done correctly and incorrectly.

12

Derivative Credit Risk (Counterparty Risk)

12.1 Basic Concepts

The points discussed in the previous chapters could give the impression that credit risk can only occur if a creditor lends money to a borrower, but this is not the case, as when a derivative is contracted this generates a new risk whereby, should the case arise, the other party in the contract fails to meet their obligations; this risk is a particular type of credit risk known as derivative credit risk or counterparty risk.

For example, imagine that two parties (A and B) are entering into a forward contract, party A as a buyer and party B as a seller, whereby they agree that party A will purchase a particular asset from party B on a future date at a price K which is fixed today. Thus, if at that time the price of the asset in question (S_T) is much lower than K, party A suffers a loss equal to the difference between K and S_T, while party B makes a profit. So far, there is nothing here that has not been discussed in previous chapters. However, at this point it could be that party A is unable to meet their obligations, that is, they do not have the agreed amount of money, and therefore party B cannot sell the asset at price K. Of course, in this scenario party A would enter a credit event (default) and, as a result,

F.J. Población García, *Financial Risk Management*,
DOI 10.1007/978-3-319-41366-2_12

should benefit from a suspension of payments or go bankrupt immediately which, one way or another, entails a loss for party B, due to credit risk. Likewise, the example can develop in the opposite direction, in which case the loss is suffered by party A.

As shown in this example, neither of the parties lends money to the other at any time, but both are subject to credit risk. Once the contract has been signed, they may make profits or losses due to market risk, and in the case of making a profit, they may not receive it because the other party defaults, that is, due to credit risk.

In this regard, note that this counterparty risk can be managed in a much simpler way than the overall credit risk, whose management can sometimes become complex. For this reason, in the next section the difference between over-the-counter (OTC) markets and organised markets will be studied.

12.2 OTC Markets Versus Organised Markets

When dealing with market risk, it is not important whether a contract is formed in an OTC market or in an exchange market; however, when dealing with credit risk, it is of vital importance.

By way of introduction, it can be said that OTC contracts are tailored, as both sides can negotiate all the terms, while contracts administered in organised markets are standard contracts where everything but the price is fixed. Like everything tailored, OTC contracts bear a higher credit risk, as only the other party responds and there is no stock exchange to fall back on to solve possible conflicts that may arise. In addition, these OTC contracts usually have liquidity problems.

12.2.1 OTC Markets

By definition, an over-the-counter contract is a bilateral contract in which two parties agree on the terms for the liquidation of the instrument. This is exactly what differentiates them from contracts traded in organised markets, where contracting does not occur between the two parties but each party contracts directly with the stock market. These OTC contracts are normally made between an investment bank and the customer directly and more often than not are implemented by telephone or electronically.

The main advantage of this type of contract is that they are not standard, that is, the parties may negotiate any and all of the clauses in order to obtain a contract that best suits their needs. Another important advantage is that, unlike in organised markets, commission payments are not required nor is it essential to provide guarantees, all of which implies higher credit and liquidity risks.

As noted in the above example, credit risk appears for one of the parties when it makes profits in its position, since this is when the other party cannot meet their obligations. Also note that, unlike in organised markets, in these markets credit risk cannot be eliminated unless the other party accepts the total cancellation of the contract, because although one of the parties takes an opposite position to the one that it already has in a new contract and in doing so eliminates market risk, credit risk remains. Liquidity risk occurs due to the fact that, by definition, these contracts are not standardised and each is defined in a different way, which means that if one party wants to get out of it, or a market agent is looking for a counterparty for an OTC contract that perfectly suits their needs, the necessary counterpart may not be found. It is also important to note that the fact that these products present credit risk also reduces their liquidity.

However, not all OTC markets are equal and present these risks to the same extent, for example, since the foreign exchange market is an OTC market which is mainly carried out between governments and large corporations, it hardly presents any credit risk problems and is the most liquid market in the world. Similarly, markets like the NYMEX have created compensation mechanisms for some commonly traded energetic OTC derivatives, a mechanism that allows counterparties of many bilateral OTC transactions to agree to mutually transfer the negotiation to a clearing house, eliminating credit risk. Equally, in the United States the OTC negotiation of shares is carried out through mediators and is monitored by the National Association of Securities Dealers (NASD).

Contrary to how they may be perceived, OTC markets are large and have grown exponentially over the past two decades, especially the very active international entities whose profits are closely linked to activity in these markets. The expansion has occurred mainly in derivative markets on interest rates, currency and Credit Default Swaps (CDSs), to be discussed in the next chapter, and, according to the International Swaps and Derivatives Association (ISDA), the volume of these OTC markets was around 600 trillion dollars at the end of 2010.

Also, many OTC contracts are held on framework agreements. A framework agreement is an agreement between two parties which specifies the standard rules that will apply to all transactions between the two parties, and in this way, with each new transaction the framework agreement standards do not need to be renegotiated and are automatically applied. The OTC derivatives traded between financial institutions usually adopt clauses of the ISDA as a framework.

12.2.1.1 International Swaps and Derivatives Association: Framework

The International Swaps and Derivatives Association is a trade organisation of participants in OTC markets which has created a standardised contract, the ISDA Master Agreement, for derivatives transactions. It is part of a framework of documents which consists of a "Master Agreement", a "Schedule", "Confirmations", "Definition Booklets" and a "Credit Support Annex".

The ISDA Master Agreement is the most commonly used master service agreement for OTC derivatives transactions internationally and it is a document agreed between two parties that sets out standard terms that apply to all the transactions entered into between those parties. Each time a transaction is entered into, the terms of the master agreement do not need to be renegotiated but rather apply automatically.

Probably the most important aspect of the ISDA Master Agreement is that the Master Agreement and all the Confirmations form a single agreement. It has crucial importance as it allows the parties to an ISDA Master Agreement to aggregate the amounts owed by each of them and replace them with a single net amount payable by one party to the other.

12.2.2 Organised Markets

An organised market or stock market is a private organisation that provides the necessary facilities for its members to conduct negotiations for the sale and purchase of securities, such as shares in companies, public and private bonds, certificates, equities and a variety of investment instruments.

The word "stock" has its origins in a building that belonged to a noble family with the surname Van Der Buërse from the European city of Bruges in the Flanders region, where meetings of a commercial nature were held. The family's coat of arms featured three leather bags, commonly used as purses at the time. Due to the volume of transactions and negotiations that were held there, it was given the name by which it is now known, the Stock Exchange, because of the surname Buërse. However, it is believed that the world's first stock exchange was established in Antwerp (Belgium) in 1460 and the second in Amsterdam (Netherlands) in the early seventeenth century, when the city became the most important centre of world trade. Much later, this leading role was conquered by the so-called London Stock Exchange which was founded in 1801. Currently these markets are located in many countries. Based on the volume of trading, the most important stock exchange in the world today is the New York Stock Exchange.

These organised markets have the following characteristics in common:

- Their regulation establishes the standardisation of the elements of the contract, such as their underlying assets, number of titles, dates of birth and strike price.
- There is also a clearing house in which the settlement of contracts is carried out without the need for direct contact between their buyers and sellers.
- Similarly, in these markets many measures are taken to minimise credit risk to ensure that the losses suffered in the clearing house are as low as possible. The daily settlement of gains and losses and the provision of guarantees may be included in these measures.

- Finally, there is the commission charged, providing a profit to compensate for the risk assumed by the house.

As a result of these characteristics, in these markets the risk of default is very small as it can only occur if the clearing house collapses. In addition, market liquidity is guaranteed because the intermediary company assumes the risk of potential defaults and contracts are standardised. Similarly, these markets provide transparent information regarding the supply and demand of both their contracts and their price, which favours liquidity. It should also be noted that these markets are regulated, supervised and controlled by nation states, although most of them were founded prior to the creation of official supervisory agencies.

However, these markets are not without drawbacks, such as commission payments and the fact that contracts are standardised and therefore cannot be adapted to the specific needs of their participants.

12.2.2.1 The Clearing House

The clearing house is an agency that acts as a counterparty of the contracting parties within an organised market, where it is the buyer to the seller and the seller to the buyer. Due to the existence of the clearing house, the negotiating parties of a contract have no obligation to each other, only to the house, which virtually eliminates counterparty risk and allows those involved in the contracting process to remain anonymous.

As indicated, this house assumes counterparty risk and, therefore, charges commission, that is, when an agent wants to buy or sell, they enter an order into the system specifying whether they want to buy or sell and at what quoted price. If another participant wants to execute the opposite order for the same price, that is, if there is a sale order and they want to purchase or there is a purchase order and they want to sell, the transaction exchange occurs. However, neither assumes counterparty risk, as both parties contract with the clearing house and no one else. Thus, a blind market is formed where trading is anonymous, as no participant knows the counterparty directly. As a result, it is possible to leave the position at any time, which is not feasible with an OTC contract.

Formally, the functions of this house are to:

- Act as a counterparty for the contracting parties, as a buyer for the seller and a seller for the buyer.
- Determine security deposits for open positions daily.
- Liquidate gains and losses daily.
- Liquidate contracts at maturity.

As the house eliminates counterparty risk for those who trade in the market, a mechanism must be established to prevent losses when faced with the possible insolvency of a market member. In order to do this, firstly, each participant is required to provide a daily settlement of profits and losses, as well as a security deposit.

The daily settlement of profits and losses involves proceeding to settlement every day once the market has closed, regardless of when the contract matures. In order to better explain this concept, the following example is presented: imagine a futures contract on an underlying asset trading today at €20 ($S_0 =$ €20) with a maturity of one year and a strike price also equal to €20 ($K =$ €20). If the price of the underlying asset rises to €21 over the next day, the party with the long position will have made €1, while the party with the short position will have lost €1. If the contract was an OTC contract, the loss or profit would be unknown until maturity. In order to avoid a situation whereby the loss at maturity has reached such an extent that the losing party cannot meet its obligations, in a futures contract traded in an organised market the participants are required to materialise the losses daily. Thus, at the end of the following day the party with the long position will receive €1 from the house, while the seller will have to pay this amount and, for all practical purposes, the contract remains a futures contract with the same maturity but with a strike price equal to €21. In this sense, it must not be forgotten that a futures contract which is traded in an OTC market is called a forward, while when it is traded in an organised market it is called a future (Fig. 12.1).

Thus, if at the end of the day a party cannot meet their obligations—in this example, the party with the short position cannot pay the house €1—the house assumes their position and the loss that has occurred on that day

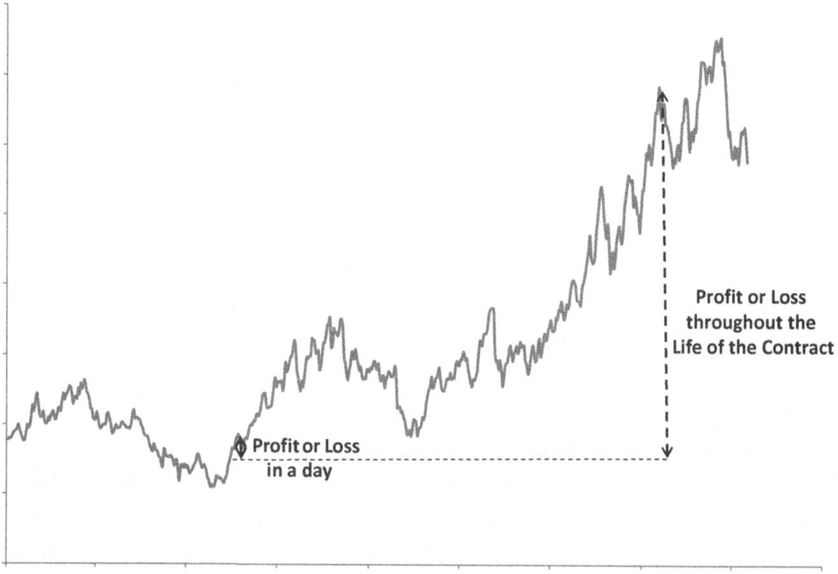

Fig. 12.1 Profit and loss over time (Author's own composition)

and the other party is unaware of this since they receive their profits from the house. Consequently, it is the house that assumes the counterparty risk but the loss they suffer is much lower than that suffered in an OTC market, as at most it assumes the loss suffered in a day, which will usually be much lower than that which occurs over a longer period of time, a year in this example. Note that when the market opens the following day, the house disposes of its position, thus avoiding having to manage its market risk.

Since the house assumes the loss caused by counterparty risk, in an organised market each participant is required to settle a security deposit determined by the number and type of contracts bought or sold. Using market research, the house estimates the maximum loss that could occur if an agent could not carry out the daily settlement of their profits and losses, and based on this estimate each participant is required to settle a security deposit. When a participant cannot satisfy the daily settlement of profits and losses, this security deposit will be executed in order to minimise the house's loss as a result of this risk. For this guarantee to remain unchanged, the clearing house adjusts it daily using deposit updates. In addition, each type of futures contract specifies the amount of money to be deposited as collateral margin concept.

Finally, it should be noted that in organised markets commission is charged precisely to offset any losses that may result from this type of event. Thus, if the house manages this type of event well, profits are made from the commission charged, while if it manages it badly, losses are suffered.

Part IV

Other Risks

13

Operational Risk

13.1 Basic Concepts

13.1.1 Definition of Operational Risk

In recent years, the improvements made to new technology and the increasing complexity and globalisation of companies has led to increased concern about operational risk. There are many examples of operational risk events, including the BP oil platform spill in the summer of 2010 off the coast of New Orleans, in the Gulf of Mexico, which was the largest spill in history; the discovery in 2002 that an Allied Irish Bank trader had hidden losses in yen/dollar transactions with subsidiaries in the United States for three years, damaging the reputation of the bank; and others.

The first step in measuring risk is to define it; however, the difficulties associated with identifying operational risk compared to market risk or credit risk have led to a lack of consensus on its definition. Three approaches can be distinguished, ranging from a broad definition to a more precise definition:

F.J. Población García, *Financial Risk Management*,
DOI 10.1007/978-3-319-41366-2_13

- The first definition is broad, since it defines operational risk as any risk that does not fall into the category of market risk or credit risk. This definition is too broad, as it includes many risks which are not market or credit risks but which, strictly speaking, cannot be considered operational risks either.
- At the other extreme is the narrow definition which defines operational risk as the risk arising from operations including "back office" problems, failures in transaction processes or systems and technology failures. However, this definition only focuses on operations and does not include other significant operational risk events, such as internal fraud, improper sales practices or model risk.
- The third definition is set out in the Basel II Accord, a global agreement for the regulation of risks assumed by credit institutions: the operational risk is the risk of loss resulting from inadequate or failed processes, staff or internal systems or as a result of external events. It includes legal risk but excludes strategic and reputational risk.

For the purposes of this book, the third definition of operational risk will be used excluding legal risk which will be discussed later. Table 13.1 defines various sources that can cause operational risk.

The definition is completed by recognising seven categories of events that generate these losses:

- **Internal fraud**: intent to defraud, steal goods or evade regulation, laws and company policy, such as self-employed insider trading.
- **External fraud:** intent by a third party to defraud, misappropriate property or evade the law, such as theft, forgery or hacking.
- **Industrial relations and security in the workplace**: acts inconsistent with employment laws or agreements on health and safety or that result in the payment of personal injury claims, such as claims for worker compensation, violation of employee health and safety rules, discrimination complaints and so on.
- **Practice with clients, products and business**: involuntary error or negligent failure to meet an obligation to a specific client or regarding the nature or design of a product, such as the misuse of confidential

Table 13.1 Various sources that can cause operational risk (Author's own composition)

Cause	Definition	Example
Internal processes	Losses from failed transactions, clients' accounts, liquidations and daily business processes	Data input errors, denied access, negligent losses/ damage to client assets
Individuals	Losses caused by an employee or which involve an employee (intentional or otherwise) or losses caused by relationships between the company and the clients, third party shareholders and regulators	Unauthorised trading, internal fraud, harassment
Systems	Losses arising from the interruption of trade or system failure due to the unviability of infrastructure	Telecommunication failure, programming errors, viruses, public service cuts
External events	Losses arising from third party shares, including external fraud, damage to property or assets or changes to regulations which alter the ability of the firm to continue doing business	Natural disasters, terrorism, extortion, credit card fraud

client information, money laundering, the sale of unauthorised products and so on.

- **Damage to material assets**: loss or damage to physical assets as a consequence of natural disasters and other events such as terrorism, vandalism, earthquakes and so on.
- **Business incidents and system failures**: examples include hardware and software failure, telecommunications problems and public services cuts.
- **Execution, delivery and process management**: failure in the transaction process or management process and relationships with business

partners and suppliers, such as data entry errors, incomplete legal documentation, access to restricted customer accounts and so on.

Ninety per cent of a credit institution's liabilities consist of depositors' resources, thus these entities are subject to special regulation and close supervision. There is no specific regulation on risks that may or may not be assumed in other companies because these companies can assume as many risks as creditors allow. However, both types of companies, banks and non-banks, are exposed to operational risk, therefore this definition is considered to be applicable globally.

This risk is closely related to others such as country risk, legal risk and reputational risk, and in many cases there is a fine line separating them. In any case, this book discusses each of these risks individually, although they are of course related.

Finally, it is important to note that this risk is conceptually different from market risk and credit risk, which were studied previously, in the following ways:

- Unlike market risk and credit risk, this risk takes place internally, making it difficult to obtain databases as companies are reluctant to acknowledge their mistakes. Additionally, the way this risk is reflected in each company is different.
- In the case of credit risk and market risk, the exposure and risk factors can be separated to ensure that exposure can be controlled and measured easily. However, with operational risk the relationship between risk factors and the size and probability of losses is not easy to establish.
- Many manifestations of this type of risk occur very rarely but when they do occur, the losses suffered by the company are such that they can, and sometimes do, lead to bankruptcy. This type of event is what is known as the "fat tails" problem, and in these situations it is difficult to reach a robust value of operational risk with a high confidence level.

13.2 Operational Risk Measurement

Once operational risk has been defined, the next step in its management is to evaluate or measure it.

13.2.1 Loss Function

Conceptually, operational risk measurement is no different from any other risk measurement. The ultimate goal is to define a loss function, that is, a function that, for each level of loss, provides the probability of obtaining this level of loss as a result of operational risk over a given time horizon. Once the loss function has been defined, as shown in Fig. 13.1, the levels of loss can be classified into three categories:

- The expected loss is the loss which, on average, is expected to occur at each time period as a result of operational risk. This is something well known by managers and is reflected in a different way in each sector. In

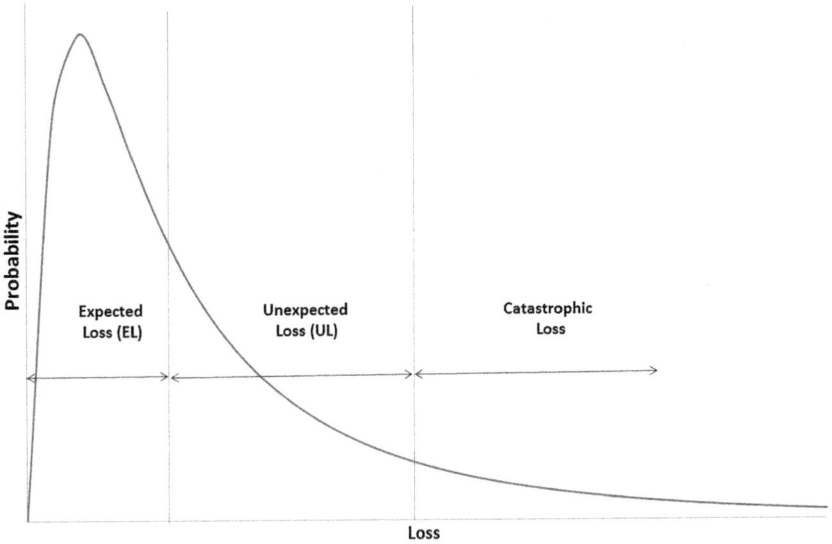

Fig. 13.1 Probability vs. loss (Author's own composition)

the department store sector, this refers primarily to the loss caused by shoplifting; in the transport and storage sector, the loss is caused by waste; in the electricity sector, it is caused by voltage reductions; and so on. This concept of expected loss is the same as that of credit risk discussed above.

- The unexpected loss is defined as a measure of the maximum loss that may be suffered due to operational risk over a time horizon and at a given probability level. The unexpected loss in the context of operational risk is the equivalent of the value at risk (VaR) for market risk and has the same concept as in the case of credit risk.
- If the probability level defined for the unexpected loss, which is usually 99.9 % in the case of operational risk, is exceeded, the level of loss that is obtained is defined as catastrophic loss.

As in the case of credit risk, there are two important distributions when estimating potential losses resulting from operational risk:

- On the one hand, the loss frequency distribution, which is simply the distribution of the number of losses observed over the horizon, is the likelihood of a certain number of events occurring which involve operational risk and is equivalent to the probability of default (PD) for credit risk.
- On the other hand, the loss severity distribution, which is simply a measure of the size of the losses, assuming the operational risk event occurs, is the probability of loss in each of these operational risk events and is equivalent to the loss given default (LGD) in the case of credit risk.

Both distributions are assumed to be independent, thus the loss function is obtained by combining the two probability distributions which allows the risk to be measured.

13.2.2 Databases

Everything studied so far in relation to operational risk, with possible variations, is common to all risks. However, the main difference between operational risk and other risks is the definition of each probability distribution, as the problem with operational risk is the lack of reliable databases. Unlike other risks, many operational risk events are very unlikely but when they occur they entail huge losses, hence the difficulty in obtaining databases. The events associated with other risks are more frequent and do not involve such high losses; consider the case of large frauds or major damages, for example, which are classic operational risk events.

It is true that in some industries there are more frequent operational risk events involving fewer losses, and consequently in these sectors it is relatively easy to measure operational risk, but this is not the most common scenario in industry. For this reason, in the Basel II Accord, credit institutions that want to measure operational risk using internal models are required to be able to prevent potentially serious events affecting the tails of probability distribution. More specifically, they are required to reach a degree of certainty comparable to a confidence interval of 99.9 % of the loss distribution with a time horizon of one year and are therefore required to combine four sources of information—model inputs—and justify the weight given to each of them. These four sources are internal data, external data, scenario analysis, and control factors and business environment.

The Basel II Accord only affects banks, because they constitute a regulated sector, but its general principles apply to any industry. In this sense, when internal databases are referred to in this agreement, a minimum observation period of five years is required; in addition, the data is required to be of good quality and to have an acceptable level of detail. The use of external data is primarily intended for when an entity or industry is thought to be exposed to rare but potentially severe losses; of these databases, the possibility of using public agency databases and also those created by some private companies is considered. Examples of this include meteorological institute databases, since very high or very low temperatures can cause operational risk events; databases developed by private companies in relation to fraud; and so on. A scenario analysis and external databases are required in order to assess exposure to rare but potentially severe losses. The quantitative development of this scenario analysis is very similar to what is carried out for other risks, such as market risk which was studied previously; however, expert judgement is required to determine the parameters (volatilities, correlations, etc.). As regards control and business factors, the main objective of introducing these factors is to allow risk assessments to be better oriented towards the future, to reflect the control environment of the institution and to recognise both improvements and deteriorations observed in operational risk profiles in a timelier manner.

13.2.3 Approaches to Operational Risk Measurement

The main approaches to operational risk measurement can be classified broadly as "top-down" or "bottom-up" models. "Top-down" models measure operational risk for the entity or industry as a whole; the results determine the amount of capital that must be reserved as a buffer against operational risk, and this amount is then divided among the business units. Conversely, "bottom-up" models start measuring risk in business units or processes and the results are aggregated to determine the risk profile of the institution. The main advantage of these approaches is that they allow for a better understanding of the causes of operational risk.

In this sense, and without being exhaustive, it can be said that the tools used to manage operational risk can be classified into six categories:

- **External audit**: involves an external audit department reviewing business processes.
- **Self-management review**: where each of the business units identifies the source and extent of the operational risk to which it is exposed. This subjective assessment includes its expected loss frequency and loss severity and the description of how to control the risk. Checklists and questionnaires are among the tools used for such processes.

- **Key risk indicators**: involve simple measures that provide indicators of changes that occur in the risks over time. These early warning signs include audit results, staff turnover, trading volumes and so on. It is assumed that operational risk events are more likely to occur when indicator values increase. These measures are objective and allow the risk manager to predict losses by, for example, applying regression techniques.
- **Volatility of revenue**: after disaggregating the effects of market risk and credit risk, this can be used to manage operational risk. This approach involves obtaining a time series of income, adjusted by trend, and obtaining a measure of volatility. This measure is easy to use, although it does come with many problems, as it includes fluctuations arising from business risks and changes in the macroeconomic environment which fall outside the category of operational risk. It is also a retrospective measure, and as such it ignores variations (positive or negative) in quality controls.
- **Causal networks**: describe how losses can occur as a result of a cascade of different causes. The causes and effects are related by conditional probabilities and the loss distribution is simulated by taking into account the relationships between different variables. These "bottom-up" models help to better understand the losses, since they are based on risk determinants.
- **Actuarial models**: combine the frequency distribution of losses with the severity distribution to obtain an objective distribution of losses due to operational risk, as noted previously in the section on determining the loss function. These models can be "bottom-up" or "top-down".

13.3 Operational Risk Mitigation Systems

Once any operational risk present in the company has been detected and measured, the company may decide to allocate resources to reduce that risk. Like all other risks, operational risk can be reduced, or even almost mitigated, but as in the case of the other risks, this entails a cost. The risk can be reduced both in the frequency with which losses occur and in the magnitude of losses when they occur.

Suppose a negotiating board of a broker agency wants to install a system that captures "front-office" operations and moves them directly to the "back-office." This avoids the possibility of human error and therefore reduces operational risk losses. The agency will buy the system if the benefits outweigh the costs. To assess whether this is the case or not, imagine that the same board performs an interest rate swap operation in five years and this product produces a large number of cash flows that may be the source of potential errors. Similarly, at the beginning the operation needs to be confirmed by the counterparty and, moreover, must be assessed in order to attribute the benefit to the business unit. Payments made by the swap must be computed accurately and, in this regard, errors may arise, from late payments to major problems such as hedging failures or the fraudulent behaviour of a "trader." Thus, analysing the potential benefits of this system and of avoiding such errors, it can be concluded whether it is beneficial to purchase that system or not.

In general, it can be said that operational risk can be reduced, or even mitigated, in many ways. The first is by methods of internal control which, roughly, involve:

- Separation of duties: employees in charge of commission operations must not carry out trade settlement or accounting operations.
- Dual inputs: inputs must be verified by two different sources.
- Reconciliations: the results or outputs must be verified by different sources. In the case of a "trading" board, these sources can be "trader" profit estimates and confirmation by "middle-office".
- Warning systems: important dates, maturities, liquidations and so on should be entered on a calendar in order to provide a reminder before the deadline.
- Amendments control: any amendment must be subject to the same controls as the original process.
- Confirmations: the ticket of the operation must be verified by the counterparty that provides an independent comparison.

- Price check: to evaluate positions, prices are available from external sources; this implies that an institution must be able to internally assess transactions before undertaking them.
- Authorisations: the counterparty must be provided with a list of people authorised to negotiate and a list of possible transactions.
- Settlement: the payment process itself may indicate whether some terms have been recorded incorrectly.
- Internal/external audits: such operations provide information about potentially weak areas in the structure of the organisation or business unit.

As indicated, these internal control methods are very useful and often partially mitigate operational risk, but it is very difficult to achieve its total mitigation; therefore, if the aim is to achieve a greater degree of mitigation, the only option is to resort to external methods. Traditionally, operational risk has been mitigated through insurance, but more recently there has been a tendency to use financial hedges based on financial derivatives on operational risk events such as the weather, theft and the like.

13.3.1 Insurance

Insurance is the traditional instrument for mitigating operational risk. Traditional insurance is based on compensating the individual who contracts it if a certain operational risk event occurs; for example, if there is a fire in a warehouse, fire insurance indemnifies the owner of the warehouse based on the value of the goods that have been burnt, or if hail spoils the harvest, the insurance pays the farmer for the difference in production between this year and last year.

Despite the obvious advantages of this type of instrument, when reducing operational risk several problems arise. One of these problems is the moral hazard, which is the risk of the insurance beneficiary behaving in a different way than they would if there were no insurance because if they are hedged against the consequences of an operational risk event, less care is taken to minimise the probability of the event occurring. For example, if they have fire insurance, the warehouse is less careful regarding precautions to minimise the chances of a fire occurring (flammable materials, smoking regulations, etc.), or a bank with theft insurance consequently takes increasingly lax security measures.

This change of attitude increases the risk for insurance companies and therefore these companies hedge the moral hazard in several ways, one of which is known as a deductible (or excess). The company introduces a clause in the insurance contract making the policyholder responsible for paying the specified first portion of losses. At other times the company introduces a coinsurance provision which means that the company pays a certain percentage less than 100 % of losses that exceed the deductible. Likewise, there is almost always a policy limit, that is, a limit to the insurer's obligations.

Adverse selection is one of the biggest problems for insurance companies. This phenomenon occurs when the insurer cannot distinguish between "good" and "bad" policyholders and offers the same price to everyone, inadvertently attracting the worst customers. Companies hedge themselves against this problem by using varying premiums depending on the information obtained about the policyholder over time but, as with moral hazard, in the absence of perfect information, this risk can never be completely removed.

Since it is not possible to elimiate fraud completely in this type of transaction, meaning that the policyholder requests more compensation from the company than the cost incurred by the damage, since the insurance company is unable to verify the actual loss suffered accurately.

In addition, insurance can generate a conflict of interest, in the sense that the expert evaluating the damages suffered as a result of the operational risk event is paid by the insurance company and therefore has an incentive to declare fewer losses than actually occurred. Similarly, insurers are not always responsible for the operational risk event occurring. The best example of this was 9/11, when the insurance companies of both the towers and the planes initially refused to pay compensation based on the fact that the damage came from a terrorist attack, although one of the main causes of planes crashing or skyscrapers collapsing is a terrorist attack. Another example is the case of insurance against the breakage of windows, where policyholders are not paid if breakage occurs as a result of riots, even though riots are one of the main causes of broken windows.

13.3.2 Financial Hedges

Due to the problems previously indicated, the mitigation of some operational risk events has now begun to be carried out through financial hedging instead of insurance. These financial hedges are based on derivatives whose underlying asset is the operational risk event, such as temperature, rain and so on. These derivatives have greatly expanded in the operational risk mitigation industry, as they have been developed to hedge catastrophic risks, usually meteorological, seismic and the like. A classic example is the derivative that pays the buyer a certain amount of money for the days that the National Institute of Meteorology declares that the temperature in a given geographical area is above a given temperature and, in doing so, the farmer can protect against drought. This can also be carried out in terms of days of rain, hail, frost and so on.

The primary advantage of this type of hedging is that it avoids many of the aforementioned problems. The main reason is that the payoff function is objective, that is, it is not based on a subjective estimate of losses. In the previous example it was established that hedging pays a certain amount of money for the days when the National Institute of Meteorology declares that the temperature in a given geographical area is above a given temperature; thus, this payment function does not depend on the views of an expert paid by the insurance company or on what the policyholder claims, and therefore it avoids moral hazard because payments do not depend on loss. It also eliminates the possibility of events occurring in which the insurance company avoids being liable for loss because the damages are not evaluated by their experts. Fraud and conflict of interest are also avoided because an independent third party with objective measures, in this example the National Institute of Meteorology, states how much must be paid and when.

However, despite these obvious advantages, these products also have disadvantages compared to insurance. Their main drawback is that since their payoff function is not directly linked to the loss, they are not always effective in hedging it. That is, in the above example, if a farmer concerned about possible drought contracts a derivative that pays a specified amount of money for the days when the National Institute of Meteorology declares that the temperature in a given geographical area is superior to a given temperature, their payment has no relation to the losses suffered by drought, which may be much higher than the payments received; therefore the effectiveness of hedging may be very low.

13.4 Approach to Operational Risk in Basel II: Determination of Regulatory Capital

Although this book is about risk management in an industrial company and, as already indicated, the Basel II Accord is an international agreement for the regulation of risks assumed by banks, this section will summarise very briefly what this agreement states regarding operational risk, as it can be useful in other types of businesses.

Banking regulation in general, and this agreement in particular, establish minimum capital requirements which must include liabilities of a credit institution depending on the risks assumed, including operational risk. In this sense, this agreement provides three methods for calculating capital requirements for operational risk: the Basic Indicator Approach (BIA), the Standardised Approach (SA) and the Advanced Methods Approach (AMA).

- **The Basic Indicator Approach (BIA)** is the simplest of all and must be applied to entities by default. With this approach, the capital requirement for operational risk is equal to 15 % of gross revenues for the preceding three years. For this calculation, gross income is defined as total net income from interest, also known as net interest income, which is defined as the excess income from loans minus interest paid on deposits and other instruments used for finance loans plus non-interest income.
- **The Standardised Approach (SA)** is very similar to the BIA, but slightly more complex. In this approach, entities are required to divide

Table 13.2 "Beta" factors (Author's own composition)

Business line	"Beta" factor
Corporate finance	18 %
Trading and sales	18 %
Retail banking	12 %
Commercial banking	15 %
Payment and settlement	18 %
Agency services	15 %
Asset management	12 %
Retail brokerage	12 %

their activities into eight lines of business: corporate finance, trading and sales, retail banking, commercial banking, payment and settlement, agency services, asset management and retail brokerage. The average gross income in recent years for each business line is multiplied by a "beta" factor for each line of business and the result is added to obtain the total amount of capital (Table 13.2).

In order to use this method, the entity must demonstrate that it has systems to distribute income among business lines and the central bank must give permission. Similarly, conditions are established which must be met for a bank to use the standard method:

- The credit institution must have an operational risk management function which is responsible for identifying, assessing, monitoring and controlling operational risk.
- They must keep track of the relevant losses by business line and create incentives to improve operational risk.
- Losses due to operational risk must be reported regularly by the credit institution.
- The system of operational risk management should be well documented.
- Management processes and operational risk assessment systems must be subject to independent periodic reviews by internal auditors; they must also be subject to periodic review by external auditors, supervisors or both.

- Finally, by using the Advanced Models Approach (MA), the capital requirement for operational risk is calculated internally by the bank through the use of qualitative and quantitative criteria. In this case the central bank must give permission and conditions are established which must be met for a bank to use the advanced models approach (MA).

14

Liquidity Risk

14.1 Basic Concepts

Liquidity is a phenomenon to keep firmly in mind when managing the risk of a firm. Formally speaking, the liquidity risk of a company can be defined as the loss that may occur due to events that affect the availability of resources needed to meet liability obligations, whether this is due to an inability to sell assets, an unexpected reduction in trade liabilities or the closure of usual sources. In other words, liquidity risk is caused by the fact that the company has to make recurring payments but the timing of these payments does not usually coincide with receiving income, and their wealth is not stored as money but, conversely, part of it is kept in assets. When the time comes to deal with a payment, a situation may arise in which the company cannot find an entity willing to finance it in market conditions, and these assets cannot be sold without offering a large discount because of a lack of interested counterparties or directly because the company cannot find a counterparty to contract with.

In order to avoid liquidity problems, positions in short-term instruments with high creditworthiness must be taken. However, as discussed in previous chapters, these instruments provide the least compensation,

F.J. Población García, *Financial Risk Management*,
DOI 10.1007/978-3-319-41366-2_14

therefore the disadvantage of liquidity is that the opportunity to obtain higher income by investing in longer terms and/or lower-rated assets must be relinquished.

It should also be noted that, like most of the risks affecting the company, liquidity risk is a risk cycle, in other words, in times of crisis liquidity is generally lower—that is, liquidity evaporates—as opposed to in good times, meaning that the measurement and management of this risk is more complicated than it might initially seem. In fact, the recent economic crisis has shown that certain assets which have traditionally been considered to be very liquid have ceased to be so, and for this reason many of the recent changes in banking regulation have focused on liquidity risk.

14.1.1 Types of Liquidity Risk and Its Relationships with Other Risks

The manifestation of liquidity risk is very different from a drop in price to zero, which is market risk. In case of a drop in an asset's price to zero, the market is saying that the asset is valueless; however, if one party cannot find another party who is interested in trading the asset, this could potentially be simply a problem of the market participants finding each other rather than an asset price problem. For this reason, liquidity risk is usually found to be higher in emerging markets or low-volume markets.

Strictly speaking, there are two types of liquidity risk: market liquidity risk and funding liquidity risk. Market liquidity risk is the risk that an asset cannot be sold due to lack of liquidity in the market, whereas funding liquidity risk arises when liabilities cannot be met when they fall due or can only be met at an uneconomic price.

Nevertheless, market and funding liquidity risks affect each other, as it is difficult to sell when other investors face funding problems and it is difficult to get funding when the collateral is hard to sell. Moreover, liquidity risk also tends to create other risks; for example, if an investment bank has a position in an illiquid asset, its limited ability to liquidate that position in a short period of time will compound its market risk. Another example could be a company that has offsetting cash flows with two different counterparties on a given day: if the counterparty that owes it a payment defaults, the company will have to raise cash from other sources to make its payment, which may not be possible or could be very difficult and could lead the company to default. In this case, liquidity risk is compounding credit risk.

Due to this propensity to compound other risks (mainly market and credit risk), it is difficult or impossible to isolate liquidity risk and consequently liquidity risk should be managed in addition to other risks. Taking what has already been said into consideration, comprehensive metrics of liquidity risk do not exist in isolation; however, certain techniques of asset liability management can be applied to measuring liquidity risk. A simple test for liquidity risk is to look at future net cash flows on a day-to-day basis and flag each day that has a sizeable negative net cash flow. These kinds of analyses can be supplemented with stress test techniques, that is, looking at net cash flows on a day-to-day basis assuming that an important counterparty defaults or some claim prices drop significantly.

However, analyses like these cannot easily take into account contingent cash flows, such as cash flows from derivatives or mortgage-backed securities. If an organisation's cash flows are largely contingent, liquidity risk can simply be assessed using scenario analysis. A general approach using scenario analysis might entail the construction of multiple scenarios for market movements and defaults over a given period of time and the assessment of day-to-day cash flows under each scenario. Because balance sheets differ so significantly from one organisation to the next, there is little standardisation in how such analyses are implemented.

14.2 Liquidity Risk Measurement

The management of liquidity risk, as with that of any other risk, involves establishing a system to identify, monitor, measure and control the degree of exposure to risk. At a basic level, the measurement of liquidity risk involves comparing the maturity of all the cash flows of its asset, liability and off-balance-sheet operations to identify the possible existence of future gaps. Thus, the measure of liquidity is simply the expression of the mismatch between assets and liabilities, whether in absolute or relative terms. The sophistication of liquidity analysis lies in the predictive behaviour models of assets, liabilities and off-balance-sheet operations and the dynamic evolution of the entity's balance sheet.

In order to determine whether the liquidity position of the company is adequate, the following items must be analysed: historical resource requirements, current liquidity position, future cash requirements, sources of funding, options to reduce resource requirements or to obtain additional resources, present and projected quality of assets, current and future capacity to generate profits and position of current and anticipated capital.

In order to compare cash flows arising from the entity's asset, liability and off-balance-sheet positions, a scale is used in which the corresponding maturities are clustered in certain periods of time; thus, the analysis of future fund requirements comes from the construction of the maturity scale and the calculation of the gap—surplus or deficit—for the periods considered and the amount accumulated over a period of time.

14.2.1 Static Measurement

The static measurement of liquidity risk is the result of flows, liabilities and assets being projected, for a period of time, in a predetermined scenario; in this way the amount of surplus or deficit can also be determined—that is, the liquidity gap—in each period. Estimation is straightforward for contractual flows, while in the case of uncertain cash flows the use of behavioural hypotheses is required.

After calculating the liquidity gap of each period, the so-called cumulative liquidity gap can be estimated by adding the gaps of the periods included within a certain period of time. The expression that would allow its calculation is:

$$C_{t_N}^{\text{Acum}} = \sum_{i=0}^{N} \left(C_{t_i}^{A} - C_{t_i}^{P} \right)$$

where C_{tN}^{Acum} is the cumulative liquidity gap for the period t_N, C_{ti}^{A} are positive cash flows for the period i and C_{ti}^{P} are negative cash flows for the period i.

The cumulative liquidity gap provides information on the requirements (negative gap) or excess (positive gap) of liquidity in the period. Contrary to how they might initially be perceived, the possibility of a positive cumulative gap is also important, since unnecessary excess liquidity may have a negative impact on the profitability of managing the balance sheet. However, in the context of a risk management function, the objective is to establish minimum levels of liquidity, operational limits or liquidity ratios, which allow losses arising from liquidity problems to be minimised.

There are many internal boundaries used by companies depending on the model of liquidity management implemented: by term, currency, maximum percentage of counterparty funding, gaps in the maturity scale, maximum position in the interbank market, and so on. Whatever the boundaries used, quantitative limits to liquidity risk must be referred to by at least establishing the maximum cumulative liquidity gap in each term of analysis.

14.2.2 Dynamic Measurement

Unlike static measurement, dynamic measurement results from considering various future scenarios for the evolution of net cash flows, which involves modelling the uncertain portion of future cash flows. That is, dynamic treatment of liquidity risk involves developing probabilistic and behavioural models for market variables and balance lines. When developing liquidity forecasts, macroeconomic, market and interest rate trends must be taken into account due to their impact on the evolution of assets and liabilities, as well as on contingent liabilities and derivatives.

By using the models it is possible to generate multiple future scenarios for the distribution of asset and liability flows, and the volatility of certain asset and liability items will be different depending on the scenarios considered, especially items without a fixed maturity, such as current accounts, those available on credit accounts and other contingent liabilities, such as guarantees.

14.2.3 Pricing Liquidity Risk

As with any other kind of risk, the higher an asset's liquidity risk, the higher the market requested return—that is, risk averse investors naturally require a higher expected return as compensation for liquidity risk. This extra return is known as the liquidity premium.

In this sense, the liquidity risk elasticity is defined as the change in the net asset value over funded liabilities which occurs when the liquidity premium on the company's marginal funding cost rises by a small amount. For banks this would be measured as a spread over Libor, whereas for non-financial companies it would be measured as a spread over commercial paper rates. The main problem with the use of liquidity risk elasticity is that it assumes parallel changes in funding spread across all maturities and that it is only accurate for small changes in funding spreads.

In financial markets, the bid–ask spread is defined as the difference between the prices quoted for an immediate sale (bid) and an immediate purchase (ask). The size of the bid–ask spread in a security is another way to measure market liquidity and the extent of the transaction cost; specifically, in comparing different products, the ratio of the spread to the product's bid price can be used: the smaller the ratio is, the more liquid the asset is.

In line with market risk, another interesting measure to price liquidity risk is the "liquidity-adjusted VaR", which incorporates exogenous liquidity risk into value at risk (VaR). It can be defined at VAR + ELC (exogenous liquidity cost), where the ELC is the worst expected half-spread at a particular confidence level. Another possibility is to consider the VaR over the period of time needed to liquidate the portfolio. In this sense, another measure is the liquidity at risk, which is defined as the maximum potential liquidity gap that a company can suffer within a certain time horizon and for a given confidence level. However, although these measures are useful, especially under mild scenarios, they face limitations when more severe liquidity shocks arise because, as stated above, liquidity risk is a low-frequency and high-impact risk, and consequently historical volatilities and correlations tend to underestimate funding risk under severe stress because severe stress is highly non-linear.

14.2.4 Methods to Assess Liquidity Risk: Liquidity Stress Test

Methods to assess liquidity risk run from the use of simple indicators to very refined and intricate systems. A usual starting point for assessing liquidity risk is through reliable indicators which provide significant information on the liquidity position of the company, which can be compared with that of its peers and over time. Among these simple indicators are ratios like the loan to deposit ratio or the public to private sources ratio. The maturity matrix is also a simple and very useful indicator.

On the banking regulatory side, considerable efforts have been made to contain liquidity risk at the bank level. Basel III has introduced two measures to contain short-term vulnerabilities and excessive maturity mismatches. The first measure is the "liquidity coverage ratio" (LCR), which requires a bank to hold sufficient high-quality liquid assets to ensure the bank's resilience against a "significant stress scenario lasting 30 days", that is, the bank should be able to survive for one month under (medium to severe) stress. Mathematically it is expressed as follows: $\text{LCR} = \frac{\text{High Quality Liquid Assets}}{\text{Total Net Liquidity Outflows over 30 Days}} \geq 100\%$. The second measure is the "net stable funding ratio" (NSFR), which requires an available amount of stable funding to exceed the compulsory amount over a one-year period of extended stress; it also aims to limit maturity mismatches, with a 12-month horizon.

Liquidity stress tests are more forward-looking, and several methods have been developed. Classical stress tests are based on cash flows (top-down and bottom-up). Another liquidity stress testing framework is one in which banks' liquidity risk arises from the impact of mark-to-market losses on banks' solvency, leading to deposit outflows and evaporating asset fire sales, and consequently sharply rising contingent liquidity risk. In both cases feedback effects, along with liquidity risk issues and other risks, mainly credit and market risk, should be taken into account.

Stress tests in the banking industry are focused on maturity mismatch approaches because the ultimate aim of liquidity stress tests is to determine the maximum level of risk that a company, usually a bank, is willing to accept under stress conditions, that is, the company's risk tolerance for liquidity risk. Sometimes this maturity mismatch approach is complemented by stochastic VaR components, liquidity at risk or liquidity-adjusted VaR, for those funding sources for which there is sufficient data.

As stated above, the classical way to stress test liquidity risk is to use cash flow level data. Taking into account that the cash flow structure and the maturity of all cash flows are monitored, the challenge is how to deal with the volatility of funding and the strategy of managing maturity mismatch. The volatility of funding comes from cash flows which don't have predefined cash flow structures; in a bank or a financial company these cash flows are contingent liabilities (e.g., credit cards or lines) on the asset side and demand deposits or short-term interbank market access on the liability side.

There are two ways to stress test liquidity risk system-wide: defining common scenarios that are run by companies, particularly banks themselves—so-called bottom-up (BU) tests—making use of granular data; or collecting data from broader liability and asset types and applying scenarios accordingly in a top-down (TD) fashion (i.e., run by authorities, particularly central banks). The results of these wide liquidity stress tests are the following: they show the ability of a company, usually a bank, to continue being a liquid company; they permit a peer comparison; and, if the feedback between solvency and liquidity risks is modelled, they can provide a link between the joint resistance to liquidity and solvency risks.

14.3 Liquidity Risk Management

Liquidity management involves estimating cash requirements to achieve the foreseen objectives, and to do so in the least costly manner possible, considering that liquidity can be obtained on both sides of the balance sheet as well as from off-balance-sheet activities.

As far as the asset is concerned, note that it is possible to maintain some liquid assets on the balance sheet—that is, assets that can be quickly and easily converted into cash at a reasonable cost or that have a maturity term earlier than the expected liquidity requirements. The basic function of these assets is to ensure liquidity, although managers also expect to obtain interest income on these assets. Money market assets are typically the most liquid assets, although the company can raise cash by other means: the maturity of assets, the sale of assets to raise cash and the use of other assets as collateral for a loan.

In terms of the liabilities, it must be noted that access to wholesale markets, especially large banks, can provide funds quickly and in large quantities in comparison to the much slower results achieved from having access to equity in the retail market; however, smaller companies rarely have the same ease of access to these large markets and this must be taken into account. On the other hand, although, as previously noted, the wholesale market is the fastest way to achieve liquidity, changes in market conditions may make it difficult for the company to obtain resources to manage its liability structure, as these markets are much more sensitive to credit risk and interest rate risk than retail markets and they react differently to changes in the economic and financial conditions of the company.

Considering these aspects, the managers, in addition to trying to get a proper structure of resources, must carefully consider the potential concentration of funding. There is considered to be a concentration where a single decision or a single factor can cause a considerable withdrawal of funding. No specific size is required to be considered as "concentration"; rather, it depends on the company and its balance sheet structure.

In addition to managing liquidity in normal situations, companies must be prepared to respond to any eventual individual or market crisis. The approach is to design different crisis scenarios, estimate how they would affect the entity and prepare appropriate contingency plans designed to ensure continuity of the entity while incurring the lowest possible cost. Although theoretically the variety of crisis scenarios is limitless, institutions tend to focus on scenarios that reflect individual circumstances to which they are most sensitive, be they internal (fraud, mismanagement, loss of reputation, IT failures, etc.) or external (wars, natural disasters, problems in a country or geographical area in which they have subsidiaries, regulatory changes, etc.). In addition, besides the degree of each entity's exposure to the causes that define each scenario, it will be necessary to formulate hypotheses about the duration of the crisis, its intensity, its generality and so on. The next step is to estimate how the most significant variables might be affected and, especially for severe crisis scenarios, the number of guaranteed days of survival must be established, taking into account that the minimum necessary horizon is 20–30 days.

After establishing the different crisis scenarios and the survival horizon to be guaranteed, a way of obtaining the necessary liquidity in these circumstances must be considered, designing procedures that guarantee sufficient liquidity at the lowest possible cost, so that these various contingency plans can be activated when the events that prefigure each crisis scenario occur. Examples of internal indicators of these events include a negative trend or significantly increased risk in a specific area or product line; the concentration of assets or liabilities; a decline in indicators of asset quality; a decrease in the levels of revenue or anticipated revenues; and rapid growth funded by volatile liabilities. Professional analysts or other market participants can also comment on the creditworthiness of the company. Examples of these assessments by third parties include the existence of rumours in the market suggesting the situation of the company is worrying; declines in its creditworthiness according to rating agencies; and speculative downward movements in the secondary market for the entity's stocks.

In addition, there are also macro-prudential approaches to managing systemic liquidity risk. These approaches provide incentives such as taxes, capital charges, the introduction of minimum liquidity ratios and haircuts, and so on to limit systemic liquidity risks. Some of them have been used, at least partially, in emerging market countries for many years; however, full implementation around the world seems unlikely, mainly owing to the complexity of measuring this risk.

14.3.1 Liquidity Crisis

Until the recent financial crisis, liquidity risk was considered a minor risk and liquidity risk management was considered to be "less of an issue". However, the recent financial crisis has demonstrated that liquidity risk is an important risk because, even though liquidity crises are very low-frequency, which greatly reduces the opportunity to draw on historical experience to calibrate models, they are very high-impact events. Moreover, as stated above, due to the propensity of liquidity risk to compound other risks, all liquidity crises are somehow different, at least if we analyse the relationship between the sources and the resulting liquidity shortfalls, reducing the usefulness of "standard" stress assumptions.

As stated above, liquidity crises typically occur very suddenly and can be triggered by various events, most notably solvency problems, but also political instability and fraud. They spread very quickly, giving firms very little time to react. Contagion can escalate idiosyncratic shocks into market-wide shocks, as seen during the recent crisis period, and it is for this reason that liquidity buffer requirements should be based on highly conservative principles. A key principle applied by US authorities during the height of the recent financial crisis was to ensure that investment banks made it through a business week so that a viable solution could be found during the weekend if necessary. As stated above, there are two liquidity risk measures in the regulatory framework established by Basel III: the "liquidity coverage ratio" and the "net stable funding ratio".

As stated above, liquidity crises may be sharp and short or more drawn out, and consequently each crisis requires different mitigating actions and considerations. However, some common ideas can be identified. Firstly, the obvious solution to counterbalancing bank-run-type outflows is to liquidate assets through fire sales; nevertheless, the dilemma for banks lies in the cost of holding high-quality liquid assets, particularly cash and "prime" government bonds. More illiquid securities are less costly due to their return but are subject to higher haircuts, or become illiquid during periods of market stress and/or may no longer qualify as eligible collateral (to ensure secured funding).

Secondly, in the case of durable liquidity problems, the maturity matrix of assets and liabilities is a very helpful indicator as maturing assets can then be used to deleverage in an "orderly" way, provided that, at least partly, maturing debt can be rolled over. In fact, the analysis of rollover risk has become an important part of liquidity risk analysis, as institutions sometimes face a "wall of funding".

Finally, in a severe crisis central bank funding plays a natural counterbalancing role since it can act as a lender of last resort. Parent banks can also step in to increase credit lines in subsidiaries if a subsidiary loses access to funding sources.

15

Country Risk

15.1 Basic Concepts

In recent years, country risk analysis has become an important subject of study in the research and risk management departments of banks, rating agencies, insurance companies and financial system regulators. The concept of country risk emerged in the 1950s in the context of the resurgence of international banking activity and gained notoriety from the early 1980s with the outbreak of the Latin American debt crisis.

Until the early 1970s, developing countries could only get funding from official sources, that is, the World Bank, regional development banks, bilateral loans and so on, usually associated with specific projects. However, after the oil crisis of 1973 the growing need for funding in oil-importing countries and the availability of funds in oil-exporting countries led commercial banks to start providing greater cash flows to developing countries. However, when the second oil crisis occurred in 1979, many of the countries that had borrowed heavily during that decade began to have trouble coping with their payment commitments abroad, with Mexico being the first country to suspend payments in 1982.

F.J. Población García, *Financial Risk Management*,
DOI 10.1007/978-3-319-41366-2_15

The debt crisis of the 1980s fuelled the concerns of financial supervisory authorities regarding the control of international banking risks, especially in the USA where bankruptcy in banks occurred as a result of default in Latin American countries. From that time the concept of country risk became increasingly important, leading to the development of specific methodologies and regulations.

Country risk is a very broad concept which includes the study of economic, financial, political, historical and sociological aspects. It also includes both the risk of default on external sovereign debt (sovereign risk) and the risk of default on external private debt, when credit risk is due to circumstances beyond the solvency or liquidity situation of the private sector. External debt refers to any debt instrument, loans or bonds, or contingent risk—that is, collateral, guarantees, deposits and so on—contracted by residents of one country with those in the rest of the world.

In a first approximation, country risk can be said to refer to the probability of a financial loss occurring due to macroeconomic, political or social circumstances or due to natural disasters in a certain country. However, this is not the only accepted definition of country risk. According to the Circular 4/2004 of the Banco de España, country risk is the credit risk, or default risk, which is associated with customers resident in a particular country due to circumstances other than normal commercial risk.

15.1.1 Country Risk in a Strict Sense

Strictly speaking, country risk comprises sovereign risk and transfer risk. Sovereign risk refers to the credit risk, or default risk, of the state as a debtor or guarantor, when this credit risk is caused by circumstances beyond solvency or liquidity in the private sector.

Sovereign risk is the default risk on state debt or the entities guaranteed by them. Sovereign debt default may occur due to a lack of public revenue, a lack of foreign exchange, or because the government is not willing to pay for political reasons.

As regards non-sovereign or private debt, default due to circumstances beyond the solvency or liquidity of the debtor may firstly be caused by the so-called transfer risk which is accrued when there is a lack of the currency in which the external debt is named. Risk transfer can occur as a result of a serious imbalance of payments, for example as a result of a high level of external debt, or due to a sudden lack of trust leading to a massive outflow of capital.

Private external debt default can also be caused by the occurrence of other risks, such as balance-of-payments crises, significant devaluations of the parity of currency which may generate a situation of insolvency, wars, revolutions, natural disasters, expropriations and nationalisations, as well as a lack of implementation of commitments and contracts by the governments of both the debtor and the creditor country. The above circumstances can lead to defaults on foreign debt due to the disappearance of institutions, the need to reserve currencies to satisfy needs more pressing than debt settlement, or the bankruptcy of enterprises as a result of excessive debt increasing in the national currency because of a very significant devaluation of the exchange rate or lack of enforcement of contracts.

This was the original meaning of the term country risk, referring almost exclusively to the default risk of private bank loans granted to public and private entities in a given country due to their own causes and not to the individual circumstances of the debtor. Later the concept was expanded to include the issue of international bonds and, more recently, with the development of international equity markets, it has also come to include portfolio investment.

15.1.2 Country Risk in a Broad Sense

Country risk is broadly defined as the risk that arises when operating in or with a given country. This risk refers to variations, regarding expectations, that monetary flows or asset values may suffer in operations in a foreign country due to changes in the conditions of that country. These changes in conditions may affect values both nationally and internationally, but the international effects are those which attract most attention.

In this broad definition of country risk two components can be found: economic and financial risk and political risk. Economic and financial risk refers to unexpected changes in the economic and financial field such as variations in the exchange rate, the interest rate or inflation, while political risk is the risk of the government in the foreign country changing the rules under which the operation is carried out, for example, the expropriation of assets, the freezing of funds or changes in the tax system. This political risk comprises socio-political risk and administrative risk. In addition, the risk associated with foreign direct investment (FDI), which includes the transfer risk in dividend payments and the product of investment liquidation, the risk of confiscation, expropriation and nationalisation of foreign investments, the risk of breach of contract and the risk of wars, political violence and natural disasters are sometimes included in this definition of country risk in a wider sense. These issues have already been addressed in both private and sovereign debt default risk, since when a nation has a high level of country risk for debt instruments, it also has a high level of country risk for foreign direct investment.

As demonstrated, the different risks encompassed within the concept of country risk are not separate categories, but are closely related and even overlapping. For example, transfer risk caused by a lack of currency affects both private and sovereign debt and thus is related to economic and financial risk; wars and political conflicts may lead to significant devaluations, again linked to economic and financial risk, which generate an increased transfer risk, affecting the payment of private and sovereign debt.

Similarly, country risk is closely related to other types of risk such as market risk or credit risk; consequently these risks are not always easily distinguishable. For example, consider a private company in a developing country with an acceptable level of external debt and a business dependent on imported raw materials, without liquidity or solvency problems. If devaluation occurs, the company may become insolvent and have to suspend payment of its foreign debt, in which case both the client's country risk and its credit risk appear and a decision must be reached as to which of the two predominates. On the other hand, the default on foreign debt by a private company as a result of the enactment of new legislation prohibiting such payments will clearly constitute a country risk default event. Thus, it is clear that this broad definition of country risk, in terms of the economic and financial risk, overlaps with other risks such as exchange risk and interest rate risk.

15.2 Variables Influencing Country Risk

Once we have presented all different concepts that can influence country risk, we are going to briefly analyse the different aspects that can influence the risk of default on external debt because of country risk.

- In the political field it is necessary to analyse political stability, government effectiveness, the strength of institutions, the risk of internal and external political conflicts, geographical location considering political or military conflicts in the area, the extent of corruption and debt payment culture. Political risk can be measured by the governance indicators of the World Bank which evaluate the set of traditions and institutions used to exercise authority in a country, including the election process, control and replacement of governments, the ability of the government to effectively formulate and implement sound policies, and the respect that the citizens and the state have for the institutions that govern economic and social interactions between them.
- In the macroeconomic sphere the following characteristics must be observed: the rate of economic growth and its potential volatility over time, the inflation rate, the credibility of monetary policy instruments, the level of the nominal and real interest rates, the public sector balance sheet and, in the event of a deficit, its financing, the level of public debt, and the degree of development in the local bond market.
- The economic structure sphere comprises the level of per capita income, income distribution, social mobility, country size, product diversification, concentration of exports in a few goods or services and energy dependence.
- In the banking sector, the following features must be noted; the proportion of poor quality bank loans, the profitability of banking, foreign bank penetration, the rate of domestic savings, access to bank credit, the balance of bank assets and liabilities in foreign currency, the

existence of a deposit insurance institution, and the degree of development and effectiveness of banking supervision.

- In the foreign sector, the features that must be analysed include the balance of trade and current accounts, the exchange rate regime, the level of foreign direct and foreign portfolio investment, the existence of exchange controls, devaluation history, the level and structure of external debt, payment history and refinancing, and the level of foreign reserves.
- Markets also provide valuable information about the country's risk of default through indicators such as the sovereign spread or the interest rate spread of sovereign debt in dollars relative to the interest rate of US Treasury bonds in ten years as measured by the JP Morgan EMBI index (Emerging Market Bond Index) and the credit default swap (CDS) spread. In addition to these indicators, the long-term sovereign credit rating in a foreign currency assigned by credit rating agencies constitutes an important reference in markets, as do the Organisation for Economic Co-operation and Development (OECD) country risk classifications.

The EMBI+ or EMBI Plus (Emerging Markets Bond Index Plus) developed by the US investment bank JP Morgan is the best known index used to measure country risk from a market perspective. The EMBI+ began publication in July 1995 with the aim of creating a reference to reflect the returns of a debt portfolio of emerging markets. In total, the index consists of 107 instruments from 16 countries: Argentina, Brazil, Bulgaria, Colombia, Ecuador, Egypt, Indonesia, Mexico, Panama, Peru, the Philippines, Russia, South Africa, Turkey, Ukraine and Venezuela. In order to be included in the EMBI, debt instruments must have a minimum live nominal value of 500 million dollars.

Brady bonds, Eurobonds, loans and debt instruments from sovereign issuers are included in the bond index denominated in foreign currencies, mainly in US dollars, and since 31 May 2002 debt under local jurisdiction has not been eligible for inclusion in the index where inclusion is limited to issuers with legal jurisdiction in a country of the G7. Since the index includes the debt of emerging countries in dollars, the sovereign credit rating of countries cannot be greater than BBB+ on the scale of the credit rating agency Standard and Poor's, or Baa1 on Moody's scale. Normally, the index is expressed as a spread in basic points on the yield of US Treasury bonds in ten years.

The JP Morgan EMBI Global index is itself an extended version of the EMBI+ created to be fully representative of the emerging countries in general by covering a wider range of debt values with lower liquidity requirements, a greater number of countries which are classified as low or middle income by the World Bank (having a per capita income below $11,116 in 2006) and countries which enjoy a higher credit rating than BBB+ or Baa1. Specifically, EMBI Global includes 27 countries, those in the EMBI+ as well as countries like Algeria, Chile, China, Malaysia, Morocco, Nigeria and Poland.

The EMBI, both in its plus version and in its global version, traditionally referred to as one of the main indicators of country risk, has recently lost some relevance as a risk indicator of emerging countries, as at present dollar-denominated bonds only represent about 28 % of outstanding sovereign debt, while the remaining 72 % of debt consists of bonds denominated in local currency, which have recently been attracting considerable interest from investors. For this reason, in 2005 JP Morgan added the Government Bond Index–Emerging Markets (GBI–EM) to its family of emerging market indexes, an index that allows the sovereign debt in the local currency of 19 emerging countries to be monitored: Argentina, Brazil, Chile, China, Colombia, Czech Republic, Egypt, Hungary, India, Indonesia, Malaysia, Mexico, Peru, Poland, Russia, Slovakia, South Africa, Thailand and Turkey.

Another market indicator used to assess country risk is the credit default swap spread. As discussed, when dealing with credit risk, this instrument is a financial derivative which allows credit risk to be transferred because it is a bilateral over-the-counter (OTC) contract which is used to transfer risk from the protection buyer to the protection seller. This is the risk of a "credit event" specified in the contract occurring, such as bankruptcy, default, restructuring, breach of obligations, repudiation and so on by a company or sovereign issuer. The protection buyer pays a periodic premium on the face value, usually expressed as an annual rate, called spread, until the expiration of the contract or until the credit event specified in the protection contract occurs. Since it is a contract which hedges credit risk, the amount of the CDS premium provides information on the credit quality of reference entities and the increases in spreads indicate increased risk, while decreases indicate decreased risk and, therefore, in the event that the reference entity is a sovereign state, the CDS premium can be used as an indicator of country risk.

Market indicators such as the EMBI Plus and CDS spread give an immediate idea of the level of country risk assigned by the market as it can be measured using the corresponding risk premium, and in that sense they constitute an important reference for issuers and investors. However, they have an important inconvenience for country risk analysts, which is the excessive value placed on short-term events which may cause significant alterations in the level of premiums but do not reflect the actual risk of the country. This evolution contrasts with the stability of the OECD's country risk ratings, which usually only vary in response to more enduring factors in the medium and long term. Furthermore, the evolution of these indicators comprises the variation in country risk attributable not only to country-specific factors but also to external factors, such as the situation of the international economy or the degree of liquidity in financial markets. Similarly, the long-term sovereign credit rating in foreign currency measures the default risk on sovereign debt in foreign currency due to the lack of ability or willingness to pay. In this case, the variables considered by agencies for the development of ratings vary in each case but coincide with important features which have already been mentioned previously. The main variables that influence country risk have been summarised in Table 15.1.

15.3 Adjustments to the Cost of Capital: The Country Risk Premium

When the net present value, NPV, of an investment project is estimated, expected cash flows must be discounted at the rate of opportunity cost of capital, which is defined as the return that could be obtained in the market assuming a similar risk to that of the aforementioned project. Assuming the investment project being evaluated has a similar risk to that of the

Table 15.1 Main variables that influence country risk (Author's own composition)

Political situation	Geopolitical risk of the region Risk of internal or external political conflicts Political stability, government efficiency, strength of institutions Debt payment culture Level of corruption
Macroeconomic situation	GDP growth rate, with consumption, investment and savings detail Inflation rate and monetary policy instruments Nominal and real interest rates Public sector balance (in % of GDP) Internal and external public debt (in % of GDP) Size of local bonds market (in % of GDP) Unemployment rate
Economic structure	GDP composition by economic sector Size of the population Profit distribution, measured by the Gini index Profit per capita in $ Exportation of one primary product (in % of total exports) Energy imports (in % of primary energy consumption)
Banking sector	Poor quality credits (in % of total credits) Solvency and profit ratios Foreign bank penetration Assets and liabilities in foreign banking currency Banking supervision and deposit insurance agency
External sector	Balance of commercial and current accounts Exchange rate regime and devaluation history Payment and refinancing history in the Paris Club Existence of exchange control Level and structure of external debt Foreign exchange reserves and import hedges (no. of months) and short-term debt Foreign direct investment and portfolio investment
Market indicators	Of sovereign debt, collected in the EMBI Plus or EMBI Global index Credit default swap spread
Long-term sovereign rating in foreign currency	Moody's Standard and Poor's Fitch Ratings

company, the opportunity cost of capital for this project can be estimated by the average cost the company pays to be financed, a cost which is known as the weighted average cost of capital or WACC.

Thus, as discussed previously, the investment project being evaluated will be accepted if the NPV of the project, discounted at the average rate of WACC, is positive or, equivalently, if the internal rate of return, IRR, that the project provides is greater than the WACC.

As will be discussed in later chapters, the WACC is calculated by

$$\mathrm{WACC} = K_e \frac{\mathrm{CAA}}{\mathrm{CAA}+D} + K_d(1-T)\frac{D}{\mathrm{CAA}+D}$$

where:

- K_e is the rate of return required by the shareholders of the company and can be estimated using the capital asset pricing model (CAPM) or the Gordon–Shapiro share valuation model.
- K_d is the cost (IRR) of debt issued by the company.
- CAA is the capital contributed by shareholders and is defined as the market value of the company's shares, that is, the market capitalisation of the company if it is traded in the stock market.
- D is the market value of debt issued by the company.
- T is the corporate tax rate.

Importantly, capital values (CAA) and debt values (D) must be expressed in market values and not in accounting values because, as is known, sometimes accounting values deviate substantially from market values. Thus, the market value of a company's shares, the capitalisation of the company, is usually considerably greater than its accounting value, since the latter is a historical cost which reflects neither the value generated by the company since its establishment nor its future growth expectations. Also, the market value of debt does not have to coincide with the accounting value; for example, if the market considers the risk of default to be high, the debt securities issued by the company will be listed in the market at a value below their accounting value. Similarly, the calculation of rates of return on equity (K_e) and debt (K_d) will be carried out using market capitalisation values and market debt values respectively.

It must also be noted that in the calculation of WACC the cost of debt is multiplied by (1 − T) due to tax savings (tax shield) which provide the company with financing through debt, that is, the more indebted a company is, the more interest it will pay; the more interest paid, the lower the taxable income; and finally, the lower the taxable income, the lower the tax payable. Therefore, the real cost of debt, after taking into account the tax savings, is not K_d, but K_d without the tax savings, that is, $K_d - K_d{*}\,T = K_d{*}\,(1 - T)$.

From the above expression it can be concluded that the two key determinants of WACC are the cost of equity (or return required by shareholders), K_e, and the cost of debt, K_d, and both values depend on the type of investment project being evaluated and the country in which the project is developed. Therefore, the WACC has a clear dependence on the country where the investment project is developed since the greater the country risk, the larger the WACC. Thus, for a given investment project the country risk premium can be defined as the difference between the WACC of this project and the WACC that the project would have if it were developed in a country of the OECD. In the same way, the risk premium of an investment project can also be defined as the difference between the WACC of the project and the risk-free interest rate, a premium in which, of course, country risk and all other risks associated with the project are included.

15.4 Regulatory Risk/Legal Risk

Regulatory risk or legal risk is closely related to country risk and is, in fact, frequently included in the same category. Regulatory risk, or legal risk, refers to the variability that occurs in the performance of an investment due to regulatory changes concerning some aspect affecting the investment project being evaluated. Therefore, regulatory risk includes aspects such as legislation involving the expropriation of assets, freezing of funds, changes in the tax system and so forth—aspects which are closely related to country risk—but also situations in which, by natural evolution, the existing regulation is changed, having an impact (usually negative) on the investment project being analysed.

The significant increase in regulation regarding environmental protection issues, which has occurred in most countries in recent years, serves as an example of a regulatory risk event, as these regulatory changes have had a negative impact on investment projects undertaken by many companies. It must also be noted in this example that this type of risk is not necessarily related to country risk, that is, it could occur in any developed country. Another notable example is that of increased regulation implemented in the banking sector in recent years. Policy changes related to public health issues are also very current, for example, laws that restrict the consumption of tobacco, alcohol and the like which may adversely affect investment projects related to the hotel and catering industry.

Other notable examples of regulatory risk events are the increased regulation of data protection and IT security. Similarly, policy changes in the renewable energy sector in Spain are highly topical and greatly affect the investments made by energy companies, as are new laws regarding the storage of raw materials or perishable goods.

The risk related to changes in accounting policies are also very notable, as the implementation of the IAS, International Accounting Standards, has been a clear detriment to many companies used to calculating results according to the rules of their own country, which are usually simpler than those of the IAS.

15.4.1 Regulatory Risk in OECD Countries

Given the above, it is clear that regulatory risk is not only present in developing countries but may be present, and in fact often is present, in OECD countries; moreover, regulatory changes are occurring more and more frequently, increasing regulatory risk in OECD countries.

In addition, it should be noted that in OECD countries not only does the regulatory risk increase due to legislative changes as a result of the natural evolution of standards but also, though in a more timely manner, another type of regulatory risk associated with expropriations, freezing of funds and changes in the tax system in highly consolidated industries can occur in these countries. Consider, for example, the regulation prohibiting building work in areas close to the coast which sometimes involves the expropriation and demolition of accommodation establishments located by the beach. Tax changes experienced in Canada in 2007 regarding oil "royalties" serve as an example of changes in the tax system. Royalties are taxes dating back many years, usually several centuries, which are mainly applied to raw materials and, generally, consist of a percentage (25 %, 50 %, etc.) of the sale value of the raw material. It is not common for royalties to change, and even less so in OECD countries; however, in 2007 they suffered a sharp rise in Canada, which was not an isolated case, since similar situations have occurred in other OECD countries.

15.4.2 The Examples of Bolivia and Argentina

Clear examples of regulatory risk that have been seen globally in recent years are those which occurred in the American Southern Cone. Coinciding with the dramatic increase in the international price of oil in the period between 2003 and 2008, the Argentine government introduced a new tax on oil, whereby almost all revenues from the sale of each barrel of crude oil at over $55/barrel was appropriated. In other words, oil companies received a maximum of $55 per barrel sold, regardless of the international price of crude oil. In addition, they still had to pay the standard taxes already established on the profits made, $55/barrel at best; that is, they had to pay corporate tax, royalties and so on.

During that period the price of oil reached around $150/barrel, so the loss suffered by the oil companies as a result of these regulatory changes was very significant. It was also established that before oil could be exported, oil and gas companies had to supply the domestic market but at prices that were usually around one-third of the international price of this oil. Among other things, these regulatory changes led to oil and gas companies failing to comply with long-term sales commitments to foreign companies, while in Argentina energy-intensive industries, such as the steel industry, started to open or planned to open production facilities, something that had not been seen previously. Note that in this case the policy change had a positive effect on investment projects in companies with intensive energy use.

In no case did the Argentine government proceed to expropriate any assets. However, in many respects, the action taken may be considered equivalent to expropriation.

In the case of Bolivia there was full-scale expropriation, as the government issued a law decree stating that, in practice, all oil reserves on Bolivian soil, which had been discovered largely thanks to capital injection from abroad, became the property of the Bolivian state. Foreign companies operating in the country could manage the extraction of reserves in exchange for a commission, so long as they provided the investments needed for this. As expected, no foreign company made an investment.

15.4.3 Risks in Accounting

Accounting has a decisive impact on risk management, but accounting regulation itself can also change. In 2005 the International Accounting Standards came into force in virtually all OECD countries and replaced the accounting standards in each country. The only exception in OECD countries was the USA, where the FAS (Federal Accounting Standards) continued to be applied as opposed to the IAS. However, the IAS are virtually identical to the FAS, and therefore it can be confirmed that from 2005 the other OECD countries adopted the US accounting standards.

Accounting regulation in most OECD countries, particularly in Spain, had been very simple and therefore allowed complex assets, such as derivatives used for hedging, to be recorded arbitrarily, though always within reason. The IAS are much more complex and elaborate accounting policies which greatly limit the share margin when companies submit their financial statements, and as a result of this change in accounting regulations, many companies have suffered very severe alterations in both their balance sheets and their income statements, confirming that there is also a regulatory risk associated with accounting standards.

15.5 Country Risk Management

As country risk is determined by the variability that occurs in performance as a result of situations or decisions, usually political, that affect business in a foreign country, in many situations it is considered to be a pure systematic risk in the sense that it is caused by factors that cannot be controlled by the company and, therefore, cannot be managed. Consider, for example, the mining industry, which depends on the existence of mines—mines that are not located in the countries where these companies would like to find them but, generally, in countries with high country risk.

However, there is also some specific risk in the sense that it can be diversified if the company divides its activities between several countries or carries out deep and systematic research to characterise the implications of this risk as accurately as possible in each of the countries in which it could invest. In this regard, it should be noted that in certain sectors the systemic component is not as strong and the idiosyncratic component is much more significant.

Part V

Financial Implications of Risk

16

The CAPM

16.1 Basic Concepts

This chapter will examine how the types of risk previously discussed affect the value of a company's shares, while Chap. 17 will examine how they affect the value of the company as a whole, shares plus debt.

In order to see how these risks affect the value of a company's shares, this chapter will analyse the capital asset pricing model, known as CAPM, one of the most common tools used in finance to determine the required rate of return for a particular asset based on its risks. Three influential economists—William Sharpe, John Lintner and Jan Mossin—worked simultaneously, but separately, on the design of the model, publishing their investigations in different journals between 1964 and 1966. What attracted them to this topic was their interest in the development of models to explain and predict the behaviour of financial assets, as all had been influenced by Harry Markowitz's portfolio theory, published in 1952 and reformulated in 1959, in which the advantages of diversifying investments to reduce risk are highlighted.

The idea of diversifying investments involves allocating resources in different areas, such as industry, construction, technology, natural

F.J. Población García, *Financial Risk Management*,
DOI 10.1007/978-3-319-41366-2_16

resources, research and development (R&D), health and so on. Markowitz called this a portfolio, and the thesis was that the better diversified the portfolio was, the better prepared it would be to face risks. The CAPM took this idea one step forward by looking to maximise the return of every share in order to achieve an even more profitable portfolio. For this important contribution to the development of financial economics, William Sharpe received the Nobel Prize in Economics (jointly with Harry Markowitz and Merton Miller) in 1990.

Before presenting the CAPM some notions of portfolio theory, also known as portfolio selection theory, must be briefly introduced.

16.2 Portfolio Theory

A portfolio is simply a combination of several shares in certain proportions. For example, a portfolio can be formed by investing 20 % of the money in asset A, 40 % in asset B and 40% in asset C; logically, these percentages or weights must always amount to the unit.

When investors choose their portfolios, they do so considering two main characteristics of the shares: the profit they expect to obtain and the risk they want to assume. When the portfolio is formed, the profits that will actually be made at the end of the investment are unknown, and thus investors focus on the profits they expect to make and the risk they are willing to assume with their investments. That is, since both the profit they expect to make and the risk to be assumed in a future period are unknown at the beginning of the process, a way of estimating them must be found. One possibility is to use the information in the time series of returns to try to estimate their expected return and risk. As an indicator of expected profitability, the average profit made during an earlier period can be used, while as an indicator of expected risk, the standard deviation of the profits made during the same period can be used.

Note that, in finance, the standard deviation of an asset's returns is called volatility and is represented by the Greek letter σ; as noted in earlier chapters, since it is the standard deviation of returns, not prices, it has no units and allows the price risk of different assets to be compared.

Table 16.1 Shares estimates (Author's own composition)

Share	Expected profit (%)	Volatility (%)
1	8.5	3.57
2	10.25	4.08
3	9.0	4.24

Once the profitability and risk have been measured, given the set of possible options, the goal is to choose the portfolios that are most attractive to the investor. In order to do this two basic assumptions are made: the first is the non-satiety assumption, in other words, investors prefer more wealth to less, an assumption which implies that if there are two shares with the same risk, investors will prefer the one offering the highest expected return; the second is the risk aversion assumption, that is, investors do not like to take risks, an assumption which implies that if there are two assets with the same expected return, they will prefer the one offering the lowest risk. Under these assumptions, investors prefer portfolios with maximum expected returns and minimal risk simultaneously; the problem is that, in practice, the higher the expected return of an asset, the greater its risk. This means that if there are two investments, one with higher expected returns but also higher risk than the other, it will not be possible to determine in advance which of the two portfolios will be preferred by investors.

In these cases, the choice will depend on how averse the investor is to risk because, as will be explained later, more risk averse investors will prefer the investment with lower risk, while those who are less risk averse will prefer the investment with the higher expected profit. Suppose there are three shares 1, 2 and 3, for which the following estimates have been made (Table 16.1):

From the data in the table, it can be concluded that more risk averse investors will prefer share 1, which is the one with the lowest volatility, while less risk averse investors will choose share 2, which is the one with the highest expected return. Thus, if the choice is between shares 1 and 2, it will not be possible to decide in advance which of the two shares will be preferable because the more risk averse investors prefer share 1, which has lower volatility, even if this means relinquishing a higher expected return, while less risk averse investors prefer share 2, which has higher profits, even if this means they must bear a greater risk. A similar situation

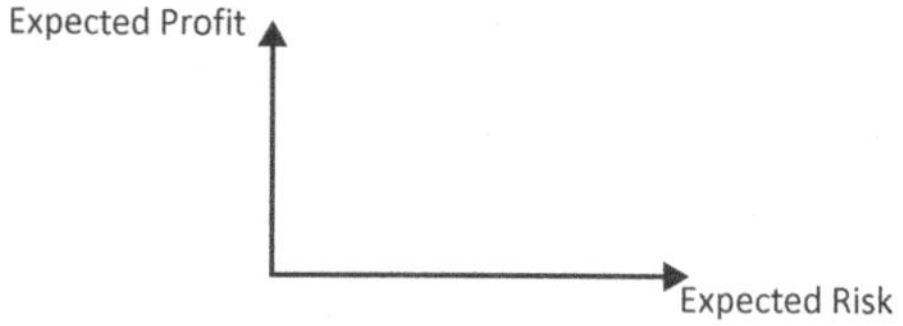

Fig. 16.1 Expected profit–risk graph (Author's own composition)

exists between shares 1 and 3, while if a choice must be made between shares 2 and 3, share 2 will be preferable for all investors because 2 has a higher expected return and a lower risk than 3.

16.2.1 Graphical Representation of Portfolios in the Mean: Standard Deviation Plan

In order to determine which of the portfolios are reasonable and which are not, a graphical representation of all the portfolios that can be formed with various assets is often made on Cartesian axes. In this way, the ordinate, the vertical axis, shows the expected profitability, while the abscissa, the horizontal axis, shows the expected risk, or the expected return volatility. That is, a graph similar to the one in Fig. 16.1 would be formed.

Once the portfolios have been marked on the graph, those with the highest profitability and, at the same time, the lowest risk must be selected. By way of example, portfolios that can be formed with shares of Banco Santander, BBVA and Inditex will be represented graphically. In this case, the average return and standard deviation of returns have been used as estimates of the expected return and risk, respectively, of these three shares during the period from 1 July to 28 September 2010. Daily profit rates have been calculated based on closing prices, and for simplicity of calculation, the dividends paid for these three shares have been ignored, thus, the rates of return have been calculated as: $R = (P_1 - P_0)/P_0$.

If C is any portfolio made up of these three shares, it must then be verified that the return is the weighted average of the profit of the three shares:

$$R_C = \omega_{\text{SAN}} \cdot R_{\text{SAN}} + \omega_{\text{BBVA}} \cdot R_{\text{BBVA}} + \omega_{\text{ITX}} \cdot R_{\text{ITX}}$$

where $\omega_{\text{SAN},}$ ω_{BBVA} and ω_{ITX} are the weights, percentages which are invested in each share, received in the portfolio of Banco Santander, BBVA and Inditex respectively. As is evident, infinite portfolios can be formed with these three assets by simply giving values to the weights $\omega_{\text{SAN},}$ ω_{BBVA} and ω_{ITX}, where, logically, the only restriction is that the sum of the three weights must be the unit.

Today, the profit that will be made from each of these three assets is unknown; thus, the value that R_C will take is also unknown, although it is possible to calculate the average return and standard deviation that this portfolio would have had in the period designated above. The average return of the portfolio can be calculated as:

$$\begin{aligned}\overline{R}_C &= \frac{1}{n}\sum_{i=1}^{n} R_C = \frac{1}{n}\sum_{i=1}^{n}(\omega_{\text{SAN}}R_{\text{SAN}} + \omega_{\text{BBVA}}R_{\text{BBVA}} + \omega_{\text{ITX}}R_{\text{ITX}})\\ &= \frac{1}{n}\omega_{\text{SAN}}\sum_{i=1}^{n}R_{\text{SAN}} + \frac{1}{n}\omega_{\text{BBVA}}\sum_{i=1}^{n}R_{\text{BBVA}} + \frac{1}{n}\omega_{\text{ITX}}\sum_{i=1}^{n}R_{\text{ITX}}\\ &= \omega_{\text{SAN}}\overline{R}_{\text{SAN}} + \omega_{\text{BBVA}}\overline{R}_{\text{BBVA}} + \omega_{\text{ITX}}\overline{R}_{\text{ITX}}\end{aligned}$$

That is, the average return of the portfolio is the weighted sum of the average returns of the portfolio's shares and, in this way, once the average profit of the three shares has been calculated, the average return on any portfolio can be calculated by simply varying the weights: ω_{SAN}, ω_{BBVA} and ω_{ITX}.

The variance calculation, or the standard deviation of the portfolio, is a little more complicated, since the variance of a portfolio is not simply the weighted sum of its share variances but covariance terms must also be taken into account. Thus, in this example the variance of portfolio C made up of these three shares can be calculated as:

$$\begin{aligned}\text{var}(R_C) = {}& \omega_{\text{SAN}}^2\text{var}(R_{\text{SAN}}) + \omega_{\text{BBVA}}^2\text{var}(R_{\text{BBVA}}) + \omega_{\text{ITX}}^2\text{var}(R_{\text{ITX}})\\ &+2\omega_{\text{SAN}}\cdot\omega_{\text{BBVA}}\cdot\text{cov}(R_{\text{SAN}},R_{\text{BBVA}})\\ &+2\omega_{\text{SAN}}\cdot\omega_{\text{ITX}}\cdot\text{cov}(R_{\text{SAN}},R_{\text{ITX}})\\ &+2\omega_{\text{BBVA}}\cdot\omega_{\text{ITX}}\cdot\text{cov}(R_{\text{BBVA}},R_{\text{ITX}}).\end{aligned}$$

Table 16.2 Variance–covariance matrix (Author's own composition)

	SAN	BBVA	ITX
SAN	0.00044	0.00038	0.00019
BBVA		0.00038	0.00016
ITX			0.00023

From the above expression it can be concluded that the lower the covariance between the return of shares in the portfolio is, the lower its variance will be. This idea is very important and is the basis of the principle of diversification studied in earlier chapters, whereby to reduce the risk of a portfolio, shares whose returns are as unrelated as possible—that is, those which have low covariance or, equivalently, lower correlation coefficient—should be selected.

As a numerical example, consider a portfolio made up of 29.41 % of Banco Santander shares, 23.53 % of BBVA shares and 47.06 % of Inditex shares. As indicated, the average return of these three shares was calculated based on a time series of their daily returns during the period between 1 July and 28 September 2010, which are 0.1 %, 0.3 % and 0.4 % for Santander, BBVA and Inditex respectively. Hence, the average daily return of the portfolio is:

$$\begin{aligned}\overline{R}_C &= \omega_{\mathrm{SAN}}\overline{R}_{\mathrm{SAN}} + \omega_{\mathrm{BBVA}}\overline{R}_{\mathrm{BBVA}} + \omega_{\mathrm{ITX}}\overline{R}_{\mathrm{ITX}} \\ &= 0.2941 \cdot 0.001 + 0.2353 \cdot 0.003 + 0.4706 \cdot 0.004 \\ &= 0.0029 = 0.29\%\end{aligned}$$

Similarly, the variance and covariance of the returns of these three shares have been estimated based on a time series of their daily returns during the period between 1 July and 28 September 2010, obtaining the variance–covariance matrix in Table 16.2.

The portfolio return variance is:

$$\begin{aligned}\mathrm{var}(R_C) &= 0.2941^2 \cdot 0.00044 + 0.2353^2 \cdot 0.00038 \\ &+ 0.4706^2 \cdot 0.00023 + 2 \cdot 0.2941 \cdot 0.2353 \cdot 0.00038 \\ &+ 2 \cdot 0.2941 \cdot 0.4706 \cdot 0.00019 + 2 \cdot 0.2353 \cdot 0.4706 \cdot 0.00016 \\ &= 0.00025\end{aligned}$$

Table 16.3 The average return and standard deviation of five portfolios (Author's own composition)

	Portfolio 1	Portfolio 2	Portfolio 3	Portfolio 4	Portfolio 5
ω_{SAN}	1	0	0	0.33	0.4
ω_{BBVA}	0	1	0	0.33	0.3
ω_{ITX}	0	0	1	0.33	0.3
Standard deviation	0.021	0.020	0.015	0.017	0.017
Average	0.001	0.003	0.004	0.003	0.003

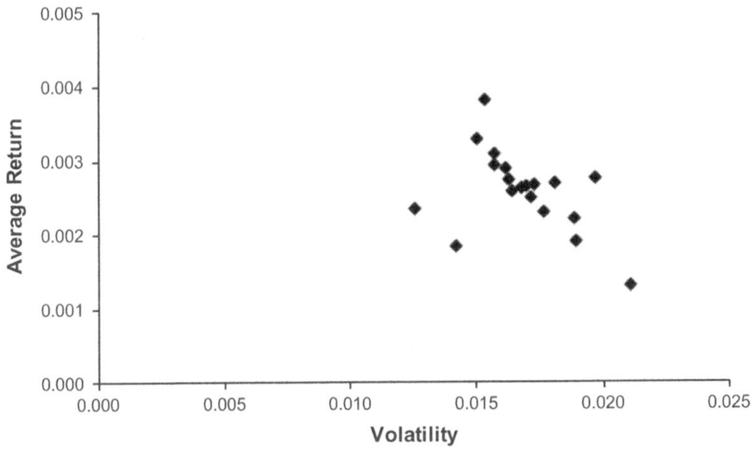

Fig. 16.2 Portfolio average return and standard deviation (Author's own composition)

The volatility of the portfolio is simply the square root of the variance: $\sigma_c = 0.0158 = 1.58\%$ daily.

Once the calculation method for the average return and volatility of a portfolio is known, it is possible to make a graphical representation of several of the infinite portfolios that can be formed with these three assets. This can be achieved by using a spreadsheet to give values to the weights ω_{SAN}, ω_{BBVA} and ω_{ITX} to obtain the average return and standard deviation of several portfolios. For example, the average return and standard deviation of five portfolios have been calculated in Table 16.3.

Plotting the two features (standard deviation, average) of these portfolios would produce the graph represented in Fig. 16.2.

Note that Fig. 16.2 only shows some, nineteen specifically, of the infinite portfolios that can be formed with these three assets. The objective is to select which of the infinite portfolios are the best, that is, those which provide the maximum expected return with minimum risk, and to that end, the portfolios located in the north-west corner of Fig. 16.2 must be selected.

16.2.2 Efficient Portfolios

As has just been noted, several of the infinite portfolios that can be formed with the three selected shares are shown in Fig. 16.2. However, many of these portfolios are unreasonable because they have the same average return as another portfolio but a higher standard deviation or volatility, or they have the same volatility but a lower average return than any other portfolio. For example, in Fig. 16.2 a perpendicular line can be drawn on the horizontal axis at point 0.016 and it is evident that there are several portfolios with a standard deviation at this point; however, of all these portfolios with a standard deviation of 0.016, investors will prefer the one with the highest average return, that is, the one which is highest in the graph.

Therefore, portfolios that are not dominated by any other portfolio in this way are called "efficient portfolios," that is, those with the highest average return for a given level of volatility or, put another way, the lowest volatility for a given level of average return.

16.2.2.1 Analytic Derivation of the Efficient Portfolio Frontier

This subsection will discuss how to analytically determine the set of efficient portfolios, known as the "efficient frontier" because it consists of portfolios that lie on the north-west frontier of the graph in Fig. 16.2. Thus, suppose you have shares of the three assets mentioned in the previous example, namely Banco Santander, BBVA and Inditex, and the problem is how to determine the set of efficient portfolios. In order to determine the efficient portfolios, remember that the profitability of the portfolio is $\overline{R}_C = \omega_1\overline{R}_1 + \omega_2\overline{R}_2 + \omega_3\overline{R}_3$, while its variance is $\omega_1^2\text{var}_1$

$$+\omega_2^2\text{var}_2 + \omega_3^2\text{var}_3 + 2\omega_1\omega_2\text{cov}_{1,2} + 2\omega_1\omega_3\text{cov}_{1,3} + 2\omega_2\omega_3\text{cov}_{2,3},$$

where ω_1, ω_2 and ω_3*are* the weights of each of these assets in the portfolio as a whole, where the subscripts 1, 2 and 3 refer to Banco Santander, BBVA and Inditex respectively. Therefore, the problem is reduced to:

$$\text{Max}\ \omega_1, \omega_2, \omega_3\ \overline{R}_C = \omega_1\overline{R}_1 + \omega_2\overline{R}_2 + \omega_3\overline{R}_3$$

s.t.

$$\omega_1^2\text{var}_1 + \omega_2^2\text{var}_2 + \omega_3^2\text{var}_3 + 2\omega_1\omega_2\text{cov}_{1,2} + 2\omega_1\omega_3\text{cov}_{1,3} + 2\omega_2\omega_3\text{cov}_{2,3}$$

$$= \sigma_e^2\omega_1 + \omega_2 + \omega_3 = 1$$

where the abbreviation "s.t" means "subject to."

This is a constrained optimisation problem, where the aim is to find the weights (ω_1, ω_2 and ω_3) of the portfolio with the highest expected return of all those with a variance level equal to σ_e^2. The second constraint simply states that for the weights to be well defined they must add up to the unit.

σ_e^2 is a parameter that can take any value between zero and infinity and, therefore, to find all efficient portfolios it is necessary to solve the previous problem for all the σ_e^2 values between zero and infinity. However, in practice, this only requires solving the problem for a small number of σ_e^2 values, around ten, which will define several points on the plane, which together will determine the efficient frontier.

Another possibility to determine the efficient portfolios is to solve the problem in reverse, in other words, efficient portfolios can be determined by finding the portfolio that has the lowest variance of all the portfolios with a given expected return ($\overline{R}_e$), that is:

$$\underset{\omega_1,\omega_2,\omega_3}{\text{Min}}\ \sigma^2{}_c = \omega_1^2\text{var}_1 + \omega_2^2\text{var}_2 + \omega_3^2\text{var}_3 + 2\omega_1\omega_2\text{cov}_{1,2} + 2\omega_1\omega_3\text{cov}_{1,3}$$

$$+2\omega_2\omega_3\text{cov}_{2,3}$$

$$s.a.$$

$$\omega_1\overline{R}_1 + \omega_2\overline{R}_2 + \omega_3\overline{R}_3 = \overline{R}_e$$

$$\omega_1 + \omega_2 + \omega_3 = 1$$

As in the previous case, this problem should be solved for infinite $\overline{R}_e$ values between zero and infinity but, in practice, it is sufficient to solve it for a small number of $\overline{R}_e$ values, no more than ten, which together will define the set of efficient portfolios.

Either of the above problems can be solved by forming a "Lagrangian," since it deals with constrained optimisation problems. However, in practice it is easier to solve the second problem, since the solution to this second problem can be found easily by solving a linear system of five equations with five unknown quantities, as will be demonstrated, whereas the solution to the first problem would involve solving a non-linear system.

This "Lagrange method" reduces the problem of minimising (or maximising) with n variables and k restrictions to one with $n + k$ variables without restrictions and, in general, if the aim is to solve the following problem: $\underset{x_1,\ldots x_n}{\min}\ f(x_1, \ldots, x_n)$ $s.a.\ g_1(x_1, \ldots, x_n)=0, \ldots, g_k(x_1, \ldots, x_n)=0$ a function called Lagrangian (L) must be formed which depends on the n variables of the original problem plus additional k variables, one for each constraint, called Lagrange multipliers ($\lambda_1,\ldots, \lambda_k$), such that: $L(x_1,\ldots x_n,\lambda_1,\ldots,\lambda_m)=f(x_1,\ldots,x_n)-\sum_{i=1}^{k}\lambda_i\cdot g_i(x_1,\ldots,x_n)$. The solution to the problem would be found by calculating the derivatives of the Lagrangian with respect to each of its $n + k$ variables and equating them to zero.

In this case, the Lagrangian depends on $n = 3$ variables of the original problem plus $k = 2$ Lagrange multipliers (λ_1, λ_2) so that:

$$\begin{aligned}\mathrm{L}(\omega_1,\omega_2,\omega_3,\lambda_1,\lambda_2) = {} & \omega_1^2\mathrm{var}_1 + \omega_2^2\mathrm{var}_2 + \omega_3^2\mathrm{var}_3 + 2\omega_1\omega_2\mathrm{cov}_{1,2} \\ & +2\omega_1\omega_3\mathrm{cov}_{1,3} + 2\omega_2\omega_3\mathrm{cov}_{2,3} \\ & -\lambda_1\left(\omega_1\overline{R}_1 + \omega_2\overline{R}_2 + \omega_3\overline{R}_3 - \overline{R}_e\right) \\ & -\lambda_2(\omega_1 + \omega_2 + \omega_3 - 1)\end{aligned}$$

As mentioned, the problem is solved by equating the partial derivatives of the previous Lagrangian to zero with respect to the five variables (ω_1, ω_2, ω_3, λ_1, λ_2):

$$\frac{\partial L}{\partial \omega_1} = 2\omega_1\mathrm{var}_1 + 2\omega_2\mathrm{cov}_{1,2} + 2\omega_3\mathrm{cov}_{1,3} - \lambda_1\overline{R_1} - \lambda_2 = 0$$

$$\frac{\partial L}{\partial \omega_2} = 2\omega_2\mathrm{var}_2 + 2\omega_1\mathrm{cov}_{1,2} + 2\omega_3\mathrm{cov}_{2,3} - \lambda_1\overline{R_2} - \lambda_2 = 0$$

$$\frac{\partial L}{\partial \omega_3} = 2\omega_3\mathrm{var}_3 + 2\omega_1\mathrm{cov}_{1,3} + 2\omega_2\mathrm{cov}_{2,3} - \lambda_1\overline{R_3} - \lambda_2 = 0$$

$$\frac{\partial L}{\partial \lambda_1} = -\left[\omega_1\overline{R}_1 + \omega_2\overline{R_2} + \omega_3\overline{R_3} - \overline{R_e}\right] = 0$$

$$\frac{\partial L}{\partial \lambda_2} = -[\omega_1 + \omega_2 + \omega_3 - 1] = 0$$

These five derivatives equalling zero form a linear system of five equations with five unknown quantities, which can be expressed in a matricial way as $A \cdot X = B$, where matrix A, with a dimension of 5×5, is the coefficient matrix of the system, the vector X, with a dimension of 5×1, is the vector of unknown quantities and the vector B, with a dimension of 5×1, is the vector of the independent terms of the system. That is:

$$\underbrace{\begin{pmatrix} 2\text{var}_1 & 2\text{cov}_{1,2} & 2\text{cov}_{1,3} & -\overline{R_1} & -1 \\ 2\text{cov}_{1,2} & 2\text{var}_2 & 2\text{cov}_{2,3} & -\overline{R_2} & -1 \\ 2\text{cov}_{1,3} & 2\text{cov}_{2,3} & 2\text{var}_3 & -\overline{R_3} & -1 \\ -\overline{R_1} & -\overline{R_2} & -\overline{R_3} & 0 & 0 \\ -1 & -1 & -1 & 0 & 0 \end{pmatrix}}_{A} \cdot \underbrace{\begin{pmatrix} \omega_1 \\ \omega_2 \\ \omega_3 \\ \lambda_1 \\ \lambda_2 \end{pmatrix}}_{X} = \underbrace{\begin{pmatrix} 0 \\ 0 \\ 0 \\ -\overline{R_e} \\ -1 \end{pmatrix}}_{B}$$

This system can be solved as $X = A^{-1} \cdot B$, and Fig. 16.3 shows the set of efficient portfolios obtained with the shares of Banco Santander, BBVA and Inditex from a time series of their daily returns during the period from 1 July to 28 September 2010. For this set of efficient portfolios to be obtained, seven different values have been defined for the parameter $\overline{R}_e$, as shown in Table 16.4, whereby seven points in the volatility – average return plane were obtained, which together define the efficient frontier (Fig. 16.3).

It is possible to demonstrate that the efficient frontier corresponds to the positive branch of a hyperbola, while the negative branch is not considered, as it would correspond to negative values of the volatility, which is impossible. If the graph had been formed in the variance–average return plane rather than in the volatility–average return plane, the figure would have been a parabola. It can also be observed that of all the portfolios on the positive branch of the hyperbola above, only those that are above the vertex of this hyperbola are efficient. Portfolios that are in this branch of the hyperbola but below the vertex are not efficient because

Table 16.4 Average return $\overline{R}_e$ and volatility (Author's own composition)

Volatility	Average return $\overline{R}_e$
0.02092988	0.001
0.01771125	0.002
0.01539228	0.003
0.01441394	0.004
0.01504015	0.005
0.01709551	0.006
0.02014726	0.007

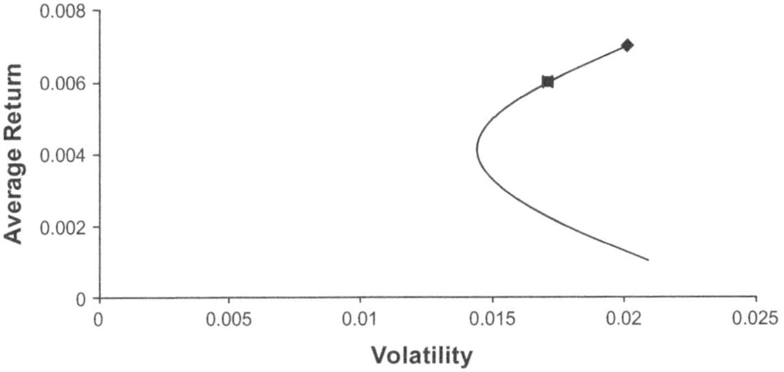

Fig. 16.3 Efficient portfolios (Author's own composition)

they have the same volatility as another portfolio located above the vertex but with a lower average return.

In this case, the efficient frontier has been constructed from three values; however, the procedure to be followed with n values would be completely analogous to the one shown above, except that instead of solving a linear system of five equations with five unknown quantities, a linear system of $n + 2$ equations with $n + 2$ unknown quantities would have to be solved.

Finally, there are two points marked on the graph above, one with a rhombus and the other with a square, both of which correspond to efficient portfolios, as they provide the maximum expected return for their level of risk. As has already been explained, whether they choose one portfolio or the other will depend on the investors' degree of risk aversion. More risk averse investors, that is, those who are more conservative, will prefer to take less risk even at the cost of relinquishing higher expected returns and will prefer the portfolio marked with a square. Similarly, less risk averse investors will prefer to obtain higher expected returns even if this means taking greater risks, and therefore they will prefer the portfolio marked with a rhombus.

Although it exceeds the scope of this book, it is also possible to demonstrate that the degree of curvature seen on the branch of the previous hyperbola depends on the degree of correlation between the returns of shares used in its construction and, thus, the lower the correlation, the greater the curvature of the hyperbola. This result is logical, since the lower the correlation between shares, the greater the risk diversification in the portfolios that are formed with them and, therefore, the lower the risk of these portfolios, causing the hyperbola to curve to the left in the graph above.

16.2.2.2 Analytic Derivation of the Minimum Variance Portfolio

In relation to the analysis presented above, it is important to note that there is a portfolio variance, or volatility, lower than all of the possible portfolios, called the minimum variance portfolio, which is the portfolio at the vertex of the previous hyperbola branch. This minimum variance portfolio has the smallest variance of all the possible portfolios, therefore it can be obtained with the same procedure as the one that was used to obtain the efficient frontier but without the first constraint, since the aim is no longer to achieve the portfolio with the smallest variance among all those with a given average return, but rather the portfolio with the smallest variance of all the possible portfolios. Thus, the problem that determines the minimum variance portfolio is:

$$\underset{\omega_1,\omega_2,\omega_3}{\text{Min}} \ \sigma^2{}_c = \omega_1^2\text{var}_1 + \omega_2^2\text{var}_2 + \omega_3^2\text{var}_3 + 2\omega_1\omega_2\text{cov}_{1,2} + 2\omega_1\omega_3\text{cov}_{1,3} + 2\omega_2\omega_3\text{cov}_{2,3}$$

$s.a.$

$$\omega_1 + \omega_2 + \omega_3 = 1$$

The procedure used to solve this problem will be completely analogous to the previous one but will consider the fact that the Lagrangian now only depends on four variables: ω_1, ω_2, ω_3, λ_2 because λ_1 disappears with the removal of the first restriction. The matrix A of system coefficients is the same as above but without the fourth row and fourth column, while

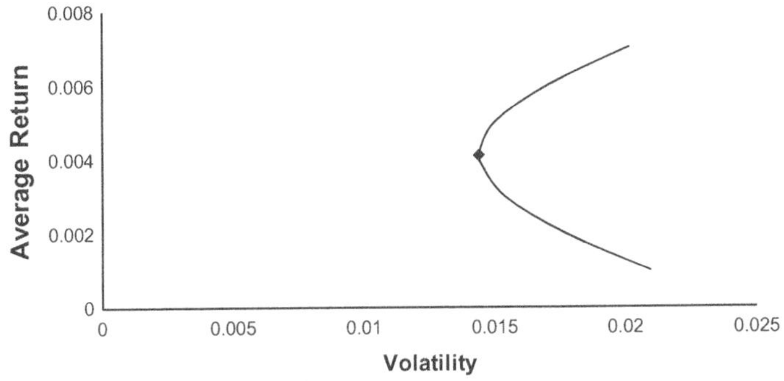

Fig. 16.4 Minimum variance portfolio (Author's own composition)

Table 16.5 Coordinates of the minimum variance portfolio (Author's own composition)

Volatility	0.01440347
Average return	0.00411255

the vector B of independent terms is also the same as above but without the fourth element ($\overline{R}_e$). The weights of the minimum variance portfolio (ω_1, ω_2, ω_3) are obtained by solving the system as a matrix expression. The coordinates in the standard deviation – average return of this portfolio can then be calculated based on these weights. The minimum variance portfolio has been obtained for the example above and is represented in Fig. 16.4 by the point marked with a rhombus.

The coordinates of the minimum variance portfolio are shown in Table 16.5.

The lower the correlation is between the shares used to construct the graph, the more curved the branch of the hyperbola will be and, for the same reason, the lower the variance of the minimum variance portfolio will be.

16.2.2.3 The Introduction of the Risk-Free Asset: The Capital Market Line (CML)

At this point the following question is appropriate: what happens if all the investors can borrow or lend at the same interest rate? The answer to this

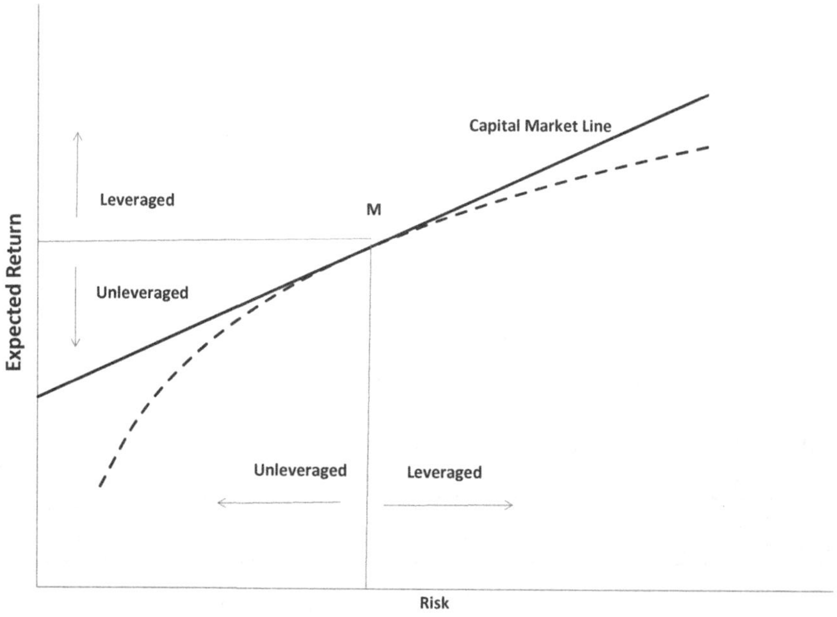

Fig. 16.5 The efficient frontier and the risk-free rate (r_F) (Author's own composition)

question can be found simply by analysing the graph in Fig. 16.5. The dotted line represents the efficient frontier and r_F is the risk-free rate; thus, it is easy to demonstrate that if investors can lend and borrow at the risk-free rate, it is possible to form portfolios along the continuous line, a line known as the capital market line (CML), which is simply the maximum slope line connecting the R_F point of the ordinate, the vertical axis, with the efficient frontier.

Thus, except for point *M*, known as the market portfolio, which can also be found on the efficient frontier, all the points on the capital market line have a greater expected return and/or a lower risk and therefore, on balance, any investor will choose a point on this line. More conservative investors will lend a portion of their money and invest the remainder in market portfolio *M*, while the less risk averse will borrow money in order to invest an amount larger than their initial funds in the market portfolio. In other words, as seen in Fig. 16.6, all investors will be on the capital

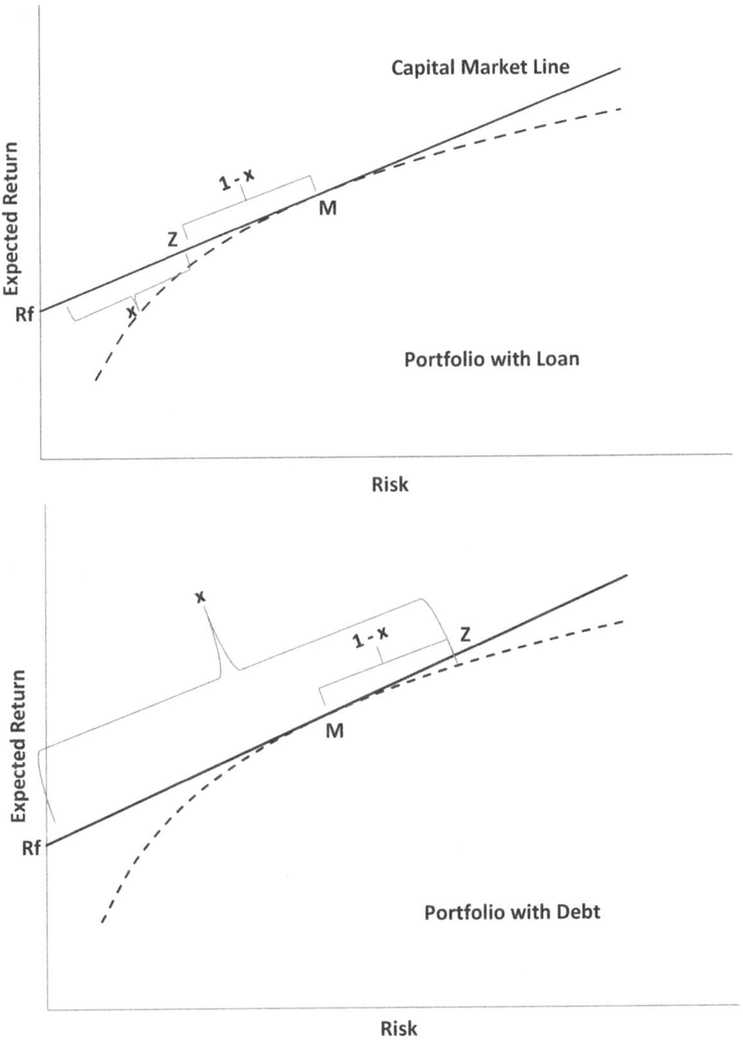

Fig. 16.6 Investors on the capital market line (Author's own composition)

market line; those that are near the ordinate, the vertical axis, at the r_F point (graph on the left) will invest a significant proportion of their wealth in the safe asset, that is, lend money, while those who are in a remote spot (graph on the right) will borrow money in order to invest more money in risky assets that provide a higher expected return but also have a higher risk. Thus, at point M nothing is lent or borrowed, that is, the safe asset is not bought or sold, and it is for this reason that it is also located on the efficient frontier.

Once the risk has been represented through the volatility (σ) in the same way as in the examples in previous sections, the return (r) of any portfolio on the capital market line can be expressed as $r = r_F + \delta^*\sigma$ where δ is the slope of this line, which is simply $\delta = (r_M - r_F)/\sigma_M$ where r_M and σ_M are the expected return and volatility of the market portfolio. In other words, $r = r_F + \frac{r_M - r_F}{\sigma_M}\sigma$, which establishes a relationship between the expected profit and the risk assumed within the portfolios that will be chosen by investors in such a way that the greater the expected return required, the greater the risk and vice versa. Another way to reach the same equation with the graph above is based on the idea that investors combine the market portfolio, M, with loans or debts at the risk-free interest rate (r_F), and therefore the expected profit of this combination will be $r = (1 - X)r_F + Xr_M = r_F + [r_M - r_F]\ X$ where X is the portion of the total budget invested in the market portfolio and $1 - X$ is the lent portion (if $X < 1$) or the borrowed portion (if $X > 1$). Moreover, the risk of such a combination measured by the standard deviation will be $\sigma = X^*\sigma_M$.

16.3 The CAPM

16.3.1 The Securities Market Line (SML)

By convention, the risk of a portfolio is usually measured by the standard deviation of its profitability and, as has just been discussed, there is a simple relationship in equilibrium between the expected return and the risk of efficient portfolios. However, this relationship is not achieved with inefficient portfolios or isolated securities and therefore it is necessary to find some other measure of risk.

In Fig. 16.7, Z represents an isolated security that lies below the CML, as it is the investment in an inefficient security. Assume that investment is divided between the market portfolio, M, and the security with risk, Z. The expected return and risk of this combination will be $r = (1 - X)r_M +$

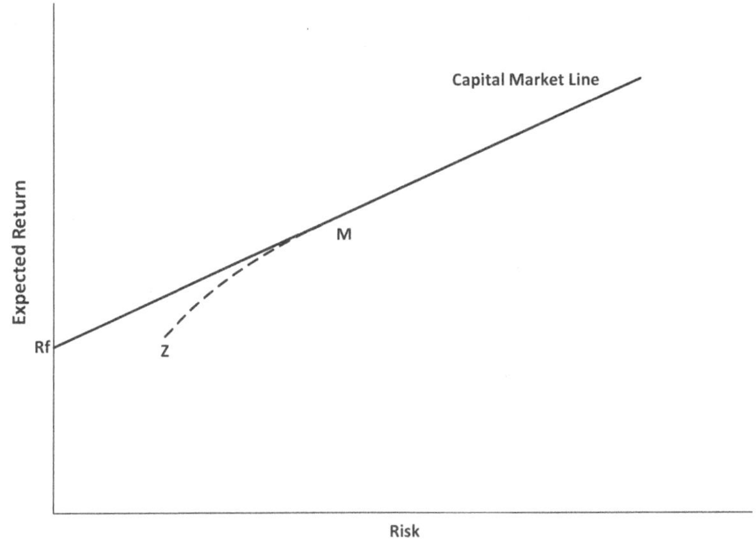

Fig. 16.7 An isolated security that lies below the CML (Author's own composition)

Xr_Z y $\sigma^2 = X^2\sigma_Z{}^2 + (1 - X)^2\sigma_M{}^2 + X(1 - X)\sigma_{ZM}$ where σ_{ZM} is the covariance between asset *Z* and market portfolio *M*. The closer value *X* is to the unit, the closer it will be to point *Z* and the closer it is to zero, the more is invested in the market portfolio.

The value of the *MZ* curve slope at point *M* will be calculated below, since it is particularly relevant to the ultimate goal and, to this end, the standard deviation of the above combination is calculated first: $\sigma = \sqrt{X^2\,\sigma_Z^2 + (1-X)^2\sigma_M^2 + X(1-X)\sigma_{ZM}}$. Then, by partially deriving the expected return and risk represented by this standard deviation with respect to X, $\frac{\delta r}{\delta X} = r_Z - r_M$ and $\frac{\delta\sigma}{\delta x} = \frac{2X\sigma_Z^2 - 2(1-X)\sigma_M^2 + (1-2X)\sigma_{ZM}}{\sigma}$ are obtained, which are used to calculate the slope $\frac{\delta r}{\delta\sigma} = \frac{\frac{\delta r}{\delta X}}{\frac{\delta\sigma}{\delta x}} = \frac{\sigma(r_Z - r_M)}{2X\sigma_Z^2 - 2(1-X)\sigma_M^2 + (1-2X)\sigma_{ZM}}$. At point *M*, $X = 0$ and the risk of the portfolio coincides with that of the market portfolio, $\sigma = \sigma_M$; thus, the former will be replaced by the latter, resulting in: $\frac{\delta r}{\delta\sigma} = \frac{\sigma_M(r_Z - r_M)}{\sigma_{ZM} - \sigma_M^2}$.

The reason for the importance of this slope is that at point M the ZM combination must be tangent to the CML when the situation is balanced, and therefore both lines will be identical $\frac{\sigma_M(r_Z - r_M)}{\sigma_{ZM} - \sigma_M^2} = \frac{r_M - r_F}{\sigma_M}$ and the securities market line (SML) equation, which is the base of the capital asset pricing model, can then be obtained: $r_Z = r_F + \frac{r_M - r_F}{\sigma_M^2} \sigma_{ZM}$.

At equilibrium, all securities and portfolios, efficient or not, will be on the SML where the covariance is between their returns and those of the market, with an appropriate measure of the risk of each asset being represented on the SML. Thus, when an investor considers adding a new security to their portfolio, they must know that they will only be rewarded for the covariance risk between the security return and the market return and not for the total risk measured using the variance or standard deviation. This can be seen most clearly if the SML equation above is replaced with the following one depending on the volatility coefficient β_Z: $r_Z = r_F + \beta_Z(r_M - r_F)$, being $\beta_Z = \frac{\sigma_{ZM}}{\sigma_M^2}$.

This coefficient β indicates the volatility of the security return in relation to changes in the market return. Securities or portfolios with a $\beta > 1$ will have a higher risk than the market portfolio risk and are called aggressive, while those that have $\beta < 1$ will have a lower risk than the market portfolio and are called defensive. Thus, the β of the market portfolio is equal to the unit, as seen in Fig. 16.8.

16.3.2 The Market Model

The CAPM is based on a number of basic assumptions which allow investors to diversify their portfolios efficiently without incurring any additional costs. These assumptions are:

- There are no transaction costs.
- All assets can be negotiated.
- Any asset is infinitely divisible.
- All investors have access to the same information.
- It is impossible to find undervalued or overvalued assets in the market.

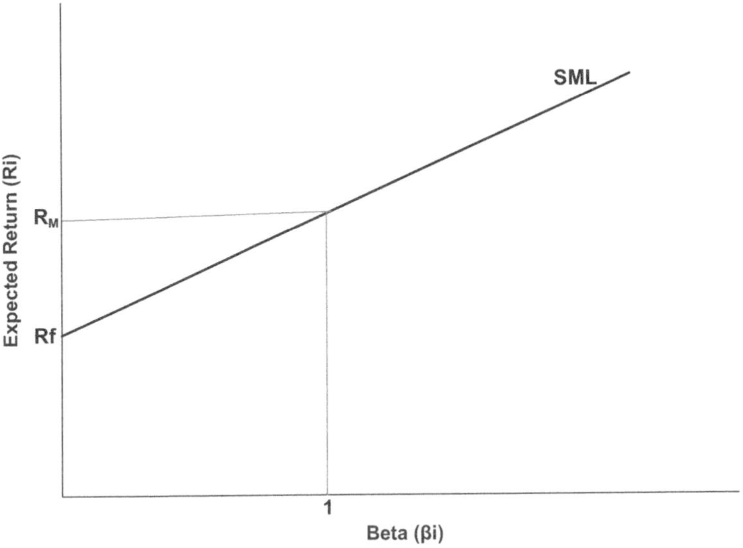

Fig. 16.8 *β and expected return* (Author's own composition)

From these assumptions, Sharpe developed a linear regression model called the market model which relates the return of the market, an independent variable, and the return of the portfolio or security, a dependent variable. This model is as follows: $r = \alpha + \beta r_M + \varepsilon$ where α indicates the average return of the security when the market return is zero, that is, when the market doesn't move up or down; β indicates the volatility of the security return with respect to a change in market return, hence its name volatility coefficient; and ε is the error indicating the random balancing disturbance of the statistical model and represents the idiosyncratic risk which has zero mean but non-zero variance and has no influence on the profitability that the market offers for this security or portfolio but does have an effect on its aggregate risk.

Once the values of α and β have been found, the expected return of a security for a future time period can be calculated. In order to achieve this, the following expression will be applied: $r = \alpha + \beta r_M$. Based on the SML, b can be obtained by dividing the covariance between the return of the security and that of the market, σ_{ZM}, by the variance of the market return,

σ_M^2, while α can be calculated from the difference in the previous equation: $b = \sigma_{ZM}/\sigma_M^2$ and $\alpha = r - b_{rM}$.

From the relationship $r = \alpha + \beta r_M + \varepsilon$ it is immediately deduced that the overall risk of the portfolio or asset in question is $\sigma^2 = \beta^2\sigma_M^2 + \sigma_\varepsilon^2$ in which there is no covariance term because, by construction, ε, which is the error term in the regression model, has no correlation with the independent variable, r_M in this case. It must also be noted that to the right of the equal sign in the previous expression there are two addends. As has already been noted, the first is systematic risk and indicates the risk of the security or portfolio which depends solely and exclusively on the market, that is, it is due to common macroeconomic factors; while the other addend represents the idiosyncratic or specific risk, that is, the portion of the total security risk which depends solely on the company itself and not on the market.

Note that β is different for each financial asset, while the variance of the market return, σ_M^2, is the same in each case; therefore, the greater the β is, the greater the systematic risk will be, that is, the more the security return will vary when the market return varies. Hence, assets that have a greater β than that of the market portfolio are aggressive, while assets that have a smaller β than that of the market portfolio are defensive.

As noted, idiosyncratic risk is important because it has the property of being diversifiable and virtually voidable; moreover, efficient portfolios have zero-specific (idiosyncratic) risk. It should also be kept in mind that it is possible to eliminate this idiosyncratic risk with good diversification by the investor, but this is not the case with systematic risk. The expected return of a security or portfolio depends mainly on systematic risk, that is, the market only remunerates the systematic risk of the investment and, therefore, if idiosyncratic risk is not eliminated, the investor may not be compensated for this risk, that is, they will not be repaid.

Finally, it must be noted that everything said so far can be applied to isolated securities and portfolios and, in addition, it is easy to demonstrate that the β, or α, of a portfolio is equal to the weighted average of the βs, or αs, of the securities that form it.

17
The WACC

17.1 Basic Concepts

Following on the discussion of the capital asset pricing model (CAPM) in Chap. 16, this chapter will examine how risks affect a company as a whole and specifically how these risks are summarised in a single parameter.

When calculating the net present value (NPV) of an investment project, its estimated cash flows must be discounted at the opportunity cost of capital rate, which is defined as the return that could be obtained in the market if a similar risk to that of this project is assumed. This same concept can be applied to a company as a whole, and in this case the cash flows of the company must be discounted using the weighted average cost of capital, better known by its acronym WACC.

The WACC is the cost of financing the business, that is, its own funding (shares) and external funding (debt), and adjustments to current tax rates (corporate tax). The WACC is the discount rate that will be applied to net cash flows generated by the company in the future, and for this reason the WACC can be understood as a measure of the company's risk. In this sense, the WACC of a company can be interpreted in three different ways:

F.J. Población García, *Financial Risk Management*,
DOI 10.1007/978-3-319-41366-2_17

- From the perspective of company assets: the rate that must be applied to discount the expected cash flows.
- From the perspective of liabilities: the cost of external financing required by a company.
- From the perspective of investors: the return expected by shareholders for investing in a particular company.

It can be deduced from the above that the WACC is calculated by a weighted average of two very different magnitudes: a cost—the cost of debt—and a required return on shares. As a result, although for the purposes of this book the WACC is defined as the cost of a company's funding, following a purist approach the cost of debt, which causes the company to go bankrupt if it is not paid off, is not the same as the required return of the share, which has less severe consequences in the case of default.

Considering the above and to conclude this section, it must be noted that although there are differences, it is also possible to define the WACC for an investment project. The differences between the WACC of a company and that of a particular project are due to the fact that for a company, the WACC is the average cost of funding and will be linked to all the risks assumed by this company, while on the other hand, if the same company is presented with the opportunity to invest in a new project, the decision will be mainly based on two parameters: its profitability and the additional risk that this project represents, that is, its marginal risk. In order to measure this marginal risk in the same way as in previous chapters, the total risk of the company must be calculated with and without the new investment project, and the difference will be the marginal risk. In terms of profitability, the WACC that the new project would have for the company in question will be calculated and the net present value of the project will be estimated by discounting the future cash flows at the WACC, where the project is still profitable if the NPV is positive.

17.2 WACC Calculation

For the calculation of the WACC, as in section 3 of chapter 15, the following nomenclature is used:

- K_e is the rate of return required by the shareholders of the company and can be estimated using the capital asset pricing model discussed in Chap. 16.
- K_d is the cost (IRR) of debt issued by the company.
- CAA is the capital contributed by shareholders and is defined as the market value of the company's shares, that is, the market capitalisation of the company, if it is traded in the stock market.
- D is the market value of debt issued by the company.
- T is the corporate tax rate.

Using this notation, the WACC is expressed as:

$$\mathrm{WACC} = K_e \frac{\mathrm{CAA}}{\mathrm{CAA} + D} + K_d(1 - T)\frac{D}{\mathrm{CAA} + D}$$

Importantly, capital values (CAA) and debt (D) must be expressed in market values and not accounting values because, as has been discussed in many parts of this book, at times accounting values differ significantly from market values. Thus, the market value of a company's shares, capitalisation of the company, is usually considerably greater than its accounting value, since the latter is a historical cost and does not reflect the value generated by the company since its establishment or the expectations of future growth. In addition, the market value of debt does not have to coincide with the accounting value because if, for example, the market perceives there to be a high risk of default, the debt securities issued by the company will be listed on the market at a lower value than the accounting value. Similarly, the calculation of rates of return on equity (K_e) and the cost of debt (K_d) will be made using the values of market capitalisation and market debt respectively.

Note that in the calculation of the WACC the cost of debt is multiplied by $(1 - T)$ due to the tax savings that the company makes through debt financing; in other words, the more indebted a company is, the more interest it will pay and the more interest it pays, the lower its taxable income will be because the taxable income is the net profit of the interest payments, and, finally, the lower its taxable income is, the lower the tax payable will be. Therefore, the real cost of debt, after taking into account these tax savings, is not K_d, but K_d minus the tax savings, that is, $K_d - K_d T = K_d(1 - T)$.

It can be deduced from the above expression that the two key determinants of the WACC are the cost of capital, or return required by shareholders, K_e, and the cost of debt, K_d. Both parameters depend on all the inherent risks to the company or the project in question but in different ways, given the different payment structure of debt and equity instruments.

The CAPM studied in Chap. 16 can be used to calculate K_e because according to the CAPM there is an increasing linear relationship between the expected return of an asset and its risk as measured by its coefficient β; that is, according to this model, the profitability that a certain share should have is $r = r_F + \beta(r_M - r_F) + \varepsilon$, but at present the profitability of the market portfolio and the value of term ε in the future are unknown, thus the required return of a particular share is simply:

$$K_e = E(r) = r_F + \beta(E(R_m) - r_F)$$

where:

- $E(r)$ is the required return of the share, that is, K_e.
- r_F is the interest rate of the risk-free asset.
- $E(R_m) - r_F$ is the expected risk premium of the market portfolio.
- β is the coefficient that reflects the degree of relationship between the profitability of the company's shares and the profitability of the market portfolio.

According to this expression, the higher coefficient β is, the higher the equity risk will be and therefore the higher the required return will be. If estimates of the expected return on the market portfolio and the beta coefficient of the shares in question are available, an estimate of the expected return on equity can be obtained. One way of estimating the return on the market portfolio and the beta coefficient of the shares is to use the time series of the return on the market portfolio and the return on the shares in question.

Aside from using the CAPM methodology, there are other alternatives to estimate K_e. One is to use the Gordon–Shapiro dividend discount model. According to this model, assuming that the dividends paid by the company will grow indefinitely at a constant rate of g, the current share price, P_0, will be equal to: $P_0 = \frac{\text{DIV}_1}{K_e - g}$, where DIV_1 is the estimated dividend that the shares will pay over the next year. However, in practice, the dividend growth rate will be higher or lower at different periods of time; therefore, to be able to use this formula, it is necessary to obtain an estimate of the long-term average dividend growth rate, and in this case, once an estimate of the company's long-term average dividend growth rate and an estimate of the next dividend have been obtained, the required return of shares can be estimated as: $K_e = \frac{\text{DIV}_1}{P_0} + g$.

As mentioned above, the cost of debt, K_d, is estimated using the IRR of the company's debt and, logically, the IRR will depend on the probability of default perceived in the market; in other words, the more likely default is to occur, the lower the market value of debt will be, which will result in a higher IRR.

17.2.1 The Risk Premium

As was established when dealing with country risk, once the WACC of a company has been defined the risk premium of this company can be defined as the difference between the WACC of the company and the risk-free interest rate of the currency in which the WACC is named, that is, the currency used to calculate the WACC. It is important to remember that the risk-free rate is different in different currency denominations, although the risk premium does not vary too much, since the WACC is also different in different currencies; thus, the extra cost of financing caused by running risks does not usually vary significantly between currencies.

This risk premium is a measure of the risks being taken by the company, that is, it includes all its systematic risks because, as discussed in previous chapters, idiosyncratic risks are not remunerated, since they are diversifiable. In this regard, note that it is possible for companies to have a negative risk premium, as long as the total risk being run by the company is opposite to that of the rest of the market and therefore allows portfolios to be diversified.

Also note that the concept of a safe asset, which gives rise to the risk-free interest rate, is a purely academic concept that does not have an exact equivalent in real life. In the real world the closest thing to a risk-free asset, and which is usually taken as such, is state debt; however, as has become evident in the recent crisis, these assets are not in any way safe. Not even the debt of countries like the USA or Germany, countries which are perceived by the market as being very safe and have never defaulted on their obligations, can be considered 100 % safe because, although small, there is a probability of default. Therefore, the risk premium of a company, calculated as its WACC minus the interest rate of US and German debt, may be negative.

17.3 The WACC of an Investment Project

As noted at the beginning of this chapter, each company has a WACC, which is a measure of the cost of its funding and is, therefore, directly related to the risks it assumes. On the other hand, when a company is evaluating the possibility of developing a new investment project, it must estimate its expected return, discounting the expected cash flows of the project through the WACC of that project, which need not coincide with that of the company.

The WACC of the project must be calculated based on how much the company has to pay to finance this project with the capital structure (debt–equity ratio) necessary to carry it out. That is, the method used to calculate the WACC for a specific project is the same as the one used for the company in general, the only difference being that the K_e, K_d, CAA, D and T parameters are linked not only to the company in question but also to the specific project. Thus, this WACC will depend not only on the company developing it, but also on the type of investment project being developed and on the country where it is being developed.

Following the same line as the previous section, the risk premium of an investment project can be defined as the difference between the WACC of this project and the risk-free interest rate, a premium which, logically, includes all systematic risks associated with the project.

17.3.1 Risk-Adjusted Cash Flows

When evaluating an investment project according to the criteria of the NPV, what matters is not the cash flows themselves but the risk-adjusted cash flows, that is, the cash flows updated at the WACC rate. Thus, if an investment project provides estimated cash flows of de $-C_0$, C_1, ... C_n over the next n years, then its NPV will be:

$$\text{NPV} = -C_0 + \frac{C_1}{1 + \text{WACC}} + \ldots + \frac{C_n}{(1 + \text{WACC})^n}$$

Logically, the higher the risk of the project is, the greater the WACC will be and the lower the risk-adjusted cash flows will be, and it is for this reason that the riskiest investment projects are required to provide significantly higher returns, WACC and cash flows than less risky projects. In particular, as discussed in Chapter 15, projects developed in countries outside the Organisation for Economic Co-operation and Development (OECD) are required to provide significantly higher returns, WACC and cash flows due to country risk than similar projects developed in OECD countries (not only because of this risk, but also due to others such as equity, commodity, credit, counterparty, operational, etc.).

In this sense, if the cash flows are compared without adjusting to account for risk, it can be concluded that riskier investment projects are required to provide much higher cash flows than less risky ones; however, if the risk-adjusted cash flows are compared, the differences are not so great.

18

Conclusions

As stated in the Introduction, in recent times risk analysis and management has gained great importance in the world of business due to a sharp increase in the size and complexity of business models. Compared to only a few years ago, there are many large multinational companies with very complex business models operating in many (and very diverse) sectors and countries.

Unfortunately, as highlighted by the recent deep economic crisis, their management has not been sufficient. From my point of view, this has been the result of several factors. One reason, as discussed in the Introduction, is that risk assessment is not always carried out using purely financial criteria, mainly due to the ignorance of it in certain areas. I hope this book has clarified the subject.

As stated above, the concept of risk refers to the degree of uncertainty regarding future net returns which are obtained by making an investment. This book started with a discussion of the most important risk for many companies, which is market risk. It is easy to understand why market risk is so important for many companies, since it is the uncertainty that exists about future earnings arising from changes in market conditions (share prices, interest rates, exchange rates, commodity prices, etc.). In other

F.J. Población García, *Financial Risk Management*,
DOI 10.1007/978-3-319-41366-2_18

words, market risk is the uncertainty that exists regarding all economic and financial variables which affect the result of a company.

Consequently, this market risk is the most "natural" risk in an industrial company because it affects production input prices and final product prices, which determine the company profit margin. Moreover, it also affects all kinds of companies, since exchange rate risk and interest rate risk are part of market risk.

After market risk, the other big risk is credit risk; however, credit risk is limited to companies which lend money in one way or another. As stated above, credit risk arises from the possibility of borrowers, bond issuers or counterparties in derivative transactions not meeting their obligations, which includes counterparty risk. Since credit risk is a dichotomous phenomenon, the study of credit risk is more complex than, and very different to, that of market risk, where risk originates from market variables, generally prices, which can take a continuum of values, usually between zero and infinity.

After these two big risks there are many others, the most important among them being operational, liquidity and country risks. The improvements made in new technology and the increasing complexity and globalisation of companies has led to increased concern about operational risk. Many recent examples of operational risk events have been presented. On the other hand, the liquidity risk of a company can be defined as the loss that may occur due to events that affect the availability of resources needed to meet their liability obligations. In other words, liquidity risk is caused by the fact that the company has to make recurring payments, but the timing of these payments does not usually coincide with receiving income and their wealth is not stored as money but, conversely, part of it is kept in assets.

Country risk refers to the probability of a financial loss occurring due to macroeconomic, political or social circumstances or due to natural disasters in a certain country. Country risk has become an important subject of study in the research and risk management departments of banks, rating agencies, insurance companies and financial system regulators, especially since Organisation for Economic Co-operation and Development (OECD) countries in the eurozone have also presented country risk.

Although other kinds of risk exist, for the sake of brevity they have not been presented in this book.

To conclude this summary, the last two chapters can be said to examine how these risks affect the value of a company's shares and how they affect the value of the company as a whole, including both shares and debts.

One interesting issue that is outside the scope of this book is the correlation among risks. In this book each risk has been studied in isolation, but all of them are related, especially during times of crisis. At such times, regardless of the risk that triggered the crisis, all risks come into play. For example, if the crisis has been triggered by a credit risk event like the 2008 financial crisis, there are not only credit risk issues, but also other risk issues. In other words, since borrowers stop paying, it is logical that banks suffer credit risk events; however, the consequences do not stop there. Since banks are in trouble, there are credit constraints which affect the rest of the economy and commodities and companies' stock exchange quotations go down, which is a market risk event. Moreover, since uncertainties arise in markets, economies and countries, liquidity evaporates and country risk increases.

In other words, once a risk event triggers a crisis, all risks are affected and the snowball effect doesn't stop until suitable measures are taken and confidence is restored.

What can be concluded from this book? As stated in the Introduction, I have attempted to show that risk is not something negative but quite the opposite, something very positive, as it is the inevitable consequence of freedom. Since this is a technical book in the risk management/finance field I haven't explained in depth why I think this. However, this final chapter is a good opportunity to expand on the idea.

As I explained in the Introduction, if there were no risk there would be no freedom, because if everything in life were deterministic to avoid risks, human beings could not make any decisions, and consequently there would be no freedom. The problem is that we tend to see only the negative consequences of risk (which are the same as the negative consequences of freedom), which are economic and financial crisis, and we miss the value added of the possibility to undertake new projects.

In other words, since we have risks, humanity can evolve and human life continues to improve. For this reason the ingenious gentleman Don

Quixote of La Mancha says that "Freedom is one of the most precious gifts granted to men from heaven", because the existence of freedom, and therefore risk, allows humankind to acquire human dignity instead of being devices or something worse. And this human dignity that we can obtain by making the most of our freedom is exactly what leads us to reach our divinity, as can be read in another bestseller completed in the Middle East almost 2,000 years ago.

It is true that an inappropriate use of freedom can lead a man or a woman to lose their human dignity, but I honestly believe this is not the final word; otherwise, taking into account humankind's capacity for destruction, humanity would have disappeared a long time ago. However, this does not mean there are no negative consequences of the inappropriate use of freedom by human beings, and the 2008 financial crisis is a very good example of it.

Why are we engaged in this financial crisis? It is a complex question from a technical point of view, and for this reason governments, central banks and regulators are currently developing laws, rules and regulations in order to make the world economy recover fully and to avoid another crisis. However, the deepest underlying reason is very clear, at least for people who use common sense: it is the inappropriate use of freedom by people.

When I say "inappropriate use of freedom by people" I do not mean an inappropriate use of freedom by some people, I mean an inappropriate use of freedom by most people, if not everyone.

Experts agree that the current financial crisis started because of a credit risk issue: people around the world (or at least in many of the most important economic areas) stopped repaying their mortgage loans and this, as has been discussed in this book, led to credit risk events, which produced losses. Since, as stated above, economic activities are closely related and therefore risks are highly correlated in crisis times, these credit losses triggered many other risks events (market, liquidity, country risks) which caused new losses, all of which led the world to the current financial crisis.

Other wiser authors have described in depth the devices which triggered each of the risk events that led to the huge losses and the current financial crisis. I will not do so. However, what is easy for me to analyse is the underlying reason: many people asked for mortgages in which there was a probability (in some cases a significant probability) of non-repayment, the banks granted them, supervisors did not stop enough them, regulators did not provide enough additional regulation in this respect, governments did nothing which worked and society as a whole did not vote for other governments.

Many people asked for mortgages in which there was a probability of non-repayment because at that time they preferred to live in a better house regardless of the consequences in the future; the banks granted the loans because they provided short-term benefits (which were translated into wages and bonuses) regardless of what happened afterwards; supervisors, regulators and governments did nothing because the economy performed well (and, consequently, they were getting a huge amount of taxes); and society as a whole didn't vote for other governments because people benefit from government expenditure.

However, this house of cards relied on the fact that many people asked for mortgages in which there was a probability—in some cases a significant probability—of non-repayment. This seems obvious now, but years ago, in the middle of the boom, everybody was focused more on the short-term benefits than on the long-term consequences.

It could be argued that it is very easy to say what we should have done in the past to avoid undesirable situations, but it is not so easy to rectify now; or, some might say that only a small group of very wise economists could have foreseen the situation in the past but no one else. However, I do not agree, firstly because when a person approaches a bank to ask for a loan, from my point of view, this is the first person responsible for repaying it. They should know the amount of money that they should pay and how likely it is that they are going to be able to repay it in the future. I honestly believe that, apart from rare outliers who shouldn't receive loans, people in the first world economy who receive a loan are and were able to carry out this type of analysis. Secondly, banks have and had in the past tools in place to carry out these types of analyses before granting a loan. Thirdly, supervisors, regulators and governments in OECD countries have technicians who are and were able to develop analyses which would have concluded that significant risk had been taken. Finally, everyone in society has the common sense (at least I would like to think so) to understand that monthly mortgage payments come with risks.

In my humble opinion, the only possible explanation for the final result that we have seen is the inappropriate use of freedom by people. As stated above, when I say "an inappropriate use of freedom by people" I do not mean an inappropriate use of freedom by some people, I mean an inappropriate use of freedom by most people, if not by everyone.

Nevertheless, as stated above, I strongly believe that the positive consequences of freedom and risk greatly outweigh the negative ones, and consequently we should continue to rely on freedom and risk and continue to think that risk and freedom are the most precious gifts granted to humankind from heaven. For this reason, as I explained in the Introduction, the fact that risk exists must not be thought of as a problem but as an opportunity, an opportunity for people to reach their full potential.

Glossary of Terms

Appreciation Appreciation is the increase in value of any asset compared with another with or without similar characteristics.

Arbitrage/Arbitration Following Ramón Tamames, arbitrage is an action whereby an arbitrator (a good person chosen by two or more parties in dispute) decides (to avoid resorting to the ordinary judiciary power) on a fair solution to a dispute.The simultaneous purchase and sale of securities between two or more markets to get the best out of the price differences.

Assets Following Enrique Ortega Martínez, assets are a set of goods and rights valuable in money with an economic unit. The asset represents the economic structure of a company and the realisation of its financial structure.Taking the asset's degree of liquidity into consideration, it is divided into a current and a non-current asset.

- Current Assets

A current asset consists of assets and rights that can be converted into cash in a short period of time, usually within a year. Liquid assets and realisable assets also fall into this category. The former includes assets and rights that are likely to become money immediately, such as cash on hand/in banks or in current accounts, acceptances, negotiable instruments in the stock market, etc. Realisable assets include goods and rights that can be converted into money in the short term, such as loans, advances to suppliers, finished goods, etc.

F.J. Población García, *Financial Risk Management*,
DOI 10.1007/978-3-319-41366-2

- Non-Current Assets, Also Known as Fixed Assets
A non-current asset, also called a fixed asset, consists of goods and rights that are intended to remain in the company over several periods. It includes tangible fixed assets and intangible fixed assets. The first type consists of different goods of a tangible nature, such as land, buildings, machinery, furniture, etc. Intangible fixed assets include the different assets of the company that do not have a tangible nature, such as depreciation, patents, etc.

Asset-Backed Securities An asset-backed security (ABS) is a security which is created by pooling non-mortgage assets and is then resold to investors. The pool of assets is typically a group of illiquid assets which are difficult to sell individually. Therefore, pooling the assets into financial instruments allows them to be sold to investors. The pools of underlying assets can include payments from auto loans, royalty payments, etc. The securitisation process of asset-backed securities is handled by an institution called a special purpose vehicle (SPV), which creates and sells the securities and uses the proceeds from the sale to pay back the institution (typically a bank) that originated the underlying assets. Over time, market practice has developed more sophisticated names for securities issued via the securitisation of specific assets, such as mortgages or debt, leaving the name ABS for the plain vanilla securitisation of low-risk bonds.

Asymmetric Information This term describes a situation in which a buyer and a seller have different information on the same transaction, leading to a situation of price discrimination, harmful to the consumer because they may be paying more than others for the same product. This asymmetric information leads the market economy to a socially inefficient macroeconomic outcome.

Autoregressive Process Autoregressive processes are a family of processes in which observations depend on previous observations. They are known as AR processes and are characterised by their order (P). The first-order autoregressive process is the simplest of the family of autoregressive processes. If a series follows an AR (1) process, each observation is based on the previous one, plus a random disturbance.

Average/Mean The arithmetic mean is the value obtained by adding all the values and dividing the result by the total number of them. The average can only be found for quantitative variables; it can be calculated whatever the range of intervals may be; it is very sensitive to extreme scores; and it cannot be calculated if there is an interval with an undetermined range.

Back Office Deloitte defines the back office as employees of companies who are not in direct contact with clients, but are responsible for performing the administrative tasks associated with the operations they request.

Balance of Payments Following Ramón Tamames, a balance of payments is a comparative statement of receipts and payments (or inflows and outflows) of all kinds in a national economy. It consists of several subcategories:
- Goods (imports and exports);
- Services (freight, insurance, tourism, etc.);
- Transfers (remittances from emigrants, donations, etc.);
- Long-term capital (direct investment in companies, stock exchange, real estate, credits, etc.);
- Short-term capital (currency movements).

The closing of balance of payments may generate a surplus, resulting in increased foreign exchange reserves, or a deficiency which is reflected in reduced reserves or increased borrowing.

Bank Deposit A bank deposit refers to an amount of money which is paid into a credit institution by a customer in the form of cash or financial assets for safekeeping and to obtain interest. Deposits may be demand, term or savings deposits depending on their availability, i.e., if they are available freely, with minimal notice, or at the end of a previously fixed term, respectively.

Bear Position/Short Position These terms are used to describe a position in options and futures transactions whereby the person who has to deliver a certain asset in the future (commodities, currencies, securities, etc.) at a fixed price does not have it at that time, as they trust that in the future the price will go down and they can buy it at a lower price before the delivery date.

Benchmark This concept was introduced into business language by the company Xerox, which has defined it as "the continuous process of measuring and comparing our products, services and practices with the strongest competitors or with companies that are recognised as industry leaders." Thus, the benchmark is simply a process or management technique through which companies or organisations evaluate the performance of their processes, systems and management procedures, comparing them with the best performances found in other organisations.

It is a reference that is used to make comparisons. In the financial sphere, it is any index which is used as a reference to assess the efficiency of portfolio management.

Cost–Benefit Analysis Cost–benefit analysis is a financial tool that measures the relationship between the costs and earnings associated with an investment project in order to assess its profitability, where the term investment project refers not only to the creation of a new business, but also to investments that can be made in an operating company, such as the development of a new product or the acquisition of new machinery. It is therefore a conceptual

framework for evaluating public or private investment projects and is also sometimes used as a criterion for selection among alternatives in many different situations.
What differentiates it from a simpler common financial analysis is that in the cost–benefit analysis all gains and profits involved in the project are taken into account; a profit is any gain in earnings, in any form, and a cost is any loss of earnings derived from the project, measured in terms of opportunity costs. Therefore, all externalities produced by the action in question must be taken into account: changes in the environment, collateral effects on other projects, etc.

Bond A bond is one way of realising the issuance of public or private borrowing. Bonds are usually bearer securities traded in the stock exchange, nationally or internationally, with fixed interest; or variable, based on the Libor or on another reference. According to issue, these are: Treasury bonds, industrial bank bonds, company treasury bonds, etc.

Bull Position/Long Position This is a situation, in options and futures transactions, which occurs when a certain asset is purchased (commodities, currencies, securities, etc.), although it does not have to be delivered until a later point in time, because it is believed that its price will rise in the future.

Business Cycle This concept refers to the regular fluctuation of economic activities over time, usually measured or expressed as changes in gross national product. Its main phases are the boom or expansion phase, where total economic activity and employment grow, and the recession or contraction phase, whereby the pace of the economy slows and these variables reduce or stagnate.

Cap A cap is a call option (purchased by the bond issuer who pays market interest rate as a coupon and sold by the buyer of that bond) which causes the issuer's final payment, i.e., the buyer's final bond collection, to have no more than a given interest rate—the exercise price, or "strike," of the option. Thus, with the cap the bond issuer is guaranteed not to pay more than a certain interest rate. The case may arise, and in fact does, that the person buying the cap is not the bond issuer or the person selling is not actually the buyer because both the buyer and the seller are speculators.

Cash Flow at Risk (CFaR) The cash flow at risk is defined as the measure of the maximum potential change that cash flow being studied may suffer (it may be that of a particular project, a division, the entire company, etc.) at a time horizon and at a given probability level.

Cash Flow Hedge Following Francisco J. Alcalá and Pablo Doménech, a cash flow hedge creates a hedge of the fluctuation in future cash flows resulting from

market-related risk. The hedged item in a cash flow hedge can take one of the two following forms:
- Future cash flows relating to an asset or liability on the balance sheet (such as future payments of interest rates on variable rate debt);
- Future cash flows relating to both risky transactions and highly probable transactions (such as an anticipated purchase or sale).

Cash In/Liquidity This concept refers to the quality of an investment which can be converted into cash immediately. For listed securities, a good degree of liquidity generally means a high volume and frequency of trading and little difference between buying and selling prices. This allows securities to be bought and sold instantly without the price of the transaction being affected by the lack of counterparties. Liquid assets are usually defined as those which can be converted into money in the short term without losing value and can be converted into cash. Economically, a liquid asset is an asset which can be converted into or exchanged for money quickly or without losing value.

Central Bank A central bank manages the running of the financial system in a country. It is in charge of issuing currency and supervising the circulation of legal tender coins and notes. It performs the function of a bank for banks, provides public debt services and other state treasury services, controls the movement of capital abroad, maintains metal and currency reserves and supervises credit and savings institutions.

Clearing Banks/Clearing House This refers to an association of local banks which liquidate reciprocal obligations resulting from documents of which each is a holder, whether on their own behalf or on behalf of their branches, agencies, clients or other banks. They are usually formal institutions with independent legal status and official sanction.

Coinsurance Insurance provided by two or more direct insurers covering the same risk. It is a system used to distribute risk in such a way that each insurer is only liable for a portion of the total risk.

Collar The collar is a combination of a cap and a floor and therefore hedges both the bond issuer, who is guaranteed to pay no more than a maximum price, and the buyer, who is guaranteed to receive no less than a minimum price.

Collateral Collateral is the name for assets that are offered as an additional guarantee on a loan or a bond issue. Since this involves a reduction of credit risk, the cost of borrowing also decreases, i.e., interest offered to the investor.

Collateralised Debt Obligation (CDO) Collateralised debt obligations (CDOs) are a type of ABS; however, they differ in the type of pool of underlying assets used to create them. Specifically, CDOs are obligations backed by a set of debt assets, such as credit card debt.

Collateralised Mortgage Obligation (CMO) A collateralised mortgage obligation (CMO) is a more complicated version of MBS. Specifically, CMOs are multi-class bonds backed by a pool of mortgage pass-through or mortgage loans. CMOs may be collateralised by either mortgage pass-through securities or mortgage loans, or a combination of them.

Commercial Bank A commercial bank is dedicated to financing the production cycle of companies without participating in their capital, as well as working with individuals.

Commodities Commodities are assets that comprise the essential raw materials of our economy and the world and are another investment alternative for different investor profiles. They are very homogeneous products which have suffered very small or insignificant transformation processes. In international financial markets they are classified as: metals (gold, silver, copper), energy (oil, natural gas), food and supplies (sugar, cotton, cocoa, coffee), grains (corn, wheat, chickpeas, beans) and livestock (pork, beef).

Competitive Advantage Competitive advantages are not related to a country's specific natural resource endowment or other similar factors, but to the skills and technology which are involved in the production process. In turn, it is any characteristic of a company that sets it apart from the rest and places it in a superior position to compete. Basic competitive advantages are cost leadership and product differentiation.

Compound Interest Compound interest is the return on capital which accrues interest at the end of each period, resulting in a new amount on which new interest will be generated.

Continuous Compound Interest This is the compound interest due on a debt at an interest rate when the number of accumulation periods is very large and can be assumed to be infinite.

Convenience Yield Consumer assets are usually products and commodities used as an energy source or in a production process, for example, crude oil or iron. Physically possessing the goods in the inventory instead of placing the asset in a forward could be considered advantageous. The benefits of this include the ability to capitalise on temporary shortages of the product and the ability to keep a production process running; this benefit is known as the "convenience yield." Since the convenience yield provides a profit for the holder of the goods, but not the holder of the forward contract, it can be modelled as a kind of "dividend yield." However, it is important to note that the convenience yield is not a cash benefit, but reflects market expectations about the future availability of the commodity.

Low commodity inventory levels imply a higher probability of shortages, resulting in a higher convenience yield. When commodity inventory levels are high, the opposite will occur and there will be a lower convenience yield.

Convexity Like that of the investment value, the duration depends on the interest rate. For this reason, the duration of an investment calculated for a given interest rate is not useful for understanding the percentage change in asset values when there are variations of one percentage point in the interest rate and the initial interest rate is different. Therefore, the duration of a bond when the interest rate is 1 % is not equal to the duration when the interest rate is 7 %. At a higher interest rate, the duration will be shorter. This phenomenon is called convexity.

Correlation The correlation between two assets measures the degree of association between their movements, whereby if the yields of these assets move, they do not always do so in the same direction. It is essential for both assets to be incorporated when ascertaining the variability or risk of a portfolio, in order to know not only how much each one moves, but how much one moves when the other moves. A correlation coefficient (r) equal to one indicates that both assets move in exactly the same way. A correlation coefficient of -1 demonstrates that when one asset rises the other falls and vice versa. A correlation coefficient of zero indicates that the movements of both assets are uncorrelated, or that when one moves in either direction, the other does not move at all. The lack of correlation between the movements of two or more assets is very important to cushion fluctuations in the value of the portfolio as a whole, therefore reducing the overall portfolio risk. The great advantage of diversification is having assets which allow the correlation coefficients of their yields to remain below one. Diversification, therefore, is not only spreading investments among different assets (due to prudence or uncertainty regarding the estimate of their future returns), but is mostly to reduce the overall portfolio risk to a given average performance level.

Counterparty This is the other party involved in a contract. In the financial sector, it is used to refer to organisations that act as a guarantee in the last instance of the transaction. It can also refer to brokers, investment banks and other dealers acting as the contracting party to complete financial transactions. The counterparty assumes the risk of potential financial loss if it proves to be difficult for the other party to meet these obligations in the market.

Coupon A coupon is a document accompanying a security which must be separated from it in order to obtain the profits made in a specific period or to exercise any other right (right of first refusal, etc.).

Credit Rating Credit ratings are prospective opinions about credit risk. They express the views of the agency on the ability and willingness of an issuer, whether a company, state or local government, to fulfil their financial obligations in a timely manner. The credit rating is an opinion issued by an independent entity (rating agency) about the ability of a debt issuer to meet their payment obligations in due time, as regards both capital and interests.Rating agencies assess the quality and risk of debt issued by corporations, states, government agencies and organisations. In doing so, the issuers are assigned a score (in the form of letters and/or numbers) which reflects their creditworthiness. This score is a mark or opinion about the issuer's ability to meet a financial obligation.

Credit Spread/Differential Rate This is the quantification of the difference between the average asset and liability interest rate of a financial institution.

Cross Currency Rate Swap (CCRS) A cross currency rate swap (CCRS) is a derivative contract in which one party pays the other an amount in currency for a certain period of time on certain dates, in exchange for another amount in a different currency.

Currency Depreciation This concept refers to a reduction in the value of a currency relative to the value of other foreign currencies. Devaluation represents a reduction in the price of products made in the country whose currency is devalued in relation to those countries whose currencies do not change in value. By contrast, products manufactured abroad are more expensive for the country whose currency has lost value. For this reason, the devaluation of a currency tends to lead to increased exports and reduced imports.

Debenture Following Ramón Tamames, in economics, and strictly speaking, debenture refers to securities that companies or organisations of all types issue to obtain credit on the capital market, with a commitment to complete repayments within a given term and normally at a fixed interest rate. Obligations placed between institutional or private purchasers through banking and the stock exchange may be convertible into shares at an exchange rate predetermined in the issue offer. In theory, bondholders have no voting rights in the issuing company but they can organise bondholders' unions to defend their rights if they feel threatened by the company's policy. Treasury obligations have been issued in Spain since the beginning of the 1980s as long-term securities with a fixed interest rate.

Debt Debt is an amount of money or property which a person, company or country owes to another and constitutes obligations to repay it within a certain time. By origin, debt can be classified into internal and external debt, in the sense that it may become public or private.

Default Default is a delay or failure in the fulfilment of an obligation.

Depreciation Depreciation is a decline in the value of an asset for different reasons: wear or physical deterioration, obsolescence, the passage of time, changing tastes, etc.

Derivative Asset (or Derivative Contract) A derivative asset is a financial instrument with a payment structure which depends on another asset or portfolio of assets known as the underlying asset. Sometimes they are referred to as derivative products (or contracts) rather than assets.

Diffusion Diffusion measurements can be defined as numerical values aiming to analyse the degree of separation of values in a statistical series with respect to the measures of central tendency being considered.There are two types of diffusion measures:

- Absolute diffusion measures include projection, mean deviation, variance and standard deviation, which are used in overall statistical analyses.
- Relative diffusion measures determine the diffusion of statistical distribution regardless of the units in which the variable is expressed. They deal with more technical parameters used in specific studies including opening coefficients, relative projection, variation coefficient (Pearson diffusion index) and medium diffusion index.

Direct Costs Direct costs are those which are directly attributable to a production centre or a particular product.

Diversification Diversification refers to investments in a wide variety of assets or securities to reduce the risk of a portfolio. The total risk or volatility of a portfolio decreases with diversification, and a portfolio made up of values which are not perfectly correlated offers a greater risk–return pattern than its individual components.

Dividend The dividend is the remuneration received by the holder of shares in a company. This remuneration is representative of the profit distribution obtained by the issuer. It is the return on the investment which a company awards to its shareholders according to the number of shares they have. It is paid with resources arising from profits made by the company during a certain period and can be paid either in the form of money or more stocks. A company's General Assembly of Shareholders is responsible for deciding when and how dividends are paid.

Duration The simple duration or Macaulay duration of a financial transaction (typically applied to a bond) is the average of the different terms or maturities in which the financial transaction will generate a cash flow where the weight is the present value of the cash flow corresponding to that period.The modified duration measures price sensitivity to a small change in the level of the interest rate.

Earnings per Share at Risk (EPSaR) The earnings per share at risk, EPSAR, is defined as the measure of the maximum potential change that earnings per share being studied may suffer (it may be that of a particular project, a division, the entire company, etc.) at a time horizon and at a given probability level.

Euribor This is a benchmark to which the remuneration of many financial contracts is linked. It is defined as the interest rate at which the financial institutions with the best ratings in the eurozone (approximately 60 institutions) lend money to each other in the interbank market. It is published monthly as a simple arithmetic average of the daily values (on the working days of the market during the month) of the spot interest rate issued by the European Banking Federation for deposit transactions in euros.

Ex Ante Following Ramón Tamames, *ex ante* is an expression which was introduced into economic language by Gunnar Myrdal (and consolidated by the neo-Wicksellian Swedish school) and is used to refer to the prospective outlook of a magnitude in economic analyses, such as how it may be expected to evolve.

Exchange Rate This is the equivalence relation between two currencies, measured by the number of a country's monetary units that must be delivered to acquire a monetary unit of another.

Exotic Options Exotic option is the name given to all options which are not standard. In order to accommodate the needs of their clients (the risk that they want to assume, required return, hedging required), financial institutions design options with new characteristics. Some of the main reasons for the existence of these options are the following:

- Costs: sometimes it is possible to design exotic options that have no initial cost and also allow the holder to cancel them when maintaining them involves high hedging costs;
- Flexibility when determining exercise conditions and financial structure;
- Complexity: they allow the investor to provide solutions to complex needs.

Two large groups of exotic options can be determined according to whether payments in the financial year depend on the evolution of the underlying asset price or not.

In order to trade in currencies, exotic options are highly specialised trading tools that allow strategies to be tailored to specific situations.

Expectation See expected value

Expected Value The expected value of a random variable is its mean value. The expected value is a number. This number is one of a set whose extremes are the minimum and the maximum value that the random variable may take.

Ex Post This is an adjective used to describe the measurement of a variable, after a certain period or at the end of a period, taken in order to obtain its value and observe any variations that may have occurred.

Face Value This is the value which is assigned to a coin by monetary authorities and which also appears on the coin itself. In the case of marketable securities, this term is sometimes used synonymously with nominal value.

Fair Value Hedge Following Felipe Herranz Martín, a derivative performs a fair value hedging function when market changes produce variations in the fair value of the hedged item but also produce the same or similar variations in the hedging derivative in the opposite direction. An example could be a loan received by a company at a fixed interest rate hedged by a "commodity–interest rate" swap.

In these cases, the changes in the derivative valuation are applied to the income statement, where they are offset by the hedged item which changes in the opposite direction.

It is important to point out that with this type of hedging, the hedged item will always be measured by its fair value, allocating valuation changes to the income statement, although its accounting treatment is different when it is not part of a hedge.

Financial Statements Financial statements are documents or reports that provide insight into the financial situation of a company: the resources it has, the results it has obtained, the returns it has generated, cash inflows and outflows, among other related financial issues.

Whether used by managers, administrators, investors, shareholders, partners, suppliers, banks, financial agents or government entities, financial statements allow relevant information to be obtained and analysed so that decisions can be made based on this analysis. Most of these reports form the end product of accounting and are produced in accordance with generally accepted accounting principles, accounting standards and financial reporting standards.

Statutory financial statements depend on each country, where the most common components are as follows: Statement of Financial Position (also known as Balance Sheet), Profit and Loss Account (also called Income Statement or Profit and Loss Statement), Statement of Changes in Equity (also known as Statement of Returned Earnings) and Cash Flow Statement (also known as Statement of Cash Flows).

Financial System This refers to a set of institutions, means and markets whose primary purpose is to channel savings generated by economic agents with lending capacity to those who need funding at a given moment. The financial system is a set of regulations, policies, instruments, individuals and institutions which run and form a part of the money market and the capital market of a country.

Fixed Income/Fixed Interest These are transferable securities whose return is constant and independent of the results obtained by the economic unit issuing them. The most typical example would be obligations. There is a wide range

of fixed-income products with different durations (maturities), risk levels and ways of perceiving the returns.
Broadly, they can be classified:
According to their issuer, including:
- Public Fixed income ("Public Debt"): when the issuer is a Stateor another public body.
- Corporate bonds: when the issuer is a private company;
According to their funding and negotiation term:
- Fixed income in the money market: short-term fixed-income assets (these do not usually exceed 18 months). These assets have very low risk and high liquidity (it is easy to buy and sell them in secondary markets);
- Fixed income in the capital market: assets which are issued in the medium and long term (more than two years).
Depending on the type of return they generate, including:
- Explicit return values, in which the interest paid (coupon) is specifically agreed. This is the case of bonds and debentures issued by the government and the private sector;
- Implicit return values, in which the return is obtained by the difference between the transfer or face value and the acquisition value. Any financial asset issued at a discount, such as Treasury bills, has an implicit return.

Floor A floor is a put option (sold by the bond issuer who pays the market interest rate as a coupon and purchased by the buyer of this bond) which causes the issuer's final payment or the buyer's final bond collection to be a minimum determined interest rate, the exercise price or "strike," of the option. Thus with the floor the bond buyer ensures that they receive a minimum specified interest rate.

Flow of Funds/Cash Flow Cash flow refers to inflows and outflows of money generated by a project, investment or any other economic activity. It is also the difference between a company's receipts and payments over a given period.

Forward Rate Agreement (FRA) A Forward Rate Agreement is a commitment between two parties who agree on a fixed interest rate to be paid by a theoretical deposit with a specific maturity on a future date. On the date the contract is signed, the fixed rate is established along with the date when the theoretical deposit transfer begins. At maturity, the seller will pay the buyer the difference if the current interest rate, i.e. the variable rate, exceeds the agreed interest rate. If, however, the current interest rate is less than the rate taken as a reference, the buyer will pay the seller.

Future Price This is the price for which an asset is traded in the future market. A price per unit of the underlying asset is agreed in a future contract on the date of the event. This will be adjusted daily for the purposes of reflecting any losses or gains that occur in the price of the underlying asset.

GDP (Gross Domestic Product) The GDP is the sum of the value of all final goods and services produced in a country (it is called domestic for this reason) in a year. Final goods and services are referred to because in this way the production is consolidated, which involves aggregation sector by sector, eliminating any possible calculation duplications. It is called gross because depreciation is not deducted. This quantity can be calculated by summing consumption, investment and exports and subtracting imports.

Guarantee A guarantee is also referred to as a deposit, bond, collateral, security and surety. It is a person or thing that ensures the fulfilment or resolution of the agreement made with a third party if they fail to meet their obligation.

Hedging Hedging refers to the act of making an investment to reduce the risk of an adverse movement in the asset in which the main investment was made. All traders should be aware that hedging is a possible method of protection and risk management. Although several hedging techniques have been developed, there are two which are more common and more important than the others: the first is to make two investments in two negatively correlated instruments, and the other is to use derivative financial instruments (usually options and futures).

Holder/Bearer Following Deloitte, in civil law, this refers to the individual or organisation that is in physical possession of something; this need not coincide with its rightful owner.

In commercial law, it refers to an individual who is in possession of a debt instrument or stock (bill of exchange, cheque, etc.), whether this is the drawer or any other person to whom it has been ceded or transferred by endorsement. In the bond market, it is the owner of a security or value.

Immunisation (Portfolio Immunisation) Portfolio immunisation is a technique that seeks to guarantee the initial yield of the portfolio regardless of the evolution suffered by interest rates over the investment horizon. It is therefore a technique that immunises the portfolio from adverse changes in interest rates.

Implicit Rate Implicit interest rates are financial costs that are expressed not by an interest rate, but by the difference between the purchase price and the amount to be received at maturity. This difference may be caused by an issue premium (when debt is underwritten, an amount lower than its face value is paid) or by a redemption premium (at maturity the investor receives an amount greater than that of its face value). When these debts are issued, they will be recorded on the balance sheet at their redemption value, and the difference between the subscription and redemption value (implicit interest) is included in an asset account, "Deferred interest expenses of transferable securities," which will continue to produce results throughout the life of the transaction.

Indebtedness Following Serfinco, indebtedness is the acquisition of external resources by companies, i.e., external funding sources, in order to be able to develop their activities. The ratio of a company's indebtedness expresses the relationship between its own funds and its total debts; in turn, the debt ratio indicates the portion of a company's asset that belongs to creditors and determines the company's ability to obtain new debt.

Indirect Costs Indirect costs are those which cannot be assigned directly to a centre or a product, as they are shared between several reference units. These costs are distributed between units based on their percentage of ownership.

Inflation Inflation is an increase in the general level of prices. Cost-push inflation is essentially caused by rising prices in production factors (wages, interest rates, land prices, energy, raw materials, etc.). Demand-pull inflation is mainly attributable to increased consumer requirements where, due to supply rigidities, the only option is to increase prices.

Input This is a term used to describe all products and services, as well as energy, which are introduced in the production process and which, once combined and transformed, result in outputs or finished products.

Institutional Investor This term refers mainly to insurance companies, pension funds and investment funds which collect savings and supply funds to markets.

Insurance This is the means by which the risks faced by individuals or companies are shared. It is the service provided by specialised companies that charge the insured an amount (premium) in exchange for a certain compensation in the event of an incident occurring.

The contract through which insurance is established is usually mutually beneficial; the insured party chooses to pay the insurer a much lower value than that of the product being ensured to hedge against the possibility of losing the product completely. This gives them peace of mind and avoids the need to keep assets that would enable them to meet the cost of the loss. The insurance company, on the other hand, can make a clear profit if it accurately estimates the probability of the risk occurring.

Interest Rate This is the price of money from a general perspective. From the debtor's point of view, it is a quantity added to the main amount which must be delivered if a certain sum of money is borrowed; and from the creditor's point of view, it is an amount received as a return on the capital that they have lent. The interest rate is usually expressed as a percentage and, although it typically refers to a period of one year, it may also refer to a shorter period such as a semester, quarter or month.

Interest Rate Swap (IRS) An interest rate swap is an agreement between two parties where each agrees to make periodic payments to the other on certain future dates in such a way that one of them is interested in receiving or paying a variable interest rate while the other party is interested in receiving or paying a fixed rate. The fixed rate payer must make payments based on a specified fixed interest rate, while the variable rate payer must make payments based on a variable interest rate. Such payments are calculated based on a theoretical nominal amount and settlements are calculated based on the differences established between the reference rates and the rates fixed in the contract.

Intermediation Costs Financial intermediation represents the activity performed by banking institutions when taking customer deposits and investments over a certain length of time and with a certain interest rate and when lending to other customers over a different term and at a different interest rate, usually higher. Consequently, intermediation margins, or brokerage costs, represent a measure of the way in which the financial sector uses the resources necessary to fulfil its intermediation role and can be considered as an indicator of efficiency.

Intrinsic Value In a derivative contract, the intrinsic value refers to the collections/payments that would occur if the maturity of the derivative was at present.

Investment Bank/Business Bank This is a bank whose principal activities include financing large companies, conducting operations abroad, managing company investments and treasuries, as well as participating in activities in the company mergers and acquisitions field.

Issuer According to Deloitte, issuers are individual investors and legal entities, public or private, who issue securities or financial assets as a way of obtaining external resources to finance their activities.

Leverage Leverage is the relationship between equity and credit comprising the total capital used in an investment or any other financial transaction. Loans, equity or debt margins, can be used as a source of credit. The use of equity can be significantly reduced by using credit and, thus, the profitability of a financial transaction can be significantly increased. The use of loans or debt generates interest costs, so the investment must generate a higher income than these interests to ensure that the balance is positive for the investor.

The leverage effect is the relationship between the investment performance and the capital invested: leverage effect = investment performance/capital invested.

Liabilities Following Enrique Ortega Martínez and Deloitte, these are a set of contracted debts and obligations that an economic unit has. Liability represents the company's financial structure or funding sources.

Depending on the degree of enforceability that liabilities have, they are divided into enforceable and unenforceable liabilities:
- Enforceable liabilities consist of debts incurred by the company which have to be cleared at different points in time. If debts are due in the short term, they are called current liabilities, while if they are due in the long term, they are called fixed liabilities or non-current liabilities;
- Unenforceable liabilities (fixed equity) consist of all the funds that have been contributed by the members of a business (capital and reserves) and that, therefore, constitute their own funds.

Long Term This is generally a period of more than twelve months, depending on the activity to which it refers.

Macroeconomic Variables These are economic aggregates which are studied in order to understand the overall running of a country or region. Macroeconomics uses categories such as overall employment, national income, consumption, aggregate supply and demand, average value of prices, etc. and generally follows the conceptualisation formed by John M. Keynes.
Their purpose is to study the influences determining the level of national income and economic growth, as well as other problems related to those mentioned previously, such as unemployment and recessions. Macroeconomists usually consider the problem of individual price formation abstractly and deal with aggregate price indices which are determined by the overall spending level. The study of macro variables is very useful to appreciate and understand the evolution of a country's economy and the way in which various public decisions affect their behaviour.Macroeconomic studies attempt to describe a country's economic activity and, in turn, the expectations for its future development. In order to do this, certain indicators are analysed, providing a better understanding of the economic situation, its structure, its competitiveness and where it is going. The most relevant macroeconomic variables or indicators are: gross domestic product (GDP), inflation, interest rate, exchange rate, balance of payments and unemployment, among others.

Marginal Utility This is the satisfaction that the consumption of a unit or an additional amount of a particular product or basket of goods gives to the consumer.

Marginal VaR The marginal VaR (value at risk) can be defined as the derivative of the VaR with respect to a specific asset, and its economic interpretation is the variation of the VaR of a portfolio on increasing the amount invested in an asset, which may or may not be part of the initial portfolio, by an infinitesimal amount of money.

Market Price This is the price that a product reaches depending on its supply and demand, a price at which the supply becomes equal to the demand. It is known as quotation in financial markets.

Mean Reversion There are different ways to define a process with mean reversion, some based on more qualitative than quantitative ideas, and others based on the opposite approach, giving much weight to mathematical concepts and making the classification of processes with mean reversion more accurate.

A first definition agrees with the idea that processes with mean reversion tend to change their behaviour of growth or decline when they reach (historical) extremes. This definition is one of the most widely accepted.

In addition to the previous definition, it has been suggested that a process with mean reversion is one in which the returns have a negative autocorrelation. This definition would prompt a procedure to examine the hypothesis of whether a process reverts to the mean or not.

Medium Term This expression is applicable to any period of time ranging from short to long term. Its duration depends on the context, but in money markets it is the term corresponding to all transactions with a maturity of more than a year, and in the Eurobond market it refers to issues with a maturity ranging from two to seven years.

Middle Office The purpose of the middle office is usually a grey area without a specific definition. From our point of view, middle office/risks perform control functions of counterparty limits, market risk limits and static and dynamic data management.

These functions usually use different modules which operate with the other systems of the entity, providing management support and a regulatory framework.

Mortgage-Backed Securities (MBS) Mortgage-backed securities (MBS) are bonds that are backed by pools or mortgage loans, such as mortgage papers, house papers or land and property papers.

Net Investment Hedge A net investment hedge involves hedging the exchange rate risk on investments in subsidiaries, partners, joint businesses and branches whose activities are based on or conducted in a functional currency different to the one used by the company that draws up the annual accounts.

Net Present Value at Risk (NPVaR) The net present value at risk, NPVaR, is defined as the measure of the maximum potential change that the net present value being studied may suffer (it may be that of a particular project, a division, the entire company, etc.) at a time horizon and at a given probability level.

Net Worth/Heritage This is the set of assets, rights and obligations of an individual investor or firm, country or entity. When used to refer to an individual person, it usually only covers material goods with a certain economic value.

Operating Cost These are the typical costs or expenses incurred when carrying out an activity.

Opportunity Cost The opportunity cost is the value of the best possible economic alternative, relinquished as a result of dedicating resources to another specific activity.

Option In the financial sphere, this is a contract which awards some of the parties paying a premium the right but not the obligation to buy or sell an asset (underlying asset) at an agreed price (strike price) on a certain date or during a certain period. The two most common objectives of option contracts are to hedge against a potential risk or to attempt to obtain a capital gain. Options are primarily traded in organised markets. Spain has had a financial options market since 1989, which is now called the MEFF (Mercado Español de Futuros Financieros).

OTC (Over-the-Counter) Market The negotiated or OTC (over-the-counter) market can be used for contracts on financial instruments established between two parties directly and also for negotiating on derivative financial instruments sold through a dealer and not through a centralised market.

For example, a futures contract is a standardised product which is traded on the futures market, while a forward contract is an OTC product.

Generally, in regards to shares, if a share is traded in an OTC context, it is usually because the company is small and does not meet the requirements to be listed on the stock exchange. Shares of companies which are not listed on the stock market are sold through brokers or dealers who negotiate directly between the investor and the company via computer networks or by telephone.

OTC contracts that are produced in these negotiations are bilateral contracts containing the agreement reached by two parties regarding the settlement of the instrument. Most OTC contracts are drawn up through banks and financial investment companies. There are also OTC derivative negotiating frameworks which are usually included in these contracts, such as the regulations of the International Swaps and Derivatives Association (ISDA).

Output/Product This is a term used to refer to final products arising from any type of process (productive, computer, etc.).

Over-the-Counter Derivatives (OTC Derivatives) Over-the-counter (OTC) derivatives are agreements between private agents and do not appear in any financial market. The terms of a contract of this type are virtually free and are tailored to the clients, meaning they are usually more complex than traded derivatives.

Overdraft Following María Moliner, an overdraft is the deficit in an account: more debit than credit.

Parity This is the relationship between the values of two currencies of different countries.

Perfect Market A perfect market is one in which information about the conditions (quality) of what is being negotiated is the same for all suppliers and demanders (there is no exclusive or privileged information) and price and volume information is also available to everyone. Put another way, it is a market in which the forces of supply and demand can act freely and which satisfies all the conditions of perfect competition.

Price/Quotation/Quote This involves publishing the price of securities or goods traded on the stock, commodities, metal, etc. market daily. The price can be given four times per session: open, low, high and close. The same principal applies for a currency in comparison with others.

Probability The word probability, derived from the Latin *probabilĭtas*, is a word that enhances the characteristic of being probable (i.e., that something can occur or is realistic). It deals with evaluating and measuring frequency, allowing a certain result in the framework to be obtained from a random process. Probability can therefore be defined as the ratio of the number of successful cases and the number of potential problems. Mathematics, physics and statistics are some of the areas that allow conclusions to be reached regarding the likelihood of potential events.

Project Finance A project finance is a financial mechanism which is aimed at realising investment projects of great magnitude which therefore require specialised funding. In project finance, financing is linked to the project itself, and the generation of its financial flows covers the financing required. The project company operates with a very high debt ratio, which makes the transaction high risk, meaning that it is unlikely that the financial institutions involved will recover the funding provided in case of default.

The types of projects to which it is usually applied are energy projects (especially renewable energy projects, which are becoming increasingly important); the construction of new motorways, airports and fishing ports; and large civil works such as hospitals, bridges and universities. The way in which it is structured depends on the characteristics of the project in question, according to factors such as the financial flows needed to develop the various stages of implementation, the scale of the project, its maturity and the contractual conditions of the pool of banks participating in it.

Random Number This is any of the numbers within a certain range in which all have the same probability of occurring.

Random Walk A random walk represents a variable whose changes are white noise and are therefore unpredictable.

Rate This is the ratio or quotient of two related magnitudes. Financial or accounting ratios are coefficients provided by financial units of measurement and comparison. Through them, the relationship between two financial data sets is established and it is possible to analyse the status of an organisation on the basis of their optimal levels.

Refunding Refunding is the extension of funding through a new credit or loan at its maturity. The term also encompasses changes in conditions agreed on a loan or credit in a manner favourable to the debtor, where this second definition is synonymous with "debt restructuring." It involves the modification of existing debt conditions (maturity modification, postponement of interest payments, cancellation of part of the debt) in order to help the debtor face a period of financial difficulty.

Repayment The repayment period or simple recovery involves establishing how long it will take for a given investment to be recovered. If the future income is the same for all periods, the calculation is performed by establishing the ratio between the initial investment and the average net income.

Replacement Cost This term refers to the current cost of replacing a particular machine or warehouse product.

Risk-Free Interest Rate The risk-free rate is a concept which states that there is an alternative investment in the economy that has no risk for the investor.

In other words, it is the rate provided by a reliable return in a particular currency unit and during a certain period. There is no credit risk or reinvestment risk because the cash will be available at maturity.

In practice, it is assumed that US Treasury bond yields are a good measure of risk-free interest rate, as the probability of default on a bond issued by the USA is considered to be very close to zero.

Risk Premium In the context of financial markets, this is the differential between the interest rate on a company's fixed-income issues and the interest rate on state issues or those which are guaranteed by the state. The interest rate is lower on state issues because of their higher security. It also refers to the differential between interest rates on debt issued by different states, depending on the security that they offer the investor. It is the difference in the required return on an asset as a result of the increased risk that this asset involves against another which is risk free.

Royalty Following Ramón Tamames, formerly this was the prerogative of the monarch to exercise their power, examples of which include minting money or obtaining a certain proportion of specific revenue (e.g. Royal Fifth).In modern times, it is the percentage that the owner of a patent, a production process, etc. is entitled to receive from the sale of a product by prior agreement.

Savings Rate The savings rate of a country is the part of GDP which is saved. The savings rate determines whether a country has sufficient resources to invest in productive resources with funds from the financial market provided by savers. Countries with low savings levels will not have available resources for the productive sector and will need external funding with the introduction of currency, which usually has two different effects: the destabilisation of the national currency with the introduction of other currencies, and the fact that part of the returns on investments financed with foreign currency have to leave the country.

Overall, the savings rate in developed countries is higher than in developing countries which do not have sufficient resources to save, making them too dependent on foreign funds to invest in productive capacity.

Securitisation This is the transformation of present and future receivables into marketable debt instruments, derecognising sold assets in the balance sheet of ceding entities. It involves converting cash flows arising from illiquid assets into securities (asset-backed securities). These securities are issued by a financial company and are placed on a stock market. It is carried out when there is an illiquid debt and this debt is converted into marketable securities in an organised market which provides liquidity to investments. These securities entitle investors to receive cash flows associated with the security, assuming the risk of its realisation, leaving the administration (collection) to the original company.

Share A share is a security which establishes the proportionate participation that its holder has in the capital of a company. Its title holder becomes an owner and partner and is granted the right to vote at general company meetings and is entitled to receive dividends corresponding to the earnings that have been obtained.

The most common types of shares are common, preferred (where shareholders have a superior right to collect money derived from their acquisition, even before the distribution of dividends to partners, if this has been agreed previously) and non-voting (which grant the shareholder economic rights [the receipt of dividends] but no other rights, such as voting on a Board).

Short Term This is the short period of time which, for economic purposes, is considered for credits, planning, etc. It must be less than twelve months.

Simple Interest In contrast to compound interest, this is the return on borrowed capital which is not added to the debt to produce new interest. It is often used in short-term transactions.

Spot Price This is the market value of a financial asset in the spot market.

Standard Deviation The standard deviation measures the spread of data around the mean. Under the data distribution hypothesis, observations ranging between the average and +/− twice the deviation are considered normal.

Stochastic Process A stochastic process is one in which all the individual steps required to perform an activity are represented, along with the forms or ways in which each of the steps can be carried out and their respective probabilities. In other words, any process involving probabilities is a stochastic process.

Stock Indexes/General Share Price Index These measure the evolution of securities listed on a particular stock exchange. They are made up of a sample of securities which are subject to higher trading volumes. The best known stock market index is the Dow Jones, which reflects the situation of the New York Stock Exchange, the world's most influential stock market, on a daily basis.

Strike Price This is the price agreed in the option contract at which the buyer of an option can purchase (if they have acquired a "call" option) or sell (if they have acquired a "put" option) the underlying asset. The seller of the option is obligated to buy or sell, respectively, if the buyer exercises their right.

Structured Bonds In recent years a complex type of bond has appeared which is aimed at transferring risk to the market through a securitisation process of certain financial assets (mortgages, credit card receivables, auto loans, etc.). This process allows financial institutions to remove certain illiquid assets from their balance sheets as well as providing investors with access to diversified asset classes. Common examples of assets created through this securitisation process, known as structured bonds, include ABS, CDO, MBS and CMS, among others.

Swap A swap is a derivative contract through which the nature of the flows generated in a financial transaction are exchanged or altered. The most important are interest rate swaps (IRS) and cross currency rate swap (CCRS).

Swaption Following "Inversionario.com," swaption defines the option contract on a financial swap whereby the buyer of the option pays a premium to be able to perform a "swap" for a certain period of time. It usually refers to an interest rate swap. A swaption gives the holder the right, but not the obligation, to enter into an interest swap. In the same way as an option, a swaption determines the price, the strike (or fixed rate) and the time to maturity. There are two types of swaptions: payer and receiver. A payer swaption gives the holder the right to receive the floating rate of the swap and pay the fixed rate. A receiver swaption gives the holder the right to receive the fixed rate (of the swap) and pay the floating rate. Investors enter into swaptions when they think they may need a specific rate at some point in the future, or to limit interest rate risk. Instead of entering into a swap, the investor buys the swaption (the option to enter into the swap).

Temporary Series A temporary series (also called historical, chronological or time series) is defined as a data set corresponding to an economic phenomenon, arranged in chronological order. The components of a temporary series are trend, cyclical variations, seasonal variations and accidental variations.

Term Structure of Interest Rates (TSIR) The graph presenting the interest rates of different bonds with the same risk, liquidity and tax but different maturities is known as the yield curve or term structure of interest rates (TSIR). More formally, the TSIR can be defined as the function relating interest rates to terms until the securities mature for bonds with similar credit ratings. Obviously, for each level of credit rating there is a curve of different rates, thus the worse the credit rating is, the higher the interest rates are and vice versa.
The term structure of interest rates can be defined with different types of bond that have very different payment structures, but for consistency, the TSIR is normally created with the interest rates of zero-coupon bonds. Thus, TSIRs that are created in this way are homogeneous and unless otherwise stated, in this book the TSIR refers to its zero-coupon bonds.

Time Value In a derivative contract, the time value refers to the extra value that a derivative has due to the fact that over time collections/payments may increase.

Trade-Off Trade-off is an expression which is widely used in international financial jargon to refer to the relationship of substitution between two or more alternatives, for example, the "risk–return trade off" for the purposes of investment in financial assets.

Trading Trading involves purchase and sale stock exchange transactions which are carried out over a very short term, usually one day, are of a speculative nature and are used in order to get an immediate return; this type of transaction presents a high risk.

Uncertainty Uncertainty is a situation which occurs when there are two or more possible outcomes for an ongoing action and the exact probabilities of these outcomes are unknown. In this sense, in economics, planning acts to reduce uncertainties.

Underlying Asset In options and futures markets, this is an asset which is normally subject to a standard contract and is to be exchanged. It may be a physical product (gold, silver, grains) or a financial asset (currency or securities), or even a portfolio of assets (stock indexes) or the interest rate of a notional bond.

Utility Following Enrique Ortega, utility is the property that goods have to meet human needs. The utility of goods cannot be determined in an absolute sense; instead, it is measured in a relative sense, comparing the different utilities of various goods with each other.

Value at Risk (VaR) There are many ways to measure risk, but for the market in general and for equities in particular, the most commonly used is the value at risk (VaR). By definition, the VaR is a measure of the maximum potential change that the value of a portfolio can suffer over a time horizon and given probability level.

Variance Variance measures the spread of a given distribution around the arithmetic mean. It is defined as the average of the sum of squared deviations from the mean of a series of numbers. The greater the variance is, the greater the spread will be.

Volatility This is a measure of the frequency and intensity of changes in the price of an asset. It measures the price variability that an asset has in relation to its mean. It is used to measure and predict the risk of investing in a particular asset and is used in financial markets to differentiate between financial assets which are stable and those which are not. In options transactions, it represents the average variability of the underlying asset price.

Weighting This is the weight assigned to each variable in a set to be measured or expressed in an index.

White Noise Process A white noise process represents a variable:

- Which oscillates around a constant mean;
- Which has a constant volatility;
- Whose past values do not contain useful information for predicting future values.

Yield/Profitability This is the ability to produce profits or income. It refers to the relationship between the value of a particular investment and the profits obtained once fees and taxes have been deducted. Profitability, unlike factors such as income or profit, is always expressed in relative terms.

Bibliography

Alcalá, F.J., and Doménech, P. Aplicación de la Normativa Internacional Contable en los Instrumentos Financieros de Cobertura.

Beninga, S. (2006). Principles of Finance with Excel. Oxford University Press.

Beninga, S. (2008). Financial Modeling. MIT Press.

Basel Committee on Banking Supervision. (2005a). Guidance on Paragraph 468 of the Framework Document.

Basel Committee on Banking Supervision. (2005b). Studies on the Validation of Internal Rating Systems, Working Paper No. 14.

Basel Committee on Banking Supervision. (2004a). International Convergence of Capital Measurement and Capital Standards. A Revised Framework.

Basel Committee on Banking Supervision. (2004b). The new Basel Capital Accord.

Basel Committee on Banking Supervision. (2013a). Liquidity stress testing: a survey of theory, empirics and current industry and supervisory practices, Working Paper 24.

Basel Committee on Banking Supervision. (2013b). Literature review of factors relating to liquidity stress – extended version, Working Paper 24.

Brealy, R.A. and Myers, S.C. (2006): Principios de Finanzas Corporativas, McGraw Hill.

F.J. Población García, *Financial Risk Management*,
DOI 10.1007/978-3-319-41366-2

CEBS. (2006). Guidelines on the Implementation, Validation and assessment of Advanced Measurement (AMA) and Internal Ratings Based (IRB) Approaches, CP 10 revised.
cn crece negocios.com
Contabilidad en Linea.
CRR, Regulation (EU) No 575/2013 of the European Parliament and of the Council.
Culp. (2001). The Risk Management Process: Business Strategy and Tactics. Wiley.
Deloitte. (2007). Economía y Negocios. Espasa Calpe S.A. Madrid.
Díaz, Rafael. Introducción a la Probabilidad, los Procesos Estocásticos y la Estadística en Ingeniería.
Diccionario Economico Financiero de la Caixa.
http://elnuevoparquet.com/
http://inversionario.com/
http://knoow.net/
http://www.abanfin.com/
http://www.bcrp.gob.pe/publicaciones/glosario.html
http://www.bmv.com.mx/es/grupo-bmv/glosario
http://www.bolsamadrid.es
http://www.cnmv.es/portal/inversor
http://www.consultingcredit.com/
http://www.definicion.org/
http://definanzas.com/
http://www.eco-finanzas.com/
http://www.economiasimple.net/
http://www.economia48.com/
http://www.economist.com
http://www.edufinet.com/
http://www.elblogsalmon.com/
http://www.eleconomista.es/
http://www.eumed.net/cursecon/dic/dic-cs.htm
http://www.euroval.com
http://www.finanzasparatodos.es/
http://www.gabilos.com/
http://www.hiru.eus/
http://www.info-forex.com/
http://www.itchihuahua.edu.mx/

http://www.gestiopolis.com/
http://www.gbmarketingcr.net/
http://www.lainformacion.com/
http://www.lasbolsasdevalores.com/
http://www.mathematicsdictionary.com/
http://www.plangeneralcontable.com/
http://www.saberia.com/conocimiento-por-materias/
http://www.ultraserfinco.com/site/
http://usuaris.tinet.cat/fllorens/tema7.htm
https://efxto.com/diccionario
https://www.bolsar.com
https://www.e-conomic.com
https://www.moodys.com/
https://www.standardandpoors.com

Froot, A., Scharfstein, D.A., and Stein, J.C. (1994). A Framework for Risk Management. Harvard Business Review, 72, 91–102.

García A., Población J., and Serna, G. (2008). A Note on Commodity Contingent Valuation. Journal of Derivatives and Hedge Funds, 13, 311–320.

García A., Población J., and Serna, G. (2012). The stochastic seasonal behavior of natural gas prices. European Financial Management, 18, 410–443.

Glosario de bolsa.

Grinblatt and Titman. (2001). Financial Markets and Corporate Strategy, Second Edition, Part VI (Risk Management).

Hull, J. (2003). Options, Futures and Other Derivatives, Fifth Edition, Prentice Hall, New Jersey.

Jerez, M., and Sotoca, S. (2010). Econometría II. Universidad Complutense de Madrid.

Morgan, J.P. (1996). Risk Metrics – Technical Document, Fourth Edition, New York.

Morgan, J.P. (1999). Corporate Metrics – Technical Document, First Edition, New York.

Kim, J., Malz, A., and Mina, J. (1999). LongRun– Technical Document, Risk Metrics Group, First Edition, New York.

López Pascual, J., and Díez, L. (2001). "Dirección Financiera. Planificación, Gestión y Control". Financial Times-Prentice Hall.

López Pascual, J., and Díez, L. (2007). "Dirección Financiera. La Inteligencia Financiera en la Gestión Empresarial". Financial Times-Prentice Hall.

Maarse, B. (2012). "Backtesting Framework for PD, EAD and LGD". Rabobank International Quantitative Risk Analytics.

Moliner, M. (2008). Diccionario de uso del español. Editorial Gredos S.A.U.

Moral, G. (2004). Validación de enfoques IRB para el cálculo del capital mínimo por riesgo de crédito, Estabilidad Financiera, 7, 75–110.

Moral G. (2006). Estimaciones de la EAD para operaciones con límites de crédito explícito. Estabilidad Financiera, 10, 55–97.

Nieto, M. (2005). El Tratamiento del Riesgo Operacional en Basilea II. Estabilidad Financiera, 8, 163–185.

Novales, A. (1993). Econometría. McGraw-Hill.

Nunes, Paulo. Definición de Benchmarking.

Ortega Martínez, Enrique. (1990). El nuevo diccionario de Marketing (y disciplinas afines). Área Editorial S.A.

Palacio Montoya, J.S. Estudio de Procesos de Reversión a la Media.

Pablo López, A. (2008). Manual Práctico de Matemática Comercial y Financiera. Tomo II. Ed. Universitaria Ramón Areces. Madrid.

Pablo López, A. (2009). Matemática de las Operaciones Financieras. Tomo II. Ed. UNED. Madrid.

Peña, D. (2000). Estadística: Modelos y Métodos. Alianza Editorial.

Peña, J.I. (2002). La gestión de riesgos financieros de mercado y de crédito. Pearson Educación.

Rouah, F.D., and Vainberg, G. (2007). Option Pricing Models and Volatility Using Excel-VBA. John Wiley & Sons.

Rating Models and Validation. Guidelines on Credit Risk Management. Oesterreichische Nationalbank (OeNB). (2004).

Ruiz Munoz, David; Manual de estadística.

Sabino, Carlos. (1991). "Diccionario de economía y Finanzas", PANAPO.

Schmieder, C, Heiko, H., Neudorfer, B., Puhr, C., and Schmitz S. (2011a). Next Generation Balance Sheet Stress Testing, IMF Working Paper 11/83.

Schmieder, C, Heiko, H., Neudorfer, B., Puhr, C., and Schmitz S. (2011b) Next-Generation System wide Liquidity Stress Testing, IMF Working Paper 12/3.

Schwartz, E.S. (1997). The stochastic behavior of commodity prices: Implication for valuation and hedging. The Journal of Finance, 52, 923–973.

Schwartz, E.S., and Smith, J.E. (2000). Short-term variations and long-term dynamics in commodity prices. Management Science, 46(7), 893–911.

Sorensen, C. (2002). Modeling seasonality in agricultural commodity futures. The Journal of Futures Markets, 22, 393–426.

Smit, H.T.J. (1997). Investment analysis of offshore concessions in the Netherlands. Financial Management, 26(2), 5–17.

Tamames, Ramón. (1988). Diccionario de Economía. Alianza Editorial S.A. Madrid.

Stulz. (1996). Rethinking Risk Management. Journal of Applied Corporate Finance, 9 (3), 8–24.

Stulz. (2002). Risk Management Derivatives, South-Western College Pub.

Index

Note: Page numbers with "n" denote notes.

F.J. Población García, *Financial Risk Management*,
DOI 10.1007/978-3-319-41366-2

E